TODAY'S CRIME AND PUNISHMENT ISSUES

Recent Titles in the Across the Aisle Series

Today's Social Issues: Democrats and Republicans
Timothy W. Kneeland

Today's Economic Issues: Democrats and Republicans
Nancy S. Lind, Erik T. Rankin, and Gardenia Harris

Today's Foreign Policy Issues: Democrats and Republicans
Trevor Rubenzer

Today's Environmental Issues: Democrats and Republicans
Teri J. Walker

Today's Health Care Issues: Democrats and Republicans
Robert B. Hackey and Todd M. Olszewski

Today's Civil Rights and Liberties Issues: Democrats and Republicans
Kara E. Stooksbury

TODAY'S CRIME AND PUNISHMENT ISSUES

DEMOCRATS AND REPUBLICANS

Edited by

Angela D. Madden

Across the Aisle

BLOOMSBURY ACADEMIC
NEW YORK • LONDON • OXFORD • NEW DELHI • SYDNEY

BLOOMSBURY ACADEMIC
Bloomsbury Publishing Inc
1385 Broadway, New York, NY 10018, USA
50 Bedford Square, London, WC1B 3DP, UK
29 Earlsfort Terrace, Dublin 2, Ireland

BLOOMSBURY, BLOOMSBURY ACADEMIC and the Diana logo are trademarks of Bloomsbury Publishing Plc

First published in the United States of America 2025

Cover image: Albund/Dreamstime.com

Library of Congress Cataloging-in-Publication Data
Names: Madden, Angela D., editor.
Title: Today's crime and punishment issues : Democrats and Republicans / Angela D. Madden, editor.
Description: New York, NY : Bloomsbury Academic, 2025. | Series: Across the aisle series | Includes bibliographical references and index.
Identifiers: LCCN 2024023631 (print) | LCCN 2024023632 (ebook) | ISBN 9781440873324 (hardback) | ISBN 9798765131435 (paperback) | ISBN 9798216172437 (epub) | ISBN 9781440873331 (pdf)
Subjects: LCSH: Criminal justice, Administration of–United States–Political aspects. | Law enforcement–United States–Political aspects. |
BISAC: LAW / Criminal Law / General | SOCIAL SCIENCE / Criminology
Classification: LCC HV9950 .T63 2025 (print) | LCC HV9950 (ebook) | DDC 364.973–dc23/eng/20240806
LC record available at https://lccn.loc.gov/2024023631
LC ebook record available at https://lccn.loc.gov/2024023632

ISBN: HB: 978-1-4408-7332-4
ePDF: 978-1-4408-7333-1
eBook: 979-8-2161-7243-7

Series: Across the Aisle

Typeset by Newgen KnowledgeWorks Pvt. Ltd., Chennai, India
Printed and bound in the United States of America

CONTENTS

Preface viii

Acknowledgments xii

Narrative Chronology of Crime and Punishment Regulation in the United States xiii

1 Bail Reform 1
Brian A. Pitman, Randy R. Gainey, and Ruth Triplett

2 Civil Asset Forfeiture 11
Chastity Blankenship and Madison Santore

3 Concealed or Open Firearm Carry 23
Sherah L. Basham

4 Corporate Crime 35
Bradley D. Edwards and Mary Smith-Tengroth

5 Crime Victims' Rights 45
Elizabeth Q. Wright

6 Cyberviolence and Online Extremism 59
Donna Ossorio

7 Death Penalty 73
Dale Wilson

8 Diversion Programs for Drug Offenders 85
Albert M. Kopak

9 Environmental Crime 97
J. Andy Hansen

10 Felon Disenfranchisement 111
Roger Byrd and Olivia A. Eason

11 Gang Violence 123
Sheri Jenkins Keenan, Jeffrey P. Rush, and Kellen McLaughlin

12 Gun Control 135
Angela D. Madden and Olivia A. Eason

13 Hate Crimes 149
Brendan Lantz and Zachary T. Malcom

14 Immigration and Customs Enforcement 161
Sean Maddan and Miguel V. Rangel

15 International Terrorism 175
Kelly A. McHugh

16 Law Enforcement Discretion 187
Luis F. Nuño

17 Mandatory Minimum Sentences 199
R. Bruce Anderson, Edward Kerr, and McKenna Marsh

18 Marijuana Legalization 211
Kyle C. Ward and Brian Iannacchione

19 Mental Health Care in the Criminal Justice System 221
Elizabeth Q. Wright and Deonna Gibbs

20 Police Militarization 235
Stephen T. Young and Brian A. Pitman

21 Prosecuting Juveniles as Adults 247
Kimberly DeTardo-Bora and Dhruba J. Bora

22 Reproductive Rights 257
Angela D. Madden

23 Sentencing for Drug Offenses 273
Zachary D. Baumann and Angela D. Madden

24 Technology in Policing 283
Kelly A. McHugh

25 Three-Strikes Policies 295
Elizabeth Gloyd, Wanda Leal, and Whitney Gass

Bibliography 307
About the Editor and Contributors 309
Index 317

PREFACE

When first asked to take on the task of *Today's Crime and Punishment Issues: Democrats and Republicans*, I was thrilled but clueless about the enormity of narrowing the myriad issues in criminal justice to twenty-five chapters while simultaneously evaluating political perspectives across time. As anyone who teaches or conducts research in this field knows, each new day seems to bring new, complex problems of concern to crime and punishment that are, or could be, impacted by policy and are, or could be, used as tools by either major political party to garner votes and political clout. One example is reproductive rights, which was not originally considered as a potential topic because *Roe v. Wade* (410 U.S. 113, 1973) had provided constitutional protection for reproductive rights for nearly fifty years. With one US Supreme Court decision, a formerly protected behavior was criminalized in dozens of states across the country. Given the striking division between Republicans and Democrats on this topic with respect to legislating that specific behaviors, specific people, and specific circumstances would warrant criminalization, I clearly could not omit it.

The first job was to be thoughtful about which issues to include to comprise twenty-five chapters. Complicating this process was an overlap in many topics. Firearms, for example, are a major concern in society and impactful at the local, state, and federal levels with respect to rising rates of firearm-involved violent gun crime, especially murders, and high rates of firearm-involved suicide. Implicit in any conversation about firearm use, whether for protection, sport, crime, or self-harm, is consideration of the Second Amendment and the right to keep and bear arms, but an ancillary issue is the circumstances under which those arms can be publicly carried on persons and in vehicles. Inherently controversial and rife with policy implications, politicians on both sides use the conflict between gun rights and gun control advocates to exploit the public's fear of crime and the gun-owner's fear of significant restrictions on perceived personal liberty.

The issue of gun control is not the only one to involve potentially divisive concerns that put Americans at odds with each other and play directly into the hands of politicians. Many topics generate strong patriotic reactions, like terrorism and immigration. Others, such as the use of technology in policing and the militarization of police, involve questions about the extent to which Americans are willing to sacrifice individual freedom and rights to privacy for the general welfare of society. Others, such as the criminalization of selected behaviors, disparities in sentencing, and felon disenfranchisement, involve questions of justice and fundamental fairness within a system that many argue is inherently prejudicial and discriminatory.

At the heart of tension between Democrats and Republicans is fundamental disagreement about the nature and extent of government power and individual rights within a complex and diverse society. Laws around crime and punishment exemplify how policymakers attempt to resolve this tension, and public support for any approach fluctuates across time with changes in societal priorities, public opinion (heavily influenced by media), political leadership, and high-profile events. Support for various approaches to punishment, for example, has shifted back and forth from more punitive approaches meant to provide retribution to more rehabilitative approaches meant to provide correction and prevent future offending. Laws related to bail reform, sentencing reform, alternatives to incarceration, and substance abuse and mental health treatment for offenders, for example, reflect more liberal (i.e., Democratic) public views about crime and punishment, whereas laws imposing mandatory minimums, "three strikes" laws, felon disenfranchisement, and allowing concealed carry of weapons reflect more conservative (i.e., Republican) views.

Capital punishment is another area in which recent changes in public perception have impacted policies and practices. According to the Death Penalty Information Center (2024), of the twenty-seven jurisdictions that still allow capital punishment, fourteen have not executed anyone in more than ten years and the number of annual executions has drastically decreased since the number peaked in 1999 at ninety-eight; the twenty-four executions in 2023 were carried out by only five states. Since 2019, there have been fewer than thirty executions per year, a trend not seen since before 1992. In the case of capital punishment and states that allow it but have not used it for decades, legislation does not seem to be guiding action, but public opinion seems to be inhibiting it.

Closely correlated with capital punishment is the practice of sentencing someone to death. Between 2002 and 2023, the number of annual death sentences dropped from 166 to 21. A recognition that mitigating factors such as age and cognitive functioning ability should be considered when sentencing someone to death reflects a swing toward more liberal thought. Jurisdictions also are swayed by strong evidence of racial bias in sentencing, generally, and in death sentences, specifically, as well as increasing public support for alternatives to capital punishment.

The overlap among critical partisan issues in crime and punishment is clearly illustrated in the capital sentencing and capital punishment discussion. Racial/ethnic bias, mental health concerns, and juvenile justice all are involved. As a result of the integrated nature of many of the topics in this volume, the reader will encounter some redundancy. Similar material may be found across chapters as the authors discuss the issues and how Democrats and Republicans respond to those issues. Likewise, the reader will read about many of the same laws across chapters. For example, the Violent Crime Control and Law Enforcement Act of 1994, signed into law by Democratic President Bill Clinton, has implications for several topics throughout this volume. This expansive and ambitious act covered a plethora of crime and punishment topics, including immigration, gangs, guns, drugs, sentencing, three-strikes laws, sex offenders, juveniles, hate crime, and crime victims, as well as proving funds for a wide variety of law enforcement activities. It is unlikely, in fact, that the reader will run across many chapters that do not mention this law.

After settling on topic areas that were somewhat distinct and approached very similar problems from different angles (e.g., mandatory minimum sentences and "three strikes" laws), my second job was to help contributors approach their respective entries and guide them through writing objectively on legislative actions about which they may have passionate (and partisan) opinions. As I learned in writing the chapter on gun control, it is difficult to avoid writing that subtly (or not so subtly) supports one perspective or the other. Throughout this process, I tried to guide contributors during the editing process toward more objectivity in presenting the major pieces of legislation within each party across time. I was successful to varying degrees because some topics are just more naturally associated with the views of one party and because, sometimes, legislation is so bad that objectivity is nearly impossible.

The reader may also find that a chapter may be missing discussion of an important piece of legislation. First, contributors were limited in their words, so they often had to choose among several "important" pieces of legislation. Second, I am not an expert in all these topics and might not have noticed an omission that is glaring to those with expertise in the area. This should in no way be a reflection on the quality of the contributors, many of whom I hounded with numerous suggested revisions in "tracked changes" documents multiple times. To the long-suffering contributors, I apologize and thank you wholeheartedly for your hard work and patience over several years to get this to print.

Since most of the chapters in this volume were written, a few events have impacted legislation in crime and punishment. The midterm elections of 2022, for example, were expected (at least by Republicans) to be a "red wave" as an incumbent president's party generally loses a substantial number of seats. This did not materialize. In House races, Republicans won the popular vote by a margin of only 2.8 percent, enough to flip the House, but Democrats gained one seat in the Senate and held several others that were expected (at least by Republicans) to flip.

Although many issues unrelated to crime and justice featured in the 2022 midterms, violent crime and gun violence was one that pundits believe influenced voter behavior at the polls. A mass shooting in May 2022 at Robb Elementary School in Uvalde, Texas, happened just weeks prior to President Biden signing into law the Bipartisan Safer Communities Act of 2022. In addition to a provision related to firearms, the legislation also contains a provision related to mental health services for families and children, particularly in schools, as well as appropriations to help fund various initiatives outlined in the Act.

While Democrats pushed for stricter gun laws and enjoyed a minor victory with the Safer Communities Act, the conservative US Supreme Court handed gun-rights proponents a major Second Amendment victory in *New York State Rifle & Pistol Assn., Inc. v. Bruen* when it held that a New York law requiring gun owners to show proper cause for licenses to publicly carry their weapons was unconstitutional. Instead of stopping at that point, the Court outlined how lower courts should approach cases involving any potential restrictions. In the majority opinion, Justice Clarence Thomas wrote that the only allowable regulations should be those that do not encroach on conduct plainly covered by the Second Amendment and that are "consistent with this Nation's historical tradition." The *Bruen* case has dramatically altered the landscape within which gun-related legislation is considered. In Delaware, for example, a federal district judge used *Bruen* to justify halting legislation prohibiting manufacture and possession of untraceable firearms (i.e., "ghost guns"), arguing that those advocating the law had not proven that such restrictions had historically existed. It is unclear how the conflict between restrictions proposed in the Safer Communities Act and loosening of restrictions because of *Bruen* will be resolved or how this conflict will impact violent gun crime.

This volume is published with the 2024 election cycle looming and several pieces of important crime and justice legislation pending at various stages in the legislative process. As Democrats and Republicans debate these policies, experience pressure from lobbyists and interest groups, wrestle for control, try to appease supporters with riders slipped into major proposals, loudly argue their positions, and try to justify election into their positions, the public must deal with crime and punishment with little effort by politicians to reach "across the aisle" to make communities safer.

ACKNOWLEDGMENTS

I thank my husband, Steven, who suffered through many days and nights of meals and social events on his own but made sure I ate and slept and generally took care of me as I devoted my attention to this project. As you always say, we're a team and I couldn't have finished this without you. Love you.

I also thank Konnor Long, Lauren Weaver, and Michelle Fletcher Hunt for their invaluable editorial assistance in proofreading and editing some of the early chapters. Although I didn't pay you, I know that helping me was its own reward and the intrinsic satisfaction far outweighed any monetary compensation that I could have offered you. Love you all.

Again, I thank the contributors with the expertise in their respective areas and the willingness to write a lot to put together this important examination of how partisan (and bipartisan) politics impact the practice of crime and punishment in the United States. Thank you for suffering my marked-up documents and often long-winded suggestions. This volume would not be possible without each of you.

Finally, I thank Kevin Hillstrom, the series editor, and all the wonderful staff at ABC-CLIO who patiently prodded me to keep going even as I tried to quit several times to enjoy semi-retirement. Thank you for your continued support and patience. I would love to work with you again, but I'm off to the beach.

NARRATIVE CHRONOLOGY OF CRIME AND PUNISHMENT REGULATION IN THE UNITED STATES

The evolution of using laws to regulate crime and punishment in the United States began well before the founding of the country. The first known set of written codified principles of behavior, literally written in stone, dates to the reign of Babylonian king Hammurabi, who ruled from 1792 to 1750 BCE. The *Code of Hammurabi* defined a set of legal precedents for various disputes and crimes, from family squabbles to contracts to serious violent acts. Based on the principle of retribution, or "an eye for an eye," the punishments outlined severe and often gruesome retaliatory reactions based on the offender's age, social class, and gender.

As time passed, philosophers debated crime and punishment, adding and refining critical components to how societies should handle those who stray from community norms. Among the most important considerations, according to Greek philosophers Plato and Aristotle, were an understanding of the reason an offense was committed and contemplation about what purpose punishment should serve. These ancient scholars argued that mitigating factors should lessen the severity of punishment. Stealing fruit from a market for one's starving child, for example, should be punished less harshly than stealing to feed oneself. Plato specifically discussed the relationship of poverty and lack of education to the likelihood of committing offenses. More than 2,000 years later, society is still learning the extent to which this is true. Aristotle argued that punishment should be used to not only prevent the offender from committing crime again, but also prevent society from engaging in similar prohibited acts. Again, more than 2,000 years later, our society still debates the relative utility of punishment as both a specific deterrent (preventing the offender from reoffending) and as a general deterrent (preventing others from committing similar offenses).

Defying religious tradition that crimes were sins worthy of punishment, ancient Rome witnessed the rise of secular law. The Romans believed crime was an affront to society, in general, so they developed their system of regulation to maintain societal order. Public safety, rather than heavenly reward, became the main concern.

During the Middle Ages and the rise of Christianity, Roman ideals were neglected in favor of more religious ideologies. Believing that punishments by man on earth were ordained by God and that crimes were sins caused by the "devil," punishments were often inhumane and violent. Guilt was not necessarily determined in any rational way, but was often "trial by ordeal," where "God's will" dictated the outcome; if the person died, they were obviously guilty, but if they lived, they were innocent.

On the North American continent, a significant event in the history of modern-day America with far-reaching implications on many laws related to crime and punishment happened in 1619. In August of that year, the *White Lion* brought about twenty to thirty Angolans kidnapped from a Portuguese slave ship to Jamestown, Virginia, and traded them for supplies. Another ship with a similar load of human cargo followed four days later. This is widely considered the beginning of the enslavement of African people in the colonies and eventually, in the United States. Enslavement of Indigenous peoples started around the same time and some settlers owned both Native American and African slaves.

In 1636, another significant event with implications for crime and justice occurred when the city of Boston became the first to implement a "night-watch" system whereby volunteers, and sometimes professional constables, rode around on horses, kept watch, and warned other citizens if there was danger. New York implemented a similar system in 1658, followed by Philadelphia in 1700.

In 1704, slave patrols began in South Carolina and quickly spread to become engrained in the antebellum south. Ostensibly to patrol for contraband, runaways, and illegal gatherings, these groups were primarily used to instill fear in Black populations and suppress slave revolts. These continued after the Civil War as former patrollers became law enforcement officers.

During colonial times, each colony determined its own crimes, punishments, and methods of adjudicating guilt. The US Constitution, however, brought an opportunity to develop a uniform system of governance, outlining specific laws and rights for the citizens of the new Republic. To accomplish this task, the framers relied heavily on European legal thought. In 1764, for example, Italian philosopher Cesare Beccaria published *On Crimes and Punishments*, which many of America's "founding fathers" had read. Along with an English counterpart, Jeremy Bentham, Beccaria advocated crime prevention through a system of laws but also swift and certain punishments that were proportionate to the offense. Swift, certain, and proportionately severe punishment would prevent future criminal behavior by impacting the "free will" of the offender. If legislators made the punishment (cost) of a criminal act outweigh its utility (benefit), then the person would be deterred and decide against the criminal act. Deterrence remains an underlying principle for punishment in the United States.

After the Declaration of Independence and the US Constitution were ratified, it became apparent that additional guidance was necessary. In 1791, the first ten amendments to the Constitution, the Bill of Rights, specified the protections guaranteed by the Constitution. It also set limits for government power in "due process" provisions. The framers, however, left significant room for interpretation by including very subjective language, leaving future case law to clarify meaning in many cases. The Second Amendment, for example, contains vague language about militia and the right to keep and bear arms. The

Eighth Amendment does not specify "excessive" bail and fines, or "cruel and unusual punishment."

Before the American Revolution, punishment was largely barbaric and retributive, based on a philosophy of an "eye for an eye." Jails were not used *as* punishment, but were filthy, disease-ridden holding facilities for the accused to await trial and punishment, which was usually physical, public, and immediate. Afterward, however, reformers from a Christian Protestant sect known as the Religious Society of Friends (colloquially known as "Quakers") advocated a more humane (and private) approach to punishment. By 1790, a Philadelphia jail was converted into a "penitentiary house," within which serious offenders were sentenced to complete isolation, which gave them time to reflect on their criminal (i.e., sinful) ways and to repent. The jail soon became overcrowded, so the Pennsylvania legislature appropriated funds in 1821 to build the Eastern State Penitentiary. It was designed with individual cells for each prisoner to serve his sentence in complete isolation, silence, and penitence, complete with toilets, sinks, Bibles, and attached recreation yards. By the 1850s, the isolation system was abandoned, and a congregate style was adopted. After scandals, high-profile escapes, and societal shifts to more rehabilitative techniques, Eastern State closed in 1971. It is a historical site today.

In the early to mid-1800s, policing evolved as a profession. Boston created America's first full-time professional police department in 1838, with other major American cities soon following suit. Within just a few decades, every major city had a police department.

Throughout the mid- to late-1800s, reformers argued for more humane punishment, and scholars and researchers began thinking about crime as partially determined by factors beyond free will. Italian psychiatrist Cesare Lombroso argued that criminal behavior was a product of heredity, evolution, and other psychological and biological factors. Lombroso's theories formed the basis for modern criminology and influenced the modern criminal justice system. The impact of factors beyond individual control are criminological foundations today and many current policies related to crime and punishment are informed by the current state of knowledge related to biological, psychological, and environmental factors.

Concepts in the Declaration of Independence clearly indicated the need for reform with respect to slavery and involuntary servitude. The belief that "all men are created equal and endowed ... with certain unalienable rights" caused abolitionists to eventually argue that slaves were "men," worthy of the same rights and protections as others. In the early 1800s, slavery began losing favor, although southern states still heavily relied upon slave labor for agricultural work. Court opinions such as *Dred Scott v. Sanford* (1857), however, reinforced the status quo when the Supreme Court held that African Americans were not and could never be citizens. This decision only fueled the division between pro-slavery advocates and abolitionists, and slavery became one of the catalysts for the Civil War (1861–5). Many southern states seceded from the Union over a debate about the expansion of slavery into the western territories. As the Civil War raged, President Abraham Lincoln issued the Emancipation Proclamation in 1863 that effectively ended slavery, and Congress followed it in 1865 with the Thirteenth Amendment, which forbade slavery and involuntary servitude "except as a punishment for crime." This exception is still controversial because it allows for deprivation of basic human rights. The "Black

Codes" passed in the antebellum south, for example, criminalized Black activities to such extent that nearly every Black person was in violation of some law at any given time. Vagrancy was the most common offense for which Black persons were eventually forced back into slavery under convict-leasing systems in which jurisdictions convicted offenders, fined them, then "leased" them to industries and farms as slave labor until they either paid off their fines or died. In the 2022 midterm elections, voters in five states (Alabama, Tennessee, Oregon, Vermont, Louisiana) voted on whether to eliminate this type of slavery from their respective state constitutions. Louisiana was the only state to vote to keep slavery and involuntary servitude as punishment for crime.

Although the death penalty was first used in the colonies in 1608, advances in technology and public sentiment moved it from public hangings to private events that took place behind prison walls. With the invention of electricity in 1882, it only took eight years before the first person was executed by electrocution. Promoted as more humane than hanging, the electrocution took several tries and about eight minutes as witnesses reported that the condemned man's body caught on fire. Despite the gruesome death, states quickly adopted electrocution to replace hanging as the primary method of execution.

As the convict leasing system lost favor, chain gangs and prison plantation systems grew in popularity. Chain gangs used groups of imprisoned laborers to conduct hard labor as the state saw fit (roads, farms, rock quarries). Prison farms like Parchman in Mississippi and Angola in Louisiana exploited prisoners as slave labor to work primarily in agriculture, picking cotton and working fields under constant threat of beatings or death, like many of their ancestors.

In 1908, nine former Secret Service agents were hired by the Attorney General as Justice "special agents," and in 1909, he issued a formal order to create a "Bureau of Investigation." In 1935, under Director J. Edgar Hoover, this agency became the Federal Bureau of Investigation (FBI) and the investigatory arm of the Justice Department.

In the early 1900s, advances in investigative technologies led to the need for law to regulate them and their uses. The US Supreme Court held in *Weeks v. United States* (1914) that evidence seized in violation of a person's Fourth Amendment rights against unreasonable search and seizure could not be used as evidence against that person. This "exclusionary rule" protects people from overeager enforcement efforts.

The first half of the twentieth century was characterized by violence and war. In 1920, the Volstead Act provided for enforcement of the Eighteenth Amendment, which authorized the prohibition of "manufacture, sale, or transportation of intoxicating liquors" in the United States. It also gave rise to a profitable black market for alcohol, underground places for consumption, and gang and mob violence within organized criminal activities. The installation of J. Edgar Hoover in 1924 as head of the Bureau of Investigation started a decades-long expansion of the agency into a premiere crime-fighting agency with somewhat morally, ethically, and legally questionable tactics. Hoover spearheaded the development of forensic labs and a centralized national repository for fingerprints. He was also instrumental in combatting gang violence that arose after Prohibition, orchestrating the capture or killing of several high-profile and deadly gangsters like John Dillinger. After gangsters using machine guns wreaked havoc across the United States in the 1930s,

Democratic President Franklin Delano Roosevelt signed into law the National Firearms Act of 1934 (NFA) and the Federal Firearms Act of 1938 (FFA). The NFA imposed a $200 tax on making and transferring certain firearms (e.g., machine guns) and required registration of those firearms. The FFA required anyone in the "business of selling firearms" to obtain a "federal firearms license" (FFL), required them to keep records on purchasers, and defined individuals prohibited from purchasing (e.g., convicted felons). After an allegation that these legislative efforts were in violation of the Second Amendment, the US Supreme Court held in *United States v. Miller* (1939) that weapons with no relation to preserving a militia can be restricted by states and the federal government.

The 1940s and 1950s were consumed by the Second World War and its aftermath, growing tensions with Russia, apprehension about atomic and hydrogen bombs, the beginning of the space race, the Cold War, and the continued civil rights struggle. In 1946, the US Supreme Court declared segregation on interstate buses to be unconstitutional and Democratic President Harry S. Truman subsequently called for an end to segregation with equal rights for all persons. However, the 1955 murder of Black teenager Emmett Till by a white mob in Mississippi proved racism was still pervasive in the south.

Although the 1960s was the decade of "peace" and "love," it also was a decade in which crime rates rose 126 percent. Legislators placed blame on drugs and violent street gangs, which resulted in harsh policies that militarized law enforcement and filled American prisons. In the 1970s, crime rates rose another 64 percent. The 1960s was characterized by several landmark Supreme Court cases that impacted crime and justice. In 1961, *Mapp v. Ohio* applied the exclusionary rule to searches by the federal government. The Court held in *Gideon v. Wainwright* (1963), that defendants had the right to free counsel. Democratic President Lyndon B. Johnson implemented a War on Crime in 1965 and advocated for the Law Enforcement Assistance Act of 1965 to improve and strengthen crime control programs and law enforcement. And while *Miranda v. Arizona* (1966) outlined protections for suspects during interrogations, and *In re Gault* (1967) applied due process protections to juveniles, *Terry v. Ohio* (1968) protected the power of the police to stop and frisk suspects. The Omnibus Crime Control and Safe Streets Acts of 1968, signed into law by Johnson, established the Law Enforcement Assistance Administration (LEAA), which eventually became the Office of Justice Programs. The Act also prohibited interstate trade of handguns and raised to twenty-one the legal age to purchase handguns. The ability to conduct wiretaps was also expanded while the strength of *Miranda* in protecting defendant rights in interrogations was diluted when the Act gave federal trial judges the ability to admit statements into evidence that were issued voluntarily, even without suspects being informed of their constitutional rights. This provision was not struck down until thirty-two years later in *Dickerson v. United States* (2000).

In the 1970s, the battle to reign in drug crime continued with the passage of the Racketeering Influenced and Corrupt Organizations Act of 1970 (RICO) and Republican President Richard M. Nixon declared a War on Drugs. First among several similar cases to restrict various forms of corporal punishment as cruel and unusual punishment, *Gates v. Collier* (1974) ended the trusty system and associated varieties of inmate abuse in a case involving Mississippi's Parchman Farm. It did not, however, end such abuses as Parchman figured prominently in similar cases up into the 2020s.

In 1972, the FBI's Behavioral Science Unit was established, and two landmark Supreme Court decisions were reached. *Furman v. Georgia* halted capital punishment in the country as arbitrary and capricious, and *Morrisey v. Brewer* extended due process protections to parole revocations. Several other landmark cases followed during the decade. *Gagnon v. Scarpelli* (1973) extended the protection of due process to probation revocations. Gary Gilmore became the first person executed after *Gregg v. Georgia* (1976) reinstated the death penalty, dying by firing squad in Utah. Capital punishment became more sophisticated when Oklahoma approved lethal injection in 1977 with the first execution by that method in 1982.

The 1980s were characterized by police battles with Columbian drug cartels in Florida and a massive legislative effort to reduce rapidly rising drug- and gang-related violence. The Comprehensive Crime Control Act of 1984, signed into law by Democratic President Bill Clinton, was the most comprehensive crime control legislation ever passed. Its twelve titles addressed a wide variety of concerns about crime and justice, from pretrial to post-conviction. Among other notable provisions, it eliminated federal parole and the federal death penalty for most crimes, established the United States Sentencing Commission, imposed mandatory minimum sentences, and amended RICO to expand properties subject to forfeiture. Also in 1984, the Victims of Crime Act (VOCA) established the Crime Victims Fund to provide restitution, compensation, and services to crime victims.

The 1990s were plagued by police violence, riots, a burgeoning anti-government militia movement, and a tragic case of domestic terrorism. In the first half of the decade, the beating of civilian Rodney King by Los Angeles police officers and their subsequent acquittal triggered protests and violent riots, and focused intense scrutiny on law enforcement power and use of force. In 1992 and 1993, incidents at Ruby Ridge (CO) and Waco (TX) focused intense scrutiny on the law enforcement power of the federal government and provided rationale for a domestic terrorist in 1995. Ruby Ridge involved agents of the US Marshals Service attempting to execute a bench warrant for a man with numerous weapons and anti-government sentiment. In an ensuing gunfight, two members of the suspect's family and one US Marshal were killed. In Waco, agents from the Bureau of Alcohol, Tobacco, and Firearms (ATF) and Texas officials were attempting to serve a search warrant at the compound of the Branch Davidians, a religious cult suspected of stockpiling illegal weapons, when a gunfight erupted. The FBI joined the melee when the ATF failed to execute the search warrant. To end the fifty-one-day siege, the FBI attacked the compound with tear gas. A fire erupted, which eventually put an end to the disaster and resulted in the deaths of four federal agents and eighty-two Branch Davidians, including twenty-eight children. The domestic terrorist who bombed the Alfred P. Murrah Federal Building in Oklahoma City on April 19, 1995, was motivated by anti-government sentiment and by the sieges at Ruby Ridge and Waco.

The first decade of the twenty-first century was rocked by foreign terrorist attacks on American soil. On September 11, 2001, two airplanes piloted by terrorists crashed into New York City's Twin Towers, one into the Pentagon in Washington, DC, and one into a Pennsylvania field after passengers thwarted its planned route to another federal building in Washington, DC. The attacks killed nearly 3,000 people and became the catalyst for the War on Terror against al-Qaeda and the Taliban in Afghanistan under the leadership of Osama bin Laden who was killed nearly a decade later by the US military in a raid on May 2, 2011. The bipartisan Uniting and Strengthening America by Providing Appropriate Tools Required to Intercept and Obstruct Terrorism Act of 2001 (USA Patriot Act) was signed into law by Republican President George W. Bush just weeks after the attack. Spurred by defects in how agencies surveilled, searched, and investigated suspects (especially barriers to interagency communication), it expanded the powers of federal law enforcement and intelligence agencies to search and surveil suspects, especially with respect to telephonic and electronic communications. It also made significant changes to the Foreign Intelligence Surveillance Court and laws around money laundering and immigration. Several new crimes were defined and penalties for many existing offenses were enhanced. Critics viewed the Patriot Act as a government shield for civil and human rights abuses in investigations and interrogations of suspected terrorists, especially with respect to First and Fourth Amendment protections. Many provisions of the Patriot Act were extended into 2015. On June 2, 2015, however, Democratic President Barack Obama signed the Uniting and Strengthening America by Fulfilling Rights and Ensuring Effective Discipline Over Monitoring Act of 2015 (USA Freedom Act), which requires the government to submit public requests to the Foreign Intelligence Surveillance Act (FISA) court to collect data.

Three landmark cases between 2002 and 2008 specified situations in which capital punishment is unconstitutional. In *Atkins v. Virginia* (536 U.S. 304, 2002), the Court forbade execution of the intellectually disabled, in *Roper v. Simmons* (543 U.S. 551, 2005), it forbade the execution of anyone who committed their qualifying crime before the age of eighteen, and in *Kennedy v. Louisiana* (554 U.S. 407, 2008), it prohibited execution in cases that did not involve homicide or a crime against the state, like treason. Also in 2008, *District of Columbia v. Heller* (554 U.S. 570) was a landmark victory for gun rights advocates when the Court ruled a DC law restricting handguns was unconstitutional under the Second Amendment.

In the second decade of the twenty-first century, courts continued to refine sentences for juveniles. In *Graham v. Florida* (560 U.S. 48, 2010), the Supreme Court held that courts cannot impose life without parole on juveniles convicted of non-homicides. Going a step further, in *Miller v. Alabama* (567 U.S. 460, 2012), the Court prohibited mandatory sentences to life without parole for any juvenile offender. Another notable case related to crime and punishment was *Riley v. California* (573 U.S. 373, 2014) in which the Court held that it is a violation of the Fourth Amendment to search a person's cell phone without a warrant.

Finally, one of the most impactful movements of the 2010s and into the 2020s relates to the constitutionality of bail. Bail was originally intended as a monetary bond to insure a defendant's appearance in court, but it has evolved to keep impoverished persons in jail to await trial while those with financial resources remain free. Bail critics have advocated for the use of pretrial risk assessments to evaluate the potential risks posed to public safety by the pretrial release of suspects. In 2019, California was to become the first state to abolish cash bail after Democratic Governor Jerry Brown signed S.B. 10 in 2018. Critics of S.B. 10, however, were skeptical of the efficacy and fairness of pretrial risk assessments. This skepticism played out in a 2020 referendum when California voters decided against such assessments and effectively nullified S.B. 10. In Illinois, lawmakers successfully proposed a bail reform law in 2021 to end cash bail. After the Illinois Supreme Court overruled an appeals court decision that lawmakers did not have the constitutional authority to abolish bail, the new law went into effect on September 18, 2023. The Illinois Pretrial Fairness Act gives courts three options for pretrial suspects: (1) release on recognizance (ROR), (2) release with conditions, such as electronic monitoring, or (3) pretrial detention if they are a flight risk or threat to public safety.

Five important cases with relevance to crime and punishment have been decided so far in the 2020s. In 2020, the US Supreme Court held that the Sixth Amendment right to a jury trial requires courts at both the state and federal levels to reach unanimous verdicts to convict a person of a serious offense (*Ramos v. Louisiana*, 590 U.S. 83, 2020). On June 23, 2022, gun rights advocates won another major victory in *New York State Rifle & Pistol Assn., Inc. v. Bruen* (597 U.S. 1, 2022). In *Bruen*, the Court held that the Second Amendment protects an individual's right to carry a handgun outside the home for self-defense with no requirement to justify a reason. The next day, on June 24, 2022, the Court overturned the landmark case of *Roe v. Wade* (410 U.S. 113, 1973), which had previously protected a woman's right to an abortion. Since that ruling, many states have passed or attempted to pass laws to criminalize abortion in most circumstances, as well as to criminalize assisting someone to get an abortion. In November 2023, the US Supreme Court heard a challenge to the Armed Career Criminal Act of 1984 (ACCA) in *Brown v. United States* (602 U.S. ___, 2024). The ACCA imposes a minimum sentence of fifteen years in prison for anyone with at least three previous convictions for violent felonies or serious drug offenses who illegally possesses a firearm. On May 23, 2024, the Court ruled that state drug convictions can trigger a longer sentence if the drug in question was a federally controlled substance at the time of conviction. On June 21, 2024, however, this ruling was constrained by the Court's ruling in *Erlinger v. United States* (602 U.S. ___, 2024) that juries and not judges should decide whether a defendant's sentence can be enhanced under the ACCA.

CHAPTER 1

Bail Reform

BRIAN A. PITMAN, RANDY R. GAINEY, AND RUTH TRIPLETT

AT A GLANCE

The Republican and Democratic Parties have held varying stances over the years on bail and bail reform. Bail reform became part of the mainstream discussion surrounding criminal justice reform with the Democratic and Republican presidential primaries in 2016 and with the Democratic primary in 2020. During the early stages of the presidential primaries in 2015, the suicide of Kalief Browder played an important role. Browder, a Black man from New York City, spent three of his childhood years at Riker's Island because his family could not afford his $3,000 bail on accusations that he stole a backpack. At Riker's, Browder was put into solitary confinement multiple times because he was subject to abuse and attacks from prisoners and prison officers. The time at Riker's took a heavy mental toll on Browder and ultimately led to his death by suicide.

Many Democrats and a few Republicans were drawn to Browder's story in advocating for bail reform. In 2016, Republican presidential candidate and senator Rand Paul (KY) had been retelling Browder's story for some time prior to his candidacy as an exemplary justification for criminal justice reform. Another Republican, presidential candidate Chris Christie, advocated for federal bail reforms similar to the reforms he helped pass while he was governor of New Jersey. Ultimately bail reform was not part of either party's platform in 2016.

After the election of Republican Donald J. Trump in 2016, members of the Republican Party at the federal and state level have held varying views on bail reform. Senator Rand Paul has been consistent in his advocacy for bail reform. Republicans in Alaska and Ohio have also been behind the bail reform push in their states. However, most Republicans in California, New York, Georgia, and Wisconsin have staunchly opposed bail reforms in their states.

Democrats had been the most vocal supporters of bail reform since 2016. They have put forth bills in cities, states, and at the federal level to decrease or eliminate cash bail. During campaigns for the 2020 Democratic Party presidential nomination, several Democrats supported the elimination of monetary bail, while a few supported reducing the use of monetary bail. Some states with Democratic leadership have also passed bail reform, while many Democratic city leaders have overhauled monetary bail at the local level (Venhuizen 2023). The state of Illinois, in 2021, for example, passed the Safety, Accountability, Fairness and Equity-Today Act that made the state the first to abolish cash bail entirely. However, these positions are far from universal within the party.

MANY REPUBLICANS...

- Have mixed feelings about bail reform. That is, some favor the same types of reforms Democrats do, while some do not.
- Favor bail reform that reduces taxpayer expenses.
- Are against bail reform, arguing that reforms take too much discretion away from judges and will result in decreased public safety.

MANY DEMOCRATS...

- Have proposed the ending of cash bail for misdemeanor and nonviolent offenses at the state and federal level.
- Support the elimination or reduction of reliance on cash bail because requirements for cash bonds criminalize poverty and are a form of wealth-based discrimination.
- Support the use of pretrial risk assessment tools to replace cash bail.

OVERVIEW

Bail is defined as the right to be released or to obtain release prior to trial for charges of unlawful activity. Historically, bail was imposed to ensure the accused returned to court to face their charges. To do this, a community member took financial responsibility for the accused returning to court, sometimes referred to as "sufficient sureties." While not legislated to do so at the time it first developed, judges have also always assessed perceived danger of the offender to the community and self and potential for committing further crimes in their bail decisions.

Virginia instituted the first bail law in 1645. Massachusetts and Pennsylvania soon followed when they codified bail for noncapital offenses. Pennsylvania's law had an explicit mention of sufficient sureties, which would later be adopted by many state constitutions. Under the Judiciary Act of 1789, the right to bail was guaranteed for noncapital offenses, and for capital offenses where proof was not "evident." The Eighth Amendment also protects the accused from excessive bail. State constitutions adopted similar language.

Initially, prepayment of sufficient sureties was not a requirement. However, this changed as community ties dissipated with Western colonization and industrialization increasing perceptions of risk of flight. These conditions gave rise to new experiments by states to ensure the accused returned to court by way of the commercial bail bond industry. The first bail bonds company was established in San Francisco, California, in 1898, and as the business was clearly lucrative it expanded quickly across the country.

Bail bonds allow the accused to pay a bail bondsperson a percentage of the overall bail (8 to10 percent of assigned bail plus fees and other collateral). In exchange, the bondsperson puts up the remaining amount of bail as a "surety" that the accused will appear for court. This is the option that poorer defendants often rely on. If the accused pays the entirety of their bail, they receive their money back if acquitted or the charges are dismissed. Those who utilize bail bonds companies do not receive their money back. Thus, the emergence of the bail bond industry presented the accused with three options if they were not released on their own recognizance: (1) pay the bail in its entirety, (2) pay a bail bonds company a nonrefundable fee, or (3) remain in jail until the trial is complete. This was authorized under the Supreme Court decision *Leary v. United States* (395 U.S. 6, 1969).

The bail bonds industry fostered corruption, as the industry incentivized bonds people to collude with criminal legal officials so that those officials would send them clients. Before the establishment of bail bonds, the accused would be responsible to someone in the community. Now the accused were monetarily exposed to the for-profit bail bonds industry. Investigations in Cleveland and Chicago, as well as Republican President Herbert Hoover's Wickersham Commission, noted the industry's corruption, collusion with criminal legal officials, and classist biases. However, the industry was able to weather the storm and largely remain intact as it generally faced relatively limited and mild reform proposals. By 1937, all states and the federal government had codified various forms of bail regulation into law, while reform efforts lost steam and dissipated.

Liberal reforms for bail nationwide began again in the 1950s as court decisions and lawmakers became aware of and concerned with protecting the accused. Under former Democratic politician and current chief justice, Fred Vinson, the Supreme Court ruled in *Stack v. Boyle* (342 U.S. 1, 1951) that bail is excessive when it was higher than a reasonable calculation to ensure the accused's return to court. Following this ruling, more studies that demonstrated case after case of discrimination in the bail system emerged. The Philadelphia Bail Study found that 75 percent of accused persons were under pretrial detention and that bail disproportionately affected poorer citizens. These findings were replicated in Washington, DC, and New York City. The Vera Institute of Justice and Manhattan Bail Project developed various release on recognizance (ROR) models, which helped identify poorer defendants with community ties for ROR and surveillance. By 1964, this was the standard ROR model nationwide. Under Democratic House and Senate majorities and Democratic President Lyndon B. Johnson, the Bail Reform Act of 1966 was passed, which required those accused of federal, noncapital offenses receive bond only if the prosecution could demonstrate the accused was likely to flee. For capital offenses at the federal level, prosecutors had to be able to show the accused's dangerousness and likelihood of fleeing. This led to a 19 percent rise in pretrial release for the accused between 1962 and 1971 from 48 percent to 67 percent.

Individual states also implemented their own bail reforms in the 1960s. In 1963, under Democratic Governor Otto Kerner, Jr., the state of Illinois began allowing defendants to pay the state 10 percent of their bail to the court, thus serving as their own bail bondsperson. Seven states would follow in passing similar laws by 1971. In 1967, under Democratic

Governor John Dempsey, Connecticut, passed a law creating a bail commission that utilized risk assessment. In 1976, Kentucky, under Democratic Governor Julian Carroll, banned the commercial bail bonds industry. Throughout the 1960s and 1970s, there was a dramatic increase in pretrial release and supervision and a dramatic decrease in bail bonds profits.

During the 1980s, increasing crime rates and southern politics fueled the conservative turn in bail policies nationwide. While ROR programs were able to keep jail populations down, critics jumped on the higher rates of failure to appear and pretrial arrests to advocate harsher bail restrictions. Also citing the supposed taxpayer burden of ROR programs, conservatives sought to reprivatize the bail system and allow judges to consider dangerousness in bail decisions. In 1984, under Republican President Ronald Reagan, the Democratic House Majority and Republican Senate passed the Bail Reform Act of 1984, which included the Bail Reform Act allowing federal judges to consider public danger and flight risk in determining bail. Within a year, thirty-four states followed in passing similar laws while eight states passed constitutional amendments. In *United States v. Salerno* (481 U.S. 739, 1987), the conservative majority court upheld the Bail Reform Act of 1984, and it would go untouched until 2006, when it was amended to mandate pretrial release conditions for those accused of federal child sex crimes.

The Battle over Money Bail in New York City

On January 1, 2020, New York City's bail reform law went into effect. This law requires judges to only consider flight risk in whether to set bail for the accused, not the perceived dangerousness of a person. It also allows for approximately 90 percent of arrests to result in release without bail, excluding certain violent felonies, sex crimes, and domestic violence arrests. Since the law went into effect, the media and political stakeholders have raised concerns about its implementation. Others, such as Kellen Funk at Columbia Law School, have called these concerns "the Willie Horton effect." (Willie Horton was a Black man convicted of murder in Massachusetts when he was out on a weekend furlough program and later convicted of raping a white woman while out on furlough; the Horton story became a Republican campaign tool during George H. W. Bush's 1988 run against Massachusetts governor Michael Dukakis.) Funk notes that there are "attention-grabbing anecdotes that sway policy much more than the statistics that tell us which policies work and which don't." Some of these headlines include "New York man arrested 3 times in one day," "Man accused of driving drunk, killing pedestrian freed due to new criminal justice reforms," and "Long Island burglary spree suspect released under bail reform, then robs another store hours later." There was also a spate of anti-Semitic and anti-Asian attacks that were weaponized to enhance political pressure. New York deputy Democratic leader of the state senate, Michael Gianaris, noted that "The hysteria around the situation completely ignores the fact that people have been released and accused of horrible things for a long time," noting that Harvey Weinstein was out of jail on a $1 million bail (Schuppe 2020).

Pretrial detainment grew as a consequence of these laws and the ensuing drug war; from 1970 to 2015, the use of pretrial detention increased 433 percent. Approximately 60 percent of people in jail are there on pretrial detention, not yet convicted of an offense, primarily for minor drug and property crimes (75 percent). More than 30 percent of those detained defendants are unable to afford the bail they were assigned. Recently, the Democratic Party has been leading discussions of bail reform at both federal and state levels while the Republican Party has primarily pushed back on those reforms. Numerous Democratic Party-led cities have begun a turn toward eliminating monetary bail and replacing it with risk assessment technologies or electronic monitoring. However, the implementation of these tools has led to an increase in pretrial detention in New Jersey and Maryland, while failing to solve the race and class biases inherent in the bail system.

REPUBLICANS ON BAIL REFORM

The Republican Party has had various opinions on bail reform at the federal, state, and local levels. When bail first faced changes at the federal level under the Bail Reform Act of 1966, only a few Republicans in Congress voted against it. The rising Civil Rights Movement that occurred alongside escalating crime, however, gave Republicans an opportunity to push back on criminal justice reforms. Republican President Richard Nixon started the War on Drugs that was continued by Republican President Ronald Reagan in the 1980s. Republicans stoked emerging social anxieties via the southern strategy that used crime as a coded language for race. In 1984, President Reagan signed the Comprehensive Crime Control Act of 1984 sponsored by Republican Senator Strom Thurmond. This bill included the Bail Reform Act of 1984. In all, twenty-three House Republicans and thirty-two Senate Republicans cosponsored the bill.

Between 1984 and 2006 bail laws remained largely unchanged. Then, in 2005 Republican Rep. James F. Sensenbrenner, Jr. (WI) introduced the Adam Walsh Child Protection and Safety Act of 2006, which included an amendment to the 1984 Bail Reform Act that enacted mandatory conditions of pretrial release for any person accused of sexual crimes against children. At minimum, charges of sex crimes resulted in electronic monitoring that limited traveling, mandatory contact with pretrial services agencies, curfew, and limits on firearm possession. This popular amendment faced no debate from either party.

As the problems of mass incarceration arose in the political consciousness, only one Republican Congressperson has actively supported bail reform. Specifically, Republican Senator Rand Paul (KY) has made bail reform part of his larger criminal justice reform platform. In 2017, he cosponsored with Democratic Senator Kamala Harris (CA) the Pretrial Integrity and Safety Act to reform bail at the federal level. In contrast, Republican Louisiana Senator and Senate Judiciary Committee member John Kennedy denounced bail reform writ large, but especially risk assessment tools and algorithms, describing them as dangerous in a Fox News op-ed in 2019.

At the state level, Republicans have made decisions that illustrate the varying positions of the party on bail reform. In 2014, Republican governor and eventual 2016 Republican presidential primary candidate, Chris Christie (NJ) signed legislation that effectively eliminated cash bail by 2017, replacing it with a risk assessment tool that utilizes an algorithm to determine a defendant's flight risk or danger to the community. In Alaska in 2016, former Republican turned independent governor Bill Walker signed into law a bipartisan criminal justice reform bill that released those in jail on pretrial detention to ankle monitoring or halfway houses. However, Walker's successor Republican Mike Dunleavy, overturned these reforms just a few years later. In Illinois, Republican Governor Bruce Rauner signed the Bail Reform Act into law in 2017. This legislation sought to move away from cash bail for defendants charged with nonviolent misdemeanors and low-level felonies. Finally, the Republican House Majority in Tennessee's House of Representatives approved a bill in June 2020, which requires release of a person who: (1) is accused of a nonviolent misdemeanor that is later eligible for expungement, (2) has not been previously convicted of a crime ineligible for expungement, and (3) is not deemed a risk to flee or commit another crime, to be automatically considered for release on their own recognizance.

However, Republicans in other states began campaigning against significant bail reform, including in places like California, New York, Georgia, and Wisconsin. In California, all but one state-elected Republican voted against a bill to eliminate cash bail in their state in August 2018. California Republicans, including the nominees for governor and attorney general, felt the bill was reckless for the community and the economy as it threatened the local bail bonds industry. While the California legislature passed the elimination of cash bail in 2018, a referendum drive garnered enough signatures to put the bill on hold until it was put on the ballot in 2020. California voters rejected it (Proposition 25), nullifying the bill passed by the legislature.

New York state also passed bail reform that went into effect at the beginning of 2020. The law eliminated bail for about 90 percent of crimes and required judges to only consider flight risk when assigning bail. Republicans, however, thoroughly utilized every opportunity to criticize the law, citing how it led to the release of accused bank robbery and anti-Semitic hate crime suspects. Democrats agreed to add some offenses back to the list where bail could be assigned, which went into effect in July 2020. In 2023, Democratic Governor Kathy Hochul negotiated updates to the bill to allow for increased judges' discretion, leading to more rollbacks of the original law.

Meanwhile, in Georgia, the GOP-led senate passed legislation that required cash or property bail for fifty-three offenses, many of them only misdemeanors. In Wisconsin, a GOP push for voters to approve allowing judges to consider past convictions of violent crime was approved, making this a part of the state constitution. Thus, the Republican Party's position on bail reform, like that of the Democrats, is far from stable.

DEMOCRATS ON BAIL REFORM

During the 1960s push for criminal justice reform, the Democratic Party was supportive of bail reform. In 1964, Robert Kennedy, while serving as Democratic president Lyndon Johnson's attorney general, testified before the Senate Judiciary Committee highlighting the injustices of the bail system. The Bail Reform Act of 1966 would pass a couple of years later, with only nine Democratic House members voting against it. Democratic Party-led states like Illinois, Connecticut, and Kentucky would follow by passing state bail reform laws.

At the federal level, the Democratic Party's support for bail reform did not last long. In the 1980s, nine Democratic senators, including 2020 Democratic presidential nominee Joe Biden, were original cosponsors of the bipartisan Comprehensive Crime Control Act of 1984, which included the Bail Reform Act. In all, fourteen Democratic senators and nine Democratic House members cosponsored the bill. However, the local Democratic leadership in Washington, DC, largely eliminated cash bail for the city, illustrating the varying opinions of the party even during the War on Drugs. In addition, many Democrats at the federal level later supported the amendment to the Bail Reform Act of 1984 under the Adam Walsh Child Protection and Safety Act of 2006, which changed bail conditions for those accused of sex crime against minors.

Democrats at the federal level have typically supported the push for bail reform in response to widespread awareness and concern over mass incarceration. Senator Kamala Harris (CA), along with Republican Rand Paul (KY) cosponsored the Pretrial Integrity and Safety Act, which would have established Department of Justice grants to incentivize localities to establish alternatives to cash bail and collect further data on bail nationwide. From 2017 to 2019, California Democratic Congressman Ted Lieu introduced the No Money Bail Act, which proposed to eliminate the use of monetary bail. His bill would require states to find alternatives to money bail or risk losing funds from the Edward Byrne Justice Assistance Grant Program. In July 2018, Senators Bernie Sanders (VT) and Kristen Gillibrand (NY) cosponsored a Senate companion bill to Lieu's No Money Bail Act. Thus far, these bills have not passed.

The 2020 Democratic presidential primary race also saw bail reform as one of the many criminal justice reform issues discussed. Only three of the thirteen major candidates were against the total elimination of cash bail. Top contenders Bernie Sanders and Joe Biden were both in favor of eliminating cash bail. Andrew Yang, Pete Buttigieg, and Michael Bloomberg were against the elimination of cash bail, though they too supported reducing the use of the system.

At the state and local levels, Democratic leadership has eliminated or severely limited cash bail. Kentucky, the first state to ban commercial bail bonds in the 1970s under Democratic leadership, has utilized mandatory risk assessment for bail decisions since a 2011 bill signed by Democratic Governor Steve Beshear. The state of Colorado eliminated cash bail for low-level offenses in 2019. Meanwhile, Democratic district attorneys in Philadelphia, Norfolk, and Richmond have either stopped requesting cash bail for low-level offenses or moved to completely eliminate the practice. Cook County, Illinois, where Chicago is located, moved away from cash bail in favor of electronic pretrial monitoring prior to the state of Illinois eliminating cash bail altogether in 2023.

In California, Democratic Governor Jerry Brown signed a bill abolishing the state's money bail system in 2018, which was eventually rejected by voters in November 2020. On April 6, 2020, with the emerging Covid-19 pandemic, state officials reduced bail to $0 for most low-level offenses under the guise of decreasing the spread of the virus in jails. This led to the jail population in California decreasing by nearly 20,000 people over a two-month period during the early months of the pandemic. Los Angeles Superior Court put an end to this rule in 2022 and other parts of the state also reversed their bail policies. San Francisco, for example, after having moved away from cash bail to "risk-based detention" under district attorney Chesa Boudin, reinstated bail for misdemeanor in bail cases after he was recalled and the mayor selected Brooke Jenkins as DA.

Party thinking on bail reform, however, has not been fully unified across the country. In April 2019, for example, New York, led by a Democratic Senate majority and a Democratic governor, passed massive bail reform that went into effect on January 1, 2020. Since its implementation though, public pressure has led to attempts to scale back the law. New York City's Democratic Mayor Bill de Blasio commented that the new bail rule was likely a cause of the uptick in crime at the beginning of the 2020 year. In April 2020, the bill was amended to allow judges to have more discretion in assigning bail for certain offenses. It went into effect in July 2020.

FURTHER READING

Ahee, William, Micaela Alvarez, Jevhon Rivers, and Grace Signorelli. "Moving Beyond Money: A Primer on Bail Reform." Report by The Criminal Justice Policy Program, Harvard Law School, Cambridge. October 2016. http://cjpp.law.harvard.edu/assets/FINAL-Primer-on-Bail-Reform.pdf.

Alexander, Michelle. 2012. *The New Jim Crow: Mass Incarceration in the Age of Colorblindness.* New York: New Press.

Baughman, Shima Baradaran. 2018. *The Bail Book: A Comprehensive Look at Bail in America's Criminal Justice System.* London: Cambridge University Press.

Brand, Jessica, and Jessica Pishko. 2018. "Bail Reform Explained." *The Appeal*, June 14, 2018. https://theappeal.org/bail-reform-explained-4abb73dd2e8a/.

Dabney, Dean A., Joshua A. Page, and Volkan Topalli. 2017. "American Bail and the Tinting of Criminal Justice." *The Howard Journal of Crime and Justice* 56, no. 4: 397–418.

Digard, Léon, and Elizabeth Swavola. 2019. "Justice Denied: The Harmful and Lasting Effects of Pretrial Detention." Vera Institute of Justice, New York. https://www.vera.org/downloads/publications/Justice-Denied-Evidence-Brief.pdf. Accessed July 31, 2024.

Friedman, Lee S. 1976. "The Evolution of Bail Reform." *Policy Sciences* 7, no. 3: 281–313.

Gonnerman, Jennifer. 2014. "Before the Law." *New Yorker*, September 29, 2014. https://www.newyorker.com/magazine/2014/10/06/before-the-law.

Koepke, John Logan, and David G. Robinson. 2018. "Danger Ahead: Risk Assessment and the Future of Bail Reform." *Washington Law Review* 93, no. 4: 1725–807.

Lay, Donald P, and JillDe La Hunt. 1985. "The Bail Reform Act of 1984: A Discussion." *William Mitchell Law Review* 11, no. 4: 929–66.

Leslie, Emily, and Nolan G. Pope. 2017. "The Unintended Impact of Pretrial Detention on Case Outcomes: Evidence from New York City Arraignments." *Journal of Law and Economics* 60, no. 3: 529–57.

Ortiz, Natalie. 2015. "County Jails at a Crossroads: An Examination of the Jail Population and Pretrial Release." National Association of Counties, Washington, DC. July 8, 2015. https://www.naco.org/sites/default/files/documents/County%20Jails%20at%20a%20Crossroads%20-%20Full%20Report_updated.pdf.

Rice, Josie Duffy, and Clint Smith III, hosts. "Justice for the Rich, Money Bail." *Justice in America* (podcast), July 25, 2018. https://theappeal.org/justice-in-america-episode-1-justice-for-the-rich-money-bail/. Accessed July 27, 2020.

Sawyer, Wendy, and Peter Wagner. 2019. "Mass Incarceration: The Whole Pie 2019." *Prison Policy Initiative*, March 24, 2020. https://www.prisonpolicy.org/reports/pie2019.html.

Schnacke, Timothy R., Michael R. Jones, and Claire M. B. Brooker. 2010. "The History of Bail and Pretrial Release." Pretrial Justice Institute, Baltimore. https://www.harryphillipsaic.com/wp-content/uploads/2018/03/HistoryofBail-Pre-TrialRelease-PJI_2010.pdf. Accessed July 27, 2020.

Schuppe, Jon. 2020. "Fair or Dangerous? Days after Ending Cash Bail, New York Has Second Thoughts." *NBC News*, January 7, 2020. https://www.nbcnews.com/news/crime-courts/fair-or-dangerous-days-after-ending-cash-bail-new-york-n1111346.

Shirazi, Nima, and Adam Johnson, hosts. "Willie Hortonism 2020—Media Attacks on Prison Reform." *Citations Needed* (podcast), February 5, 2020. https://citationsneeded.libsyn.com/episode-100-willie-hortonism-2020-media-attacks-on-prison-reform. Accessed July 27, 2020

Smith, Rachel. 2018. "Condemned to Repeat History? Why the Last Movement for Bail Reform Failed, and How This One Can Succeed." *Georgetown Journal on Poverty Law and Policy* 25, no. 3: 451–473.

Van Brunt, Alexa, and Locke E. Bowman. 2018. "Toward a Just Model of Pretrial Release: A History of Bail Reform and a Prescription for What's Next." *The Journal of Criminal Law & Criminology* 108, no. 4: 701–74.

Venhuizen, Harm. 2023. "Republican Bills Push Cash Bail, Subvert Democratic Changes." AP News, March 13, 2023. https://apnews.com/article/cash-bail-crimes-republican-legislation-348362a8484828500e01a545ec58e28f.

Wykstra, Stephanie. 2018. "Bail Reform, Which Could Save Millions of Unconvicted People from Jail, Explained." *Vox*, October 17, 2018. https://www.vox.com/future-perfect/2018/10/17/17955306/bail-reform-criminal-justice-inequality.

Zeng, Zhen. 2018. "Jail Inmates in 2016." *Bureau of Justice Statistics*. Washington, DC: Department of Justice. https://www.bjs.gov/index.cfm?ty=pbdetail&iid=6186. Accessed July 27, 2020.

CHAPTER 2

Civil Asset Forfeiture

CHASTITY BLANKENSHIP AND MADISON SANTORE

AT A GLANCE

Asset forfeiture refers to the seizure of property involved in a crime (e.g., money, weapons, vehicles) by law enforcement officers or other government officials (e.g., state or federal prosecutor). There are two main types of asset forfeiture, criminal and civil. In criminal cases, forfeiture *in personam* (order against a person) applies. If a criminal defendant is convicted, they may be ordered to forfeit any monetary gain from the crime and any property purchased traceable to the crime. In civil cases, *in rem* (order against a thing or property) applies. Like criminal forfeiture, civil asset forfeiture (CAF) is designed to help disrupt the operation of a crime. Unlike criminal forfeiture, however, third parties may have an interest in confiscated property. Civil forfeiture allows the government to bring an order against a "thing or property" without bringing an action against each party with interest in the assets or property involved in a crime.

To clarify, under CAF, property can be seized even if an owner is unaware that those assets or property were involved in the commission of a crime. For example, in *Bennis v. Michigan* (516 U.S. 442, 1996), a car was seized by Michigan officials after a husband engaged in a sex act with a prostitute. While the husband was arrested, he was not charged or convicted of any crime. The wife, who had no knowledge of her husband's activities, sought to recover her share of the vehicle without financial penalty. She was denied recovery of the vehicle with the US Supreme Court finding that an innocent owner defense is not constitutionally mandated by the Fourteenth Amendment (e.g., arbitrary denial of life, liberty, or property by the government).

CAF proceedings are regulated by statute and take place at state and federal levels. Currently, all CAF statutes include provisions of the Civil Asset Forfeiture Reform Act of 2000 (CAFRA). CAFRA established general rules of civil forfeiture proceedings, including the requirement that the government must send the involved party proper notice as soon as practicable and within sixty days after the date of the seizure. CAFRA also explains procedures for filing claims for seized property, and it places the burden of proof on the government to establish that the property is subject to forfeiture. Property is seized based on the idea that it has been put to improper use, not based on the belief that the owner was involved in any wrongdoing (i.e., *in rem*).

While CAF was originally meant to stop criminal activity by seizing the resources used to commit the crime, it is criticized by both sides of the political spectrum. Civil libertarians disagree with taking property from otherwise innocent citizens, while progressives oppose the impact of forfeiture on low-income families and minorities. Another common criticism is that law enforcement agencies use CAF as a profit-generating tool (i.e., "for profit" policing). Although some argue that CAF is unconstitutional because owners of seized properties do not need to be arrested for their belongings to be permanently taken by the government, the US Supreme Court disagrees. Due process, however, is another matter. In October 2023, the Court heard oral arguments in *Culley v. Marshall* (Docket 22-585), a class action Alabama case involving vehicle seizures. At issue is whether due process requires a post-seizure probable cause hearing if CAF is used to seize property from innocent owners, and if so, whether the due process test from *Mathews v. Eldridge* (424 U.S. 319, 1976) or the speedy trial test from *Barker v. Wingo* (407 U.S. 514, 1972) should be used. Although ostensibly about due process, this case may be "a fig leaf for a debate over the legitimacy of widespread civil forfeiture itself" (Jacobson 2023).

MANY REPUBLICANS...

- Historically supported the use of asset forfeiture to take away the tools of the trade for drug cartels.
- Support asset forfeiture for criminal convictions.
- Believe profiting from property seizure could entice law enforcement agencies into unethical behavior when faced with high crime rates and budget cuts.

MANY DEMOCRATS...

- Believe asset forfeiture targets racial minorities since most seizures are related to selling drugs. For example, selling marijuana from a car means the car could be confiscated since it was involved in the commission of a crime.
- Are against civil forfeiture that does not require a criminal conviction for confiscation of property.
- Support the elimination or reduction of "equitable sharing," which is the ability to transfer an asset forfeiture court case to the federal government. Equitable sharing is problematic because federal forfeiture laws are less stringent and the court is more likely to rule in the prosecution's favor.

OVERVIEW

Asset forfeiture is rooted in English common law, but there is debate about whether it is even older. Some scholars view the beginning of asset forfeiture as stemming from an Old Testament biblical passage that justified taking an animal from its owner and killing it. The passage reads, "If an ox gore a man or a woman, that they die: than the ox shall be surely stoned, and his flesh shall not be eaten; but the owner of the ox shall be quit" (Rogin 2014, 3). Early English common law allowed contraband or facilitating property to be seized, but not proceeds of any criminal acts. This standard stayed in place until the late twentieth century.

At the beginning of English sea exploration, England established a practice that more closely resembles the modern American practice. The Navigation Acts of 1660 stated that a single crewman's misconduct could cause the entire ship to be forfeited. In the early Republic of the United States, *in rem* forfeiture actions continued to focus mostly on customs and maritime issues. Courts applied a negligence rationale, which allowed policymakers to justify the forfeiture of property that would otherwise appear unjust. If a court determined that an otherwise innocent owner had allowed illegal use of his property, it helped justify the loss of the property, even if the owner was unaware. During the Civil War, Congress created the Confiscation Act of 1826 to "suppress insurrection, to punish Treason and Rebellion, [and] to seize and confiscate the Property of Rebels." It was considered "the duty of the President of the United States to cause the seizure of all the estate and property, money, stocks, credits, and effects" from anyone who participated in the Confederate government or those who provided "aid and comfort to [the] rebellion." The Confiscation Act represents the first time that Congress applied forfeiture principles to all property with a punitive intention rather than only applying them to admiralty or customs cases. During Prohibition (1920–33), the property involved in illegal alcohol transport was added by the federal government to be subject to forfeiture. Forfeiture cases during Prohibition were more like early admiralty forfeiture cases than modern forfeiture actions because the seizure of property came from the misuse of the property itself.

The case of *Boyd v. United States* (1886) played an important role in CAF proceedings. In this case, the US Supreme Court decided that an *in rem* forfeiture action was a criminal procedure and should be protected under the Fourth Amendment (i.e., unreasonable searches and seizures), and the Fifth Amendment (i.e., the right to a grand jury). Ten years later, the case of *United States v. Zucker* (1896) led to the Court's decision that civil forfeiture was not "technically criminal," so the Sixth Amendment (i.e., the right to public trial without unnecessary delay, the right to a lawyer, and the right to an impartial jury) was not applicable. Then, in *One 1958 Plymouth Sedan v. Pennsylvania* (1965), the Court clarified that civil forfeiture is a civil action, but the proceeding has a quasi-criminal character. This means the proceeding has some qualities of a criminal prosecution, but not all.

Only a few years later, President Nixon's administration passed the Comprehensive Abuse Prevention and Control Act (1970). This act expanded seizure regulations and allowed for drug-related CAF. As part of the War on Drugs, one goal of this act was to remove the economic incentives from cartels or individuals primarily involved in organized crime. It does not make sense to just seize illegal drugs while a criminal gets to enjoy a lavish lifestyle based on the fruits of their wrongdoing. This act took away the tools of the trade (e.g., property and assets) making it more difficult for the criminal to engage in similar acts.

Under President Reagan, the Comprehensive Crime Control Act (1984) passed with nearly unanimous support. This act also expanded asset forfeiture, by specifically entitling local law enforcement to share sized property with federal agencies through equitable sharing. More specifically, equitable sharing means a local or state law enforcement agency that is directly involved in a federal forfeiture case may request to either put that property into official use or share the seized assets. This was a significant step, since federal statues were, and continue to this day, to be more lenient in the type of forfeiture allowed by law in comparison to state law. Additionally, federal agencies typically have more resources available to help them prosecute a case than state or local governments, which in turn makes it more difficult for defendants to fight asset forfeiture.

During the 1990s, President George H. W. Bush's administration continued using asset forfeiture. However, toward the end of his term in office, public officials began to openly speak out against the use of asset forfeiture. In 1993, Supreme Court Justice Clarence Thomas voiced concerns over the growing use of CAF. Several years later, while Democratic President William J. "Bill" Clinton's administration also used CAF, calls for reform could no longer be ignored. President Clinton signed into law the Civil Asset Forfeiture Reform Act of 2000 (CAFRA). This act was passed by Congress in response to Illinois representative Henry Hyde, who believed that CAF laws at the time were being used unjustly. Congress' objective was to carry out President Nixon's War on Drugs in a fairer manner.

CAFRA established general rules of civil forfeiture proceedings, including the requirement that the government must send the involved party proper notice as soon as practicable and within sixty days after the date of the seizure. CAFRA also explains procedures for filing claims for seized property and places the burden of proof on the government to establish that the property is subject to forfeiture. Property is seized based on the idea that it has been put to improper use, not based on the belief that the owner was involved in any wrongdoing (i.e., *in rem*). Additionally, CAFRA shifted the burden of proof to the government rather than the owner, who previously had to establish the property's innocence.

Only one year later, in 2001, less than two months after the terrorist attacks on September 11, the USA Patriot Act was passed. This expanded the federal government's ability to seize property and assets related to the commission of acts of terrorism. During the 2000s under President George W. Bush and later President Barack Obama, forfeiture by the federal government continued with increased revenue from asset forfeiture. Eventually, fears of international terrorism cooled, and public opinion swayed toward concerns of prison overpopulation. Increasingly, the public began to decry punishment for nonviolent drug offenses especially for the use of marijuana. Some state and local areas began to decriminalize marijuana possession, and some went even further by allowing for medical or recreational use. At the same time, Attorney General Eric Holder announced forfeiture would only be used for the most serious illegal banking transactions after a defendant was criminally charged.

Timbs v. Indiana

One of the most famous civil forfeiture cases occurred following the seizure of a luxury vehicle. An Indiana man, Tyson Timbs, legally purchased a Land Rover vehicle in 2012 with life insurance money he received following his father's death. In 2013, Timbs was arrested by undercover officers after selling them around $200 in drugs. Applying CAF law, Indiana state authorities confiscated the Land Rover from Timbs. Timbs and the Institute for Justice challenged this seizure in court. They argued the confiscation of the Land Rover violated the excessive fines clause of the Eighth Amendment. A Grant County Superior judge found the value of the vehicle, which was over $40,000, to be over four times the maximum penalty for his drug conviction and ruled in Timbs's favor. However, the Indiana Supreme Court reversed this decision and argued the Eight Amendment only applied for federal and not state actions. Following the reversal, Timbs petitioned the US Supreme Court to hear his case. They agreed and oral arguments began in November 2018. At the heart of this court battle was whether the Eighth Amendment excessive fines clause was a right to be incorporated by the states. In February 2019, the US Supreme Court unanimously ruled the Eighth Amendment excessive fines clause is an incorporated protection in local and state law (*Timbs* 2019).

At the time of the presidential election in November 2016, both Republican and Democratic party platforms endorsed forfeiture reform. The Republican Party stated that, while forfeiture was originally designed to disrupt organized crime, it has become a tool abused by law enforcement for profit at the expense of innocent citizens. Similarly, the Democratic Party platform aimed to protect the American public and remove incentives for law enforcement agencies to profit from forfeiture. In July 2017, however, Republican lawmakers became angry when a Justice Department directive allowed the federal government to take assets that were lawfully seized by local or state law enforcement officials. Critics claimed it encouraged law enforcement agencies to take property from people who were only suspected of engaging in criminal activity, which would be a violation of due process. This directive allowed local law enforcement to avoid state regulations that put limits on forfeitures. The state or local agency would then be eligible to keep most of the proceeds, ignoring state laws that require assets to go into general funds for the state.

At the beginning of his presidency, however, Republican Donald Trump disagreed with lawmakers who wanted to make changes to civil asset forfeiture laws. Under Trump's command, the Justice Department's Equitable Sharing Program was revived. Additionally, in October 2018, the Supreme Court unanimously assumed that civil *in rem* forfeiture was constitutional. Instead, the focus was on whether the Eighth Amendment (i.e., no excessive fines or cruel and unusual punishment inflicted) applied to civil asset forfeiture. Consequently, the Supreme Court has not yet decided on the constitutionality of the standard of proof for civil asset forfeiture.

In general, there has recently been bipartisan support for civil asset forfeiture reform. Republicans have called for greater accountability and tracking of seized property, while Democrats tend to call for greater restrictions in equitable sharing programs. While Republicans and Democrats may disagree on who (or if) forfeiture laws target specific groups, they seem to agree that left unchecked, seizing property could encourage law enforcement agencies to engage in this process to financially support their departments. In 2020, neither Republican nor Democrat Party platforms included updated forfeiture reform plans. Republicans did not create a new party platform and continued to work on their 2016 goals, and Democrats shifted focus to revamp and detail their fight for racial justice and national health care in America. It is expected that the 2024 Republican platform will remain virtually unchanged from 2016/2020 and that Democrats will focus primarily on the economy, social justice issues, and healthcare, including abortion rights.

REPUBLICANS ON CIVIL ASSET FORFEITURE

One of the most vocal supporters of CAF is former Republican Alabama senator and former Trump attorney general Jeff Sessions. In 1999, Senator Sessions, along with Democratic New York Senator Charles Schumer and others, introduced the Civil Asset Forfeiture Reform Act of 1999, also known as the Sessions/Schumer Bill. The failed Sessions/Schumer Bill attempted to address loopholes that could be used by local and state law enforcement officials. In particular, the bill addressed raising the burden of proof from "probable cause" to a "preponderance of the evidence." The Sessions/Schumer Bill would have allowed defendants to collect attorney's fees from the government and tightened the timeframe in which state and local agencies could request federal adoption of forfeiture cases. With federal adoption of a case, a federal agency with more resources would take over the prosecution of a case, while still allowing a state and local agency to share revenue generated from the confiscated property or assets.

One of the most controversial elements of the Sessions/Schumer Bill was that it continued to allow federal adoption through *equitable sharing*. Equitable sharing allows state and local agencies to transfer cases to a federal agency and provides incentives for doing so. Primarily, federal forfeiture laws are typically less stringent compared to state regulations. Secondarily, state officials can still receive a vast majority of the proceeds from forfeiture cases. According to Sessions, proceeds from civil forfeiture is one of the main tools that allow law enforcement to take material support from criminals and fund law enforcement efforts. For many agencies, this is a win-win-win situation—fewer resources are allocated to prosecuting forfeiture cases, they receive the lion's share of the proceeds, and with relatively lax policies, federal agencies are more likely to secure a judgment in their favor.

The Sessions/Schumer Bill did not address some concerns the public had regarding civil forfeiture. Two conservative organizations, the Institute of Justice and the Heritage Foundation, concluded that modern forfeiture violates due processes specifically because the burden of proof was lower for civil forfeiture than for criminal conviction. This means the government could seize property at a much lower standard, which is more likely to result in the court siding with prosecutors rather than defendants. Additionally, the Sessions/Schumer Bill would have continued to allow innocent victims to have their property seized. For example, if a family member was arrested for selling drugs from a borrowed car, the state or federal government could seize the vehicle. In other words, if the property was involved in a crime that the owner was unaware of, the property could legally be seized through *in rem* forfeiture.

In addition to sponsoring the Sessions/Schumer Bill as a senator, Sessions also acted to support CAF during his year-plus appointment as Trump's attorney general. He rescinded some modest changes made to CAF by Eric Holder, attorney general for Democratic President Barack Obama. For example, Holder limited Equitable Sharing proceeds obtained without criminal charges or warrants, but Sessions reversed those policies and stated in a press release that, "President Trump has directed this Department of Justice to reduce crime in this country, and we will use every lawful tool that we have to do that. We will continue to encourage civil asset forfeiture whenever appropriate."

Sessions is unique among Republicans who generally are more likely to introduce legislation that limits CAF. In 2015, several states passed Republican-supported legislation to tighten forfeiture requirements in 2015. Michigan's Republican Governor Rick Snyder passed legislation requiring agencies to track seized property, the underlying offense that caused the forfeiture, and whether the property owner was charged and/or convicted of that crime. New Mexico's Republican Governor Susana Martinez signed House Bill 560, requiring a criminal conviction before property can be forfeited. Additionally, the state must now show by clear and convincing evidence the property owner had "actual knowledge of the underlying crime giving rise to the forfeiture" (Snead 2016). Further, Equitable Sharing can only occur under limited circumstances such as when property value exceeds $50,000, or the criminal conduct is interstate.

In Montana, Republican Senator Bob Keenan and Republican Representatives Matt Regier and Ryan Lynch introduced House Bill 463, which requires a criminal conviction before forfeiture. The state also must prove, "the property was either an instrumentality of the criminal offense or constitutes the illicit proceeds of the offense," by clear and convincing evidence (Snead 2016). Requiring a criminal conviction before forfeiture essentially abolishes *in rem* forfeiture. There are exceptions, such as if the seized property is a controlled substance or the property owner is unknown, deported, flees, or dies.

These pieces of legislation have increased restrictions for the use of CAF, making it more difficult for agencies to use this tactic for disrupting criminal activities. Nebraska's Republican Governor Pete Ricketts signed House Bill 560 in 2016, which has one of the strictest civil forfeiture statues in the United States in that property may only be seized when the defendant is convicted of drug, child pornography, or illegal gambling offenses. Equitable Sharing is also limited to cases in which a federal agent physically seizes the property, the defendant is facing federal prosecution, or the property value exceeds $25,000.

In the same year, Florida's Republican Governor Rick Scott signed State Bill 1044, which reduced the state's ability to use civil forfeiture to seize property. This bill raised the standard for a seizure to "beyond a reasonable doubt," and required the state to prove the defendant had actual knowledge of the criminal activity involving their property. State Bill 1044 also requires the seizing agency to pay a $1,000 filing fee and post a $1,500 bond that is payable to the defendant if they win (Snead 2016). These changes could act as an effective deterrent to bringing cases based on dubious or little evidence.

More recent changes continue to reduce the likelihood that agencies will seize property through civil forfeiture. Michigan Republican Senators Peter Lucido and Lee Roberson Chatfield supported a forfeiture reform bill to reduce the reach of agencies using civil forfeiture to seize property. In this case, police must charge someone with a crime to seize their property. Maryland's Republican Governor Hogan signed House Bill 336 in which law enforcement agencies may forfeit cash only in connection with the illegal manufacture, distribution, or dispensing of controlled substances. Cash seizures based on simple drug possession would not qualify for forfeiture.

At the federal level, the 2016 Republican Party platform (2016, 15) contained a statement condemning the use of civil forfeiture without much-needed changes. As mentioned in their 2016 platform,

> Civil asset forfeiture was originally intended as a way to cripple organized crime through the seizure of property used in a criminal enterprise. Regrettably, it has become a tool for unscrupulous law enforcement officials, acting without due process, to profit by destroying the livelihood of innocent individuals, many of whom never recover the lawful assets taken from them. When the rights of the innocent can be so easily violated, no one's rights are safe. We call on Congress and state legislatures to enact reforms to protect law-abiding citizens against abusive asset forfeiture tactics.

Overall, Republicans were originally some of the first to push for greater use of forfeiture. They did this through acts passed under President Nixon's War on Drugs, and by Presidents Reagan and George H. W. Bush's continuation of a tough on drug crime policies. In the 2000s President George W. Bush shifted the use of asset forfeiture from drugs to terrorism. However, more recently both Republicans and Democrats became increasingly suspect of the use of civil forfeiture without a criminal conviction. More specifically, some of the major changes introduced by Republicans shifted the burden of proof from the defendant to the state by requiring beyond a reasonable doubt the property owner knew about the illegal activity. Further, many bills introduced by Republicans limited local and state agencies' ability to transfer a case under equitable sharing.

DEMOCRATS ON CIVIL ASSET FORFEITURE

Similar civil forfeiture bills have been introduced by Democrat legislators and signed into law by representatives in executive branches of government. In 2014, Democratic Minnesota Governor Mark Dayton signed a bill that requires a criminal conviction for property to be seized. Two years later, New Hampshire's former governor and current Democratic senator Maggie Hassan also signed a bill requiring a criminal conviction in most forfeiture cases. A criminal conviction sets a higher standard for forfeiture than legislation, which requires a person to be charged with a criminal offense. When only a criminal charge is required, a defendant could win their criminal case (i.e., be acquitted) but still must fight for their property in a civil forfeiture court case. This could be problematic for the defendant if the state they live in allows for *in rem* forfeiture. In other words, a defendant could win their criminal trial and lose their property through civil forfeiture proceedings. In Minnesota and New Hampshire, this loophole is closed by requiring a conviction for property to be seized.

In a 2015 Department of Justice press release (Number 15-400), Attorney General Eric Holder announced forfeiture would only be used for the most serious illegal banking transactions after the defendant was criminally charged or engaged in additional criminal activity. He stated:

> Appropriate use of asset forfeiture law allows the Justice Department to safeguard the integrity, security, and stability of our nation's financial system while protecting the civil liberties of all Americans. And as we continue our comprehensive review of the Asset Forfeiture Program, we will stay focused on deterring criminal activity, assisting victims of wrongdoing and defending the rights of our citizens.

One of the most comprehensive bills was signed into law by Democratic California Governor Jerry Brown. The bill was written by Democratic Senator Holly Mitchell and Republican assembly member David Hadley to prevent law enforcement agencies from profiting from property gained through civil forfeiture. In a press release through the Drug Policy Alliance (2016), this bill prevents "agencies from receiving a share of the federally forfeited property unless there is a conviction in an underlying case involving seized property that is up to $40,000 in cash or for cars and homes." The bill also requires a criminal conviction in most cases of property seizure.

In 2016, the Democrat Party platform included a brief statement that indicated they would push to reform civil asset forfeiture; however, they failed to explain how or what type of changes they would make. Related to asset forfeiture law, their 2016 platform did include a detailed plan to have the federal government remove marijuana from the list of Schedule 1 controlled substances. Democrats also stated they would like the federal government to create a pathway toward future legalization of marijuana. Linking these platforms together, by removing marijuana from the federal list of controlled substances, states may continue to adopt or change penalties for marijuana possession. For example, asset forfeiture laws have been used to seize a vehicle when the driver of the car is arrested for marijuana possession. By abolishing marijuana possession as an offense at the federal level, this could eliminate the possibility of a criminal conviction. At the state level, some may decide to follow the federal government's lead and remove marijuana possession from their list of criminal offenses. In turn, this would mean federal, state, and local agencies would be unable to seize property for possession alone.

At that state level, in 2019, Michigan Attorney General Dana Nessel (D) stated she would not use civil forfeiture to seize assets. Like others, Nessel has called civil forfeiture a violation of due process. Nessel also opened a criminal investigation into the Macomb County Prosecutor Eric Smith's (D) use of forfeiture funds during the same year. Smith and a few friends schemed to use funds obtained through forfeiture for personal expenses and activities, which resulted in Smith's arrest and resignation in March 2020. He was charged with ten state felonies ranging from racketeering and embezzlement to improper use of office, and with federal obstruction of justice. Smith served six months of a twenty-one-month federal sentence and reached a plea deal on the state charges for which he was sentenced to one year in prison and ordered to pay fines, restitution, and forfeit a portion of his pension. He currently is serving four years on probation.

Also during 2020, at least one forfeiture reform bill in Arizona stalled due primarily to Democrats voting against it. Arizona Senate Bill 1556 would have required a criminal conviction before property could be permanently seized. Several Arizona Democrats who voted against this bill explained their reasoning. For example, both Representatives Diego Rodriguez (D) and Reginald Bolding (D) said they did not support Senate Bill 1556 due to the financial impact this bill would have on funding. More specifically, passing this bill would remove funding from agencies who rely on seized assets for their budgets. During the vote on this bill, the Covid-19 pandemic had just started, which meant many agencies did not have adequate funds to meet public needs. For these representatives, they were not willing to take away funds and hoped they would be replaced in the future.

Other Democrat representatives, Kirsten Engel and Jennifer Jermaine, had concerns about rushing the bill through without proper vetting. More specifically, they cited concerns if a prosecutor would still be able to seize property and hold it before a criminal conviction. Currently, prosecutors can prevent offenders from selling or shielding assets while a criminal case plays out in court. Depending on the wording of the bill, prosecutors may be stripped of that ability, which may allow individuals to sell or shield assets before they are convicted of an offense during their trial. Beyond the financial impact on agencies and prosecutors, if those illegal funds are sold off or shielded from seizure, it would further deprive victims of compensation.

Overall, while Democrats favor eliminating or drastically reducing the reach of civil forfeiture, other issues are likely more pressing. From 2020 through 2022, the Covid-19 pandemic negatively impacted law enforcement activities and left local, state, and federal agencies scrambling to find resources. As a result, it would not be surprising if reforms to asset forfeiture continue to stall. With reduced revenue, some Democrats may decide to continue to use seized property and assets to meet the needs of their constituents.

FURTHER READING

"Asset Forfeiture Abuse." n.d. American Civil Liberties Union. https://www.aclu.org/issues/criminal-law-reform/reforming-police/asset-forfeiture-abuse?redirect=issues/criminal-law-reform/reforming-police-practices/asset-forfeiture-abuse. Accessed March 16, 2023.

"Attorney General Restricts Use of Asset Forfeiture in Structuring Offenses." 2015. The United States Department of Justice, March 31, 2015. www.justice.gov/opa/pr/attorney-general-restricts-use-asset-forfeiture-structuring-offenses.

"Attorney General Sessions Issues Policy and Guidelines on Federal Adoptions of Assets Seized by State or Local Law Enforcement." 2017. The United States Department of Justice, July 19, 2017. www.justice.gov/opa/pr/attorney-general-sessions-issues-policy-and-guidelines-federal-adoptions-assets-seized-state.

Barker v. Wingo, 407 U.S. 514 (1972).

Bennis v. Michigan, 516 U.S. 442 (1996).

Boyd v. United States, 116 U.S. 616 (1886).
"California Governor Brown Signs Bill Protecting Californians from Civil Asset Forfeiture Abuse." 2016. Drug Policy Alliance, September 28, 2016. https://drugpolicy.org/news/california-governor-brown-signs-bill-protecting-californians-civil-asset-forfeiture-abu/.
Censky, Abigail. 2019. "Civil Asset Forfeiture Reform Bill Clears State Senate with Bipartisan Support." WKAR, February 13, 2019. www.wkar.org/post/civil-asset-forfeiture-reform-bill-clears-state-senate-bipartisan-support#stream/0.
"Civil Asset Forfeiture." n.d. Bill of Rights Institute. https://billofrightsinstitute.org/educate/educator-resources/lessons-plans/civil-asset-forfeiture/. Accessed July 31, 2024.
Culley v. Marshall, Docket 22-585 (2023).
Detroit Free Press. 2019. "Gretchen Whitmer Signs Bills to Limit Asset Forfeiture in Drug Cases." *Detroit Free Press*, May 9, 2019. www.freep.com/story/news/politics/2019/05/09/gretchen-whitmer-signs-bills-limit-asset-forfeiture-drug-cases/1155329001/.
Ford, Matt. 2017. "Justice Thomas's Doubts about Civil Forfeiture." *The Atlantic*, May 3, 2017. www.theatlantic.com/politics/archive/2017/04/clarence-thomas-civil-forfeiture/521583/.
Jacobson, Jill. 2023. "Procedure in Practice: *Culley v. Marshall* and the Future of Civil Asset Forfeiture." The Federalist Society, November 9, 2023. fedsoc.org/commentary/fedsoc-blog/procedure-in-practice-culley-v-marshall-and-the-future-of-civil-asset-forfeiture
Lampard, Ronald J. 2016. "New Hampshire Becomes Latest State to Overhaul Civil Asset Forfeiture Process." American Legislative Exchange Council, June 30, 2016. www.alec.org/article/new-hampshire-becomes-latest-state-to-overhaul-civil-asset-forfeiture-process/.
Mathews v. Eldridge, 423 U.S. 319 (1976).
Nelson, Caleb. 2015. "The Constitutionality of Civil Forfeiture." *Yale Law Journal* 125: 2446.
One 1958 Plymouth Sedan v. Pennsylvania, 380 U.S. 693 (1965).
"An Overview of Recent State-Level Forfeiture Reforms." 2016. The Heritage Foundation, August 8, 2016. www.heritage.org/crime-and-justice/report/overview-recent-state-level-forfeiture-reforms.
"Party Platform." 2016. *Democrats*, July 8, 2016. democrats.org/where-we-stand/party-platform/.
Rogin, Alexandra D. 2014. "Dollars for Collars: Civil Asset Forfeiture and the Breakdown of Constitutional Rights." *Drexel Law Review* 7, no. 1: 45+. https://link.gale.com/apps/doc/A417570552/AONE?u=lake33936&sid=AONE&xid=0e220c95. Accessed July 31, 2024.
"Schumer to Join Sessions to Introduce Civil Asset Forfeiture Reform Act: Bill Will Protect Innocent Citizens Without Undermining Law Enforcement." 2010. U.S. Senator Chuck Schumer of New York, April 28, 2010. www.schumer.senate.gov/newsroom/press-releases/schumer-to-join-sessions-to-introduce-civil-asset-forfeiture-reform-act.
Snead, Jason. 2016. "An Overview of Recent State-Level Forfeiture Reforms." The Heritage Foundation, August 8, 2016. www.heritage.org/crime-and-justice/report/overview-recent-state-level-forfeiture-reforms.
Teigen, Anne, and Lucia Bragg. 2018. "Evolving Civil Asset Forfeiture Laws." National Conference of State Legislatures, February 2018. https://perma.cc/5JDB-2YNH. Accessed July 31, 2024.
Timbs v. Indiana, 586 U.S. 146 (2019).
"The 2016 Republican Party Platform." 2016. GOP, July 18, 2016. gop.com/the-2016-republican-party-platform/

United States Department of Justice. 2017. "Attorney General Sessions Issues Policy and Guidelines on Federal Adoptions of Assets Seized by State or Local Law Enforcement." Office of Public Affairs, July 19, 2017. https://www.justice.gov/opa/pr/attorney-general-sessions-issues-policy-and-guidelines-federal-adoptions-assets-seized-state.

United States v. Zucker, 161 U.S. 475 (1896).

CHAPTER 3

Concealed or Open Firearm Carry

SHERAH L. BASHAM

AT A GLANCE

Laws pertaining to the carry of firearms are established by states and vary from one state to another. Each state legislature defines statutes to regulate the carry of firearms within its borders, including whether a permit or license is required, and the requirements to obtain a permit or license. Requirements for a permit or license typically include a minimum age, an application, a criminal background check, and a gun safety course. While laws surrounding the carry of a weapon may include knives, chemical sprays, and/or electronic devices, the discussion of "open" or "concealed" carry typically refers to firearms.

States with "open carry" allow residents to carry firearms in plain sight but vary as to whether a permit is required or not. However, states that do not require a permit may still have regulations in place to dictate the minimum age for the individual, those who may be restricted based on criminal history, state residency requirements, and other protocols. Additionally, states that do not require a permit for open carry within their borders may issue permits for their residents to carry in other states. "Concealed carry" refers to carrying a weapon in a hidden or concealed manner, such as in a bag or purse, or underneath one's clothing.

Concealed carry is one of four types: (1) unrestricted, (2) shall issue with no discretion, (3) shall issue with limited discretion, and (4) may issue. Unrestricted states, often called "constitutional carry" states, require no permit to carry a concealed weapon but may provide a permit in certain circumstances (e.g., for a resident who wants to also carry in another state or for a nonresident who wishes to carry in the permitting state). Currently, only Vermont does not provide or require a concealed carry permit of any kind. States that "shall issue with no discretion" grant permits to any applicant who meets the requirements, removing any discretion from the permitting authority. States that "shall issue with limited discretion" allow the granting authority to have some discretion in determining to whom to grant a permit. Finally, decision-makers in "may issue" states have complete discretion to grant or deny a permit, even when an applicant meets all the requirements. Currently, four states are "may issue," and twenty-three are "shall issue," but vary widely in their strictness. In California, for example, rural counties regularly issue concealed carry permits while more urban and suburban counties rarely approve them.

Between 1987 and 2006, over 70 percent of states shifted from more restrictive "no issue" concealed carry statutes to "shall-issue" states. By 2010, the only "no issue" states were Illinois and Wisconsin, and by 2019, many states had loosened their concealed carry statutes further, shifting from "shall-issue" to "unrestricted" statutes. By 2024, nearly half of the states had implemented some form of "unrestricted" or "Constitutional carry" statutes.

MANY REPUBLICANS...

- Advocate for reduced government oversight of gun ownership. The general argument provided is that according to the Second Amendment, citizens are guaranteed the right to own firearms and utilize firearms to defend themselves.
- Believe that the public is safer when more citizens carry firearms. This is based on the assertion that citizens can defend themselves and/or protect others when lives are threatened by carrying a firearm.
- Support the expansion of concealed carry laws. This would include allowing concealed carry in more places and permitting K-12 teachers and staff to carry on campus.

MANY DEMOCRATS...

- Support gun restrictions such as regulations on gun ownership and the licensing to carry firearms. They argue that the Second Amendment applies only to maintaining a militia, and therefore, states and cities have the power to entirely ban personal gun ownership.
- View increased control and restriction over the carrying of guns to be essential to the safety of the public.
- Advocate for stricter guidelines for obtaining concealed carry permits and more significant restrictions of where weapons may be carried concealed.

OVERVIEW

It is difficult to allocate views on gun ownership and concealed carry to one political party or another. While the right to own and carry a firearm is perceived as a conservative stance, it is grounded in constitutional rights and influenced by culture and lifestyle. The Commonwealth of Virginia, for example, traditionally votes Democrat in presidential elections, elected a Democratic governor in 2017, and usually has Democrats in crucial government positions. Despite this, most of its counties and municipalities have voted to become Second Amendment "sanctuaries" where any legislative attempts at gun control would not be enforced.

Debate over gun control is not necessarily political but constitutional and focused on individual rights. Gun ownership and the right to carry firearms have long been among the most controversial topics in American politics, legislation, and policy. Each gun-related tragedy spawns polarizing opinions among those supporting carry for personal protection versus those in favor of gun control to reduce the occurrence of similar events. However, state legislatures determine the implementation of concealed carry at the state level, and the ultimate interpretation of the Second Amendment as it relates to concealed carry is by the US Supreme Court, a nonpartisan entity.

The US Constitution is integral to arguments related to the right to carry firearms, particularly the Second Amendment. According to the Second Amendment, "A well-regulated militia being necessary to the security of a free state, the right of the people to keep and bear arms shall not be infringed." While the Bill of Rights does not explicitly address types of firearms, personal protection, or carrying openly or concealed in public, it is frequently the basis for both case and statutory law surrounding the use of firearms.

At the center of the Second Amendment debate is whether the right to bear arms is a collective or an individual right. The individual right perspective is the crux of the argument to support the open/concealed carry of firearms. In contrast, those who advocate stricter gun law more often utilize the collective right argument. When the founders established the government in America, their perspective was that to deprive citizens of their weapons would increase the potential for federal oppression and tyranny. This perspective was due to events in England. The monarchy had seized the weapons of the citizens to suppress their uprising against taxes in 1642, when the parliament confiscated firearms in 1659, and continued disarmament throughout the 1670s. English judge, Sir William Blackstone, stated that the right to keep arms was the right of every person. This was later echoed by James Madison, one of the founders of the United States. Their shared view was that through citizen firearm possession, the people's rights would be protected from oppressive government control.

Historically, political party views about gun control have been deeply divergent, with Republicans supporting a less restrictive approach and Democrats supporting a more restrictive approach. Although the current debate about concealed and open carry reflects those conflicting views, laws in the 1800s tended to favor the prohibition of concealed carry consistently. The earliest recorded law prohibiting the carrying of a concealed weapon was in Kentucky in 1813. Southern states such as Virginia and Tennessee followed suit, along with Indiana and Ohio. By the late 1800s, western territories and states such as Montana and Oklahoma were passing laws banning citizens from carrying any form of concealed weapons. Some researchers suggest that these laws were efforts to control violence.

However, the first attempt to provide gun control at the national level did not come until the passage of the Uniform Firearms Act of 1926, which included a provision to allow states to require citizens to obtain a license to carry a concealed weapon. The National Conference of Commissioners proposed this act to create uniformity in state laws. Several states adopted versions of the law, established waiting periods to purchase firearms, and instituted state-issued concealed weapon permits. After widespread adoption of the Uniform Firearms Act, there was little change to state laws regarding concealed carry for over the next fifty years. The state of Washington shifted to a shall issue state in 1961, and Indiana became a shall issue state in 1980. Through the 1980s, eight states shifted to shall carry laws. However, in the early 1990s, a new perspective arose, asserting that the intention of the Second Amendment was referring to a collective right, focusing on the operations of a militia, and not an individual right. This led to seventeen more states adopting shall issue laws between 1990 and 1996.

During the early 2000s, two important US Supreme Court decisions significantly influenced the interpretation of laws regarding personal gun ownership, and subsequently, the carrying of weapons. In the first case, *District of Columbia v. Heller* (554 U.S. 570, 2008), Heller challenged the District of Columbia's handgun ban, arguing that it violated his Second Amendment right to own firearms. Another issue in the case was a provision that firearms within one's residence must be locked, which Heller argued effectively eliminated his right and ability to protect himself in his own home.

While court decision-making is a nonpartisan process, an existing mechanism allows those who are not party to the case to make a statement about the issues under court review. *Amicus curiae* ("friend of the court") briefs are written statements submitted to a court during its deliberation to convey the opinion of government officials, special interest groups, and other groups of concerned citizens not directly party to the case, but who have an interest or stake in the outcome. These briefs often provide expertise or information about issues being argued in the case, and support or opposition for one outcome or the other. Prior to the Court's decision in *Heller*, 305 members of the House and Senate (75 percent of which were Republican) submitted an *amicus* brief on behalf of Heller. It argued that the Second Amendment applied to private ownership and allowed for carrying of firearms in one's home for personal defense, notwithstanding military obligations. Furthermore, it explained that the Second Amendment "declares a political principle and then guarantees a substantive right." The significance here is that state and federal governments do not have rights, but have power bestowed by the people; only people have rights. To illustrate, the *amicus* brief used the Fourth and Ninth Amendments. The Fourth Amendment grants "*The right of the people* to be secure in their persons, houses, papers, and effects, against unreasonable searches and seizures," and the Ninth Amendment explains that "certain rights, shall not be construed to deny or disparage others retained *by the people*" (emphases in original) (NO. 08-1521, 2009, 6).

The Supreme Court agreed, determining that the firearm rights provided in the Second Amendment applied at the state level. In its decision, the Court agreed that self-defense is a basic right of all citizens, and the District of Columbia's claim that citizens' right to bear arms dissipated upon formation of full-time armed services contradicted the Bill of Rights. Therefore, the Court ruled, it was unconstitutional for the District of Columbia to ban the ownership of handguns and to apply in-home access restrictions.

In the second case, *McDonald v. Chicago* (561 U.S. 742, 2010), McDonald challenged Chicago's ordinance that banned citizens from possessing handguns. This case received the largest bicameral *amicus* brief to date, filed with 309 signatures. While most signatories were Republican, nearly one-third of those who signed the brief were Democrat. In the *McDonald* brief, they argued that "firearms prohibitions at issue infringe on the rights of the law-abiding citizens of the District of Columbia as guaranteed by the Second Amendment." The court interpreted the *Heller* decision at the state level by applying the Fourteenth Amendment, affirming that Second Amendment rights to keep and bear arms applied to the states. During this time, state Supreme Courts in both Utah (2006) and Colorado (2010) established case laws determining that colleges did not have the authority to restrict the right of students, faculty, and staff from carrying concealed weapons, provided they possessed a concealed weapons permit.

In 2023, there were approximately 21.8 million concealed weapon permits in the United States, which represents 8.4 percent of the adult population. Florida contains the largest number with 2.56 million permit holders, while Alabama has the highest rate of permit holders, with an estimated 27.8 percent of residents possessing a permit.

REPUBLICANS ON CONCEALED OR OPEN FIREARM CARRY

Nationwide implementation of the Uniform Firearms Act of 1926 provided state laws for concealed carry, which were effective for over fifty years. In 1983, Republican President Ronald Reagan approved federal regulations that restricted the carrying of weapons in national parks. Even firearms in private vehicles were required to be unloaded. Over a quarter of a century later, these provisions were overturned. Republican Senator Tom Coburn (OK) introduced a rider to the Credit Card Accountability Responsibility and Disclosure Act of 2009 (CARD), which permitted the possession and carrying of a firearm in the National Park System and the National Wildlife Refuge System, as permitted within the state and local laws. The CARD Act was passed by Congress with bipartisan support (361 to 64), approving the main intent of the Act (credit card legislation), as well as the rider. The Act was then signed into effect by Democratic President Barack Obama.

From 1987 to 2006, multiple states that traditionally voted Republican enacted gun laws permitting the concealed carry of a weapon with a license. Most of these states moved from either "may-issue" or "no-issue" language, to become "shall-issue" states. These states included: Alaska, Arizona, Florida, Idaho, Montana, North Carolina, and Wyoming. Prior to 2010, only Alaska permitted "constitutional carry." However, after the *Heller* decision in 2008, states began to shift again, but this time toward "constitutional carry."

From 2010 to 2019, many states began to further remove restrictions on carrying concealed weapons. In 2010, Arizona became the second state to permit open carry without a license. By 2011 Republicans had taken control of Wisconsin's government and approved a law to permit and license the carrying of concealed weapons. Between 2013 and 2015, three more states, Arkansas, Maine, and Kansas, approved open carry. The shift in party control of states and subsequent change in gun laws was also seen in West Virginia. West Virginia had historically voted Democratic in state and national elections, but since 2000 they have voted Republican in presidential elections. In 2015, for the first time in over eighty-five years, Republicans were the majority in both the West Virginia state legislature and in its representatives to the US Congress. Subsequently, in

2016, West Virginia approved constitutional carry. That same year, Idaho, Mississippi, and Missouri signed laws removing the requirement of a concealed carry license for residents to carry a firearm. Moreover in 2017, both New Jersey Republican governor and North Dakota Republican governor signed bills providing constitutional carry rights to residents to carry firearms for self-protection without a state permit. In 2019, the Oklahoma Senate and House legalized permitless carry of a firearm, both concealed and open, with bipartisan support. Also, in 2019, Republican Governor Kristi Noem of South Dakota signed into effect South Dakota's Constitutional Carry law, allowing residents to carry weapons—both open and concealed for self-defense without requiring a permit. When the bill was first introduced and passed by South Dakota legislators in 2017, then Republican governor, Dennis Daugaard, vetoed the bill, citing that the current permitting process was "simple and straightforward" and not a violation of the Second Amendment.

Republicans Introduce National Reciprocity Act

Since 2015, Republican Senator John Cornyn (TX) has consistently introduced the Concealed Carry Reciprocity Act to Congress. Reciprocity is the practice of recognizing the laws or permits of another. Each state determines if they will honor concealed carry permits of other states, and if so, which states will be recognized. This issue is vital to those who carry a firearm during interstate travel, ensuring that they are not committing a crime when carrying a gun. The bill is sponsored in the House of Representatives by Republican Representative Richard Hudson (NC). If passed, any person who holds a concealed carry permit in their home state would be allowed to legally carry concealed in any other state, which also has concealed carry laws. According to Senator Cornyn, "This bill focuses on two of our country's most fundamental constitutional protections—the Second Amendment right of citizens to keep and bear arms and the Tenth Amendment's right of states to make laws best-suited for their residents" (Cornyn 2019).

National Reciprocity received support from former president Donald Trump. Prior to his election in 2016, then-candidate Trump supported both concealed carry and national reciprocity. Trump equated reciprocity of carry permits to driver's licenses, stating that "a concealed carry permit should work in every state" (Trump n.d.). Trump supported the perspective that concealed carry is a privilege protected by the Second Amendment. In its various forms, the bill has been supported primarily by Republican senators but has gained some approval by Democrats.

Since 2015, legislation to allow some form of concealed carry on college campuses has been introduced and passed. Texas, which has held a Republican governor for over twenty-five years, passed a bill in 2015, allowing concealed carry for students and faculty on college campuses, provided they possessed valid permits. Several states have relaxed restrictions on campus carry but vary from state to state regarding whether that includes students, or just faculty and staff, while others still restrict carrying weapons in certain buildings or large events. In 2020, Republican legislators in at least ten states have introduced some form of legislation to repeal restrictions of concealed carry on campus. While Republican lawmakers and pro-gun groups advocate for allowing concealed carry on college and university campuses, numerous studies indicate that most students, faculty, and administration do not support or are not comfortable with campus carry.

Nonpartisan groups such as Gallup and Pew Research conduct national surveys regarding gun ownership, gun control, and concealed carry, among other topics, in efforts to obtain impartial perspectives of important issues. A 2015 Gallup poll, for example, found that most (56 percent) respondents believed that the United States would be safer if more people carried concealed weapons. More than eight in ten of those were Republicans (48 percent) or Independents (38 percent). While it is difficult to obtain specific numbers about gun ownership and carry permits, a 2023 study by Pew Research found that 45 percent of surveyed Republicans were gun owners. Of these, 71 percent of the Republican gun owners supported the expansion of carry laws in terms of location, but 60 percent opposed permitless concealed carry (Schaffer 2023). In terms of support for carrying firearms on college campuses, a 2024 Gallup study found that the majority of students, regardless of party identification, preferred banning or creating more restrictive gun laws on college campuses (Hrynowski 2024).

DEMOCRATS ON CONCEALED OR OPEN FIREARM CARRY

As stated previously, after the widespread influence of the Uniform Firearms Act of 1926, state concealed carry laws did not change for many years. In 1961, Washington state became the first to make a change. At that time, Washington was run by a primarily Democratic government (governor, state legislature, and US Congress), and passed laws to become a shall issue state.

The Democratic Party traditionally has supported stricter gun control; however, their support for concealed and open carry has varied over the past fifty years. In 1976, Georgia Democrat Lieutenant Governor Zell Miller, developed legislation authorizing the carrying of concealed weapons with a permit. The bill was passed by the Georgia General Assembly and was signed by Democrat Governor George Busbee. This law also changed Georgia from being a "may-issue" to a "shall-issue" state. The new law became the model for many states to transition into "shall-issue" states. Between 1989 and 2006, over a dozen Democratic states voted to change their concealed carry laws to become "shall-issue" states. Among these states were Arkansas, Mississippi, Nevada, Oregon, Pennsylvania, Tennessee, Utah, Virginia, and West Virginia.

In 2012, Illinois, a Democratic state, became the last state to give up its "no issue" policy, in favor of a "shall-issue" policy. Illinois had long not permitted the carrying of weapons in public—open or concealed. However, in *Moore v. Madigan* (702 F.3d 933, 2012), the 7th Circuit Court of Appeals addressed appeals in which the district court found that the right to bear arms in public was not a core component of the Second Amendment, supporting the state's ban of concealed carry. The 7th Circuit 2012 decision determined that the state's ban on concealed carry was unconstitutional, citing the previous Supreme Court's 2008 decision in *Heller*.

Democrat Governor Strengthens Ban on Guns on Campus

In 2015, during a time when many states such as Texas, Ohio, and Tennessee, were relaxing restrictions for concealed carry on college campuses, Democrat Governor Jerry Brown (CA) approved more stringent laws. The new law prohibits the carrying of a firearm, open or concealed, not only on campus but within 1,000 feet of a school or college campus. California Democrat State Senator Lois Walk, who sponsored the bill, provided reasoning: "The sentiment behind this law is our strong belief that law enforcement truly are the ones who need to be in control of arms on the campus. And they are the only ones on campus that should be armed" (Nagourney and Turkewitz 2015).

In 2017, Governor Brown further increased the control of concealed carry on K-12 school campuses, removing provisions giving school superintendents the authority to grant special permission for employees to carry concealed on campus. Only law enforcement, armed security officers, and school authorized activities such as shooting sports are exempt from the firearm ban. As of 2023, only eleven states allow concealed carry on college campuses in some form.

In November 2019, Virginia elections shifted political control from the Republican Party to the Democrats. Heading into the election, 75 percent of Virginia's voters, regardless of party, reported that gun policy was a very important issue. Virginia's Democrat Governor Ralph Northam, among other Virginia lawmakers, detailed plans to increase gun control in Virginia, including items such as "Red Flag" laws, restricting gun sales, and banning specific types of guns and firearm parts. When an individual is perceived as a threat to themselves or others, Red Flag laws permit family members, law enforcement, and/or medical professionals to request that a judge remove firearms and concealed weapons from the individual's possession, as well as restrict their ability to purchase firearms temporarily. The components of Red Flag laws vary across jurisdictions.

When Governor Northam indicated his intention to pursue these changes, Virginia residents responded by petitioning their local governments to take a political stand against potential gun laws by declaring counties and cities as "Second Amendment Sanctuaries." Residents express their right to own guns for personal protection, sports, and hunting, while the underlying argument is that the "right to bear arms" is a constitutional right. Those governments that support sanctuary status assert that, should lawmakers enact gun laws deemed to be unconstitutional, law enforcement in the sanctuaries will not enforce the laws. While sanctuary resolutions hold no legal standing, they do establish a definite position on controversial issues. Between November 6 and December 31, 2019, over 90 percent of the counties, along with numerous cities and towns in Virginia, had voted to designate themselves as Second Amendment Sanctuaries. Through the end of 2019 and into 2020, counties and communities in other states such as Florida, Georgia, Kentucky, Arizona, and Wisconsin began to declare themselves as Second Amendment Sanctuaries over concerns of restrictive gun legislation that may arise in their own states.

In January of 2020, approximately 22,000 people attended a pro-gun rally on Virginia Lobby Day. The rally was organized by the Virginia Citizens Defense League, an organization dedicated to protecting Virginian's gun rights. In April of 2020, Governor Northam signed multiple bills and amendments, increasing firearm control in Virginia. The changes included mandatory background checks on all firearms, restricting residents to purchasing only one handgun a month, mandatory reporting of lost or stolen firearms, an Extreme Risk Protective Order, which is a form of a red flag law, providing law enforcement the right to take firearms away from those deemed a danger to themselves or others.

Pew Research's 2017 poll found that only 20 percent of surveyed Democrats owned guns. Of those, 41 percent of Democrat gun owners supported changes to concealed carry laws, and most (55 percent) never carry a firearm (Parker et al. 2017). In an more recent poll, only 20 percent of surveyed Democrats owned firearms and 91 percent opposed permitless concealed carry (Schaffer 2023). These statistics are not surprising as prior research indicates that the most common gun owner is white, male, middle class, lives in the South, Protestant, and holds conservative political views.

FURTHER READING

Alexander, Robert. 1976. "General Assembly Closes Shop." *The Red and Black*, March 11, 1976.

Arnold, Larry. n.d. *The History of Concealed Carry, 1976-2011*. Texas Handgun Association. https://txchia.org/wp-content/uploads/2024/04/The-History-of-Concealed-Carry-1976-2011.pdf. Accessed August 5, 2024.

Blackstone, William. 1783. *Commentaries on the Laws of England*. 4 vols. Oxford: Clarendon Press.

Congress.gov. n.d. *H.R.38—Concealed Carry Reciprocity Act of 2019*. 116th Congress. https://www.congress.gov/bill/116th-congress/house-bill/38. Accessed March 3, 2023.

Congress.gov. n.d. *S.69—Constitutional Concealed Carry Reciprocity Act of 2019*. 116th Congress. https://www.congress.gov/bill/116th-congress/senate-bill/69. Accessed March 3, 2023.

Cornyn, John. 2019. "Cornyn, Senate GOP Introduce Concealed-Carry Reciprocity Bill." John Cornyn, United States Senator for Texas. https://texasborderbusiness.com/cornyn-senate-gop-introduce-concealed-carry-reciprocity-bill/?amp. Accessed December 1, 2019.

Cramer, Clayton E. 1999. *Concealed Weapon Laws of the Early Republic: Dueling, Southern Violence and Moral Reform*. Westport, CT: Praeger Publishers.

Cramer, Clayton E., and David B. Kopel. 1994."'Shall Issue': The New Wave of Concealed Handgun Permit Laws." *Tennessee Law Review* 62: 679–757.

Ellison, Christopher D. 1991. "Southern Culture and Firearms Ownership." *Social Science Quarterly* 72: 267–83.

Grossman, Richard S., and Stephen A. Lee. 2008. "May Issue versus Shall Issue: Explaining the Pattern of Concealed-carry Handgun Laws, 1960–2001." *Contemporary Economic Policy* 26, no. 2: 198–206. https://doi.org/10.1111/j.1465-7287.2007.00094.x.

Hamilton, Alexander, James Madison, and John Jay. 1787. *The Federalist Papers*. 2 vols. New York: J. and A. McLean.

Hrynowski, Zack. 2024. "Most Students Prefer Colleges that Restrict Guns on Campus." *Gallup*, March 14, 2024. https://news.gallup.com/poll/611459/students-prefer-colleges-restrict-guns-campus.aspx.

Kleck, Gary. 1996. "Crime, Culture Conflict and the Sources of Support for Gun Control: A Multilevel Application of the General Social Surveys." *American Behavioral Scientist* 39: 387–404. https://doi.org/10.1177/0002764296039004004.

Kleck, Gary. 1997. *Targeting Guns: Firearms and Their Control*. New York: Aldine De Gruyter.

Nagourney, Adam, and Julie Turkewitz. 2015. "As Campus Fears Rise, So Do Efforts to Enact School Gun Laws." *New York Times*, October 19, 2015. https://www.nytimes.com/2015/10/20/us/as-campus-fears-rise-so-do-efforts-to-enact-school-gun-laws.html.

National Conference of State Legislatures. 2018. "Guns on Campus: Overview."August 14, 2018. http://www.ncsl.org/research/education/guns-on-campus-overview.aspx.

Newport, Frank. 2015. "Majority Say More Concealed Weapons Would Make U.S. Safer." *Gallup*, October 20, 2015. http://www.gallup.com/poll/186263/majority-say-concealed-weapons-safer.aspx?g_source=Politics&g_medium=newsfeed&g_campaign=tiles.

Northam, Ralph S. 2019. *Governor Northam Unveils Gun Violence Prevention Legislation Ahead of July 9 Special Session*. Press release, July 3, 2019. https://bluevirginia.us/2019/07/governor-northam-unveils-gun-violence-prevention-legislation-ahead-of-july-9-special-session.

Parker, Kim, Juliana Menasce Horowitz, Ruth Igielnik, J. Baxter Oliphant, and Anna Brown. 2017. "America's Complex Relationship with Guns: An In-depth Look at the Attitudes and Experiences of U.S. Adults." Pew Research Center, June 22, 2017. https://www.pewsocialtrends.org/wp-content/uploads/sites/3/2017/06/Guns-Report-FOR-WEBSITE-PDF-6-21.pdf.

Ruben, Eric. M., and Darrell A. H. Miller. 2017. "Preface: The Second Generation of Second Amendment Law & Policy." *Law & Contemporary Problems* 80: 1.

Schaeffer, Katherine. 2023. "Key Facts About Americans and Guns." Pew Research Center, September 13, 2023. https://www.pewresearch.org/short-reads/2023/09/13/key-facts-about-americans-and-guns/.

Trump, Donald J. n.d. "Second Amendment Rights." https://assets.donaldjtrump.com/Second_Amendment_Rights.pdf.

Vandercoy, David E. 1994. "The History of the Second Amendment." *Valparaiso Law Review* 28: 1007–39.

Virginia Citizens Defense League. n.d. https://vcdl.org/.

The Washington Post. 2019. "Washington Post-Schar School Virginia Poll." September 25–30, 2019.

Winkler, Adam. 2011. *Gunfight: The Battle Over the Right to Bear Arms in America*. New York: W. W. Norton.

Wood, Robert H. 2015. "A History of Firearms Legislation at the State and Local Levels." In *Guns and Contemporary Society: The Past, Present, and Future of Firearms and Firearm Policy*, edited by G. H. Utter, 67–82. Santa Barbara, CA: ABC-CLIO.

CHAPTER 4

Corporate Crime

BRADLEY D. EDWARDS AND MARY SMITH-TENGROTH

AT A GLANCE

Conventional wisdom suggests that the ultimate goal of any company is to maximize profits. However, there is a growing debate about how much social responsibility companies share in relation to common goals that extend beyond profits. We can likely all recognize that if there were no regulations in place upon corporations, the amount of social inequality, pollution, and workplace injuries would likely be higher than they are today while the safety of our products and food would likely be lower. Corporate crime occurs when a company's executives create a scheme to avoid compliance with these regulations or otherwise simply ignore their duty to comply.

While it is obviously important for corporations to maintain compliance with the law, there is also a legitimate political debate about how far-reaching these regulations should be. Critics assert that when regulations become too extensive, the cost of compliance with these regulations can become suffocating to businesses. This could cause companies to unknowingly violate a rule that they were unaware of, or to go out of business due to the cost of compliance. Thus, some politicians advocate for deregulation, which involves the reduction of government restrictions in a particular industry.

Historically, Democrats and Republicans have agreed on many issues surrounding corporate crime. However, the accounting and financial scandals of the early twenty-first century have created a much more partisan environment. The political discord regarding corporate crime involves two primary issues: (1) how much corporate regulation should be in place and (2) the appropriate response to take when corporations violate the law. Substantial disagreement has arisen between the two political parties regarding these questions.

MANY REPUBLICANS...

- Support the notion of a more *laissiez faire* (hands off) approach to regulations, which assumes that consumers can protect themselves from corporate wrongdoings.
- Wish to roll back many regulations put into place by previous administrations, as they argue that the cost of compliance with these regulations could be damaging to the economy.
- As with Democrats, support entering into non-prosecution and deferred-prosecution agreements with corporations who have engaged in misconduct or fraud to prevent future wrongdoing.

MANY DEMOCRATS...

- View sensible corporate regulations as a necessary intervention to protect the American public, workers, and the environment.
- Support increasing the severity of penalties placed on corporate executives whose companies have engaged in wrongdoing.
- Support entering into non-prosecution and deferred-prosecution agreements with corporations who have engaged in misconduct or fraud to prevent future wrongdoing.

OVERVIEW

In the United States, laws prohibiting certain business practices have evolved over time in response to the increasing influence that corporations have on our lives. The corporate world was largely unregulated until the mid- to late nineteenth century. The first federal law regulating businesses dates back to the Civil War, when the Union Army found itself purchasing merchandise that was inferior to expectations, like boots that wore out after a mile of walking or uniforms that disintegrated once becoming wet (Helmer 2013). It was clear that these incidents were not simply the result of poor craftsmanship, but rather an attempt by dishonest suppliers to profit off of the war. As a response to these reports, Congress quickly passed, and President Lincoln signed, the False Claims Act (1863), which imposed a fine for companies who committed fraud against the government. Over the next forty years, several more keystone pieces of regulatory legislation were passed. Most notable among these was the Sherman Antitrust Act (1890), which prevented price fixing and the formation of monopolies.

Corporate laws are most often enforced by administrative agencies, such as the Environmental Protection Agency (EPA) and the Securities and Exchange Commission (SEC), which have been given jurisdiction to enforce designated areas of the law. Depending on the specific regulation, the overseeing agency will either enforce the law through civil litigation or by referring the case to criminal prosecutors. However, corporate offenses have historically received little attention from news media, politicians, and scholars. Corporate crime continued to be overshadowed by more traditional forms of crime until the early 2000s. However, over the past two decades, attention toward corporate misconduct has increased as a series of events has highlighted the potentially ruinous economic impacts of such misconduct.

The first wave of corporate scandals began in 2001 with the highly publicized accounting frauds involving Enron and Worldcom. Enron was a large energy company that had been engaging in multiple forms of misconduct, including reporting false profits to inflate stock prices. The following year, another fraudulent accounting scheme was uncovered at Worldcom, a large telecommunications company. Worldcom also had engaged in fraudulent accounting practices that allowed the company to report profits when it had actually incurred financial losses.

Top executives from both Enron and Worldcom were arrested on charges of conspiracy and fraud, forcing both companies into bankruptcy. The financial fallout from these bankruptcies negatively affected millions of Americans. The devastating impact left many government officials asking what actions should be taken to prevent a similar catastrophe from occurring again. In response, Congress passed the bipartisan Sarbanes-Oxley Act of 2002, which placed stricter scrutiny on corporations and enhanced the criminal penalties for corporations that file misleading financial reports. At the bill's signing, George Bush clearly placed much of the blame on greedy executives, stating "for the sake of our free economy, those who break the law, break the rules of fairness, those who are dishonest, however wealthy or successful they may be, must pay a price" (Bumiller 2002, 1). One of the most important aspects of the Sarbanes-Oxley Act was the creation of additional protections for whistleblowers. Specifically, the Act required employers to create a straightforward procedure for employees to be able to disclose potential criminal activity and protected these individuals from retaliation by their employer.

The financial crisis of 2008 marked a shift in views on the role of the US government in regulating corporations. Much of the instability leading to the financial crisis originated from the mortgage industry. As described by Hellwig (2009), mortgage loans are unattractive for many financial institutions that generally do not want to hold on to a particular investment for fifteen to thirty years. To assist these financial institutions, a secondary mortgage market developed in which banks that originate home loans package several loans together and sell the packages to investment companies willing to take on the longer-term investment. In this way, the originating bank no longer has the risk associated with the loans and frees up money to sell new mortgage loans.

The two largest purchasers of mortgage loans on this secondary market, Fannie Mae and Freddie Mac, operate as private companies but are really heavily backed, government-sponsored entities. Essentially, this arrangement creates a government-sponsored monopoly in the secondary mortgage market. As could be expected, the criteria (e.g., required credit score, debt to income ratios) established by Fannie Mae and Freddie Mac to determine which mortgages they would purchase have been also widely adopted by the mortgage originators.

This process allowed politicians to influence Fannie Mae and Freddie Mac's guidelines to achieve certain policy goals. For example, a 1995 initiative by former president Bill Clinton sought to extend mortgage options to minorities and those with low income. This National Homeownership Strategy was an unprecedented public-private partnership that encouraged banks to loosen guidelines for those borrowers who came from low-income areas and encouraged Fannie Mae and Freddie Mac to buy more of these loans. In 2002, George Bush's Blueprint for the American Dream initiative continued the goal of assisting home ownership for low-income borrowers, largely by providing federal down payment and closing cost assistance (McDonald 2012). While both administrations shared the laudable goal to benefit those populations, it ultimately resulted in the approval of a high number of risky loans.

During the early 2000s, mortgage interest rates fell while housing prices increased substantially. In this environment, banks began to approve an increasing number of mortgage loans to higher-risk clients, often with adjustable rates or terms in which the borrower's monthly payment went only to pay for the interest on the loan instead of the principal. This system worked well for a while. Homeowners were able to build wealth (at least on paper) with increasing housing values and low interest rates, while lenders could continue to originate large quantities of loans to be sold on the secondary market. However, the housing bubble finally burst. When interest rates eventually rose in late 2004 and housing prices began to fall in 2006, homeowners who had adjustable rates were left with increasing payments that they could no longer afford. To make matters worse, they often owed more on their homes than they were worth, making it impossible to sell the home. Unfortunately, the only viable option available to many of these homeowners was to default on their loan. The substantial rise in mortgage defaults during this time nearly brought the entire financial sector to a halt. Large financial companies went bankrupt, and those who were unable to pay their mortgages lost their homes.

The "Great Recession of '08," as it has come to be known, was the worst financial crisis the United States had seen since the Great Depression. Many Americans were shocked when virtually none of the large bank executives were criminally prosecuted. Although the actions taken by these financial institutions were reckless and detrimental, they were mostly legal. The harshest punishments faced by the banks were mostly civil penalties related to failing to conduct due diligence during the loan origination process or for not disclosing how risky these loans were to those on the secondary market (mostly to Freddie Mac and Fannie Mae).

The responses to these crises exemplify the two most prevalent legal responses to corporate crime. While the criminal justice system became involved in the accounting scandals, the financial crisis was mostly handled by the administrative agencies who brought civil penalties on corporations that violated existing regulations. Although the criminal prosecution of corporate crime has become increasingly aggressive in recent decades, it is important to remember that corporate entities cannot be sentenced to prison. It is rare for a prosecutor to take a corporate entity to trial due to the inherent complexity of these cases and the possibility that such a move would likely force the company into bankruptcy. Instead, prosecutors prefer to enter into deferred and/or non-prosecution agreements with the corporation. In these agreements, prosecutors agree not to file criminal charges in exchange for the implementation of various control mechanisms designed to ensure the company's future compliance with the law.

REPUBLICANS ON CORPORATE CRIME

The Republican Party tends to support deregulation of business, contending that overregulation can result in job losses, inefficiency, and can be particularly hurtful for small businesses with modest financial assets. Republicans also tend to view corporations as fully capable of preventing and responding to instances of fraud and misconduct without overburdensome regulations. The reputation of a company is very important, and the news of controversial actions can spread extensively in the era of social media. Thus, corporations should have some incentive to prevent misconduct and maintain their public image.

Multiple Republican administrations have chosen to rollback corporate regulations. In the early 1970s, the Nixon administration initiated a trend of deregulation that would continue for forty years. Several Republican presidents including Nixon, Ford, Reagan, and George W. Bush proposed legislation that reduced regulations placed on the financial industry. In 1999, the Republican Party spearheaded the move to repeal the Glass-Steagall Act, a 1930s-era law that prevented commercial banking industries from engaging in investment banking. The Act's intent was to ensure that deposits made into local banks were not lost by the banks' participation in risky investments.

During George W. Bush's term, multiple corporate regulations were rolled back, specifically those targeting pollution (Lynch, Burns, and Stretesky 2010). This effort began during Bush's first official day in office, when his chief of staff sent a memo to the administrative agencies asking them to freeze any regulation that had been under review but had not yet been implemented. Ultimately, the Bush administration rewrote and relaxed several rules related to air pollution and energy efficiency. During the final year of the Bush administration, the Department of the Interior also revised a regulation that had protected clean-water ways from mountaintop mining pollution. The revision effectively removed a buffer zone that had previously been required between coal mining operations and waterways.

Following the 2008 financial crisis, Republicans also attempted to stunt efforts to pass the Dodd-Frank Act, a comprehensive bill aimed at increasing regulations on the financial industry. Republicans argued that the bill would have a negative impact on small banks. Ultimately, only three Republicans supported the bill. A particularly controversial outcome of the Dodd-Frank Act was the development of the Consumer Financial Protection Bureau (CFPB). Housed within the Federal Reserve, this agency's mission is to: (1) create rules ensuring that consumer financial products and services are fair and transparent, (2) serve an oversight function to ensure compliance with federal financial laws, and (3) investigate and bring resolutions against companies that violate consumer finance laws (Consumer Financial Protection Bureau 2013).

The controversy surrounds the CFPB's structure, which was intentionally set up in a way that isolates it from political pressure. Specifically, the agency does not rely on the normal appropriations process for funding, meaning that the agency is isolated from political backlash in terms of their annual budget. Republicans, who generally oppose most of the actions taken by the CFPB, argue that removing the Bureau's structure from the normal appropriations process unconstitutionally disrupts the role of the legislative branch to regulate administrative agencies. In 2022, the Fifth Circuit Court of Appeals agreed that the funding mechanism violated the Constitution's separation of powers. In 2023, the Supreme Court agreed to hear the case and their decision is currently pending.

The agency was also designed to be led by a single director, who could only be removed by the president for cause. This differs from other administrative agencies, whose executives serve at the will of the president. In 2020, the Supreme Court ruled that the president must be able to fire the director of the CFPB at their will. This is an important ruling, as the CFPB has come under intense political scrutiny since its inception. Republican critics argue that this agency regularly overreaches its power, and potential overregulation by the CFPB is likely to increase prices on goods and services, thus harming the very consumers that it intends to protect.

House Minority Leader John Boehner Calls for Dodd-Frank Repeal

Speaking at a press conference minutes after the passage of Dodd-Frank in 2010, House Minority Leader John Boehner explained his opposition to the bill:

> I think the financial reform bill is ill conceived, going to make credit harder for the American people to get, clearly harder for businesses to get and the fact that it's going to punish every banker in America for the sins of the few on Wall Street is unwise. On top of that I think it institutionalizes "too big to fail" and gives far too much authority to federal bureaucrats to bail out virtually any company in America they decide ought to be bailed out. (Graves 2010)

President Donald Trump's administration continued the Republican administration trend of rolling back corporate regulations and prosecutions. During his second year in office, Trump signed into law the Economic Growth, Regulatory Relief, and Consumer Protection Act. The Act effectively lessened many of the restrictions put into place by the Dodd-Frank Act, particularly those aimed at small banks. Though the legislation was initiated by Republicans, the final bill managed to receive moderate bipartisan support.

Many opponents of deregulation contend that it may allow for, and in some cases encourage, corporations to engage in practices that may endanger the public. For example, many argue that the deregulatory actions of the George W. Bush administration allowed corporations to more freely pollute waterways and the air, which could threaten public health. Others argue that the Trump agenda to deregulate corporate crime resulted in devastating consequences to vulnerable social groups. For example, some have suggested that the pullback of Dodd-Frank protection was responsible for the failure of Silicon Valley Bank and Signature Bank in March 2023 (Enrich 2023). Ultimately, it is difficult to determine the full impact of Trump's deregulation agenda. Despite its modest success at rolling back regulations, many of the proposed changes were either struck down by federal courts or otherwise failed to be enacted (Benson, Stadler, and Pontell 2019). Instead, Trump largely focused on slowing down the pace of new regulations as well as tactics such as executive orders and reducing enforcement of existing regulations, which were later reversed by President Biden.

Research also has revealed a distinct difference between Republicans and Democrats in their views of corporate crime prosecution. Although presidents are typically not able to directly intervene in a specific corporate investigation, they can indirectly affect federal agencies' broad enforcement priorities in two important ways (Arlen 2022). First, presidents can appoint the heads of administrative agencies as well as fire them without cause. Second, the budget process can be used to incentivize enforcement priorities congruent with the president's preferences. An analysis of the number of corporate fines and penalties collected by the Securities and Exchange Commission and Justice Department during the Trump administration showed a significant reduction compared to the Obama administration (Protess, Gebeloff, and Ivory 2018). Following President Biden's election in 2020, enforcement action against corporations became more aggressive.

It is important to note that total corporate prosecutions have been on the decline since early in the Obama administration, as prosecutors have started to rely more heavily on deferred prosecution agreements (Garrett 2020). In these agreements, the government will agree not to move forward with the prosecution of a case in exchange for the company agreeing to certain conditions that are designed to prevent future wrongdoing. These conditions often include the termination of executives who have engaged in wrongdoing as well as agreed to submit to increased monitoring to ensure that the company no longer engages in misconduct.

DEMOCRATS ON CORPORATE CRIME

Until the early 2000s, many Democrats, including Presidents Carter and Clinton, supported legislation that reduced regulations and restrictions placed on businesses. One high-profile example was the Gramm-Leach-Bliley Act (1999). This law included a provision requiring financial institutions to disclose their information-sharing practices with customers. However, perhaps the most influential component of this law was the effective repeal of the Glass-Stegall Act. The Glass-Stegall Act was a 1930s law that prevented commercial banking industries from engaging in investment banking by ensuring that deposits made into local banks were not lost by those banks' participation in risky investments. By the late 1990s, however, most politicians viewed the law as unnecessary and a burden on the financial sector. In 1999, Democrats joined with Republicans to repeal the Glass-Stegall Act.

Democratic views on government regulation changed after a number of accounting fraud schemes were uncovered in the early 2000s, the most notable taking place at Enron. Following the Enron collapse, Democrats introduced the aforementioned Sarbanes-Oxley Act. A year later, discovery of the Worldcom scheme motivated bipartisan support for the bill's eventual passage. Democrats also proposed the Dodd-Frank Act following the financial crisis of 2008, which placed numerous regulations on banks and lending companies with the intention of protecting consumers from risky lending and financial practices. In addition to the creation of the Consumer Financial Protection Bureau mentioned earlier, the Dodd-Frank Act also reinstituted many of the basic elements of the Glass-Stegall Act. Democrats view the Dodd-Frank Act as an essential protection to prevent risky financial industries activities from leading to a repeat of the 2008 recession. Likewise, they view the CFPB as an important agency to protect consumers from predatory practices within the financial services industry.

Some Democrats thought that the Dodd-Frank Act might have gone too far in enacting regulations. In a speech given at the Community Bankers Symposium in 2014, Daniel Tarullo, a Democrat and former member of the board of governors of the United States Federal Reserve Board, remarked that the Dodd-Frank Act may be more effective if tailored to cover larger corporations. Doing so, he argued, would take away the burden placed on smaller banks to abide by the Act's strict policies. Despite these criticisms, Democrats largely supported the Dodd-Frank legislation and other government regulation of the finance industry. Support for such legislation demonstrates the shift that has occurred within the Democratic Party over the past two decades regarding regulation of large corporations.

Within the party, Democrats differ on their beliefs about criminally prosecuting corporate entities. In 2013, Barack Obama's attorney general Eric Holder made headlines by suggesting that charging corporations might have negative collateral consequences on the economy. Holder received considerable pushback for this statement, with critics arguing that large corporations were receiving special treatment from the law simply due to their size. As previously mentioned, deferred prosecution agreements have emerged as a way in which prosecutors can attempt to prevent future wrongdoing without officially filing charges. The available evidence thus far suggests that these agreements can be effective at reforming the corporation and ensuring future compliance with the laws while minimizing the collateral consequences associated with a criminal prosecution (Xiao 2013). Nonetheless, some of the more progressive-leaning Democrats are critical of prosecution agreements.

Attorney General Suggests that Corporations Are Too Big to Jail

Speaking to the Senate Judiciary Committee in March 2013, Attorney General Eric Holder addressed the difficulties of prosecuting large corporations:

> I am concerned that the size of some of these institutions becomes so large that it does become difficult for us to prosecute them when we are hit with indications that if we do prosecute—if we do bring a criminal charge it will have a negative impact on the national economy, perhaps even the world economy. I think that is a function of the fact that some of the institutions have become too large ... The greatest effect is not to prosecute a corporation—although that is important—the greatest deterrent effect is to prosecute the individuals in the corporations that are responsible for the decisions. (US Congress 2013)

While Democrats and Republicans have disagreed on the specific responses to corporate crime, it is important to highlight the areas where agreement exists. Both parties publicly advocate for tougher punishment of corporate executives who are responsible for wrongdoing. Likewise, both parties largely support the use of deferred prosecution agreements as an effective way to reduce corporate misconduct without putting the company's operations at risk. Political support for corporate regulation appears to depend somewhat on how far society is removed from an economic crisis. Republicans are typically hesitant to support new regulations, though they ultimately supported the Sarbanes-Oxley Act after it became clear that Enron was not an isolated event. Democrats initiated the passage of the Dodd-Frank Act but joined Republicans to repeal parts of the bill eighteen years later so that small and medium-sized banks are no longer subject to increased federal oversight.

FURTHER READING

Arlen, Jennifer. 2022. "Countering Capture: A Political Theory of Corporate Criminal Liability." *The Journal of Corporate Law*, 47: 861–86.

Benson, Michael L., William A. Stadler, and Henry N. Pontell. 2019. "Harming America: Corporate Crime in a Context of Deregulation." *Victims & Offenders* 14, no. 8: 1063–83. https://doi.org/10.1080/15564886.2019.1671286. Accessed March 3, 2023.

The Brookings Institution. 2020. "Tracking Deregulation in the Trump Era." June 24, 2020. https://www.brookings.edu/interactives/tracking-deregulation-in-the-trump-era/.

Bumiller, Elisabeth. 2002. "Bush Signs Bill Aimed at Fraud in Corporations." *New York Times*, July 31, 2002. https://www.nytimes.com/2002/07/31/business/corporate-conduct-the-president-bush-signs-bill-aimed-at-fraud-in-corporations.html.

Clinard, Marshall, and Peter Yeager. 2017. *Corporate Crime*. New York: Routledge.

Consumer Financial Protection Bureau. 2013. "Consumer Financial Protection Bureau Strategic Plan." https://files.consumerfinance.gov/f/strategic-plan.pdf. Accessed July 9, 2023.

Edwards, Bradley D., and Michael C. Braswell. 2020. "Corporate Misconduct and Ethics." In *Justice, Crime, and Ethics*, edited by Michael C. Braswell, Belinda R. McCarthy, and Bernard J. McCarthy, 436–60. New York: Routledge.

Enrich, David. 2023. "Back-to-Back Bank Collapses Came after Deregulatory Push." *New York Times*, March 13, 2023. https://www.nytimes.com/2023/03/13/business/signature-silicon-valley-bank-dodd-frank-regulation.html.

Fligstein, Neil, and Alexander F. Roehrkasse. 2016. "The Causes of Fraud in the Financial Crisis of 2007 to 2009." *American Sociological Review* 81, no. 4: 617–43. https://doi.org/10.1177/0003122416645594. Accessed March 18, 2023.

Garrett, Brandon L. 2020. "Declining Corporate Prosecutions." *American Criminal Law Review*, no. 57 (February): 109–53. https://ssrn.com/abstract=3360456. Accessed June 16, 2023.

Garrett, Brandon L. 2014. *Too Big to Jail: How Prosecutors Compromise with Corporations*. London: Harvard University Press.

Graves, Lucia. 2010. "Boehner: Repeal Wall Street Reform." *Huffington Post*, July 15, 2010. https://www.huffpost.com/entry/boehner-repeal-wall-stree_n_647606.

Hellwig, Martin F. 2009. "Systemic Risk in the Financial Sector: An Analysis of the Subprime-Mortgage Financial Crisis." *De Economist* 157, no. 2: 129–207. https://doi.org/10.1007/s10645-009-9110-0. Accessed May 15, 2023.

Helmer, J. B. 2013. "False Claims Act: Incentivizing Integrity for 150 Years for Rogues, Privateers, Parasites and Patriots." *University of Cincinnati Law Review* 81: 1261–82.

Kaal, Wulf A., and Timothy Lacine. 2014. "The Effect of Deferred and Non-Prosecution Agreements on Corporate Governance: Evidence from 1993–2013." *The Business Lawyer* 70, no. 1: 61–119. https://doi.org/10.2139/ssrn.2486570. Accessed March 8, 2023.

Lucas, Deborah, and David Torregrosa. 2010. *Fannie Mae, Freddie Mac, and the Federal Role in the Secondary Mortgage Market*. Washington, DC: Congressional Budget Office.

Lynch, Michael J., Ronald G. Burns, and Paul B. Stretesky. 2010. "Global Warming and State-Corporate Crime: The Politicalization of Global Warming under the Bush Administration." *Crime, Law and Social Change* 54, no. 3: 213–39. https://doi.org/10.1007/s10611-010-9245-6. Accessed March 23, 2023.

McDonald, Oonah. 2012. *Fannie Mae and Freddie Mac: Turning the American Dream into a Nightmare*. New York: Bloomsbury Academic.

McDonald, Oonagh Anne. 2016. "Holding Banks to Account for the Financial Crisis?" *Journal of Financial Crime* 23, no. 1: 45–69. https://doi.org/10.1108/jfc-08-2015-0041. Accessed March 22, 2023.

President's Commission on Law Enforcement and Administration of Justice. 1967. "The Challenge of Crime in a Free Society." Washington, DC: United States Government Printing Office. https://www.ncjrs.gov/pdffiles1/nij/42.pdf. Accessed March 22, 2023.

Protess, Ben, Robert Gebeloff, and Danielle Ivory. 2018. "Trump Administration Spares Corporate Wrongdoers Billions in Penalties." *New York Times*, November 3, 2018. https://www.nytimes.com/2018/11/03/us/trump-sec-doj-corporate-penalties.html.

Segal, Troy. 2019. "Enron Scandal: The Fall of a Wall Street Darling." Investopedia. https://www.investopedia.com/updates/enron-scandal-summary/. Accessed March 20, 2023.

US Congress. 2013. Hearing of the Senate Judiciary Committee. "Oversight of the U.S. Department of Justice." March 6, 2013. https://www.congress.gov/event/113th-congress/senate-event/LC55681/text

Walsh, Anthony, and Craig Hemmens. 2019. *Law, Justice, and Society: A Sociolegal Introduction*. Oxford: Oxford University Press.

Woolley, John T. 2012. "Persistent Leadership: Presidents and the Evolution of U.S. Financial Reform, 1970-2007." *Presidential Studies Quarterly* 42, no. 1: 60–80. https://doi.org/10.1111/j.1741-5705.2012.03941.x. Accessed March 20, 2023.

Xiao, Michael Yangming. 2013. "Deferred/Non-Prosecution Agreements: Effective Tools to Combat Corporate Crime." *Journal of Law and Public Policy* 23, no. 1: Article 7. https://scholarship.law.cornell.edu/cjlpp/vol23/iss1/7. Accessed March 24, 2023.

Zywicki, Todd J. 2013. "The Consumer Financial Protection Bureau: Savior or Menace?" *George Washington Law Review* 81, no. 3: 856–928. https://doi.org/10.2139/ssrn.2130942. March 21, 2023.

CHAPTER 5

Crime Victims' Rights

ELIZABETH Q. WRIGHT

AT A GLANCE

The crime victims' rights movement evolved when individuals in three independent social movements with the "common experience" of crime victimization came together to cope with their situations and to improve future crime victims' experiences (Karmen 1992). Two of the social movements were more aligned with more liberal political causes (i.e., the women's movement and the civil rights movement), and one was more aligned with more conservative political ideologies (i.e., the "law and order" movement). Crime victims in each of these movements were from diverse backgrounds, demographically and politically, which was quite unusual. Despite their different initial base causes, they all agreed on the following five premises: (1) the criminal justice system ignored their needs, (2) victims often were blamed by the public and criminal justice officials for the crimes that occurred, (3) criminal justice agencies in the United States needed to develop a standard way to deal with victims and witnesses, (4) crime victims should be compensated to assist them in their recovery and (5) crime victims needed formal rights to ensure they were treated fairly within the criminal justice system.

Although the crime victims' rights movement received opposition from criminal justice system actors, Republicans and Democrats often have aligned on their support, have strong histories of supporting victims' rights, and have had considerable impact on the evolution of victims' rights since the 1960s. While both parties tend to support the same types of legislation (advocating for better services for crime victims, highlighting crimes against women and children, financial fraud crimes, evolving technology crimes, enhancing victims' rights in the criminal justice process), and legislation backed by both parties has improved the lives of victims, the parties' underlying philosophies on crime victims differ in some substantial ways.

MANY REPUBLICANS...

- Favor the rights of crime victims over defendants when victim rights intersect with defendant constitutional rights.
- Favor a retributive philosophy, focusing on legislation that promotes protection of crime victims in the form of stricter penalties for offenders.
- Support federal legislation to provide for a victims' rights amendment to the US Constitution, as well as various legislation at the state level.
- Have worked to expand protections for different groups of victims as crime has evolved over time, such as expanding protections for child victims of abuse, women victims of violence, victims of financial crimes, victims of terrorism and human trafficking, and cybercrime victims.

MANY DEMOCRATS...

- Seek to ensure that rights are more balanced and that the constitutional rights of defendants are not usurped by victims' rights.
- Favor a restorative philosophy when it comes to crime victimization, seeking out remedies to decrease crime through understanding and addressing the root causes of crime, be they social and/or economic problems, mental health related, or issues within the criminal justice system itself.
- Have sought to expand protections for additional groups of crime victims, including homosexual and transgender victims, women and children victims of violence, and financial fraud victims.
- Support stronger legislation for gun control laws as a victims' rights issue to decrease the amount of violent victimization perpetrated with firearms.

OVERVIEW

In a word, the Republican perspective on crime victims' rights could be stated as championing. Beginning in the 1960s, efforts by noted Republicans brought attention to the ignorance of victims' perspectives in the justice process. President Reagan's Task Force on Victims of Crime, created in 1982, was unprecedented and remarkable in its contribution to the understanding of the impact of crime on victims. It provided revelations from numerous interviews with crime victims across the country, highlighting how poorly victims were treated. The Task Force provided sixty-eight recommendations to criminal justice and other victim-serving groups to set the stage for action and to shift perspectives for the treatment of crime victims overall. While the sixty-eight recommendations focused exclusively on how victim-serving groups could better treat victims, policies also began to be developed that purported to be victim-focused, but were actually offender-focused, to hold offenders more accountable and to incarcerate them for longer periods of time, thus reducing the risk of victimization.

States acted on the Task Force recommendations by creating victims' "bills of rights" or constitutional amendments reflecting rights of victims, instituting new policies on informing victims of court proceedings and changes in offender status, assisting crime victims with applying for crime victim compensation (when applicable), among other improvements. At the federal level, the Task Force recommendations led to the proposal of a constitutional amendment supporting the rights of victims, as had been developed at the state level across the nation. Beginning in 1996, the constitutional amendment was submitted for consideration repeatedly, to no avail. Despite having both Congressional and presidential support, a constitutional amendment never passed. Instead, the Justice for All Act of 2004 solidified a federal victims' "bill of rights" along with recourse when federal criminal justice agents failed to abide by the provisions of the Act. This Act eliminated the need for a constitutional amendment.

In general, Republicans prefer a small government to a large one and a lack of imposition into the daily lives of the citizenry. They generally support strong-handed responses to criminal offending and prioritize protection of the public while also supporting legislation to support those harmed by crime. This is best illustrated in the 2012 Republican Party platform statement (2012, 1711):

> Liberals do not understand this simple axiom: criminals behind bars cannot harm the general public. To that end, we support mandatory prison sentencing for gang crimes, violent or sexual offenses against children, repeat drug dealers, rape, robbery and murder. We support a national registry for convicted child murderers. We oppose parole for dangerous or repeat felons.

During the 2016 presidential election, the Republican Party held firm to the position that the American people needed to be protected against criminal victimization and continued to refer back to the findings of the 1982 Presidential Task Force as the best practices guidelines for how victims *should* be treated. The Republican influence on victims' rights has helped to establish a strong foundation for respecting the impact of crime on those it directly touches. In turn, this has provided opportunities for Democrats to focus on more distinct crime victims' rights concerns, such as ensuring that the rights are available to all victims across crime types and demographic characteristics.

While the general ideologies of both parties seemed very similar from the 1970s to the 1990s in support of tough policies on offenders, Democrats pulled back and started focusing on criminal justice reform as research began to show the unintended consequences of "tough on crime" policies such as mandatory minimums, three strikes, and truth-in-sentencing laws. Democratic approaches tend to focus on using government policies to assist those afflicted by the social ills that appear to contribute to a criminal lifestyle. In this sense, it appeared as if Democrats were focusing more on defendants'/offenders' rights versus victims' rights, in some cases. In 1988, for example, Massachusetts governor and Democratic presidential candidate Michael Dukakis was heavily criticized as "soft on crime" after Willie Horton, a convicted murderer serving a life sentence in a Massachusetts prison, committed several violent felonies, including rape, after being released on weekend furlough. Although Dukakis did not institute the weekend furlough program, he lost his presidential bid to Republican George H. W. Bush, whose party exploited the Horton incident and the weekend furlough policy in negative campaign ads.

As a result, post-1988 Democratic platforms once again purported the "tough on crime" stance with Bill Clinton's praise for three strikes policies and funding promises for more prisons and police. Over the years, Democrats have supported various pieces of legislation that advocate for stronger protections for child abuse victims, homosexual and transgendered victims of crime, female victims of interpersonal violence, and victims of the criminal justice system itself. In early 2020, for example, after the killing of George Floyd at the knee of Minneapolis (MN) police officer Derek Chauvin while other officers observed, many Democrats have called for a complete overhaul of American policing.

Perhaps the most notable ideological distinction between the parties with respect to victims' rights is that Democrats generally ascribe to restorative justice philosophies whereas Republicans generally follow retributive justice philosophies. Restorative justice principles seek to identify and address the causes and the impacts of crime, and to foster cooperation among victims, offenders, and the community to resolve issues. To many Republicans, restorative justice appears to favor criminal defendants or offenders over crime victims. This view is illustrated by Republican New York Senator Thomas O'Mara, who admonished New York Democrats for scheduling a vote on items that appeared to be pro-offender (e.g., allowing felons to sit on juries, allowing bail from charitable organizations, and providing a mechanism by which inmates would have access to identification in order to vote) on the same day as the Police Officers Memorial Remembrance Ceremony (O'Mara 2019).

At the same time, New York Senate Republicans were calling for a "Victims' Justice Agenda," which would keep violent criminals incarcerated without parole options and would restructure the parole process to make it easier on victims and victims' families. This type of legislation illustrates a more retributive justice policy that purports to protect crime victims from motivated offenders by producing a high degree of deterrence through strict legislation and harsh sentencing.

The differences between Republican and Democratic platforms with respect to crime victims' rights primarily lie in how each party promotes what it stands for and how to accomplish protections for crime victims. The crime victims' rights movement was informed by both Democratically aligned, left-wing, grassroots movements and the law and order movement of Republicans. The women's movement and the "law and order" movement seemed to have found common ground in the pursuit of aggressive policing, prosecution, and stricter sentencing for rape and sexual assault offenders. Both groups wanted crime victims to be protected throughout the judicial process, from intimidation by defendants or defendants' loved ones to using a crime victims' nonessential background to discredit their testimonies. This common ground shaped the victims' rights movement into an interesting, bipartisan movement. To illustrate this common ground, Republican Representative Ted Poe (TX), Democratic Representative Jim Costa (CA), and former Republican congresswoman Katherine Harris (FL) founded in 2005 the Congressional Victims' Rights Caucus, now called the Congressional Crime Survivors and Justice Caucus, to "introduce bipartisan legislation to address the rights of crime victims and promote education and collaboration to increase the awareness of crime victims' needs and interests" (CSG Justice Center Staff 2014, para.1). The Caucus has been integral in ensuring that victim service organizations, including law enforcement, have the funding and resources necessary to provide needed services to crime victims. The Caucus also recognizes victim service organizations across the country by presenting annual awards to five such organizations or individuals for their recognition in supporting crime victims.

During the 2012 presidential race, the Democratic National Convention's platform included statements supportive of reauthorization of the Violence Against Women Act and highlighted the need to address human trafficking. It supported the rights of victims to be heard, respected, and compensated. The Republican platform focused on the need for active prosecution of child pornographers, pointing to the close connection between internet child pornography and human trafficking. It pointed to the need for states to do a better job of protecting victims by following the example of federal systems. It also indicated that perpetrators harmed during their criminal acts should not be given any type of federal or state assistance (Chammah 2016).

During the 2016 presidential campaign, the Democratic Party platform focused attention on campus sexual assault in secondary and post-secondary environments. It also highlighted commercial sexual exploitation and forced labor as part of human trafficking, calling for increased collaboration with foreign governments in identifying and prosecuting public officials who played a part in human trafficking. The Republican platform raised pornography to the level of a public health crisis, commending social networking sites that aggressively sought to protect children by identifying and restricting sex offenders from using their sites for nefarious purposes. It called for a more formal adjudication process for campus sexual assault allegations. It emphasized victims' rights in judicial proceedings, including receiving information about the case, being present at trial, having a voice in sentencing and parole hearings, receiving legal and social services as necessary, and compensation from the Crime Victims Fund (Chammah 2016).

During the 2020 presidential campaign, the Democratic Party platform again focused effort on changing the way campus sexual assault was dealt with, while expanding protections to women with disabilities, transgender women and other LGBTQ+ people, and all groups disproportionately affected by interpersonal violence and sexual assault/abuse. Additionally, lethality assessment training for law enforcement and other criminal justice personnel was a significant desire. A large emphasis was placed on victims of the criminal justice system itself, with a call to increase funding and accountability measures to reduce deaths and excessive force perpetrated by law enforcement. The 2024 Democratic Party platform has not yet been issued. In 2020, the Republican National Committee did not post a grand platform, largely due to the ongoing response to and impact of Covid-19. According to a Milwaukee Journal Sentinel article dated March 27, 2024, it is likely that there will be a convention platform posted prior to the Republican convention closer to the meeting date in the summer of 2024 (Dirr 2024).

REPUBLICANS ON CRIME VICTIMS' RIGHTS

The Republican focus on crime victims may have taken root as early as 1964 when Republican Barry Goldwater spoke during his presidential campaign about the need for the Republican Party to espouse a position of being "tough on crime." Crime rates were starting to increase significantly in the 1960s and the initial underpinnings of the "tough on crime" stance were based on dealing with the increase in violent offenders. In the early 1980s, Republican President Ronald Reagan created a Violent Crime Task Force to study violent crime, which illuminated the fact that crime victims were being treated badly by the criminal justice system. In response, Republicans broadened their "tough on crime" perspective to include an examination of the treatment of crime victims and further bolster their "law and order" stance. As a result of this broadened perspective, Reagan created the President's Task Force on Victims of Crime in 1982 to focus solely on the treatment of crime victims, and appointed as its head the Honorable Lois Haight Herrington, a superior court judge in Contra Costa County, California. In the Task Force's final report, Herrington wrote (as quoted in Hook and Seymour 2004, para. 8):

> Something insidious has happened in America: Crime has made victims of us all. Awareness of its danger affects the way we think, where we live, where we go, what we buy, how we raise our children, and the quality of our lives as we age. The specter of violent crime and the knowledge that, without warning, any person can be attacked or crippled, robbed or killed, lurks at the fringes of consciousness ... The lessons of the victims run like a threat throughout and are the foundation of all the proposals that follow. Please take the time to learn, as we have, the depth and the human aspects of this grave social problem, then join in seeking and implementing the solutions.

The Republican record on crime victims' rights demonstrates a pattern of protection and a no-nonsense approach, with a great deal of activity occurring in the first part of the 1980s during the Reagan administration. In 1981, President Reagan established the first National Crime Victims' Rights Week to recognize the work of activists, advocates, criminal justice practitioners and academics, and the victims/survivors. Perhaps the most significant contribution of the Republican Party was the creation of the President's Task Force on Victims of Crime, which led to groundbreaking recommendations to improve the rights and quality of life of crime victims nationally. The Task Force's recommendations established within the Victims of Crime Act of 1984 from which a funding base was established which solidified the development of (1) professional/paid victim advocacy organizations and (2) the Crime Victims Fund, which provides compensation to qualifying crime victims through the collection of offender fines, fees, and forfeitures primarily. In 1983, Reagan's attorney general William French Smith established the Task Force on Family Violence, which held hearings across the country to better understand the implications and effects of family violence. During that same year, Smith produced a guideline document on how best to protect federal victims and witnesses in accordance with the newly passed Federal Victim and Witness Protection Act of 1982. Throughout his presidency, Reagan continued to honor crime victims in yearly White House Rose Garden ceremonies and declared a National Missing Children's Day after the disappearance of Etan Patz, at that time the latest in a series of highly publicized child abductions. Furthermore, in 1984 and 1985, several other important developments impacted the treatment of crime victims. These included:

- The Missing Children's Assistance Act was passed, which led to the establishment of the National Center for Missing and Exploited Children;

- The Justice Assistance Act was passed, which provided funding for 200 new victim service agencies;
- Victim/witness coordinator positions were launched across the United States in U.S. Attorneys' Offices under the direction of the U.S. Department of Justice;
- The National Center for Victims of Crime (originally the National Victim Center) was developed to focus on the rights and needs of crime victims;
- Domestic violence was declared a major public health problem; and
- Real attention was paid to the emotional toll of victimization.

In 1991, Florida Republican Representative Ileana Ros-Lehtinen introduced a US Constitutional Amendment to address victims' rights (Office for Victims of Crime 2023). During Republican President George W. Bush's administration, there appeared to be a great deal of push in the U.S. Attorney General's office to incorporate victims' rights into the operations of the criminal justice system. The terrorist attacks of September 11, 2001, however, caused Bush's focus to shift away from general crime victims' rights to more specific focus on victims of terrorist attacks. By changing the Victims of Crime Act, Bush expanded the definition of crime victim to include victims of terrorist acts. Victims of human trafficking also received precedence, as new guidelines were published on how to better deal with human trafficking victims within various federal government agencies. Bush's 2004 Justice for All Act, referred to in the previous section, provided rights to crime victims as well as remedies if said rights were not upheld. While states' victims' bills of rights provided specific duties of the justice system in regard to their treatment of crime victims, they often did not supply a remedy if the rights were not respected. The Justice for All Act of 2004 addressed this by indicating that specific action could be taken against justice agents/agencies if victims' rights were denied. In 2006, President Bush also reauthorized the Violence Against Women Act (VAWA), which expanded services for sexual assault victims, ensured that women victims of domestic violence would not become homeless as a result of their victimization, and provided funding to address the mental health impact on children witnessing domestic violence in violent homes. Finally, Bush enacted the Adam Walsh Children Protection and Safety Act of 2006, which enhanced supervision of sex-offenders and provided prosecutors more latitude to be able to prosecute child sex abuse cases. During the latter part of Bush's second term, his administration focused more on cybercrime issues, including identify theft, internet crimes against children, and reparations for cybercrime victims.

Republican Senator Suggests That Republicans Are the Only Ones Supporting Crime Victims

In February 2020, Senator Joe Sanfelippo of Wisconsin posted a memo on his Congressional webpage indicating that the "Tougher on Crime" package that went to the Wisconsin State Assembly focused on increasing protections for crime victims and witnesses while enhancing punishments for repeat and violent offenders and improving transparency and oversight of state courts and corrections. Senator Sanfelippo stated that Assembly Democrats were focused more on the rights of offenders and getting people out of prison instead of balancing the rehabilitation of prisoners and the safety of the public. He proposed that Assembly Democrats and Republicans held fundamentally different beliefs about the purpose of the criminal justice system. The bill was passed by the Assembly, largely with the support of Republicans, but Governor Evers vetoed the portions of legislation highlighted by Sanfelippo, stating that signing those parts of legislation into law would have cost taxpayers \$55 million in year one to cover the costs of building two new prisons and \$156 additional annually to support those prisons. Governor Evers encouraged Assembly members to work on a more bipartisan effort similar to other states to reform the justice system (White 2020).

The administration of Republican President Donald J. Trump, sworn into office in January 2017, continued the Republican tradition of legislation to protect victims. In 2017, as the result of several high-profile scandals involving the sexual assault of minor athletes, Trump signed into law the Protecting Young Victims from Sexual Abuse and Safe Sport Authorization Act to protect minors who participated in sports organizations recognized by the International Olympic Committee. The Trump administration also focused legislation and funding on underserved populations, including Native Americans and Alaska Natives through the proclamation of May 3 as a day of remembrance for murdered individuals within those groups. Additionally, funding was made available to increase training, needed resources, and positions for Village Public Safety Officers and Tribal Police. By 2020, the Trump administration also provided resources to increase confidence in law enforcement by addressing job stress, improve officer recruitment and training, and to examine the impact of social conditions on the operations of law enforcement agencies.

DEMOCRATS ON CRIME VICTIMS' RIGHTS

Democratic President Lyndon Johnson conducted the first national survey of crime victimization in the 1960s to understand the prevalence of crime across the country, the dynamics of those crimes, reporting habits of crime victims, and the impact of crime on the victims. For the first time, it was recorded that victims did not report crime because of a general distrust of the criminal justice system itself. In response, President Johnson created the Law Enforcement Assistance Administration in 1966 to generate funding to support victim/witness liaisons in law enforcement and prosecutors' offices to assist crime victims with the judicial process. It remained business as usual for crime victims in terms of treatment by the justice system, but across the nation, grassroots victim advocacy organizations were developed utilizing volunteers, specifically to provide service to women victims of domestic violence and sexual assault, and child victims of abuse and neglect. Republican and Democratic Congresses passed a number of bills specific to women and child victims.

Democratic President Bill Clinton, elected in 1992, campaigned as "tough on crime" and was a staunch supporter of victims' rights, including support for a victims' rights amendment to the US Constitution. In 1993, he signed the Brady Bill, which required mandatory background checks and a mandatory five-day wait period for the purchase of handguns, in response to the attempted assassination of President Reagan and the subsequent permanent disability incurred by White House Press Secretary James Brady in 1981. The Brady Bill sought to protect future victims of violent crime, in particular from homicide, and was seen as a great progress toward protecting the public (Office for Victims of Crime 2023). President Clinton also enacted the Violent Crime Control and Law Enforcement Act of 1994, which included VAWA and created a National Child Sex Offender Registry. In 1999, Democratic Senator Joe Biden (DE) submitted a revision to VAWA to include stronger enforcement of "stay away" orders, more assistance for battered women, and an increase in penalties for offenders who use Rohypnol for date rape purposes, which President Clinton authorized in 2000. Federal laws were developed throughout the early 2000s that established a .08 blood alcohol concentration (BAC) national standard with the support of Mothers Against Drunk Driving, that increased funding for the Crime Victims' Fund, and that developed additional organizations to better address burgeoning areas of victimization, such as cybercrime and human trafficking (Office for Victims of Crime 2023).

Democratic President Barack Obama, elected in 2008, created in 2009 a new position of White House Advisor on Violence Against Women in support of crime victims. Victims of financial crimes, including fraud, also were a focus of the Obama administration with the creation of a Financial Fraud Enforcement Task Force and new legislation aimed at addressing the impact of a variety of financial crimes on victims. Under the Obama administration, protections for hate crime victims and LGBTQ victims were expanded. President Obama signed into legislation the Matthew Shepard and James Byrd, Jr. Hate Crimes Prevention Act to expand the scope of individuals who were eligible for protections under federal law. Victimizations experienced by those in the military and peace corps was also a focus of the Obama administration, demonstrated in the passing of a number of pieces of legislation, including the Coast Guard Authorization Act of 2010, the Skelton National Defense Authorization Act for Fiscal Year 2011, and the Kate Puzey Peace Corps Volunteer Protection Act. In line with protections for those in governmental agencies, the Prison Rape Elimination Act was enacted in 2013 calling for the collection of information related to rape of those confined in correctional institutions, and a recognition and plan for treatment by jail and prison administrators.

The 2013 reauthorization of the Violence Against Women Act also extended protections for specific classes of previously unprotected potential crime victims—same-sex couples involved in domestic violence and specific groups of immigrants. In 2019, Congressional Democrats pushed forward the Violence Against Women Reauthorization Act with an addendum that would bar individuals with domestic violence and/or stalking misdemeanors from purchasing a gun. This legislation would also close the "boyfriend loophole" by adding non-married/dating partners or ex-partners as subject to the Act. At the time of this proposal, the prohibition only applied to felony domestic violence or stalking offenders who: (1) lived with their partner/ex-partner, (2) had children with their partner/ex-partner, or (3) were married to their partner/ex-partner.

Democratic Senator Proposes Legislation to Create a Property Crime Victims' Compensation Fund

On May 19, 2019, the Associated Press reported that Democratic Senator Nate Libby of Lewiston, Maine, proposed that a property crime victims' compensation fund be created to assist property crime victims replace or repair items lost or damaged due to a property crime victimization (Associated Press 2019). Property crime victims are typically not allowed to claim state funded crime victim compensation except in very rare cases in which a personal/violent crime led to property damage as well (and only for specific states) (Wright and Brightman 2018). The laws that existed in Maine at the time allowed for restitution for property crime victims, but restitution may not be readily forthcoming.

It is important to note that while there are differences, Republican and Democratic positions on crime victims' rights are more similar than dissimilar. An April 4, 2020, news article by *Wisconsin State Journal* reporter Riley Vetterkind illustrates how similar political perspectives are on crime victims' rights. Vetterkind reported that the Marsy's Law in Wisconsin had wide support from both Republicans and Democrats. The law aimed to better protect crime victims' rights throughout the judicial process by reinforcing and/or ensuring that victims were given due respect by the justice system, including privacy regarding information not pertinent to the crime under investigation. The opposition, while slight, was also represented equally on both sides of the aisle. Opponents argued the law repeats protection offered to victims by existing statues and that it threatens the rights of defendants because it may limit their access to information that could aid in their defense. As of mid-2024, Marsy's Law had been adopted by twelve states and is under consideration in at least two others, including Idaho and Tennessee. It has long been reported that politicians use crime victims' rights bills to bolster their claims that they are "tough on crime" and/or sympathetic to crime victims' needs. In fact, the failure to support a victims' rights bill with a crime victim's name attached to it has been used against politicians to illustrate they are soft on crime. A legislator's support or opposition to a piece of legislation, however, may be due to add-ons that have nothing to do with the crime victims' right being promoted. Additionally, support of any given crime victims' rights bill may be primarily symbolic. Megan's Law, for example, required sheriff's or district attorney's offices to notify communities about the presence of sex offenders, which required adjustments to county and local budgets to cover a variety of costs, such as payroll for personnel and costs to maintain the internet sex offender registry. A study of the impact of this law in New Jersey found that some of the costs were covered using federal grant funding, but the counties were responsible for the overall funding of the sex offender registries (Zgoba et al. 2008).

FURTHER READING

Associated Press. 2019. "Maine Eyes Law Change to Better Serve Property Crime Victims." WABI, May 19, 2019. https://www.wabi.tv/content/news/Maine-eyes-law-change-to-better-serve-property-crime-victims-510143541.html.

Bazelon, Lara A., and Bruce A. Green. 2020. "Victims' Rights from a Restorative Perspective." *Ohio State Journal of Criminal Law* 17, no. 1: 1–41.

Camhi, Natasha. 2016. "Criminal Justice Reform Has Made It into Both Party Platforms. That's a big deal." Brennan Center, August 1, 2016. https://www.brennancenter.org/our-work/analysis-opinion/criminal-justice-reform-has-made-it-both-party-platforms-thats-big-deal.

Chammah, Maurice. 2016. "Two Parties, Two Platforms." The Marshall Project, July 18, 2016. https://www.themarshallproject.org/2016/07/18/two-parties-two-platforms-on-criminal-justice.

"The Congressional Victim's Rights Caucus: An Advancement for Victims of Crime." n.d. Police Chef Magazine. Accessed July 6, 2020. https://www.policechiefmagazine.org/the-congressional-victims-rights-caucus-an-advancement-for-victims-of-crime/.

CSG Justice Center Staff. 2014. "The Congressional Victims' Rights Caucus Presents Awards." CSG Justice Center, September 19, 2014. https://csgjusticecenter.org/the-congressional-victims-rights-caucus-presents-awards/.

Davis, Susan. 2019. "House Passes Bill Protecting Domestic Abuse Victims; GOP Split over Gun Restrictions." NPR: Morning Edition, April 4, 2019. https://www.npr.org/2019/04/04/707685268/violence-against-women-act-gets-tangled-up-in-gun-rights-debate.

Democratic Party Platform, 2020. https://www.presidency.ucsb.edu/documents/2020-democratic-party-platform. Accessed July 31, 2024.

Dirr, Alison. 2024. "RNC May Again Adopt a Party Platform This Year after Not Having One in 2020, Lara Trump Says." *Milwaukee Journal Sentinel*, March 27, 2024. https://www.jsonline.com/story/news/politics/elections/2024/03/27/rnc-may-again-adopt-party-platform-in-2024-lara-trump-says/73106453007/.

Frum, David. 2015. "The Coming Democratic Crack-Up." *The Atlantic*, September 21, 2015. https://www.theatlantic.com/politics/archive/2015/09/the-democrats-looming-dilemma/406426/.

Garland, David. 2001. *The Culture of Control: Crime and Social Order in Contemporary Society*. Chicago: University of Chicago Press.

Henderson, Lynne. 1985. "The Wrongs of Victim's Rights." *Stanford Law Review* 37: 937–1021.

Henderson, Lynne. 1999. "Revisiting Victim's Rights." Scholarly Works. Paper 863. https://scholars.law.unlv.edu/cgi/viewcontent.cgi?article=1886&context=facpub. Accessed July 31, 2024.

Hook, Melissa, and Anne Seymour. 2004. "Retrospective of the 1982 President's Task Force on Victims of Crime." NCJ No. 248460. December 2004. Washington, DC: Office for Victims of Crime. https://www.ojp.gov/ncjrs/virtual-library/abstracts/retrospective-1982-presidents-task-force-victims-crime.

Kane, Paul, and John Wagner. 2020. "Democrats Unveil Broad Police Reform Bill as Floyd's Death Sparks Protests Nationwide." *The Washington Post*, June 9, 2020. https://www.washingtonpost.com/powerpost/democrats-unveil-broad-police-reform-bill-pledge-to-transform-law-enforcement/2020/06/08/1ed07d7a-a992-11ea-94d2-d7bc43b26bf9_story.html.

Karmen, Andrew J. 1992. "Who's against Victims' Rights? The Nature of the Opposition to Pro Victim Initiatives in Criminal Justice." *Journal of Civil Rights and Economic Development* 8, no. 1: 157–75.

Latzer, Barry. 2020. "Democrats Prefer 'Reforming' the Criminal Justice System to Punishing Criminals." *National Review*, February 17, 2020. https://www.nationalreview.com/2020/02/democrats-prefer-reforming-criminal-justice-system-to-punishing-criminals/.

Lepore, Jill. 2018. "The Rise of the Victims'-Rights Movement: How a Conservative Agenda and a Feminist Cause Came Together to Transform Criminal Justice." *The New Yorker*, May 21, 2018. https://www.newyorker.com/magazine/2018/05/21/the-rise-of-the-victims-rights-movement.

Maciag, Mike. 2016. "Who Crime Victims Are and How They View Criminal Justice Reform." August 10, 2016. https://www.governing.com/topics/public-justice-safety/gov-national-crime-victimization-survey-data.html.

Marshall, Sandra E. 2004. "Victims of Crime: Their Station and Its Duties." *Critical Review of International Social and Political Philosophy* 7, no. 2: 104–17. doi:10.1080/1369823042000266549.

McHarris, Philip V. 2020. "Democrats Are Ignoring a Key Piece of Criminal Justice Reform—Slicing Police Budgets." *The Washington Post*, January 16, 2020. https://www.washingtonpost.com/outlook/2020/01/16/democrats-are-ignoring-key-piece-criminal-justice-reform-slicing-police-budgets/.

Mears, Daniel P., and Joshua C. Cochran. 2014. *Prisoner Reentry in the Era of Mass Incarceration*. Thousand Oaks, CA: Sage Publications.

National Crime Victim Law Institute. 2011. "Fundamentals of Victims' Rights: A Brief History of Crime Victims' Rights in the United States." *Victim Law Bulletin* (November): 1–4. Ncvli.org.

Office of Justice Programs. April 2006. "OVC Fact Sheet: The Justice for All Act." FS 000311. https://ovc.ojp.gov/sites/g/files/xyckuh226/files/publications/factshts/justforall/welcome.html. Accessed August 5, 2024.

Office for Victims of Crime. 2020. "Resource Guide: Landmarks in Victims' Rights and Services." https://ovc.ojp.gov/sites/g/files/xyckuh226/files/ncvrw2020/info_flyers/2020-NCVRW-Landmarks-in-Victims-508.pdf. Accessed July 31, 2024.

Office for Victims of Crime. 2023. "Landmarks in Victims' Rights and Services." https://ovc.ojp.gov/ncvrw2023/landmarks.pdf. Accessed July 31, 2024.

O'Mara, Thomas. 2019. "O'Mara Blasts Senate Democrats for Ongoing Actions to Favor Criminals over Crime Victims: Criticizes Scheduling Votes on Day That State Honors Fallen Police Officers." New York Senate, May 7, 2019. https://www.nysenate.gov/newsroom/articles/2019/thomas-f-omara/omara-blasts-senate-democrats-ongoing-actions-favor-criminals.

Orvis, Gregory P., and John David Reitzel. 2008. "Balancing Criminal Victims' and Criminal Defendants' Rights." In *Controversies in Victimology*, 2nd edition, edited by Laura J. Moriarty, 1–19. Cincinnati, OH: Anderson Publishing.

Republican Party Platform, 2012. https://www.presidency.ucsb.edu/documents/2012-republican-party-platform#we. Accessed July 31, 2024.

Riley, John. 2019. "Democrats Shoot Down Anti-transgender Amendments to Violence Against Women Act." MetroWeekly, March 14, 2019. https://www.metroweekly.com/2019/03/democrats-shoot-down-anti-transgender-amendments-to-violence-against-women-act/.

Rizer, Arthur, and Lars Trautman. 2018. "The Conservative Case for Criminal Justice Reform." *The Guardian*, August 5, 2018. https://www.theguardian.com/us-news/2018/aug/05/the-conservative-case-for-criminal-justice-reform.

Vetterkind, Riley. 2020. "Voters to Decide on Crime Victim Constitutional Amendment on Tuesday's Ballot." *Wisconsin State Journal*, April 4, 2020. https://madison.com/wsj/news/local/govt-and-politics/voters-to-decide-on-crime-victim-constitutional-amendment-on-tuesdays-ballot/article_b2f962e9-f12f-5f1a-9b3a-167addcf8da7.html.

White, Laurel. 2020. "Evers Vetoes GOP's 'Tougher on Crime' Bills: Republican-backed Proposals Would Have Increased Some Criminal Penalties in Wisconsin." Wisconsin Public Radio, February 28, 2020. https://www.wpr.org/evers-vetoes-gops-tougher-crime-bills.

Wright, Elizabeth Q., and Sara Brightman. 2018. *Crime Victimization: A Comprehensive Overview*. 2nd edition. Durham, NC: Carolina Academic Press.

Zgoba, Kristen, Philip Witt, Melissa Dalessandro, and Veysey Bonita. 2008. *Megan's Law: Assessing the Practical and Monetary Efficacy*. The Research & Evaluation Unit, Office of Policy and Planning, New Jersey Department of Corrections. NCJ 225370.

CHAPTER 6

Cyberviolence and Online Extremism

DONNA OSSORIO

AT A GLANCE

Social media has evolved as the world's primary means of communication. Aggression and hostility toward individuals or groups in this social environment tend to promote extreme ideology and propaganda with a degree of anonymity. People can efficiently and strategically use social media platforms to communicate extremist ideology through various forms (websites, social media, chatrooms, listservs, blogs, videos, downloadable video games, music, and various internet communities). The term "cyberviolence" is intertwined within the context of "online extremism," also called virtual extremism, which consists of cyberhate or online hate.

Cyberviolence elements consist of the use of virtual or digital communications to disseminate hate based on race, national origin, religion, ethnicity, gender, gender identity, or sexual orientation, or differing group characteristics (Blazak 2009; Hawdon, Oksanen, and Rasanen 2017). The simplistic definition defines cyberviolence as aggressive and volatile behavior on public mediated spaces (Boyd 2014, 137), including, but not limited to, social platforms such as Facebook, Twitter, Snapchat, and various websites. Online extremism is the most dangerous and formidable social media platform usage because it breeds social support for individuals who explicitly advocate violence and the promotion of harmful ideology and divisive strategies on a domestic and international level.

Terrorism can be perpetuated as a form of cyberviolence and online extremism. Schmid (2004) defines terrorism as an extreme political expression or ideology that plans and plots acts of violence against civilians and governments to support a political or social agenda. The twenty-first century has seen the passage of legislation aimed at preventing terrorist acts, including those associated with online extremism and cyberviolence. The Uniting and Strengthening America by Providing Appropriate Tools Required to Intercept and Obstruct Terrorism Act (USA Patriot Act, herein after called "the Patriot Act"), the USA Freedom Act (H.R. 2048), the Homeland Security Act (HSA), and the Center for Strategic Counterterrorism Communication were implemented to combat extremist ideology, which promotes and contributes to domestic and international terrorism. In 2018, Texas Republican Representative Michael McCaul introduced H.R. 3359, which established the Cybersecurity and Infrastructure Security Agency (CISA) to combat various forms of cyberviolence and online extremism. H.R. 3359 amended the Homeland Security Act of 2002 and focuses on threats against US infrastructure on digital technology platforms, as well as other terroristic acts.

In the immediate aftermath of the tragic September 11, 2001, terrorist attacks, the United States undertook significant legislative and governmental initiatives to bolster national security and counter emerging threats. A pivotal piece of this effort was the introduction of the USA Patriot Act by Republican Senator Jim Sensenbrenner of Wisconsin. Aimed at expanding the capabilities of law enforcement agencies, the Act enhanced the government's authority to surveil and intercept potential terrorist communications, including monitoring the online activities of individuals within the United States. Passed swiftly with bipartisan support, the Act reflected a unified commitment to strengthening the nation's defenses against terrorism. However, the reach and implications of the Patriot Act, particularly regarding personal privacy and civil liberties, sparked a complex dialogue about the balance between security and individual rights.

As certain provisions of the Act approached their expiration, the dialogue led to the enactment of the USA Freedom Act. This subsequent legislation aimed to refine and continue the surveillance capabilities established under the Patriot Act while addressing growing concerns over privacy and transparency. The USA Freedom Act served as a legislative adjustment, restoring and modifying specific measures to ensure ongoing vigilance in monitoring communications while attempting to safeguard civil liberties. Parallel to these legislative efforts, the establishment of the U.S. Department of Homeland Security (DHS) marked a significant organizational response to the multifaceted challenges of national security. As the youngest cabinet department, the DHS was tasked with a broad array of responsibilities, with anti-terrorism and cybersecurity emerging as focal points of its mandate. This focus underscores the government's recognition of the evolving nature of threats, including those emanating from cyberviolence and online extremism. Complementing these initiatives, the Center for Strategic Counterterrorism Communication, instituted by an executive order from President Barack Obama, underscored the strategic imperative to counteract extremist ideologies and actions that pose threats to national security. This effort highlighted the growing acknowledgment of the need for complex strategies that not only intercept and prevent potential threats but also address the ideological battles waged in digital arenas.

The legislative and governmental responses to the threats posed by terrorism, highlighted by the enactment of the Patriot Act, the USA Freedom Act, the establishment of the DHS, and initiatives like the Center for Strategic Counterterrorism Communication, represent critical dimensions of the US strategy against cyberviolence and online extremism. These measures reflect an evolving understanding of security in the digital age, where threats not only take the form of physical attacks but also manifest in the virtual domain, challenging societal norms and national security. Exploring the complexities of cyberviolence and online extremism, it is essential to consider these responses as part of a broader framework aimed at safeguarding both the physical and cyber realms, highlighting the intricate balance between ensuring security and preserving the foundational values of privacy and freedom.

Social media continues to dominate as a primary communication channel worldwide, increasingly being utilized to propagate extremist ideologies and cyberviolence with a concerning level of anonymity. Cyberviolence and online extremism encompass digital communications to disseminate hate and promote ideologies that advocate violence against civilians based on various characteristics. Recent years have witnessed significant legislative efforts to combat these phenomena, including updates to existing laws and the introduction of new policies aimed at curbing the influence of extremist content online while balancing concerns over free speech and privacy rights.

MANY REPUBLICANS...

- Believe that the Patriot Act preserves life and liberty in part by allowing the federal government to monitor online activity for extremism that contributes to domestic and international terrorism.
- Recognize the rights of citizens and the need to balance the First Amendment (freedom of speech) with efforts to address the dangers of online extremism.
- Oppose diplomacy in cases of international terrorism and related cyber activities.
- Support the use of force against domestic and international terrorist threats, including those revealed through cyber investigations.

MANY DEMOCRATS...

- Support "sneak and peek" search warrants that require no statutory authorization, allowing the government or law enforcement to conduct online surveillance or investigations.
- Believe legislation like the Patriot Act is a slippery slope with respect to unauthorized online surveillance violating constitutional rights.
- Support allowing investigators to use the same strategies and methods that are available to investigate organized crime, some of which were not authorized before the Patriot Act.
- Believe that some investigative tactics, including some online surveillance, impinge on individual privacy rights and liberties of citizens.

OVERVIEW

Cyberviolence can elicit emotional distress and fear, the same as real-world violence (Bocij 2004; Finn 2004; Wall 2001). The ability to send threatening and harmful messages, engage in posting unsolicited or embarrassing information (including pictures and videos) on a social platform, and exchange hurtful and damaging messages, employs indirect and direct cyberviolence (Wall 2001). A constant barrage of social media and access to a plethora of personal information via online channels creates an opportunity for personal attacks, and disparaging information creates the opportunity for harm (Holt et al. 2011).

Social media platforms allow communication across time and place with few constraints. Virtual social groups are formed in various states and countries simultaneously and develop like communities in a physical landscape. Ideology, beliefs, and points of view are the magnets that draw like-minded people into social media groups; these groups then associate themselves with labels that define their central perspectives. Identifying with a social support group is critical in forming a collective identity, which can change the group's social climate and attitudes.

Within this social platform, a vast amount of information and ideas are shared as fact-finding truths. Many members absorb those data and do not question the validity or reliability of the information, which causes a myopic view of the facts. "Flocking" is a concept that explains the learning process by which extremist ideologies and attitudes are presented and reified with those individuals who share similar experiences and worldviews (Hawdon, Bernatzky, and Costello 2019). Extremist groups such as Stormwatch operate in this manner. Stormwatch operates a website that promotes white supremacy and claims that Dr. Martin Luther King, Jr. was an advocate for Jews and Communists, an idea contradictory to King's activist role in the pursuit of justice and equality. Stormwatch attempts to convince website visitors that the information conveyed therein represents the work of a great artist, painting a picture comprised of unfounded truths and historical inaccuracies. Cyberviolence and online extremism can be traced back to the early 1980s when Tom Metzger, the White Aryan Resistance leader, created a bulletin board with the group's specific ideology. This presence has been continuously active online since that time.

Initially, al-Qaeda and other extremist groups were not very active on social media platforms, but their presence has grown since the 1990s. These radical groups avoid planning or organizing attacks online but are very innovative and creative in using social media platforms for recruitment, ensuring the group's ideology message is continuously conveyed locally and globally, in addition to soliciting money. There is a continuous threat of homegrown extremist and violent individuals joining extreme right-wing philosophical views and ideologies. Groups identified by the United States as a Foreign Terrorist Organization and far-right groups utilizes social media platforms to promote and gain sympathizers toward their specific causes. The anonymity and the accessibility that social media platforms provide create easy access to individuals and groups in the most remote and most impoverished nations. Access to social platforms can foster extreme ideology that can stream to diverse groups of individuals simultaneously. It can slowly change one's perspective or introduce new principles and core beliefs based on insufficient and inaccurate information.

Misinformation or lack of accurate information may transform an individual's cognitive thought process into an extremist ideology (Gerstenfeld, Grant, and Chiang 2003). A constant barrage of ill-informed ideology has the propensity for specific individuals to adopt a different identity or ideology, regardless of their background. The popular website Stormfront.org engages individuals with neo-Nazi ideologies, providing discussions on daily events and activities from a "white-power" perspective (Gerstenfeld, Grant, and Chiang 2003). The forum connects people with similar perspectives in the United States and spreads distorted information to others around the world.

The Palestinian Islamic Jihad, or simply "the Jihad," which is Arabic for a struggle or fight against the enemies of Islam, is a group that strives to maintain Islamic principles and beliefs, maintains a presence on social media platforms and has assimilated groups from different nations and languages to resist Western ideology and domination. Its main grievances are the Western occupation of Iraq, the continuation of a Western military presence in the Middle East, America's support of Israel, and the Western nations' lack of respect for Jihad Islamic norms and values. Long-engrained loathing of the West and past diplomatic failures breed a contentious and hostile environment. This is demonstrated by physical terrorist acts and is a cultivated, harmful, and extremist ideology that disseminates violent messages through online platforms.

Violent acts by extremist groups to promote their ideologies are also a means of conveying messages to their members and non-members. In 2002, a terrorist group in Pakistan kidnapped Daniel Pearl, a journalist for the *Wall Street Journal*. The group used a Hotmail email address to demand the release of Pakistani terror detainees, among various other demands. It posted a video of Pearl stating his name and heritage and condemning America for their foreign policy in the Middle East. The captors slit Pearl's throat immediately afterward and beheaded him while sending a threatening message that more deaths would ensue if their demands were not met. This video of an egregious act was propaganda, to incite their followers and motivate their extremist movement.

Downloadable music and video games are socially acceptable tools to attract individuals with specific extreme ideologies and perspectives. The record label Resistance Records produces and distributes music that promotes "white power" and right-wing extremist ideologies. Producing messages subtly shrouded in music geared toward young people is profitable. National Alliance, a "white power" group, owns the record label and profits from distributed music sales. This accomplishes a two-fold goal of spreading the group's message and securing monetary gain. Video games have become a vital resource in promoting extremism and a socially acceptable and expeditious means of engaging a younger audience. Resistance Records released a game called *Ethnic Cleansing*, a "first-person shooter" game in which the primary player viewpoint is that of a skinhead or Klansman who kills Blacks, Jews, and Latinos in ghetto or subway environments (Anti-Defamation League 2002). Comparably, Islamic Jihad extremists have released video games with the primary player viewpoints emulating jihadist ideology, killing Jews, Westerners, and members of the US military. Additionally, videos and publications distributed on the internet allow individuals to obtain detailed information on making bombs, improvised weapons, gunplay, and various information that could potentially lead to violence.

The United States does not have national countering violent extremism (CVE) guidelines on terrorism and targeted violence prevention. Roles and responsibilities have not been established nationally, for law enforcement or non-law enforcement entities. Creation and implementation of such guidelines are vital to ensure that health, education, local, and state officials, as well as community organizations, partner across the country to prevent cyberviolence and online extremism. The UN has called on governments to develop a framework toward a comprehensive approach to preventing terrorism and violence. Online extremism is becoming a significant concern across the globe. Exposure to extremist and violent views online can instigate or perpetuate violent behavior. Though there is no one path toward radicalization, and repeated exposure to extremist views does not necessarily elicit violence, research shows that continuous exposure does play a significant role in the radicalization process (Lacquer 1999). There must be a clear and concise message from all federal and state governments regarding extremist violence and the consequences of such actions in any form—online or physical manifestation.

The digital landscape has increasingly become a fertile ground for the spread of extremist ideologies and cyberviolence, affecting individuals' mental health and societal harmony. Social media platforms, while enabling global connectivity, also serve as arenas for the spread of harmful ideologies, misinformation, and cyberbullying. Efforts to combat these issues have been multifaceted, involving legislative measures, technological solutions, and community engagement strategies to prevent radicalization and address the root causes of online extremism. The complexity of cyberviolence and its intersection with online extremism necessitates a nuanced approach that respects free expression while protecting vulnerable communities from harm.

REPUBLICANS ON CYBERVIOLENCE AND ONLINE EXTREMISM

Radicalization is a serious threat to the US national security. Silber and Bhatt (2007) argue that it is intuitive and plausible that radical ideals produce radical behaviors. Historically, the US Congress has prioritized policy to prevent and counter violent extremism. Coined initially as a policy to "prevent and counter violent Islamic extremism" (P/CVIE) during the administration of Republican President George W. Bush, the term was subsequently modified during the Obama administration to prevent and counter violent extremism (CVE). During the implementation phase of CVE, Texas Republican Representative Michael McCaul, former chair of the House Homeland Security Committee, described the policy as "failed" and argued that it should be repealed and replaced with something new. However, The House Committee on Homeland Security operated in a bipartisan manner in its passage. The administration of Republican President Donald J. Trump considered renaming the Task Force from "countering violent extremism" to "countering Islamic extremism" or "countering radical Islamic extremism." Bipartisan concern was that extremist ideology that threatens the United States is not only concentrated among individuals from international geography but also can originate domestically. Due to the urgency to prevent and counter extremism, many House members and interested parties encouraged the Trump administration to focus on countering violent extremists, given that CVE was not a priority during the first half of the Obama administration. Until the Boston Marathon bombings in 2013, in which the perpetrators were associated with a domestic Islamic extremist organization, CVE was underfunded and lacked rigid leadership (Levitt 2017). CVE began to wither as the Trump administration planned to modify the program to eliminate targeting white supremacists and to rescind a grant to fight against neo-Nazism. Since the latter part of 2018, the CVE has been inactive.

US Government Aims to Reduce Cyberbullying

StopBullying.gov is a website that reflects the work of several federal partners (the U.S. Departments of Education, Justice, Health and Human Services, Agriculture, Defense, the Interior, the Federal Trade Commission, and the White House Initiative on Asian Americans and Pacific Islanders) to "coordinate policy, research, and communications on bullying topics." Cyberbullying is a form of bullying that happens through digital devices (e.g., cell phones, computers, tablets). It can be facilitated by text messaging systems, apps, and online social media such as forums and gaming sites where people create, view, and share content. Cyberbullying includes "sending, posting, or sharing negative, harmful, false, or mean content about someone else," and "can include sharing personal or private information about someone else causing embarrassment or humiliation." According to StopBullying.gov, "some cyberbullying crosses the line into unlawful or criminal behavior," although violation of law is generally a misdemeanor. All fifty states, the District of Columbia, and American Territories have taken steps to prevent bullying, with forty-eight states referencing bullying through electronic means.

The dilemma that arises when Congress is addressing cyberviolence is the issue of freedom of speech. Democratic California Representative Linda Sanchez introduced legislation in 2009 to criminalize cyberbullying (a form of cyberviolence). The Megan Meire Cyberbullying Prevention Act would "amend the federal criminal code to impose criminal penalties on anyone who transmits in interstate or foreign commerce a communication intended to coerce, intimidate, harass, or cause substantial emotional distress to another person, using electronic means to support severe, repeated, and hostile behavior." Of the twenty representatives who cosponsor the legislation, there were only two Republicans. Republicans' viewpoints emulated the Democrats on this issue; many were concerned that this law would interfere with silencing the political opponents and free speech. In addition, violating this law would be classified as a felony, which caused this piece of legislation to stall. Texas Republican Representative Michael McCaul, former chairman of the House Homeland Security Committee, argued the need for a legislative approach that respected constitutional freedoms while still addressing the harm caused by online activity. He referenced both foreign and domestic acts of violent extremism to highlight the broader context within which harmful behaviors online connect to larger patterns of violence.

September 11, 2001 (9/11), directly impacted legislation addressing violent extremism. Wisconsin Republican Representative Jim Sensenbrenner introduced the USA Patriot Act, comprised of three main components:

- Expanded abilities of law enforcement to surveil, including by tapping domestic and international phones

- Eased interagency communication to allow federal agencies to use all available resources in the counterterrorism effort more effectively
- Increased penalties for terrorism crimes and an expanded list of activities that qualify someone to be charged with terrorism

This Act allowed law enforcement to retrieve names and addresses, billing records, duration of calls, communication devices, and other related data to trace the user's activities efficiently. The most important and controversial element of the Patriot Act is the immediate accessibility law enforcement has to the above information from an internet service provider (ISP). If an ISP deems an emergency disclosure is necessary to protect the public safety, in instances where extreme physical or virtual threats are apparent, the ISP will expeditiously contact law enforcement.

The USA Freedom Act (H.R. 2048) was enacted to revise and modify the Patriot Act's provisions set to expire. Representative Sensenbrenner, who introduced the Patriot Act, conveyed that the National Security Agency (NSA) overstepped the Act's original intent by having metadata on American citizens' phone, internet, and social media information. Section 215 of the Patriot Act was amended to ensure only essential information was obtained by the intelligence agencies when that investigation involves terrorism or espionage. The USA Freedom Act faced scrutiny from Democrats and ISPs, who argued the revision impinged on America's Fourth Amendment, which protects citizens from unlawful searches and seizures. After a modified version was reintroduced, Republican Senator Mitch McConnell stated that revising the bill would hinder NSA's ability to collect the necessary data to fight terrorism. The Act's importance was to ensure terrorist activities were investigated efficiently and effectively. The Act passed in the House (338 votes for and 88 against) but was defeated in the Senate (57 votes for and 42 against), as 60 votes were necessary to pass this Act.

The implementation of the Department of Homeland Security (DHS) was created in response to 9/11; the purpose was to develop a national strategy in response to terrorist attacks and threats to the United States. President George W. Bush (R) established this department by incorporating twenty-two government agencies into one department, eliminating inadequate information sharing among federal entities. This department's implementation received majority support among Republicans and American citizens, who saw this as an aggressive method to combat terrorist activities. Though many noted that the Homeland Security Act's enactment was during a lame-duck session of the 107th Congress, the creation of the DHS was one of the most significant reorganization maneuvers in the federal government over several decades. Due to law enforcement concerns regarding political violence by anti-government extremists and Islamist extremists, the DHS's role in obtaining and assimilating necessary information is imperative to Americans' public safety.

The Center for Strategic Counterterrorism Communication (2011), an executive order by Democratic President Barack Obama, was met with high scrutiny. Section 1 covered the commitment to "counteractions and ideologies of al-Qa'ida, its affiliates and adherents, other terrorist organizations, and violent extremists overseas that threaten the interest and national security of the United States." The Republicans' disagreement was not based on the executive order's language but on the perception that the president was "legislating from the Oval Office."

To combat violent extremism, the Trump administration increased funding directly to law enforcement agencies to assist in gathering intelligence. Still, this funding is intertwined with community-based programs. Due to the privacy and security concerns within the CVE program, the appropriation gives law enforcement a broad platform for utilizing such funding. The Trump administration modified the CVE to target terrorism and violence, with an emphasis placed on "racially, ethnically, and religiously motivated violence" and a "whole-of-society" method to include mental health professionals, social service providers, local professionals, and community-based organizations, which can assist in deterring violent extremist behavior. The Trump administration enacted a more comprehensive approach to implementing the newly designed CVE program. Under Trump, the DHS committed $35 million toward research on terrorism and violent extremism, emphasizing public and private collaboration, interventions/prevention programs, and rehabilitation/reintegration programs. This update was viewed with much scrutiny within the Muslim communities; suspicions of over-surveillance and current stigmatization caused reservations regarding modifying the CVE programs.

Unfortunately, the Trump administration failed to provide clarity in defining "violent extremism," which hinders law enforcement's ability to successfully identify and prosecute it. Trump's CVE policies focused on social media Islamist movements and minimized the potential harm from violent online extremism originating from other ethnic and racial groups. As a result, online Homegrown Violent Extremism (HVE) and cyberviolence increased, although it is difficult to detect due to inadequate monitoring.

During the Trump administration, thirty-nine of fifty-one hate-motivated murders were committed by white supremacists. An Anti-Defamation League study found murders committed by white supremacists increased from three deaths in 2016 to seventeen in 2018. In El Paso, Texas, after twenty-three victims were killed, users of the social media site 8chan supported the action and temporarily posted a manifesto online with noted extreme ideology. Due to the egregious and heinous information promoting cyberviolence and online extremism, Cloudflare (a content delivery network) terminated website services to 8chan. Significant increases in the removal of extremist content from YouTube, Twitter, Facebook, and other online platforms are effective, but the majority of extreme online content remains undetected. The DHS noted that individuals with extremist ideology are now moving to secretive, smaller, and hard-to-detect online platforms.

Republicans have historically emphasized national security concerns in their approach to cyberviolence and online extremism, advocating for robust legislative and surveillance measures to prevent terrorist activities. This includes support for acts like the Patriot Act and its successors, which are seen as crucial tools in monitoring and intervening in potential extremist activities online. In the wake of the 2022 midterms, the party has continued to advocate for a balance between security measures and protecting civil liberties, with a renewed focus on the potential threats posed by domestic extremists. There is a growing recognition within the party for the need to address all forms of extremism, including those that originate domestically, without compromising individual freedoms.

DEMOCRATS ON CYBERVIOLENCE AND ONLINE EXTREMISM

To combat cyberviolence (cyberbullying and harassment), US Senator Frank Lautenberg (D-NJ) and Representative Rush D. Holt, Jr. (D-NJ-12) introduced the Tyler Clementi Higher Education Anti-Harassment Act in 2011. Tyler Clementi was an eighteen-year-old freshman at Rutgers University in Fall 2010. Clementi's roommate posted an intimate video of Clementi and another male. A few days later, Clementi committed suicide. Opponents of this bill point out that harassment on university campuses, including harassment based on sexual orientation, is already prohibited by law. Concerns regarding restrictions on free speech echo those discussed earlier in relation to the Megan Meier Cyberbullying Prevention Act, introduced by Democratic California Representative Linda Sanchez in 2009.

Texts Lead to Suicide

In 2014, eighteen-year-old Conrad Roy was found dead in his truck, a victim of suicide. Investigators found a slew of text messages and other electronic communications from Roy's seventeen-year-old girlfriend, Michelle Carter, encouraging him to end his life and providing instructions on how to do so. Roy, who had struggled with depression his entire life, thought he had found a kindred spirit in Carter, who also had mental health issues. While Carter was supportive at first, her texts and communications with other friends about Roy indicated her increasing frustration with Roy's inaction in ending his own pain through suicide. In 2015, Carter was indicted for involuntary manslaughter in Roy's death. At the 2017 trial, prosecutors were able to prove that Carter had a duty to alleviate the risk of Roy's suicide and that her failure to do so caused Roy's death. She was convicted, and the Massachusetts Supreme Court upheld that conviction on appeal in 2019. Her initial sentence of two and a half years was reduced to fifteen months, and she ultimately served eleven months. She has been on probation since 2020 (Margaritoff 2022).

The War on Terror, as it was characterized after the 9/11 attacks, was not considered a policy priority until ISIS and Jihadist threats and terrorism became an increasing domestic concern. Though the Patriot Act passed by a vote of 357-66 in the House and 98-1 in the Senate, some Democratic responses to the Act were negative based on the pressure to hurry the bill without the opportunity to review the document in its entirety. Some Democrats and other interested parties viewed the law as unconstitutional and that it intruded on American citizens' private communications. During the latter part of the Obama administration, CVE was launched to the forefront in dealing with cyberviolence and online terrorism. The Patriot Sunsets Extension Act of 2011 was signed by Obama to revise specific provisions in the Patriot Act, but it failed to pass Congress. As parts of the Patriot Act expired on June 1, 2015, particular sections were reenacted by the USA Freedom Act Extension of 2011 until November 2019. Both bills were met with bipartisanship support; the USA Freedom Act passed by a vote of 338-88 in the House and

67-32 in the Senate. Section 702, part of the Patriot Act that allows the government to monitor internet communication with foreign nationals was opposed by many Democrats. However, many Democrats signed on to the agreement during an open vote. There were attempts by the Democrats to include additional oversights and limits to Section 702, but this attempt failed.

The Obama administration implemented various CVE programs with differing results. It created an office within the DHS and funded approximately thirty programs with a two-year funding expiration date for combating extremist recruitment. During this period, the National Counterterrorism Center, working with various security agencies, employed a Community Awareness Briefing regarding radicalization and terrorist threats in local regions. Programs were geared toward partnering with communities, yet community contributions were scarce due to limited support and assistance. Democrats viewed CVE as violating the civil liberties of American Muslims. A lack of research and failure to track the results of CVE programs led to skepticism among Democrats who, although keenly aware that cyberviolence and online extremism are continually increasing, felt that the legislative acts contained flaws that threatened First Amendment rights. In 2010, Democratic senators warned that the way the Patriot Act was being interpreted would alarm American citizens as well as some in Congress.

According to a letter from Senators Ron Wyden and Mark Udall to Attorney General Eric Holder in March 2012, the Attorney General and the American citizens would be "stunned" if they knew how the government was interpreting the Patriot Act. The Justice Department opposed disclosing information that might damage national security if specific information was released to the public; there are currently two Freedom of Information Act lawsuits regarding the interpretation of the Patriot Act. Democrats took exception to Section 215 of the Patriot Act, which entails agents' ability to obtain a court order from the Foreign Intelligence Surveillance Court to gain access to "tangible items" that are deemed "relevant" to a terrorism or espionage investigation. It has been used to collect metadata regarding US citizens' communications.

President Barack Obama held a CVE Summit meeting in February 2015 to address leaders from the local, federal, and international levels to discuss DHS's Office of Community Partnerships (September 2015) and the DHS-housed CVE Task Force (January 2016), both newly implemented initiatives, to lay the foundation for CVE grant programs to address CVE from a private and public institutions perspective. Homeland Security was tasked with formulating the ground rules for CVE grants. Approximately $10 million was awarded before Trump took office. Once President Trump was in place, many recipients declined to accept grants awarded, concerned about the direction of the policy.

After the Boston Marathon bombing in 2013, the Obama administration's approach toward HVE and CVE were at the forefront of various programs and grant initiatives. In an attempt to combat extremist ideology, including Islamist extremism online, the Global Engagement Center (GEC) was employed in 2016 to "lead the coordination, integration, and synchronization of Government-wide communications activities directed at foreign audiences abroad to counter the messaging and diminish the influence of international terrorist organizations" (U.S. Department of State n.d.). Yet, an aggressive approach to eliminate extremist information on online platforms domestically is lacking.

Democratic President Joseph R. Biden's approach to cyberviolence and online extremism is captured in the interwoven components of the National Strategy for Countering Domestic Terrorism. This strategy clearly defines a framework to ensure a comprehensive approach to online violence without impeding individuals' civil liberties. The purpose is to develop a multilateral approach to eliminating online extremist content and ideology. The strategy consists of four pillars:

1. Understand and share domestic terrorism-related information.
2. Prevent domestic terrorism recruitment and mobilization to violence.
3. Disrupt and deter domestic terrorism activity.
4. Confront long-term contributors to domestic terrorism.

The second pillar addresses online violence and extremism. According to the Biden administration strategy, "efforts to address online terrorist recruitment and mobilization to violence by domestic terrorist through increased information sharing with the technology sector and the creation of innovative ways to foster digital literacy and build resilience to recruitment and mobilization" (The White House 2021). The Biden administration joined a New Zealand-initiated global pledge for countries and technology companies to work together to address online extremism—the Christchurch Call to Action to Eliminate Terrorist and Violent Extremist Content Online. The Call to Action was initiated after a video of a terrorist attack on a mosque in Christchurch, New Zealand, on March 15, 2019, appeared online in real time.

Violent extremist online content has the propensity to incite more violence. The Biden administration supports freedom of expression but called on technology companies "to develop and enforce terms of service and community standards that forbid the use of their platforms for terrorist and violent extremist purposes" (The White House 2021). This request reflects the goal of the administration's fourth pillar, to confront long-term contributors to domestic terrorism. The most crucial aspect of this strategy is to reduce racial, ethnic, and religious hatred, which are the core components of cyberviolence and extremism. Eliminating bias within law enforcement when policing extremism is essential to the Biden administration strategy, which emphasizes finding ways to counter polarization that is often fueled by disinformation, misinformation, and dangerous conspiracy theories online.

The Democratic Party's position on all forms of violence and extremism demonstrates a clear focus on CVE. The Biden administration has contributed over $77 million toward preventing and responding to violent extremisms. Currently, the Democratic Party understands the importance of combating terrorism and cyberviolence. However, balancing American civil liberties with law enforcement powers granted by the Patriot Act has become increasingly challenging. During the Trump presidency, New York Democrat Jerry Nadler proposed to reauthorize the Patriot Act with the support of 152 Democrats. An amendment for Section 215 stated that individuals' internet browsing or search history cannot be obtained and passed with a 59-37 vote in the Senate. However, due to the threat of a presidential veto, the House of Representatives issued an indefinite postponement and the Patriot Act expired.

The Biden administration asserted that the critical elements of extremism emerge from racially/ethnically or anti-government/anti-authority motivated violent ideology. The National Strategy for Countering Domestic Terrorism indicates that "Internet-based communications platforms such as social media, file-upload sites, and end-to-end encrypted platforms, ... can combine and amplify threats to public safety—This is the domestic terrorism threat America faces today." The administration's strategy to counter cyberviolence and online extremism may be the blueprint for future administrations.

Democrats have increasingly focused on the intersection of online extremism with issues of social justice and civil liberties, advocating for policies that address the root causes of radicalization without infringing on free speech. Following the 2022 midterms, there has been a push within the party to refine and expand community-based approaches to prevent online radicalization, emphasizing education, digital literacy, and the promotion of counternarratives to extremist ideologies. Democrats have also called for greater accountability from social media platforms in policing content, advocating for transparent policies that prevent the spread of extremist material while safeguarding user privacy and freedom of expression.

FURTHER READING

Anti-Defamation League. 2002. Report on Murder and Extremism in the United States. https://www.adl.org/resources/tools-to-track-hate/heat-map. Accessed July 8, 2022.

Blazak, Randy. 2009. "Toward a Working Definition of Hate Groups." *Hate Crimes* 3, no. 1: 133–62.

Blazakis, Jason. 2018. "American Terrorists: Why Current Laws Are Inadequate for Violent Extremists at Home." *Lawfare*, December 2, 2018.

Bocij, Paul. 2004. *Cyberstalking: Harassment in the Internet Age and How to Protect Your Family*. Westport, CT: Praeger.

Boyd, Danah. 2014. *It's Complicated: The Social Lives of Networked Teens*. New Haven, CT: Yale University Press.

Doyle, Charles. 2002. "The USA Patriot Act: A Sketch." https://apps.dtic.mil/sti/citations/ADA467148. Accessed July 10, 2022.

Finn, Jerry. 2004. "A Survey of Online Harassment at a University Campus." *Journal of Interpersonal Violence* 19, no. 4: 468–83.

Geltzer, Joshua A., Mary B. McCord, and Nicholas Rasmussen. 2019. "The Christchurch Shooting: Domestic Terrorism Goes International." *Lawfare*, March 19, 2019.

Gerstenfeld, Phyllis B., Diana R. Grant, and Chau-Pu Chiang. 2003. "Hate Online: A Content Analysis of Extremist Internet Sites." *Analyses of Social Issues and Public Policy* 3, no. 1: 29–44.

Hawdon, James, Colin Bernatzky, and Matthew Costello. 2019. "Cyber-Routines, Political Attitudes, and Exposure to Violence-Advocating Online Extremism." *Social Forces* 98, no. 1: 329–54.

Hawdon, James, Atte Oksanen, and Pekka Rasanen. 2017. "Exposure to Online Hate in Four Nations: A Cross-National Consideration." *Deviant Behavior* 38, no. 3: 254–66.

Holt, Kristoffer, Adam Shehata, Jesper Strömbäck, and Elisabet Ljungberg. 2011. "Age and the Effects of News Media Attention and Social Media Use on Political Interest and Participation: Do Social Media Function as Leveller?" *European Journal of Communication* 28, no. 1: 19–34.

Laqueur, Walter. 1999. *Fanaticism and the Arms of Mass Destruction. The New Terrorism.* Oxford: Oxford University Press.

Levitt, Matthew. 2017. *Defeating Ideologically Inspired Violent Extremism: A Strategy to Build Strong Communities and Protect the US Homeland.* Washington, DC: Washington Institute for Near East Policy.

Margaritoff, Marco. 2022. "Inside the Twisted Relationship of Michelle Carter and Conrad Roy and How it Ended in Suicide." *ati*, January 6, 2022. https://allthatsinteresting.com/michelle-carter.

McCord, Mary B. 2018. "It's Time for Congress to Make Domestic Terrorism a Federal Crime." *Lawfare*, December 5, 2018.

Schmid, A. 2004. "Terrorism—the Definitional Problem." *Case Western Reserve Journal of International Law* 36, 375.

Silber, Mitchell D., and Arvin Bhatt. 2007. *Radicalization in the West: The Homegrown Threat.* New York: New York City Police Department.

StopBullying.gov. www.StopBullying.gov. Accessed May 5, 2022.

U.S. Department of State. n.d. "About Us—Global Engagement Center." https://www.state.gov/about-us-global-engagement-center-2/. Accessed May 11, 2022.

Wall, David S., ed. 2001. *Crime and the Internet.* New York: Routledge.

The White House. (2021, June 15). Fact Sheet: National Strategy for Countering Domestic Terrorism. https://www.whitehouse.gov/briefing-room/statements-releases/2021/06/15/fact-sheet-national-strategy-for-countering-domestic-terrorism/.

CHAPTER 7

Death Penalty

DALE WILSON

AT A GLANCE

Few aspects of our criminal justice system are more controversial than capital punishment. Europeans brought the practice of capital punishment with them as they settled the "new world," with the first execution taking place in 1608 in the Jamestown colony of Virginia. Across time, states would enact and repeal capital punishment legislation as technology modified the mechanisms of death. Often, states would enact death penalty statutes, sentence people to death, but let them languish in prison. By the mid-1960s, every state had abolished mandatory capital punishment for everything except a few crimes that were rarely committed, and public support for the practice had waned. After public support waned, several landmark US Supreme Court cases in the 1970s set legal precedents for capital punishment. In *Furman v. Georgia* (408 U.S. 238, 1972), the Court held that Georgia's statute, which gave juries complete sentencing discretion without any guidance on how to exercise that discretion, potentially resulting in arbitrary sentencing. As a result, the court invalidated all states' death penalty statutes and established a moratorium (i.e., ban) on executions until state statutes could be rewritten to eliminate the death penalty's "arbitrary and capricious" nature. This moratorium was lifted in 1976, however, when the Court heard another case (*Gregg v. Georgia*, 428 U.S. 153) in which it ruled that the state statutes had been significantly revised to constitutional standards, effectively reinstating the use of death as a penalty. Executions resumed in 1977 with Utah executing Gary Gilmore by firing squad. After annual death sentences peaked at more than 300 and annual executions peaked at more than 98 in the 1990s, they have both steadily declined as more states have abolished the death penalty or have maintained a de facto abolition by simply not using it.

According to the Death Penalty Information Center (2023a), at the end of 2023, thirty-seven states had either abolished the death penalty or had not executed anyone in at least ten years. Two other states had not executed anyone in at least five years, and the

District of Columbia and the US military had not executed anyone in at least ten years. Of the 1,582 executions since the moratorium was lifted, more than half (52 percent) were carried out by only three states and 37 percent (587) by Texas alone. Clearly, states are not united in their perspectives on the use of capital punishment. While some debates about its utility are political, many involve elements of race and socioeconomic status. Although ideological perspectives were more likely to define historical stances on the death penalty, more contemporary debates revolve around wrongful convictions, race, economics, and fairness.

MANY REPUBLICANS...

- Believe the death penalty deters crime and makes everyone safer. This includes its use with those who sell drugs that result in a death, and with drug "kingpins" who tend to run major drug import and trafficking operations.
- Believe the death penalty is effective when humanely carried out and should be left to the discretion of each individual state. They tend to decry the fact that the issue has become overly federalized and believe that the US Supreme Court has settled the constitutionality of the death penalty.
- Believe people exercise free will in choices and decisions; this belief feeds into the notion that punishment should fit the crime since it was the result of a conscious decision.

MANY DEMOCRATS...

- Believe the death penalty continues to be arbitrarily administered despite the aforementioned *Gregg* decision that purported to eliminate the arbitrary and capricious nature of death sentences. Many believe it is deeply flawed at the prosecutorial level and used disparately against persons of color or of lower socioeconomic status.
- Believe execution constitutes cruel and unusual punishment and has no place in a humane society. They point to the fact that most European countries have eliminated its use and that many states continue to struggle with methods of execution thought to be safe and humane.
- Believe the criminal justice system is flawed to the extent that execution cannot be a valid option for juries; a number of inmates have been exonerated and freed from death row.

OVERVIEW

On August 11, 1967, William Furman burglarized the home of William Micke in Savannah, Georgia. Depending on the version of events one believes, Furman either half-turned and shot wildly as he ran away from Micke, or he tripped and the gun went off accidently, striking and killing Micke. Because the shooting occurred during the commission of a felony (burglary), Georgia's felony murder rule was invoked, making Furman eligible for the death penalty. The US Supreme Court combined this case with two rape cases (*Jackson v. Georgia*, 225 Ga. 790, 1969; *Branch v. Texas*, 447 S.W. 2d 932, 1969). In all three cases, the condemned was a person of color. In a 5-4 *per curiam* decision, the Court decided that the death penalty was disproportionately applied to the poor or otherwise disadvantaged. A *per curiam* decision is one in which each Justice writes an opinion because of an inability to agree on the underlying rationale for the opinion.

Politics often drive opinions about appropriate punishment for criminal activity. Capital punishment is obviously an absolute measure and cannot be overturned so it naturally receives much political attention. Republican President Richard Nixon's landslide reelection in 1972 may have been a mandate for his continuing war on crime, including the use of capital punishment. Beginning with the execution of Gary Gilmore in 1977, post-*Gregg* executions ramped up slowly with only eleven through 1983. Perhaps the explosion of cocaine, its abuse, and the accompanying violence in the 1980s signaled a desire for a more aggressive approach to "crime fighting." From 1984 through the peak in 1999, 587 individuals were executed in the United States. Interestingly, this period spanned the administrations of both major political parties. Both party platforms advanced the idea that lawlessness was something that should be addressed. While many Republicans feel the decision to use capital punishment should be left to individual states, many Democrats believe the death penalty is an inherently cruel and unusual punishment and needs to be seen as an issue of constitutionality.

As the 1992 presidential campaign unfolded, America was reeling from historically high murder rates. Many Republicans supported the reinstatement of a federal death penalty and limited appeals for those condemned to death, and still sought death as a viable option for drug traffickers. The Democratic platform held a focus on combatting the dangerous flow of drugs into society but contained no mention of the death penalty as a deterrent. Many Democrats still held to the belief that capital punishment violates the constitution; crime and its impact dominated the conversation as the nation elected a Democrat who would serve for the next eight years. Many Democratic candidates for office find themselves defending against allegations that they are seen as "soft on crime." While still campaigning for the presidency, Democratic Governor William Jefferson "Bill" Clinton made sure to return to his home state of Arkansas to preside over an execution, seen by many as an attempt to counter any of those soft on crime assertions.

The condemned man, Ricky Rector, had been convicted of killing a police officer and another man. Rector shot himself in the head, resulting in brain injury that eventually rendered him intellectually impaired. His attorneys argued that he was not mentally competent to stand trial, much less be executed. As an example of this, Rector declared that he would "save part of his last meal for later." Many felt that Clinton, then still the Arkansas governor, used the opportunity to counter previous mistakes on crime policy made by other Democratic candidates for national office. Although the Supreme Court had ruled in *Ford v. Wainright* (477 U.S. 399, 1986) that executing someone who could not understand the implications of the death penalty violated the Eighth Amendment, Rector was found competent and executed in 1992. Later actions by President Clinton would challenge any notion that, as a Democrat, he was soft on crime.

Science in general and DNA in particular changed the way in which both Democrats and Republicans viewed crime, sentencing, the death penalty, and the way race and socioeconomic status impact our criminal justice system. In 1992, Barry Scheck and Peter Neufeld founded The Innocence Project to exonerate those wrongfully convicted using DNA testing. As of January 2022, 375 people have been exonerated, including 21 who had been sentenced to death, for crimes they did not commit. Studies have estimated that 3 percent to 5 percent of incarcerated inmates are innocent of the crimes for which they have been convicted. Considering the current prison population hovers around 1.5 million, this means between 45,000 and 75,000 could potentially have been wrongfully convicted. If the same math applies to those on death row, the number is more than 100. It is sobering to think that the system has almost certainly executed innocent persons in the past, and despite political divisions, we can eliminate this possibility.

Did Texas Execute an Innocent Man?

On February 17, 2004, the state of Texas executed Cameron Todd Willingham for the 1991 arson murder of his three young daughters. Local fire department officials determined that the fire was intentionally set, resulting in Willingham's arrest. At trial, the prosecution was able to prove its case for murder as Willingham was convicted and sentenced to death. Willingham maintained his innocence until he was executed, stating the fire started accidentally as he and his daughters slept. This case has spawned a documentary (*Death by Fire*, PBS, 2010), a theatrical documentary (*Incendiary: The Willingham Case*, 2011), a movie (*Trial by Fire*, 2019), and has been picked up by The Innocence Project, all in an attempt to posthumously reverse the conviction. Key evidence at trial was later tainted by the witness' recantation of his testimony and assertion that the testimony was essentially extorted from him in exchange for a lighter sentence for his robbery charge. The witness had been a cellmate of Willingham and was being held for robbery. Additionally, in 2004, prior to the scheduled execution, forensic fire science investigators, using technology not available in 1991, presented a report to then Texas Governor Rick Perry asserting that the fire was indeed accidental. Perry rejected the report and declined to grant a stay for Willingham; the investigators had been appointed by the state of Texas and were summarily dismissed when they issued their report.

Many Republicans still supported tough penalties, including death, for drug traffickers, child rapists, and murderers. While the Supreme Court had struck down capital punishment for those convicted of raping an adult in *Coker v. Georgia* (433 U.S. 584, 1977), it was still permissible to seek death for someone when convicted of raping a child under the age of twelve. Many Democrats favored a "get-tough" approach to violent crime as well, albeit tempered with a desire to ensure basic freedoms and civil rights are preserved. At the same time, Democratic platforms supported a continued focus on rehabilitation and smoother reintegration of inmates into society when released from prison. As alluded to earlier, many Democrats also supported the increased use of DNA and post-conviction efforts to help ensure accuracy before the system commits the unpardonable act of executing an innocent person. As the United States progressed through the middle 2000s and toward another presidential election, Republican platforms still touted capital punishment as an option for capital murder and other heinous crimes. Many Republicans still opposed needless post-conviction appeals when there was little doubt about guilt. Interestingly, few prosecuting attorneys ever have any doubt about the guilt of those they prosecute. Many Democrats were turning away from the death penalty as concerns about efficacy combined with perceived inequalities in the justice system made the death penalty seem too arbitrary.

The work of The Innocence Project, in part, exposed growing concerns of racial and socioeconomic disparities in the criminal justice system. As the number of exonerees grew, highlighted by the fact that nearly 70 percent were persons of color, members of both major parties started to see a system that had flaws. Seeking a process that removed any doubt of guilt, many Democrats continued to support the use of DNA in "appropriate circumstances," according to party platforms in 2016. Many Republicans still supported capital punishment to keep neighborhoods safe; they were bolstered by a firm belief in the accuracy of court decisions and the equality of the criminal justice system. Still a few years away from Black Lives Matter, *The New Jim Crow*, and other efforts to highlight disparities toward persons of color, one could already see a massive shift in Democratic attitudes toward capital punishment. The first decade of the 2000s brought a renewed interest in abolishing the death penalty completely and refreshed the arbitrary and capricious argument that drove the moratorium in 1972.

Republicans believe the constitutionality of the death penalty is well established and seek protection for states to carry out executions to enable them to protect their citizens. Democrats wish to abolish capital punishment because it is not an effective deterrent and believe the criminal justice system needs to be overhauled with an eye on equality and civil protections. These stark distinctions will likely be emphasized during the 2024 election cycle. Presumptive Republican nominee and former president Donald Trump has called for federal drug traffickers to be executed and Florida's Republican Governor, Ron DeSantis recently authorized capital punishment as a sentencing option for anyone convicted of raping a child under the age of twelve. This is currently unconstitutional, but advocates hope that any Supreme Court challenge would overturn the precedent set in *Kennedy v. Louisiana* (554 U.S. 407, 2008) given that the Court's composition has significantly changed since 2008. DeSantis also signed a law allowing Florida juries to return a death sentence with a majority of only eight out of twelve jurors, which is the lowest in the country. President Biden's 2020 campaign website explicitly mentioned working toward eliminating the federal death penalty, but his campaign website going into the 2024 campaign season has nothing related to capital punishment.

REPUBLICANS ON THE DEATH PENALTY

Republicans are considered reliably conservative on social issues, but were founded under the idea of classical liberalism, or the belief in economic freedom and civil liberties under the color of law. Republican support for capital punishment, although still based on a belief in its deterrent value, has always been rooted in classical theory. Classical theory emerged in the eighteenth century and posits that rational people make conscious decisions after weighing the costs and benefits of a situation. Classical theory is compatible with conservative crime policy that has prevailed since the 1970s. The belief that a person is responsible for their own actions feeds into the idea that punishment should fit the crime and be swift and severe. Capital punishment is a natural progression for classical theorists. While classical theory is thought to inform criminal justice policy even today, it has lost support to proponents of rehabilitation and reform efforts intended to reduce the prison population. While classical theory has its place, the reality is that there are a number of factors that influence criminality, including environmental and social conditions, mental health disorders, and peer relationships. As such, the solutions to crime are probably more complicated than execution and incarceration.

After the Great Depression and the New Deal, Republicans came to be associated with conservatism on social issues like the death penalty. A recent poll found that 77 percent of Republicans and independents who lean Republican favor the death penalty for persons convicted of murder, while only 46 percent of Democrats express the same support (Pew Research Center 2021). Conservative values have long been associated with conservative religious values and since the earliest system of codified laws and punishments originated in Biblical times with King Hammurabi of Babylon, it is not a stretch to correlate those values with support for capital punishment. A study in 2015 found that 56 percent of Evangelical Christians lean Republican, while only 27 percent lean Democrat. Support for capital punishment has remained steady and high among Evangelical Christians in the modern death penalty era (1976–present) although it has been tempered in recent years by a decline in crime and exonerations related to wrongful convictions (Pew Research Center 2015).

Death Penalty Reinstated

Furman v. Georgia (1972) resulted in a moratorium on the death penalty until states could rework their statutes, precisely defining the crimes for which death could be sought, reducing jury discretion and bias, or abolishing the death penalty. A group of three cases that were combined into one decision, *Gregg v. Georgia* (428 U.S. 153, 1976) was the answer to the issues raised in the *Furman* decision. The Court held that the death penalty did not constitute cruel and unusual punishment in violation of the US Constitution when it was fairly and judiciously applied. Georgia required a bifurcated trial process where the trial and sentencing decisions were made in separate deliberations. It also required specificity as to crimes/circumstances that "qualified" a person for death penalty consideration. Many states refer to these as "aggravating circumstances." This case had the effect of lifting the moratorium and opening the door for executions to resume. Many felt that *Gregg* ushered in the modern era of capital punishment. Republican President Nixon's War on Drugs in 1971 may have contributed to the concurrent War on Crime and a position in support of the death penalty. Opinion 7-2: Majority: Burger-R, Stewart-R, White-D, Blackmun-R, Powell-R, Rehnquist-R, Stevens-D; Dissent: Marshall-D, Brennan-D.

Many Republicans believe the death penalty (and the system as a whole) is "over-federalized" and should be left to the states. Declaring the matter to be settled law with its constitutionality unquestioned after *Gregg*, they argue that it should be the right of the American people to decide whether to impose death as the ultimate punishment.

As violent crime increased throughout the 1970s and 1980s, it was easy to favor capital punishment. Support for capital punishment was similar among Republicans and Democrats during the 1980s and 1990s. In general terms, many Republicans have always supported the death penalty as an effective method for deterring crime, while accepting its flaws. Many Democrats have supported capital punishment for the most heinous murders but have generally tempered this with support for the appeals process as a check on the court of original jurisdiction and its decision. Possibly because of the exponential rise of the violent crime rate, political attitudes changed during the 1990s.

When homicides reached their peak of more than 24,000 in 1991, many Americans believed that only a tough approach to crime would make citizens safer. It would not be until many years later that research would indicate increasing executions does not lower murder rates. The steady decline in violent crime through the 1990s did not necessarily diminish the appetite for tough punishments, including the death penalty. In 2000, many Republicans supported the recently renewed federal death penalty and continued to call for its use with major drug traffickers. Signaling a bit of a change in the air was Republican support for crime victims' rights and restitution. Many Republicans still supported limiting habeas corpus petitions (post-conviction requests to have a case reviewed); these were seen as extending the period before a victim's family could achieve justice.

In 2019, Republican President Donald J. Trump's attorney general, William Barr, changed Department of Justice (DOJ) policies and federal execution protocols to facilitate the scheduling and fulfillment of federal executions. In July 2020, federal executions resumed for the first time in seventeen years. Across the subsequent six months, thirteen federal death row prisoners were executed at United States Penitentiary, Terre Haute in Indiana (Death Penalty Information Center 2023b). The changes made by Barr were largely rescinded by Democratic President Joseph R. Biden's attorney general, Merrick Garland. Garland also paused federal executions until all the policies and protocols can be reviewed and updated.

Support for capital punishment among state-level Republicans may be waning, however. Citing belief in a limited government, demand for fiscal responsibility, and pro-life stances, Republican legislatures across the country are reconsidering their support. A national advocacy group called "Conservatives Concerned About the Death Penalty" tracks conservative abolitionist actions and believes that "the trend is beyond dispute" (Bates 2024). In January 2024, Republican legislators in Missouri, led by Representative Chad Perkins from Bowling Green, filed legislation to abolish capital punishment in the state and to commute the lives of those on death row to life in prison without parole. Missouri was one of only five states to execute anyone in 2023, executing four people. Two people were executed by Missouri in 2022. Perkins is hopeful, but the bill has not been referred to any House committee yet.

In Ohio, a trifecta state where they occupy the office of governor as well as hold majorities in both the House and Senate, Republicans also are struggling to resolve conservative conflicts via legislation. The Ohio attorney general is pushing legislation (H.B. 392) that would "kickstart" executions by adopting the use of nitrogen hypoxia as a state-approved alternative to lethal injection due to difficulties in getting the drugs required for lethal injection. Governor Mike DeWine and Gary Mohr, a former director of the Ohio Department of Rehabilitation and Correction who supervised fifteen executions during his tenure, however, express misgivings about the utility of the death penalty, in general, and the use of nitrogen hypoxia, specifically. Competing with H.B. 392 is a package of bipartisan abolition bills (S.B. 101, H.B. 259) that are currently pending. One sponsor of the House abolition bill, Republican Representative Jean Schmidt used pro-life arguments in her defense of the bill, stating that "life begins at conception, and it ends with natural death ... the death penalty is anything but natural" (Death Penalty Information Center 2024a).

DEMOCRATS ON THE DEATH PENALTY

Democratic views on capital punishment evolved from the Age of Enlightenment and Thomas Hobbes. Hobbes believed that rational people will democratically establish a system of governance with rules to follow and a consensus by everyone to follow those rules. This social contract required mutual respect between citizens and leaders; the notion that members of a society invest in the laws of a society in exchange for protection from others who violate them is a central tenet of all enlightenment thinking. Philosophers of this era also believed everyone should have a say in the government and that the governing authority should practice fairness in determining guilt and meting out punishments. Prior to this, it was common for thieves to be subject to execution, which violated enlightened rules of common sense. When members of a society see an individual being punished unfairly or not being punished at all for conduct that has been mutually agreed to be criminal, the result can be a breakdown of the social contract.

According to a Pew Research Center poll in 2021, 46 percent of Democrats and Democratic-leaning independents expressed support for the death penalty. Although the Democratic party was originally more conservative in nature, the Great Depression and the resulting New Deal ushered in a more socially liberal party. Originally in support of a smaller government and increased states' rights, post-Depression society created a Democratic Party that focused more on social justice and civil rights. As a result, many Democrats did not support capital punishment. Civil unrest from enforcement of the Civil Rights Act of 1964, Voter Rights Act of 1965, and anti-war protests challenged Democratic notions about crime and punishments. Republican President Richard M. Nixon's War on Drugs that kicked off in 1971 coincided with the desire to punish more severely, and eventually led to a belief that the death penalty may even be appropriate for drug traffickers. Support for capital punishment has always been a mixed bag for Democrats. Because the general perception was that they opposed capital punishment, most candidates for national office had to be mindful not to appear to be too soft on crime. At the very least, they had to appear to support tougher punishments for criminals.

Death Not Appropriate for the Rape of a Child

Kennedy v. Louisiana (2005) held that execution for a crime that did not result in a death was cruel and unusual, violating the Eighth Amendment of the US Constitution. Patrick Kennedy was convicted of raping his eight-year-old stepdaughter and was sentenced to death. His sentence was upheld by the Louisiana Supreme Court but was overturned in this decision by the US Supreme Court in a 5-4 decision. Even among those who oppose the death penalty, some still believe that execution for raping a child is appropriate. Republican dissent focused on a belief that the Court should not make a blanket decision that ignores the facts or the potentially heinous nature of the crime. Interestingly, in a study that analyzed the impact of the original amendment to the Louisiana's rape statute, West (2002) found the law's only impact was to reduce the number of rape trials and she argued that prosecutors used the threat of death to elicit plea bargains and avoid costly and drawn-out trials. Majority: Stevens-D, Kennedy-R, Souter-R, Breyer-D, Ginsburg-D; Dissent: Roberts-R, Scalia-R, Thomas-R, Alito-R.

Beginning in the early 1980s, many Democrats began to focus on rehabilitation in the penal system. Prison reform, sentencing laws, and protecting civil liberties were the stated Democratic platform during the 1980 presidential campaign. Conversely, the Republican platform stated a belief that execution was an effective deterrent to crime. As executions steadily increased throughout the 1980s and 1990s, so too did the rates of violent crime across the country. Although the homicide rate in the United States doubled between the early 1960s and late 1970s, it peaked in 1980 then declined until the late 1980s (Cooper and Smith 2011). It reached 1970s-era levels in the early 1990s and began a gradual decline that has continued since then. A graphic depiction of violent crime and executions would look remarkably similar between the early 1980s and 2000, throwing caution to the idea that the death penalty is much of a deterrent to violent crime. Of note here is that while murders peaked in 1992, executions did not peak until 1999; this may have less to do with political differences and more to do with the length of time it takes to conduct an execution in the United States.

In 1988, Democratic presidential candidate and Massachusetts Governor Michael Dukakis famously stated that he would still oppose capital punishment even if the victim was his own wife. As governor, he championed a prison furlough program for murderers that resulted in the release of Willie Horton, who committed a rape and assault once released. Although prison furlough programs were common, Dukakis's Republican opponent, Vice President George H. W. Bush used Horton's crimes to ruthlessly portray Dukakis as soft on crime. Ironically, one of the most liberal prison furlough programs at the time was in the federal prison system under Republican President Ronald Reagan and Vice President Bush. Dukakis carried only ten states and the District of Columbia, losing to Bush rather soundly.

Democratic President Joseph R. Biden's 2020 campaign website promised that he would work to eliminate the federal death penalty and encourage states to do the same.

Coming into the 2024 campaign season, that promise has disappeared from his website. Federal Democratic legislators, however, are attempting to fulfill Biden's 2020 promise. Democratic Representative Ayanna Pressley (MA) and Democratic Senator Dick Durbin (IL) reintroduced the bicameral Federal Death Penalty Prohibition Act in July 2023 (S.2299, H.R. 4633). Originally proposed in 2019 after thirteen federal executions under the Republican Trump administration, and then again in 2021, the bill would prohibit death as a sentence for any federal law violation and require resentencing for all those currently on death row at USP Terre Haute (U.S. Senate Committee on the Judiciary 2023). As of April 2024, each bill has been referred to each chamber's respective Committee on the Judiciary. Although Attorney General Merrick Garland instituted a moratorium on federal executions in 2021, individuals who commit eligible federal crimes still can be sentenced to death. During the Biden administration, the DOJ has sought the death penalty for only one person, Payton Gendron, who killed ten Black people at a supermarket in Buffalo, New York, in 2022. Another man, Robert Bowers, was sentenced to death in July 2023, but he was initially charged during the Trump administration (Death Penalty Information Center 2024b).

State-level Democratic efforts related to capital punishment also struggle with inconsistencies in party support. California Governor Gavin Newsom signed an executive order to halt executions in California during his term as governor. While falling short of abolition, the effect is the same in the short term. Between 2019 and 2021, Democratic-majority legislators in Colorado, New Hampshire, and Virginia abolished the death penalty, but similar efforts in Nevada faced challenges (Metz 2021). Nevada's outgoing Democratic Governor Steve Sisolak sought in December 2022 to commute all fifty-seven state death sentences to life without parole after a Democratic bill failed to pass the Senate. Although blocked by a Nevada judge, Sisolak's request represented a reversal in his prior support for capital punishment. Oregon's Democratic Governor Kate Brown was more successful in her outgoing effort; she commuted the sentences of all seventeen people on Oregon's death row (Selsky 2022).

FURTHER READING

Alexander, M. 2012. *The New Jim Crow: Mass Incarceration in the Age of Colorblindness*. New York: New Press.

Amidon, E. 2018. "Politics and the Death Penalty; 1930-2010." *American Journal of Criminal Justice* 43: 831–60.

Bates, Clara. 2024. "Group of Republican Lawmakers Raise Concerns about Missouri Death Penalty." *Missouri Independent*, January 10, 2024. https://missouriindependent.com/2024/01/10/group-of-republican-lawmakers-raise-concerns-about-missouri-death-penalty/.

Baumgartner, F. R. 2011. *The Decline of the Death Penalty and the Discovery of Innocence*. Cambridge, England: Cambridge University Press.

Cooper, Alexia, and Erica L. Smith. 2011. "Homicide Trends in the United States, 1980-2008." November 2011. NCJ 236018. https://bjs.ojp.gov/content/pub/pdf/htus8008.pdf.

Death Penalty Information Center. 2023a. "Executions Overview: States With No Recent Executions." August 16, 2023. https://deathpenaltyinfo.org/executions/executions-overview/states-with-no-recent-executions.

Death Penalty Information Center. 2023b. "In New Podcast, 'Rush to Kill' Documents 6-Month Federal Execution Spree Under President Donald Trump's Administration." October 23, 2023. https://deathpenaltyinfo.org/news/in-new-podcast-rush-to-kill-documents-6-month-federal-execution-spree-under-president-donald-trumps-administration.

Death Penalty Information Center. 2024a. "Ohio Officials Divided on Death Penalty as Attorney General Pushes New Bill to Legalize Nitrogen Hypoxia for Executions." February 2, 2024. https://deathpenaltyinfo.org/news/ohio-officials-divided-on-death-penalty-as-attorney-general-pushes-new-bill-to-legalize-nitrogen-hypoxia-for-executions.

Death Penalty Information Center. 2024b. "U.S. Department of Justice Authorizes First Federal Death Penalty Case for Payton Gendron, Teen Who Killed Ten Black People in 2022." January 16, 2024. https://deathpenaltyinfo.org/news/u-s-department-of-justice-authorizes-first-federal-death-penalty-case-for-payton-gendron-teen-who-killed-ten-black-people-in-2022?__cf_chl_tk=bKY.Msu4YNlLWZY5PhV.PNtf2E6Ly7u7m4I.Bh_56E4-1713147655-0.0.1.1-1983.

Metz, Sam. 2021. "Blue States Chart Diverging Paths on Death Penalty Debate." *AP News*, April 22, 2021. https://apnews.com/article/race-and-ethnicity-government-and-politics-nevada-legislature-las-vegas-mass-shooting-f96adbb830e8757bc501f919b276bddc.

Pew Research Center. 2015. "Less Support for Death Penalty, Especially Among Democrats." April 16, 2015. https://www.pewresearch.org/politics/2015/04/16/less-support-for-death-penalty-especially-among-democrats/.

Pew Research Center. 2021. "Most Americans Favor the Death Penalty Despite Concerns About its Administration." June 2, 2021. https://www.pewresearch.org/politics/2021/06/02/most-americans-favor-the-death-penalty-despite-concerns-about-its-administration/.

Selsky, Andrew. 2022. "Oregon Governor Commutes All 17 of State's Death Sentences." *AP News*, December 13, 2022. https://apnews.com/article/crime-prisons-oregon-kate-brown-salem-eca820b1dcd2b51f0ad623f13f9e0387.

U.S. Senate Committee on the Judiciary. 2023. "Durbin, Pressley Reintroduce Bill to End Federal Death Penalty." July 13, 2023. https://www.judiciary.senate.gov/press/releases/durbin-pressley-reintroduce-bill-to-end-federal-death-penalty.

West, Angela D. 2002. "Death as Deterrent or Prosecutorial Tool? Examining the Impact of Louisiana's Child Rape Law." *Criminal Justice Policy Review* 13, no. 2: 156–91.

CHAPTER 8

Diversion Programs for Drug Offenders

ALBERT M. KOPAK

AT A GLANCE

Diversion programs for drug offenders have been operating in the United States for many decades, and their support has been intricately connected to several important factors. Unlike more controversial criminal justice initiatives, the endorsement of diversion as a viable approach to address criminal activities among adults who use drugs has fluctuated more in concert with the nature of current public concerns regarding the use of specific drugs and less with the view of the political majority. In general, diversion programs for drug-involved offenders have expanded and received steadily increasing levels of political support and funding since 1973, when the National Advisory Commission on Criminal Justice Standards and Goals recommended jurisdictions adopt programs focused on the pretrial phase of the court process rather than delaying programmatic options until after any court judgment. Criminal justice policies in the 1980s and 1990s were characterized by their strict emphasis on crime control strategies, especially concerning drug offenders, which contributed to an explosion in the nation's jail and prison populations. Diversion programs continued to operate during this period, but most drug offenders were subject to mandatory periods of incarceration and the dramatic growth in the number of adults in the nation's correctional centers ballooned state and federal budgets, which also enhanced the appeal of diversion programs. Interest in diversion programs has been renewed as community leaders develop responses to the current opioid epidemic.

Although Republicans and Democrats endorse diversion programs designed for drug-involved offenders according to different sets of priorities, reducing the deleterious public health effects of substance use in a fiscally responsible fashion has broad appeal to members of both parties. Diversion programs represent a unique criminal justice initiative in the way they garner support from both sides of the political aisle, especially as leaders desperately search for ways to respond to contemporary drug issues.

Support for diversion programs for drug offenders has certainly waxed and waned, but it has also persisted through drastic changes in political positions. Providing these programs for vulnerable populations has been a priority for politicians in both parties. This has been tempered, however, by the strict sanctions embedded in many diversion programs.

MANY REPUBLICANS...

- View diversion programs for drug offenders with the capability to hold participants accountable for their criminal behavior while also providing services to address substance use.
- Support diversion programs for their fiscal benefits, especially when compared to the costs of incarceration.
- Support the use of strict graduated sanctions (i.e., punishments that move from less harsh to more harsh with repeated offenses) to ensure that people who participate in diversion programs comply with the requirements.

MANY DEMOCRATS...

- View diversion programs as public health-oriented approaches capable of stemming the spread of infectious diseases associated with drug use.
- Recommend the use of diversion programs, especially law enforcement-led initiatives, to provide an alternative to incarceration and the stigma associated with involvement in the criminal justice system.
- Focus on harm reduction practices that rely less on punishment and more on enhancing the health and well-being of people who use drugs.

OVERVIEW

The nation's War on Drugs is rooted in the political attitudes and legislative actions of the early 1970s. When Republican President Richard Nixon took office, he openly shared his "reflexive disgust for illegal drugs and the people who used them" (Massing 1998, 97). The tumultuous events of the previous decade, which included extensive anti-Vietnam War demonstrations and widespread public drug consumption (primarily cannabis and LSD) by rebellious young adults, were confronted with his strong will to assert political authority. Nixon openly spoke about drugs as the "modern curse of the youth ... Just like the plagues and epidemics of former years they are decimating a generation of Americans." As part of an exercise of political might, Congress approved the Comprehensive Drug Abuse and Prevention Act of 1970, creating a clean slate with the replacement of all previous federal drug laws. This sweeping legislation contained provisions to increase funding for drug research, education, and treatment, but these priorities were superseded by the more popular law and order approach of the time.

As lower priorities, drug education and especially treatment were reserved for specific groups. In the early 1970s, young adults who had served in the military were returning from Vietnam, and many had developed an addiction to heroin during their tours of duty. This group was viewed much differently from the countercultural youth involved in disrespectful and illegal drug use. Rather than prosecute veterans, an empathetic call to legislative action was issued to help the country's patriots overcome the scourge of heroin dependence.

The response came in the form of the Drug Abuse Office and Treatment Act of 1972. Guided by the Democratic majority, Congress appropriated $120 million to establish Community Mental Health Treatment Centers, which were specifically identified as providers of drug abuse treatment in areas with demonstrated need. There are several noteworthy considerations regarding this piece of legislation, including its emphasis on providing services for veterans. Funding was earmarked specifically for inpatient services, outpatient programs, psychiatric care, vocational training, and other services designed for recently discharged military personnel. These initiatives served as precursors to the modern Veteran's Court, which is a popular diversion program offering an alternative to incarceration specifically designed to address substance use, mental health, and other behavioral health needs among veterans involved in the criminal justice system. The political support and subsequent expansion of contemporary diversion programs for drug-involved offenders can be traced to this important culmination of historical events.

The election of Democratic presidential candidate Jimmy Carter in 1976 was initially viewed as a great potential for progressive criminal justice reforms according to his left-leaning approach, but this optimism was short-lived. It was during this time that attention shifted away from a small population of heroin-using veterans toward the 39 percent of high school students who were reported as using illegal drugs (Johnston et al. 2019). This information mobilized parents and helped to create the nonprofit organization, National Families in Action, one of the strongest conservative influences of drug policy for the next several decades.

This right-of-center approach extended well into the 1980s with the election of Republican President Ronald Reagan, a staunch conservative who was "tough on crime." The Reagan administration presumed drugs were unequivocally criminal, assuming treatment for drug offenders condoned substance use. Law enforcement was the leading response to the problem, but diversion quietly remained an option for a select group of drug offenders. This approach was deeply embedded in the dubiously named Anti-Drug Abuse Act of 1986. First-time drug offenders could be diverted to probation without entering a guilty plea, but stipulations indicated one diversion opportunity was available and those with multiple convictions were subject to mandatory minimum sentences. Anyone with a criminal conviction was automatically disqualified from participation, highlighting its selectivity.

Drugs fell from the top of the list of Americans' primary concerns in the late 1980s, which was reflected in Republican President George H. W. Bush largely glossing over the issue. The approach of the time cemented the narrow focus of previous efforts exclusively on populations that seemed to be more vulnerable and thus more deserving of diversion, such as homeless individuals, adolescents, pregnant women, racial and ethnic minority group members, and rural populations.

The contradictions embedded in the broader drug control strategy continued through the 1990s and into the administration of Democratic President Bill Clinton. The Violent Crime Control and Law Enforcement Act of 1994 issued appropriations for states, state courts, local courts, and local governments to adopt programs with: (1) continued judicial supervision over nonviolent offenders with substance use disorders, and (2) the integration of sanctions and services mandating testing for drug use, prosecution or incarceration for cases of noncompliance, and programs delivering relapse prevention, educational opportunities, job placement, housing options, and family services for participants. Programs were expanded for drug-involved offenders, which had the potential to address behavioral health needs, but also mandated the use of formal sanctions. This conservative approach to the issue was further reinforced by the Personal Responsibility and Work Opportunity Reconciliation Act of 1996. This consequential law rendered any individual convicted of a felony for the possession, use, or distribution of a controlled substance ineligible (along with other family members) for any food stamp benefits of Temporary Assistance for Needy Families (TANF). Despite the continued use of diversion programs for select drug-involved populations, those convicted of certain offenses were now subject to unprecedented formal sanctions that disqualified them from many forms of social support.

The National Alliance for Model State Drug Laws (NAMSDL) Develops Model Diversion to Treatment Act Legislation

The nonprofit NAMSDL was established in 1993 when a group of legislators was joined by judges, community leaders, law enforcement representatives, and community behavioral health treatment providers to develop better policies to address substance use across the nation. This would be no easy task. The chair of the NAMSDL, Ralph Brown, identified the goal of the commission: "To talk to people on the front lines of the alcohol and other substance abuse problem and talk to those who have done some of the next thinking on the subject and then to cull and collect good ideas and programs and distill these ideas and experiences into model drug laws." The organization continues to advocate for policy reforms specifically related to addressing substance use in communities across the United States. The NAMSDL is currently promoting a model piece of comprehensive legislation related to the expansive use of law enforcement-led diversion programs, which states,

Due to their constant presence in the community interacting with the public, law enforcement officers have a unique opportunity to facilitate connections to community-based behavioral health interventions that provide substance use disorder and mental health treatment and can help save and restore lives; help reduce substance use, overdose incidence, criminal offending, and recidivism; and help prevent arrests

> and convictions that destabilize health, families and communities, as well as increase self-sufficiency. (National Alliance for Model State Drug Laws 2019)

Ironically, this legislation was passed while the most popular form of diversion programs for drug offenders were expanding. The first drug court was started in Dade County, Florida, in 1989. The program emphasized a collaborative approach between court administrators, service providers, and criminal justice personnel to connect drug-using offenders with services through an alternative to incarceration. The court was novel in its use of judicial decision-making that was therapeutic and acknowledged substance use disorder as a chronic disease that contributed to criminal behavior. The federal mandates passed in the 1990s to test diversion participants for the use of illegal drugs during the program are readily observed in current drug court procedures, relying heavily on testing to ensure compliance. Fast-forward thirty years, and there are more than 3,800 drug treatment courts diverting offenders from imprisonment to community supervision programs (U.S. Department of Justice 2023).

Formal testing for drug use became such a core component of drug court programs that the USA Patriot Improvement and Reauthorization Act of 2005, which was signed into law under the majority Republican Congress and presidential administration of George W. Bush, allowed drug court funding to be restricted solely to those courts that documented mandatory periodic testing. Attorney General John Ashcroft specified standards for testing to ensure that: (1) each participant was tested for every controlled substance that the participant has been known to use and for any other controlled substance the court may require and (2) testing was accurate and practicable. The law also specified funding could be used only for drug courts that imposed graduated sanctions based on increasingly punitive measures whenever a participant failed a drug test. The medical and social control models remained at odds with each other, especially considering the increased understanding that substance use disorder is a chronic relapsing condition, yet positive drug tests were grounds for increasingly harsh sanctions.

A radical shift in this perspective was observed after Democratic President Barack Obama entered office in 2009 and the US Department of Health and Human Services formally declared in 2016 that the nation was in the midst of an opioid epidemic. According to the Centers for Disease Control and Prevention (CDC), opioid use increased 109 percent among adults aged eighteen to twenty-five years and 58 percent among those twenty-six years and older (2020). Opioid-related treatment admissions also doubled between 2005 and 2015 (Substance Abuse and Mental Health Services Administration 2017), as did the rate of emergency department visits related to opioids (Weiss et al. 2016). The same trend was observed among male arrestees, with 10 percent testing positive for opioids at the time of jail booking, making it imperative to develop treatment-oriented initiatives for this population of drug-using offenders (Office of National Drug Control Policy 2014).

The initial political response to opioid use came in the form of the Comprehensive Addiction and Recovery Act of 2016 (CARA). The law authorized the Department of Justice to support "community-based substance use diversion program sponsored by a local law enforcement agency" (Part LL, section 3021). This represents the first progressive step toward merging law enforcement efforts targeting drug offenders with treatment alternatives for people who use drugs. Although the historical link to programs for Vietnam veterans cannot be overlooked, the CARA set a new benchmark with its dedication to "enhancing collaboration between criminal justice and substance abuse agencies; as well as developing, implementing, or expanding programs to prevent, treat, or respond to opioid abuse." Nonviolent drug offenders remained the preferred target population for these diversionary efforts, but the law also required a "report on the collateral consequences for individuals with convictions for nonviolent drug-related offenses, including the effect of those consequences on individuals resuming their personal and professional activities and the justifications for imposing those consequences." This development rolled back previous policies preventing access to services among drug offenders convicted of certain offenses. This legislation also fostered the next evolutionary phase of diversion programs.

Diversion programs continued to be attractive as opioid use and fatal overdoses continued to rise during Obama's terms. The passage of the 21st Century Cures Act established a pilot program to determine the effectiveness of diverting offenders from federal prosecution and placing them in drug courts. Appropriations for the courts and training for personnel specified the programs must include content regarding individuals with co-occurring substance abuse and mental health conditions. This additional support for programs for drug treatment alternatives to incarceration reflected the growing understanding that adults involved in drug offenses tend to have complex behavioral health profiles with an array of needs. It also represented a revitalization of alternatives to incarceration for drug users.

The 2017 election of Republican Donald Trump was followed by renewed tough on crime rhetoric reminiscent of the 1970s and 1980s. Despite the ardent conservatism of President Trump, Attorney General Jeff Sessions, and the majority Republican House of Representatives, treatment courts for veterans were fortified. A 2018 law expanded the Veterans Justice Outreach Program by adding a peer support specialist to justice teams in these treatment courts dedicated to veterans.

REPUBLICANS ON DIVERSION PROGRAMS FOR DRUG OFFENDERS

In 2020, the political climate can be characterized by its marked polarization, which reached record levels at the time Donald Trump was elected president. Results from an opinion poll conducted by the Pew Research Center (2017) demonstrated that partisan gaps more than doubled across a range of issues, from an average of about 15 percent to about 36 percent. Recent trends have generated a broader understanding of drug use as a chronic health condition among many Americans, with nearly half of the US adults reporting they have a family member who is currently or has previously been substance-dependent (Gramlich 2017). Individual experience and empathy toward friends and family members with substance use problems likely override ardent political views of the issue.

In a national poll sponsored by the American Civil Liberties Union's "Smart Justice" campaign, 87 percent of Democrats and 68 percent of Republicans agreed that "sending someone to prison for a long sentence increases the chances that he or she will commit another crime when they get out because prison doesn't do a good job of rehabilitating problems like drug addiction and mental illness" (ACLU 2017). Republicans have responded with widespread support to expand the Law Enforcement Assisted Diversion (LEAD) program, cosponsored by Senator Shelley Capito (WV). Specifically designed for drug offenders who are repeatedly stopped by police, LEAD was initiated in King County (Seattle) Washington in 2011, to address persistent offending among adults with severe substance use disorders. The program diverts offenders from the traditional prosecutorial process prior to arrest toward a case management system to address the underlying causes of drug use, including homelessness, unemployment, and behavioral health needs. LEAD emphasizes two traditional Republican values, individual accountability and fiscal conservatism, by closely supervising participants, prosecuting those who do not comply with the conditions of the program, and reducing the costs of incarceration. This $2.5 million federal appropriation has led to LEAD's expansion into more than thirty jurisdictions across the United States (LEAD National Support Bureau 2020).

This pivotal event also represents the larger movement among Republican leaders to adopt softer language related to substance use disorders and related offenses. Republican Governor Chris Christie (NJ) in his 2015 State of the State Speech emphasized the compassion required for adults suffering from substance use disorders by appealing to conservative religious values and urging mandatory treatment for nonviolent drug offenders with the claim that, "every life is an individual gift from God and no life is disposable." In this speech Christie also said, "Treatment is the path to saving lives. And I want to make this very clear. For as long as I am governor of New Jersey, treatment will be mandatory in our system and that system will not yield to the scourge of drugs in our society."

The Republican position is exemplified by the justification that diversion for drug offenders should not be interpreted as weak and lenient. Instead, diversion represents a responsible and informed crime control model. The conservative American Legislative Exchange Council (ALEC) also has adopted this position, drafting model legislation to endorse pre-arrest diversion programs for low-level, nonviolent drug offenders that can be easily adapted across states, and several have either proposed, or signed into law, legislation based on this template.

Florida was one of the first to pass legislation mandating the use of diversion programs. In March 2018, Republican Senator Jeff Brandes sponsored Bill 1392, which specifically identified pre-arrest diversion programs as preferred alternatives to incarceration. Republican Governor Rick Scott signed the bill making it state law to divert offenders who met the criteria. Georgia's Pre-Arrest Diversion for Drug and Mental Health Treatment Act (H.B. 716), proposed by Republican Representatives Rakestraw, Powell, Petrea, and Pruett was similar, except for its explicit reference to diverting eligible drug offenders to community-based treatment programs. This bill, however, was not signed into law by Republican Governor Nathan Deal.

Illinois, on the other hand, adopted the most comprehensive legislation to expand and implement diversion programs. Ten Illinois Republicans sponsored The Community-Law Enforcement Partnership for Deflection and Substance Use Disorder Treatment Act (S.B. 3023), which was signed in August 2018 by Republican Governor Bruce Rauner.

The mandate provides a roadmap for partnerships between law enforcement, substance use treatment providers, and community members to guide the development of law enforcement-led diversion programs. Details specify program types and their key features, and offer guidance and a range of options to municipalities to foster adaptation to the unique context of any given community.

DEMOCRATS ON DIVERSION PROGRAMS FOR DRUG OFFENDERS

The Democratic record on diversion programs is varied, due in part to President Bill Clinton's decidedly conservative approaches that lasted through the 1990s. Clinton was dedicated to displaying the power of the criminal justice system to "break the drug habits of our prisoners, and to break the cycle of drugs and crime for all time" (U.S. Department of Justice 1999). To accomplish this far-fetched goal, funding was primarily allocated toward the Zero Tolerance Drug Supervision Initiative to support state, local, and tribal governments in testing, treating, and supervising drug-involved offenders. These approaches relied almost entirely on universal drug testing for offenders, combined with treatment and graduated sanctions for failure to comply. This approach also fostered the expansion of drug courts for nonviolent offenders. The stated goal of these courts was to "effectively use the coercive power of the criminal justice system to break the cycle of drug abuse and crime by combining drug testing, treatment, and sanctions" (U.S. Department of Justice 1999).

The Obama administration adopted a different tact when the president convened the Task Force on 21st Century Policing to address the tenuous relationship between communities and law enforcement agencies. The Task Force was charged with identifying best policing practices that also enhanced trust in the community. The final report made several recommendations, including "Law enforcement agencies should consider adopting preferences for seeking 'least harm' resolutions, such as diversion programs or warnings and citations in lieu of arrest for minor infractions" (President's Task Force on 21st Century Policing 2015, 43).

Democrats have historically held this position on the use of diversion, and California's Substance Abuse & Crime Prevention Act of 2000 (SACPA), also widely known as "Prop 36," is a perfect example. Endorsed by Democratic Governor Gray Davis, the publicly approved referendum stated that the purpose and intent of the act was to "divert from incarceration into community-based substance abuse treatment programs nonviolent defendants, probationers, and parolees charged with simple drug possession or drug use offenses." According to the law, both first-time and repeat drug offenders became eligible for programs based on integrated treatment and supervision, and this initiative also aimed to enhance public safety by reducing drug-related crime. This marked a significant and lasting shift from a crime control model to the medically oriented public health approach characterizing much of the recent diversion-related approaches to drug offenses.

This shift in focus is highlighted by progressive law enforcement officials who have changed the narrative concerning drug-related crime with the commonly used phrase,

"We cannot arrest our way out of this crisis" (MacQuarrie 2017). Democratic district attorneys are among these reformers citing many important reasons to support diversion programs, not only for their harm reduction potential, but also to address issues related to disproportionate arrest and incarceration of racial and ethnic minority group members. Milwaukee, Wisconsin, is one jurisdiction confronting profiling of its diverse drug using population and Democratic criminal justice officials have appealed to diversion as a viable option to rectify these practices (Choudhury 2018). Milwaukee County District Attorney John Chisolm, has reported that diversion can "reduce crime, cut costs, and still keep the community safe, all while paying close attention to issues of racial disparity in prosecution and policing that for too long plagued our city" (Thompson et al. 2016).

Democratic leaders in certain states also have supported the expansion of diversion programs for more severe felony drug offenses. North Carolina's Justice Reinvestment Act of 2011, signed by Democratic Governor Bev Purdue, extended previous efforts by offering diversion programs with close supervision and treatment resources to felony drug offenders exhibiting the greatest risks and needs. This initiative was not necessarily novel given previously passed federal legislation that had identified this target population as diversion-eligible, but its passage coincided with the closure of four prisons, marking a historic turning point when previous policies were replaced with more progressive practices in the state.

The Republican and Democratic records diverge most when it comes to the harm reduction strategies and associated outreach efforts that seek to engage and divert drug offenders from the criminal justice system. The all-time high number of more than 70,000 fatal drug overdoses recorded by the CDC in 2017, many of which were attributed to injection drug use, led to a vociferous call for syringe exchange, supervised injection sites, and safe syringe disposal programs. The number of fatalities decreased by 4.1 percent in 2018, most likely due to restrictions on opioid prescription practices and increased availability of overdose reversal medication (Hedegaard, Miniño, and Warner 2020), however, the number rebounded to a record high of nearly 71,000 in 2019 (Ahmad, Rossen, and Sutton 2020). Overdoses also spiked in 2020, as the Covid-19 pandemic worsened, and continued to rise steadily (National Institute on Drug Abuse 2023). The public discussion of these initiatives by Republican leaders harkens back to the early 1970s and the notion that these programs condone drug use. Democrats, on the other hand, value these programs for their ability to address pressing public health needs while also offering the opportunity to engage drug offenders in treatment-based diversion programs.

FURTHER READING

Ahmad, Farida B., Lauren M. Rossen, and Paul Sutton. 2020. "Provisional Drug Overdose Death Counts." National Center for Health Statistics, July 28, 2020. https://www.cdc.gov/nchs/nvss/vsrr/drug-overdose-data.htm?source=email#nature_sources_of_data.

American Civil Liberties Union. 2017. "Smart Justice Campaign Polling on Americans' Attitudes on Criminal Justice." November 16, 2017. https://www.aclu.org/publications/smart-justice-campaign-polling-americans-attitudes-criminal-justice.

Auslen, Michael. 2016. "Lawmakers Overhaul System to Create 'No Wrong Door' to Mental Health Treatment." *Tampa Bay Times*, March 28, 2016. https://www.tampabay.com/news/politics/stateroundup/lawmakers-overhaul-system-to-create-no-wrong-door-to-mental-health/2270771/.

Centers for Disease Control and Prevention. 2020. "Heroin Overdose Data." July 28, 2020. https://www.cdc.gov/drugoverdose/data/heroin.html.

Choudhury, Nusrat. 2018. "New Data Reveals Milwaukee Police Stops Are about Race and Ethnicity." February 23, 2018. https://www.aclu.org/blog/criminal-law-reform/reforming-police/new-data-reveals-milwaukee-police-stops-are-about-race-and.

Gramlich, John. 2017. "Nearly Half of Americans Have a Family Member or Close Friend Who's Been Addicted to Drugs." Washington, DC: Pew Research Center, October 26, 2017.

Hedegaard, Holly, Arialdi M. Miniño, and Margaret Warner. 2020. "Drug Overdose Deaths in the United States, 1999–2018." NCH Data Brief No. 356, January 2020. Hyattsville, MD: National Center for Health Statistics.

Johnston, Lloyd D., Richard A. Miech, Patrick M. O'Malley, Jerald G. Bachman, John E. Schulenberg, and Megan E. Patrick. 2019. "'Monitoring the Future' National Survey Results on Drug Use 1975–2018: Overview, Key Findings on Adolescent Drug Use." Ann Arbor, MI: Institute for Social Research, University of Michigan.

LEAD National Support Bureau. 2020. "LEAD: Advancing Criminal Justice Reform in 2020." July 28, 2020. https://www.leadbureau.org/.

MacQuarrie, Brian. 2017. "'Angel' Opioid Initiative Thrives Despite Exit of Gloucester Police Chief." *The Boston Globe*, February 21, 2017. https://www.bostonglobe.com/metro/2017/02/21/angel-opioid-initiative-thrives-despite-exit-gloucester-police-chief/hvH14GgG0dRYTXJOpGEswO/story.html.

Massing, Michael. 1998. *The Fix: Solving the Nation's Drug Problem*. New York: Simon & Schuster.

National Alliance for Model State Drug Laws. 2019. "Model Deflection to Treatment Act." National Alliance for Model State Drug Laws. July 1, 2019. https://namsdl.org/wp-content/uploads/Model-Deflection-to-Treatment-Act.pdf.

National Institute on Drug Abuse. 2023. "Drug Overdose Death Rates." National Institutes of Health. September 1, 2023. https://nida.nih.gov/research-topics/trends-statistics/overdose-death-rates.

Office of National Drug Control Policy. 2014. "2013 Annual Report, Arrestee Drug Abuse Monitoring Program II." Washington, DC: Executive Office of the President.

Pew Research Center. 2017. "The Partisan Divide on Political Values Grows Even Wider." Washington, DC: Pew Research Center.

President's Task Force on 21st Century Policing. 2015. "Final Report of the President's Task Force on 21st Century Policing." Washington, DC: Office of Community Oriented Policing Services.

Scholl, Lawrence, Puja Seth, Mbabazi Kariisa, Nana Wilson, and Grant Baldwin. 2019. "Drug and Opioid-involved Overdose Deaths—United States, 2013–2017." *Morbidity and Mortality Weekly Report (MMWR)* 67 no. 5152: 1419–27.

Substance Abuse and Mental Health Services Administration. 2017. "Key Substance Use and Mental Health Indicators in the United States: Results from the 2016 National Survey on

Drug Use and Health." HHS Publication No. SMA 17-5044, NSDUH Series H-52. Rockville, MD: Center for Behavioral Health Statistics and Quality, Substance Abuse and Mental Health Services Administration.

Thompson, J. Scott, John Chisholm, Leah Garabedian, Barbara Broderick, and Sallie Clark. 2016. "Five Voices on Reforming the Front End of Justice." The Marshall Project, July 17, 2016. https://www.themarshallproject.org/2016/07/17/five-voices-on-reforming-the-front-end-of-justice.

Tiger, Rebecca. 2013. *Judging Addicts: Drug Courts and Coercion in the Justice System*. New York: New York University Press.

U.S. Department of Justice. 1999. "The Clinton Administration's Law Enforcement Strategy: Breaking the Cycle of Drugs and Crime." Washington, DC: U.S. Department of Justice.

U.S. Department of Justice. 2023. "Drug Treatment Courts." NCJ 238527. Washington, DC: U.S. Department of Justice, Office of Justice Programs.

Weiss, Audrey J., Anne Elixhauser, Marguerite L. Barrett, Claudia A. Steiner, Molly K. Bailey, and Lauren O'Malley. 2016. "Opioid-related Inpatient Stays and Emergency Department Visits by State, 2009–2014." Statistical Brief #219, December 2016. Rockville, MD: Agency for Healthcare Research and Quality.

CHAPTER 9

Environmental Crime

J. ANDY HANSEN

AT A GLANCE

In the United States, environmental crimes are delineated by a host of laws and statutes at the federal, state, and local levels. This chapter focuses on the views of the nation's politicians toward environmental crimes at the federal level. As such, it includes many examples from the Environmental Protection Agency (EPA) because they are the primary regulators of the environment in the United States, and from the Department of Justice (DOJ), because they prosecute environmental crimes at the federal level.

Democrats generally have held more favorable attitudes toward environmental regulations than Republicans. However, most US presidential administrations since Republican President Richard Nixon have consistently supported the prosecution of environmental crimes and some of the most influential presidents in US history, in terms of protecting the environment, were Republicans. For instance, President Nixon passed a dozen environmental laws and established the EPA. And although President George W. Bush undermined environmental protections in many areas, his administration's EPA and DOJ investigated and prosecuted a record number of environmental crimes. This trend changed during the administration of Republican President Donald J. Trump, as official data from the federal government demonstrates that the number of environmental crime prosecutions plummeted to levels far below the administrations of Republican President George W. Bush and Democratic President Barack Obama.

Since taking office in January 2021, the administration of Democratic President Joseph R. Biden and the 117th Congress has been highly critical of former President Trump and the practices of the DOJ, EPA, and other federal agencies under his watch. As president, Biden has adopted many policies advocated by other leading Democrats to strengthen environmental protections and increase environmental prosecutions. The Inflation Reduction Act of 2022, for example, has been touted as the "most significant action Congress has taken on clean energy and climate change in the nation's history"

(The White House 2023). More recently, the Biden-Harris administration established a national drinking water standard and took other regulatory actions to enhance public health and prosecute environmental wrongdoers.

MANY REPUBLICANS...

- Prefer less emphasis on environmental regulations, global environmental policies, and negative environmental effects on humans and animals. They argue that an emphasis on these things operates to the detriment of US businesses, the nation's standing in the global economy, the rights of states, and the rights of individuals to operate businesses and act on private properties as they wish.
- Would like fewer actions to be defined as crimes. Instead, they would like to use incentives to encourage environmentally friendly behaviors by individuals and businesses.
- Would like environmental crimes to be addressed by the states and not the federal government.

MANY DEMOCRATS...

- Prefer less emphasis on free market capitalism and the wishes of businesspeople to reduce environmental regulations to the point of harming the health of humans and other inhabitants of the earth, disproportionately the most vulnerable.
- Would like stricter environmental regulations to encourage good behavior.
- Would like the federal government to have an active role in prosecuting environmental crimes because states have an economic incentive to reduce regulations, thereby creating a race to the bottom.

OVERVIEW

Environmental crime, also known as green crime or conservation crime, has not received as much attention from politicians, criminologists, and other social scientists in the United States as violent crimes such as homicides or drug crimes. This relative inattention is unfortunate considering the negative impact environmental crimes such as air and water pollution have on our lives every day. For example, air and water pollution are linked to a host of serious diseases and illnesses that result in lower average life expectancies. Illegal harvesting of plants and animals has contributed to the decline of species and even extinctions.

An important first step toward understanding environmental crime is defining exactly what is, and is not, encompassed by this term. Unfortunately, a common definition of environmental crime has not been adopted or used in the past. Clifford (1998) devoted an entire chapter to the difficulty in defining environmental crime in her seminal book on the topic. Later, Clifford and Edwards (2011) suggested that students use the following as a good definition of environmental crime: "An act committed with the intent to harm or with a potential to cause harm to ecological and/or biological systems and for the purpose of securing business or personal advantage" (26). For practitioners, the authors suggested a working definition as follows: "Any act that violates an environmental protection statute" (Clifford and Edwards 2011, 26).

According to the United Nations and the Interpol, "Although the definition of 'environmental crime' is not universally agreed, it is often understood as a collective term to describe illegal activities harming the environment and aimed at benefitting individuals or groups or companies from the exploitation of, damage to, trade or theft of natural resources, including serious crimes and transnational organized crime" (Nellemann et al. 2016, 7). Although various definitions may be located, almost all contain two elements: harm (or risk of harm) to the environment and violation of the law. Common examples have usually included water pollution, air pollution, and illegal harvesting of plants and animals.

In addition to the lack of a common definition, the lack of reliable and valid environmental crime statistics is among the primary issues plaguing research on this important topic. The most commonly used sources of data on criminal offending and victimization in the United States for the past several decades, the Federal Bureau of Investigation's Uniform Crime Reports (UCR) program and the National Crime Victimization Survey (NCVS), have not included environmental crimes. The National Incident Based Reporting System (NIBRS), which is replacing the UCR, does not specifically include an environmental crimes category, but the FBI (2020) has suggested they could be included among the "other offenses" category. Unfortunately, combining a host of different offenses into one category creates problems for those who want to isolate and focus on environmental crimes. Beginning in 2020, NIBRS added a thirteenth category, "federal resource violation," to the list of group B offenses (Federal Bureau of Investigation 2020). Although this will provide a summary of environmental crimes, the data will be limited to arrests for federal offenses only. NIBRS data on other offenses, such as homicide and aggravated assault, are collected regardless of whether arrests are made, and crimes reported to local and state law enforcement agencies are included as well.

The Rivers and Harbors Act of 1899, which made discharging pollutants into navigable waterways without permits misdemeanor offenses, is often cited as the first environmental law in the United States. However, the Rivers and Harbors Act was more concerned with negative effects on waterborne commerce than the environment, so others contend that environmental legislation, and the longstanding behaviors these laws criminalize, should be traced to the early 1970s.

It is important to note that the 1970s is not the beginning of environmental crime in the United States. In fact, water pollution and numerous other actions harmful for the environment have been widespread practices across many generations of Americans. The Rivers and Harbors Act was merely the first time that these actions were added to the nation's legal codes and thereby considered criminal and subject to prosecution by the US criminal justice system.

It was during the early 1970s that US lawmakers passed a wave of environmental legislation that effectively created environmental crimes in the nation. Prior to that time, actions such as unpermitted discharges of hazardous chemicals into US waterways were considered civil or administrative, but not criminal, problems. In fact, these were standard business practices in many American industries. Among the landmark pieces of legislation during the early 1970s were the National Environmental Policy Act (1970), Clean Air Act (1970), Clean Water Act (1972), Ocean Dumping Act (1972), and Endangered Species Act (1973). The EPA was created in 1970 to enforce the new laws. Overall, the series of new federal environmental legislation was passed in response to increased public concern about the environment, attributable to books including Rachel Carson's (1962) book *Silent Spring* and several ecological disasters in the United States. Despite support from both parties and the public, environmental crimes were rarely prosecuted during the 1970s, partly because they were all misdemeanor offenses and prosecutors with limited resources tend to focus on more serious crimes (felonies). It also took time to implement changes required by the new laws, creating a further lag.

In the following years and decades, Congress passed additional environmental laws, such as the Resource Conservation and Recovery Act (1976), the Comprehensive Environmental Response, Compensation, and Liability Act (1980), and the Pollution Prevention Act (1990). A listing of federal environmental crimes, categorized as wildlife or pollution offenses, is available from the DOJ (see United States Department of Justice 2015). Importantly, Congress also amended much of the earlier environmental legislation and reclassified most environmental crimes from misdemeanors to felonies. For example, the Clean Water Act amendments of 1987 added felonies for knowingly discharging pollutants, knowingly making false statements in discharge monitoring reports, and knowingly tampering with monitoring devices. Combined with shifting legal norms, the numbers of environmental crimes prosecuted by the federal government increased dramatically during the 1980s and 1990s.

Environmental Crime Prosecutions Drop Sharply during Trump Presidency

There are few sources of data on environmental crimes in the United States, but one of the best is the Environmental Crimes Project (ECP) at the University of Michigan Law School. The ECP has compiled fourteen years of pollution prosecution data including the second term of the Republican George W. Bush administration, the entire Democratic Obama presidency, and the first two years of the Republican Trump administration. Analyses by the ECP have shown that criminal prosecutions of environmental crimes dropped dramatically in 2017 and 2018 under Trump. More specifically, the average number of defendants charged with environmental crimes during the second Bush administration was 149, dropped to 139 in the eight years under Obama, and fell precipitously to 83 during the first half of the Trump presidency. The decline in criminal prosecutions is even more dramatic when comparing numbers of cases. During the Bush and Obama years, the average number of cases filed annually was eighty-eight and seventy-seven, respectively, but subsequently decreased over 50 percent to thirty-eight per year under Trump. Official data from the EPA, reported by fiscal year, suggest that the second half of the Trump presidency was not unlike the beginning. In fact, EPA data show the average number of annual criminal environmental cases was seventy-five in fiscal years 2017 and 2018 but dropped to an average of sixty-eight cases in 2019 and 2020. Nor does it appear that the decrease in enforcement was limited to criminal cases, as comparisons of the first nine months of the G. W. Bush, Obama, and Trump administrations by the *New York Times* also found steep declines in civil cases during 2017 (EPA 2020; Lipton and Ivory 2017; Uhlmann 2020).

The EPA and DOJ have had staff dedicated to environmental crimes since October 1982. At the federal level, environmental crimes are investigated by agents of the EPA's Criminal Investigation Division, the Fish and Wildlife Service, the National Oceanic and Atmospheric Administration, the Department of Agriculture's Office of the Inspector General, the Federal Bureau of Investigation, and other law enforcement agencies. Federal environmental crimes are prosecuted by members of the Department of Justice's Environmental Crimes Section (ECS), which was created in 1987 and is located within the Environmental and Natural Resources Division (ENRD). In 2004, federal wildlife crime prosecutors were transferred to the ECS, and in 2011, the EPA was forced to eliminate approximately 950 enforcement positions due to budget cuts. In 2015, the ECS had forty-three prosecutors working on a variety of pollution and wildlife criminal cases.

It is important to note that the heads of the EPA and DOJ are presidential appointees, so the perspectives of US presidents are reflected in their policies and practices. More specifically, the EPA administrator can influence the investigation of environmental crimes, and the attorney general can influence the prosecution of environmental crimes. This became apparent from 2017 to 2020 during the presidency of Republican Donald J. Trump as his administration engaged in "business-friendly easing of the way the federal government enforce[d] scores of environment and public health protections" (Knickmeyer 2020).

After more than a decade of budget cuts and a resulting reduction in on-site EPA inspections, especially through the coronavirus pandemic from 2020 to 2022, the EPA aimed to reinvigorate its enforcement program. During 2023, the EPA conducted more inspections of polluting industrial sites than in recent years, opening nearly 200 new criminal investigations, an increase of 70 percent over 2022 (Daly and Phillis 2023). Democratic President Joseph R. Biden entered office in 2021 with an ambitious climate and environmental protection agenda, from making environmental justice an administration priority to boosting clean energy strategies. Currently, many of his proposals face legal challenges and significant resistance from Congressional Republicans.

REPUBLICANS ON ENVIRONMENTAL CRIME

The Republican party has a long history of environmental protection in the United States, and some of the most significant presidents, in terms of conservation, have been

Republicans. For instance, Republican Presidents Ulysses S. Grant and Benjamin Harrison created the first national parks and national forests, respectively. Republican President Theodore Roosevelt made natural resources a priority in the White House and protected more public land than any previous US president, and Republican President Richard Nixon signed a dozen environmental laws and created the EPA by executive order. Other Republican presidents of the past fifty years, including George H. W. Bush and George W. Bush, remained supportive of prosecuting environmental crimes, even as they declawed some of the legislation prosecutors relied on. Although some of his policy ideas had been simmering in the Republican party for years, the most recent Republican president, Donald J. Trump was an outlier even among Republican lawmakers in his attacks on the environment. Research conducted by the news media and academic researchers, detailed below, demonstrates that the Trump administration dramatically reduced criminal prosecutions of environmental crimes.

During the early 1970s, President Nixon benefitted from a great deal of bipartisan support for protecting the environment from moderate Republicans and Democrats. The Clean Air Act was passed in 1970 with a 73-0 vote in the Senate and 375-1 vote in the House. A draft of the Clean Water Act was approved by an 86-0 vote in the Senate and 380-14 vote in the House; the final version received a 74-0 vote in the Senate and 366-11 vote in the House. William Ruckelshaus, the first EPA administrator, was a Republican environmentalist who was respected by both parties. In the run-up to the 1972 midterm elections, Republicans criticized Democrats who controlled Congress for not supporting more of Nixon's environmental agenda, and touted Nixon's successes, which included creating the National Oceanic and Atmosphere Administration and EPA. In fact, there was public support for environmental laws from a variety of diverse constituency groups that Republicans traditionally court. Republican Ronald Reagan governed California from 1967 to 1975 with support from environmentalists and proposed a clean air law for that state before Congress passed the Clean Air Act at the federal level.

President Nixon was replaced in 1974 by Gerald Ford, a Republican who inherited a difficult economy highlighted by the 1973 and 1974 energy crisis. Ford was known for his dislike of federal bureaucracies including the EPA, and his administration's response to the energy crisis emphasized energy production over the environment. Still, Ford had a positive impact on environmental crimes when he passed the Resource Conservation and Recovery Act and the Toxic Substances Control Act in 1976, which criminalized improper storage and disposal of hazardous and solid wastes.

The degree of Republican support for environmental legislation and increasing punishments for committing environmental crimes during the 1970s may be surprising given more recent Republican actions. In fact, some have called "the Republican reversal on the environment ... one of the most profound and far-reaching transformations in modern American political history, on par with the transformation of twentieth-century Democrats from the part of states' rights and segregation to the part of the New Deal and civil rights" (Turner and Isenberg 2018, 6). The decline in Republican concern for the environment has been traced to the administration of President Ronald Reagan, who took office in 1981 with the support of business leaders and corporate donors, states' rights activists who distrusted federal regulations, and evangelicals who believed God granted power over the Earth to man. Economic anxiety from the late-1970s also reduced support for environmental regulations from the public.

Ronald Reagan's presidential campaign was based on a platform opposing federal bureaucracies including the EPA. As president-elect, Reagan chose an environmental plan from the Heritage Foundation over one drafted by moderate Republicans. President Reagan did not uphold the tradition of appointing subject-matter experts; for instance, he appointed Anne Gorsuch to lead the EPA. Gorsuch was a corporate lawyer and state lawmaker from Colorado who had been an outspoken critic of the agency she was appointed to lead. Although the Democrat-controlled House was able to temper some attacks on the EPA, Gorsuch and Reagan reduced the overall budget by 27 percent from 1980 to 1983. Gorsuch quit after investigations into corruption and other misconduct at the EPA. The first EPA head, Ruckelshaus, replaced her and was able to restore some of the EPA budget. Despite the impact his administration had on the Republican party's shift away from environmental protection, Reagan provided some degree of support for prosecuting environmental crimes with his DOJ creating the Environmental Crimes Section in 1987.

George H. W. Bush campaigned to be the "environmental president," and today he is credited with strengthening the Clean Air Act. President Bush's EPA administrator, William K. Riley, was a conservationist who had led nonprofits and was supported by Republicans and Democrats. Although he is credited with boosting the Clean Air Act, he also approved a decision by the DOJ to reduce enforcement of strip-mining laws. Despite rising anti-environmentalism and conservatism in the party, the large number of moderate senators and governors in the Republican party, many from the Northeast who supported environmental regulations, continued to protect the environment in certain areas. However, the Republican Party moved geographically toward the rural south and west during the 1990s and 2000s, and became more conservative philosophically, which decreased the power of moderate Republicans.

President George W. Bush is not remembered for his environmental legislation, but his record on environmental crime is more favorable. On one hand, his administration attempted to rewrite the Clean Air Act in a way to prevent future cases. Further, EPA agents were diverted to the EPA administrator's security detail after 9/11, which created morale issues (Uhlmann 2008). Also, the chief of the ECS from 2000 to 2007 wrote that he believed Attorneys General Ashcroft and Gonzalez were not committed to prosecuting environmental crime (Uhlmann 2008). On the other hand, Bush followed in his father's footsteps by appointing a respected EPA head, Christine Todd Whitman. Funding for the ECS increased under George W. Bush, as did the number of environmental crime prosecutors. The EPA's database of criminal prosecutions from 1983 to 2020 illustrates that the years with the highest numbers of cases (2003 with 138 cases; 2006 with 143 cases) were during the administration of President G. W. Bush. In addition, record criminal fines were paid for illegally transporting hazardous materials and for violating the Clean Air Act during his administration.

During his presidential campaign, the most recent Republican president, Donald J. Trump remarked about the EPA, "What they do is a disgrace. Every week they come out with new regulation." When asked who would protect the environment, candidate Trump responded, "We'll be fine with the environment. We can leave a little bit, but you can't destroy businesses" (Fox News 2015, 1). President Trump took office while Republicans controlled Congress in 2017. He appointed Scott Pruitt as EPA director, a Republican attorney general from Oklahoma with a record of hostilities toward the EPA, just as Reagan had done decades earlier. The same month President Trump was inaugurated, a Republican representative introduced a House resolution to "permanently abolish" the EPA. The following month, President Trump directed Pruitt to reduce the areas covered by the Clean Water Act. It should be noted that such changes can have a dramatic effect on the scope of environmental crimes in the United States, not by addressing the polluting actions, but by limiting the range of actions considered to be criminal. Later, Pruitt borrowed an earlier idea and reassigned EPA environmental crime prosecutors to his personal protection detail. Overall, during the first two years of his presidency, Trump and the 115th Congress undermined environmental regulations and reduced resources available for holding individuals and corporations accountable for violating environmental laws.

The Republican Party did not adopt a new policy platform in 2020, opting instead to continue supporting their 2016 agenda. In terms of the environment, the 2016 platform preamble stated, "We believe that people are the ultimate resource—and that the people, not the government, are the best stewards of our country's God-given natural resources." Similarly, the most recent Republican platform opined, "States, not Washington bureaucrats, are best equipped to engage farmers and ranchers to develop sound farm oversight policies" (Republican Party Platform 2016, 18). The platform said the EPA was a "regulatory juggernaut" that had harmed agriculture, and also called the "Waters of the United States" Rule, which extended CWA protections to streams and wetlands, a "travesty." As had been advocated by Republicans in the past, the party platform proposed, "to shift responsibility for environmental regulation from the federal bureaucracy to the states" (21). Another telling statement of the 2016/2020 Republican platform concerning environmental crime was the following: "We firmly believe environmental problems are best solved by giving incentives for human ingenuity and the development of new technologies, not through top-down, command-and-control regulations that stifle economic growth and cost thousands of jobs" (Republican Party Platform 2016, 22). It is likely that the 2024 Republican platform will remain virtually unchanged since former president Donald J. Trump is the presumptive nominee for the 2024 presidential election.

DEMOCRATS ON ENVIRONMENTAL CRIME

In 1970, the Democratic party was extremely supportive of environmental regulations, even though their monopoly was not as complete as it had been in the previous 100 years. Although the White House witnessed Republican presidents from 1970 to 1977, Democrats controlled the Senate and House from 1970 to 1981, and this decade was remembered for bipartisan environmental progress. It should be noted that ideas that materialized into environmental laws during the 1970s can be traced to Democratic President Franklin D. Roosevelt's New Deal of the 1930s that emphasized individual rights over business interests (Turner and Isenberg 2018). President Jimmy Carter enjoyed Democratic control of Congress during his term from 1977 to 1981 and shortly after taking office, Carter signed a bill that regulated strip mining, previously vetoed by former Republican President Gerald R. Ford. In 1980, Carter signed the Comprehensive Environmental Response, Compensation, and Liability Act that gave the EPA more power over hazardous substances. The EPA's criminal prosecution summary database does not include data for the Carter era.

As a Democratic presidential candidate, William Jefferson "Bill" Clinton debated Republican President George H. W. Bush about who had a stronger environmental record. President Clinton was extremely supportive of environmental legislation, certainly influenced by Vice President Al Gore, who had a very strong record on the environment as a US representative and senator from Tennessee. Clinton's attorney general, Janet Reno, also emphasized the prosecution of environmental crimes. A former employee and leader reflected that the ECS had a difficult time during the Clinton years, though, after the Republican Congress cut funding to the ENRD, the number of prosecutors dropped from thirty-five in 1995 to twenty-nine in 2002 (Uhlmann 2008). Furthermore, interviews conducted with EPA employees found that the respondents felt 1994 was the tipping point when environmental issues started becoming political and polarizing (Fredrickson et al. 2018). This timeline corresponds roughly with analyses conducted by the League of Conservation Voters, which annually issues scorecards for members of Congress based on their environment records in Washington. Overall, these scorecards show steady bipartisan support for the environment from 1970 until roughly 1991, when scorecards for Republicans in Congress begin a steady decline, and those for Democratic members of the House and Senate begin to steadily increase. Still, the number of environmental crime cases according to the EPA increased from forty-eight in 1997 to ninety-two in 1998 while Clinton was in the White House and Republicans controlled the Senate and House. The Clinton administration also focused on pollution by ships and prosecuted cases that led to then-record criminal fines. According to the EPA's criminal prosecution summary database, the number of annual environmental crimes prosecutions ranged from 115 to 136 during fiscal years 2010 to 2015.

As a US senator and presidential candidate, Barack Obama was critical of the G. W. Bush White House and the Republican-controlled 108th and 109th Congresses. Shortly after taking office, the Obama administration overturned a Bush-era removal of wolves from the Endangered Species Act that made hunting them crimes in certain states again. In September 2009, the *New York Times* reported that over 500,000 violations of the Clean Water Act had occurred in the previous five years, but less than 3 percent had resulted in any punishments (Duhigg 2009). At a House committee hearing the following month, EPA administrator Lisa Jackson acknowledged that agency officials, "are falling short of this administration's expectations for the effectiveness of our clean water enforcement programs" (Duhigg 2009, 1). She added that, "the time is long overdue for E.P.A. to re-examine its approach to Clean Water Act enforcement" (Duhigg 2009, 1). Researchers have found that environmental crime prosecutions began to decline toward the end of the Obama administration. Specifically, the number of annual environmental crime cases fell from 191 in 2011 to 106 in 2014 (Uhlmann 2020). However, a former leader of the ECS stated his belief that the decline was due to declining resources at the EPA and not a lack of support for the program (Uhlmann 2020). In summary, the Obama administration prosecuted an average of seventy-seven environmental crime cases each year, which involved an average of 139 defendants (Uhlmann 2020). For context, the average number of prosecutions was fewer than former Republican president G. W. Bush, but far more than former Republican president Trump.

In fact, the former lead prosecutor at the ECS felt that political support for prosecuting environmental crimes was amazingly strong and consistent throughout his tenure at the EPA that spanned the administrations of George H. W. Bush, Bill Clinton, George W. Bush, and Barack Obama (Uhlmann 2020). Data reported by the EPA online provide some support for the argument that environmental crime prosecutions have been relatively bipartisan at the federal level, even if party views toward environmental legislation have diverged sharply. For instance, the two fiscal years with the highest number of criminal cases were under Republican President G. W. Bush, while the third and fourth most productive fiscal years based on the EPA's criminal enforcement summary database occurred during Democratic President Barack Obama's terms. And while annual fluctuations existed, research by the ECP found annual environmental crime cases never dropped below 100 during G. W. Bush's second term or during the Obama presidency.

The 2020 Democratic Party platform did not specifically address environmental crime in the section dedicated to criminal justice. However, the platform included a chapter titled "Combating the Climate Crisis and Pursuing Environmental Justice," with the following statement: "Communities of color, low-income families, and Indigenous communities have long suffered disproportionate and cumulative harm from air pollution, water pollution, and toxic sites" (Democratic Party Platform 2020, 49). These platform papers further explain that "Every American has the right to breathe clean air, drink clean water, and live without fear of exposure to toxic waste ... Democrats will create an environmental justice fund to make historic investments aimed at eliminating legacy pollution, which disproportionately causes illness and premature death in communities of color, low-income communities, and Indigenous communities" (Democratic Party Platform 2020, 53).

In November 2020, Democrat Joseph R. Biden was elected president and benefitted from Democrat control of the House and Senate during the 117th Congress. President Biden's plans for addressing environmental crime enforcement were provided online under the heading "The Biden Plan for a Clean Energy Revolution and Environmental Justice." Although Biden was criticized for not supporting the Green New Deal espoused by some Democrats in the lead up to the 2020 elections, his plan includes the following statement:

> Biden believes the Green New Deal is a crucial framework for meeting the climate challenges we face. It powerfully captures two basic truths, which are at the core of his plan: (1) the United States urgently needs to embrace greater ambition on an epic scale to meet the scope of this challenge, and (2) our environment and our economy are completely and totally connected.

> In terms of environmental crime specifically, Biden's website states that: Vulnerable communities are disproportionately impacted by the climate emergency and pollution. The Biden Administration will take action against fossil fuel companies and other polluters who put profit over people and knowingly harm our environment and poison our communities' air, land, and water, or conceal information regarding potential environmental and health risks. (Democratic Party 2020, 1)

The Biden plan also highlighted his Republican predecessor's lack of action with respect to enforcement of environmental laws. It noted that, during the Trump administration, the EPA referred the fewest number of criminal anti-pollution cases to the DOJ in thirty years. It decried the Trump administration's ineffectiveness by stating that "allowing corporations to continue to pollute—affecting the health and safety of both their workers and surrounding communities—without consequences perpetuates an egregious abuse of power" (18). In terms of actual steps, Biden's website claimed that he would "direct his EPA and Justice Department to pursue these cases to the fullest extent permitted by law and, when needed, seek additional legislation as needed to hold corporate executives personally accountable—including jail time where merited" (18). At the end of 2022, the Biden administration defined "waters of the United States" to include small streams, wetlands, and other types of waterways under the Clean Water Act, repealing a rule imposed during the Trump administration that had removed protections for most streams and wetlands in the nation. In April 2024, the Biden administration's EPA announced its "national legally enforceable drinking water standard" for polyfluoroalkyl substances (PFAS), known as "forever chemicals" that are linked to many serious health problems, such as cancers, organ damage, and developmental impediments in children (White House 2024). This rules sets health safeguards and requires public agencies to monitor and reduce PFAS in drinking water and to notify the public whenever those limits are exceeded. Funding is also being provided to help agencies meet the new standards' requirements.

FURTHER READING

Biden for President. 2021. "The Biden Plan for a Clean Energy Revolution and Environmental Justice." https://joebiden.com/climate-plan/. Accessed July 4, 2022.

Clifford, Mary. 1998. *Environmental Crime: Enforcement, Policy, and Social Responsibility*. Gaithersburg: Aspen Publishing.

Clifford, Mary, and Terry D. Edwards. 2011. *Environmental Crime*. 2nd ed. Sudbury, MA: Jones & Bartlett Learning.

Daly, Matthew, and Michael Phillis. 2023. "After Years of Decline, the Biden Administration Says Environmental Enforcement is on the Upswing." *AP News*. December 18, 2023. https://www.apnews.com/article/epa-enforcement-inspections-pandemic-environmental-justice-0c4898bbe21dc123f8636768b9e988f3.

Democratic Party. 2020. "2020 Democratic Party Platform." https://www.demconvention.com/wp-content/uploads/2020/08/2020-07-31-Democratic-Party-Platform-For-Distribution.pdf. Accessed November 3, 2022.

Duhigg, Charles. 2009. "E.P.A. Vows Better Effort on Water." *New York Times*, October 16, 2009. https://www.nytimes.com/2009/10/16/business/energy-environment/16water.html.

Environmental Protection Agency. 2020. "Summary of Criminal Prosecutions." https://www.epa.gov/enforcement/summary-criminal-prosecutions. Accessed September 27, 2023.

Federal Bureau of Investigation. 2020. *2019.2.1 National Incident-Based Reporting System User Manual*. Washington, DC: U.S. Department of Justice.

Fox News. 2015. "Donald Trump Talks Taxes, Trade, 9/11 and Why He Takes Personal Shots at Political Rivals." *Fox News Sunday*, October 18, 2015. https://www.foxnews.com/transcript/donald-trump-talks-taxes-trade-9-11-and-why-he-takes-personal-shots-at-political-rivals.

Fredrickson, Leif, Christopher Sellers, Lindsey Dillon, Jennifer Liss Ohayon, Nicholas Shapiro, Marianne Sullivan, Stephen Bocking, et al. 2018. "History of U.S. Presidential Assaults on Modern Environmental Health Protection." *American Journal of Public Health* 108, S95–S103. https://doi.org/10.2105/AJPH.2018.304396.

Knickmeyer, Ellen. 2020. "Trump Agencies Steadily Push Rollbacks as Pandemic Rages." *AP News*. March 24, 2020. https://apnews.com/article/wa-state-wire-environment-tx-state-wire-ny-state-wire-public-health-9bc2a961143dee11fcef847be3312bc0.

Lipton, Eric, and Danielle Ivory. 2017. "Under Trump, E.P.A. Has Slowed Actions Against Polluters, and Put Limits on Enforcement Officers." *New York Times*, December 10, 2017. https://www.nytimes.com/2017/12/10/us/politics/pollution-epa-regulations.html.

Nellemann, Christian, Rune Henriksen, Arnold Kreilhuber, Davyth Stewart, Maria Kotsovou, Patricia, Raxter, Elizabeth Mrema, and Sam Barrat. 2016. "The Rise of Environmental Crime—a Growing Threat to Natural Resources, Peace, Development, and Security." United Nations Environmental Programme and Interpol. https://wedocs.unep.org/bitstream/handle/20.500.11822/7662/The_rise_of_environmental_crime_A_growing_threat_to_natural_resources_peace%2C_development_and_security-2016environmental_crimes.pdf.pdf?sequence=3&isAllowed=y. Accessed September 27, 2023.

Republican Party. 2020. "Republican Party Platform." https://prod-cdn-static.gop.com/docs/Resolution_Platform_2020.pdf. Accessed October 3, 2022.

Schwartz, John. 2020. "Under Trump, Criminal Prosecutions for Pollution Dropped Sharply." *New York Times*, October 13, 2020. https://www.nytimes.com/2020/10/13/climate/pollution-lawsuits-trump-environment.html.

South, Nigel, and Avi Brisman, eds. 2013. *Routledge International Handbook of Green Criminology*. London: Routledge.

The White House. 2023. "Inflation Reduction Act Guidebook." November 28, 2023. https://www.whitehouse.gov/cleanenergy/inflation-reduction-act-guidebook/.

Turner, James Morton, and Andrew C. Isenberg. 2018. *The Republican Reversal: Conservatives and the Environment from Nixon to Trump*. Cambridge: Harvard University Press.

Uhlmann, David M. 2008. "Strange Bedfellows." *Environmental Forum* 25, no. 3 (May/June): 40–4. https://repository.law.umich.edu/articles/1682/.

Uhlmann, David M. 2020. "New Environmental Crimes Project Data Shows that Pollution Prosecutions Plummeted During the First Two Years of the Trump Administration." University of Michigan Public Law Research Paper, no. 685: 1-16.

United States Department of Justice. 2015. "Federal Environmental Crimes, by Statute." https://www.justice.gov/enrd/federal-environmental-crimes-statute. Accessed October 8, 2022.

White House. 2024. "Fact Sheet: Biden-Harris Administration Takes Critical Action to Protect Communities from PFAS Pollution in Drinking Water." April 10, 2024. https://www.whitehouse.gov/briefing-room/statements-releases/2024/04/10/fact-sheet-biden-harris-administration-takes-critical-action-to-protect-communities-from-pfas-pollution-in-drinking-water/.

CHAPTER 10

Felon Disenfranchisement

ROGER BYRD AND OLIVIA A. EASON

AT A GLANCE

Felon disenfranchisement is the legal process by which felons are deprived of their ability to vote. In the United States, this practice is determined by individual state laws. In most states, felon voting rights are automatically restored after the completion of a person's sentence, including any probation or parole. However, in some states, felons must complete additional steps, such as paying all outstanding fines and court fees before their voting rights are restored. Felon disenfranchisement disproportionately affects minority communities. In the United States, African Americans are significantly more likely to be incarcerated than any other demographic group, and as a result, they are also more likely to be disenfranchised.

Significant debate surrounds felon voting rights in the United States. Historically, felon disenfranchisement began in America's early days. Kentucky was the first state to pass a felony disenfranchisement law in 1792. Within fifty years, four states had felony disenfranchisement policies and by the time of the American Civil War, about twenty-four states had either statutorily or by amending their state constitution enacted some form of felon disenfranchisement. The trend toward easing disenfranchisement began in the 1990s and by 2008 twenty-eight states had moved to restore rights or to simplify the process of restoration of rights.

Across time, Republicans have generally argued that felons have forfeited their rights by breaking the social contract, and that allowing them basic rights such as voting erodes societal order, particularly the electoral process. Democrats counter that felon disenfranchisement, because it affects people of color disproportionately, is reminiscent of the age of Jim Crow and a form of voter suppression.

MANY REPUBLICANS...

- Consider voting a privilege, subject to good behavior and demonstrated ability to conform to societal standards, that can be revoked either temporarily or permanently in response to felonious acts.
- Support "tough on crime" policies that increase the number of citizens who are ineligible to vote and oppose sweeping efforts to restore voting rights.
- Believe that allowing lawbreakers to vote endangers law-abiding citizens, viewing felons as untrustworthy individuals who need their ability to participate in the creation of laws and penalties restricted for public safety.

MANY DEMOCRATS...

- Believe that the right to vote is fundamental and should not be infringed except in the most extraordinary circumstances. Attempts to limit ballot box access are often viewed as an attempt to suppress voting for political purposes.
- Support policies that facilitate alternatives to incarceration, which emphasize reentry and re-inclusion into the greater community. These efforts oppose "civil death" (Kennedy 2022) and encourage participation by the population, including previous offenders.
- Tend to embrace the notion that expanding the right to vote to include felons reduces crime by fostering a sense of inclusion and hastens the restoration of offenders. Such inclusion and restoration, they believe, makes society safer.

OVERVIEW

No federal law prohibits previously convicted felons from voting. As with many other aspects of voting, such as primary dates and distribution of electors, this is an issue the US federalist system has left up to individual states. Theoretically, all states could fully restore voting rights to all felons. There is, however, constitutional protection for most states that impose severe restrictions or have an outright ban on felon voting.

One of three "Reconstruction Amendments," the Fourteenth Amendment guarantees the right to vote to all adult male citizens (later extended to all adult female citizens), with the exceptions of those who have engaged in certain unlawful behaviors. This has been interpreted to mean that a person must be convicted of a felony in order to lose voting rights.

All states impose some restrictions on voting for felons, but the details vary widely. Maine and Vermont, for instance, only disenfranchise people convicted of felonies related to elections. Other states, such as Alabama, have a wide range of offenses that disqualify a person from voting. Currently, no state permanently disenfranchises all felons, although some require extraordinary actions, such as a pardon for those convicted of violent crime, for voting rights to be restored.

To understand the fragmented laws regarding felon disenfranchisement in America, as well as the views of the two major political parties, some history is necessary regarding the origins of removing a right considered fundamental to democracy as a form of punishment. The concept of disenfranchising citizens who commit grave offenses originates in Ancient Greece, and by colonial times at least half of colonial states had some mechanism for disenfranchising those who committed the most serious crimes (Powell 2017). From this point forward in American history, it becomes impossible to discuss felon disenfranchisement without examining racial disparities and the reasons behind those disparities.

It was not until the Reconstruction period following the Civil War, when former slaves were granted the right to vote, that states began compiling long lists of crimes that constituted felonies or disenfranchised all those who committed vaguely defined crimes of "moral turpitude." Invariably, these laws managed to target freed slaves and their descendants at a vastly disproportionate rate to white people, both robbing African Americans of their political power and helping to craft the stereotype that they were dangerous and incapable of being good citizens.

While the US Supreme Court has rejected laws that specifically target African Americans or other minorities for disenfranchisement as a violation of the Equal Protections Clause, modern felon disenfranchisement laws have been written to be facially neutral, meaning they do not outright discriminate based on membership in any protected class. Historically, minority groups have been disproportionately impacted by disenfranchisement. Many factors create an uneven playing field for minorities, especially African Americans. In our federalist system of governance, states primarily regulate conditions. Even plaintiffs who use the language in the federal Voting Rights Act that prohibits disparate impact to challenge felon disenfranchisement laws have not had much success (Powell 2017).

At every stage of the criminal justice system, African Americans are overrepresented. Minority communities are policed more heavily, leading to more arrests and prosecutions across America. Black men comprise about 13 percent of the US male population, but nearly 35 percent of all men under state or federal jurisdiction with a sentence of more than one year (Hinton, Henderson, and Reed 2018).

In many states, African Americans receive longer sentences, affecting their right to vote in states where restoration of rights is contingent on being released from a custodial sentence. Racial economic disparities also mean that minorities, especially African Americans, are less likely to afford bail and therefore more likely to plead guilty to a felony in exchange for a relatively light term of confinement, disadvantaging them in states where voting rights are tied to completion of community supervision.

Economic disparities among races are also relevant due to the nature of crimes that often result in permanent disenfranchisement or require more stringent actions to obtain restoration. Offenses known as "crimes of poverty" are frequently classed as violent and treated differently in laws pertaining to felon voting than white-collar crimes that are primarily committed by wealthier white people. Lastly, many states now require the complete payment of court costs, supervision fees, and restitution before voting rights can be restored, further disadvantaging historically economically marginalized communities. Partially due to such facially neutral but practically discriminatory laws, 33 percent of African American men have felony convictions, imperiling their right to vote. Of the total male US population, 3 percent have been incarcerated compared to 15 percent of the African American male population (Shannon et al. 2017).

These racial disparities affect the debate surrounding to whom voting rights should be restored and how that should be done. Partisan fighting and concerns over which political party benefits by re-enfranchisement efforts have historically made the restoration of voting rights difficult in state legislatures. While politicians themselves rarely voice these concerns, pundits are vocal about the fact that African Americans, and most other racial minorities, tend to vote Democratic. However, while minority communities are disproportionately affected by felon disenfranchisement laws, depending on the racial makeup of a state, it does not necessarily mean that they will comprise a greater total number than white voters. Election experts in Florida, for example, during a push to re-enfranchise many released felons, were unsure which party was more likely to benefit from such a mass restoration of voting rights.

The Fight Over Re-enfranchisement of Felons in Florida: "Florida Man Wants to Vote"

In November 2018, 64.5 percent of Florida voters supported an amendment to the state constitution to restore voting rights to many of the state's felons. The amendment, however, required the Republican-controlled legislature to pass a specific bill to be signed by Republican Governor Ron DeSantis.

Republican opponents quickly used vague language in the amendment to limit the scope of the voting rights expansion. The term "sexual offense," for example, was expanded to include offenses like prostitution, which does not require sex offender registration. Most controversial was the interpretation of sentence "completion" to include payment of all fines and restitution, even if all other community supervision requirements were completed. Although this portion of the law was challenged as an unconstitutional poll tax, it was upheld by the Court of Appeals for the Eleventh Circuit and the US Supreme Court denied certiorari.

A University of Florida study estimated that this will disqualify 775,000 offenders with outstanding financial obligations, with Black Floridians disproportionately affected. While advocates have launched initiatives, and high-profile donors like billionaire Mike Bloomberg have pledged millions in support to help former offenders pay these debts, many felons are unsure of what they owe. Record-keeping is decentralized and outdated (one prospective voter found records were stored on index cards in old shoe boxes), and the Division of Elections, which must approve application for re-enfranchisement, has a limited capacity for review. Despite these challenges, by the first day of early voting for the 2020 presidential election, an estimated 67,000 felons had successfully registered to vote in Florida (Gardner 2019; *Guardian* 2020; Visser 2020; *NBC News* 2020).

During the election cycle of 2020, the debate of felon voting rights proved to be a heated issue, especially in battleground states. Incumbent Republican President Donald

Trump lost the popular vote in 2016 but won the electoral college by an estimated 80,000 votes across multiple states. To put that in perspective, this is less than 10 percent of the number of Florida felons eligible for the restoration of the voting rights, according to some estimates. Perhaps in response to his perceived vulnerability with African American voters, Trump signed the First Step Act passed by Congress, which gave federal judges greater flexibility in sentencing some drug offenders and increased efforts to reduce recidivism by providing enhanced rehabilitation services. It also reduced to twenty-five years previous life sentences for some drug offenders sentenced under "three strikes" provisions. One significant provision of the legislation provided 2,600 inmates being held for federal crack offenses convicted before August 2010 the opportunity to petition for a reduced penalty. Bipartisan support for the First Step Act notwithstanding, use of its provisions still became a point of criticism by Republican members of the Senate against Federal Appeals Court judge Ketanji Brown Jackson during her confirmation hearings for the Supreme Court in March 2022.

In 2021, the Biden administration promised to incentivize states for automatically restoring voting rights to felons who have served their sentences. H.R. 1 was a comprehensive bill to restore felons' voting rights in federal elections after they left prison. It passed the House in March 2021, but failed to reach debate in the Senate. Subsequent bills have been proposed in both the House and the Senate during the 118th Congress. Both House and Senate versions of the Democracy Restoration Act seek to restore voting rights in federal elections. However, as of April 2024, both have been introduced and referred to each chamber's respective Committee on the Judiciary.

REPUBLICANS ON FELON DISENFRANCHISEMENT

The views of Republicans on the general subject of crime are complicated and, at times, paradoxical. Following the bipartisan tough on crime era of the 1990s, soaring incarceration rates and the subsequent economic devastation in communities caused some fiscal conservatives to rethink the policies that led to the "land of the free" becoming the nation with the highest per capita number of prisoners in the world. Similarly, libertarian-leaning Republicans, whose distrust of government intervention and state control over the populace became uncomfortable with the ever-increasing number of crimes on the books. The latter concern made its way into the 2016 Republican Party platform, which was adopted without change for 2020, even amid language despairing at increasing murder rates in some locales during the administrations of Democratic President Barack Obama and calls to fully support and fund law enforcement. Missing from the official manual of concerns and goals of the Republican Party was any mention of voting rights for previously convicted felons.

To understand the Republican Party stance on felon disenfranchisement, it is illustrative to listen to elected leaders such as former Republican President Donald Trump and Republican Senate Majority Leader Mitch McConnell (KY). The former president vacillated between touting reform and requesting accolades for laws such as the First Step Act while continuing to build on the narrative of "American Carnage" made famous in his inauguration speech. On felon disenfranchisement, he has remained consistent in his opposition, often referring to Democrat-led efforts to restore voting rights as attempts to "rig" elections against Republicans.

During the 2020 election cycle, Senator McConnell came out as vehemently against a Democratic-led effort to restore the voting rights of felons who have completed their sentences. He proffered two primary arguments against the legislation. First, he stressed that felon disenfranchisement is an issue of states' rights to determine how their elections will be run. He then claimed that the bill was an effort by Democrats to win reelection and unseat Republicans, implying that he believes the majority of felons would not vote for Republicans. On the issue of states' responses to calls for re-enfranchisement, McConnell's home state of Kentucky made national news when Republican Governor Matt Bevin suspended an executive order made by the previous Democratic governor that granted the automatic restoration of voting rights to felons upon the completion of their sentences (Clark 2019).

Still, it is important to remember that the Republican Party is not a monolith and there are voices that oppose this manner of thinking, some loudly on the national stage and some quietly, voting for modest reforms in their home states. Republican Senator Rand Paul, also from Kentucky, previously supported Kentucky legislation to restore voting rights to certain nonviolent felons, although he has not prioritized this issue since the 2016 election. In Louisiana, the incarceration capital of the United States and, by extension, the world, the Republican-controlled House and Senate narrowly passed a bill that permits most felons still on probation and parole to vote if they have been out of prison for five years. In August 2020, Iowa Republican Governor Kim Reynolds signed an executive order restoring the rights of many felons who had completed all terms of their sentences, even if they are unable to pay fines and fees associated with their offense. Excluded from the order were people convicted of murder, manslaughter, and abortion after the second trimester. Previously, restrictions had disenfranchised nearly one-tenth of the state's African American population. Iowa's Republican legislature has resisted efforts to permanently end the policy. Senator Ted Cruz was even more blunt when he declared that "convicted felons tend to vote Democrat" (Beckwith 2021).

In the aftermath of the 2020 election, in which Republicans lost the presidency, the Senate, and failed to gain control of the House, Republicans made numerous attempts to limit voting rights, including blocking the expansion of voting rights for felons. In the first two months of 2022, when most states legislative sessions began, more than 250 bills were introduced to limit voting in some capacity. Most of these bills were introduced by Republicans and focused on limiting mail-in ballots and other nontraditional voting methods, which is consistent with former president Trump's mantra that the 2020 election was stolen (Brennan Center for Justice 2022). None specifically targeted felon voters. However, conservatives have successfully opposed multiple attempts to broaden voting rights for felons, including some previously bipartisan movements. In Virginia, Republicans defeated an attempt to amend the state's constitution to automatically re-enfranchise felons upon the completion of their sentences. One of the bill's original sponsors, Republican delegate Karen Grennhalgh, now opposes it after a conservative campaign against the reform (Moomaw 2022). Republicans in Congress defeated a Democratic bill in the Senate that would have restored felon voting rights nationwide (Beckworth 2021).

Conservative think tanks, which often contribute to the development of Republican legislation and talking points, have also spoken on the subject. One highly influential such organization is the Federalist Foundation. Back in 2008, they published a white paper authored by Roger Clegg, Kenneth Lee, and notable "Never-Trumper" George Conway, discounting arguments that felon disenfranchisement disproportionately harms people of color and condemning efforts to make changes to state-level disenfranchisement laws at the national level.

In the years since, Clegg, the president of the Center for Equal Opportunity, has remained in opposition to efforts to expand voting rights for felons and has been published multiple times by the Heritage Foundation, directly reaching voters and lawmakers. In an article cross-posted in the ultra-conservative *National Review*, Clegg and von Spakovsky (2018) opined an argument frequently repeated by Republican politicians, "If you're not willing to follow the law, then you should not have a role in making the law for everyone else, which is what you do when you vote—either directly (in the case of a referendum or ballot initiative) or indirectly (by choosing lawmakers and law enforcers)."

The Heritage Foundation has also posted articles with commentary proposing to allow felons the right to vote after the completion of all probation and parole, no matter how lengthy, and the payment of all fines and restitution, no matter how much. The Federalist Foundation has continued to oppose various proposed reforms that re-enfranchise felons, calling former Democratic presidential candidate and Vermont senator Bernie Sanders "crazy" for the suggestion that incarcerated felons be permitted to vote. Their argument against Sanders's suggestion is that removing the right to vote is an appropriate method of punishment for law breakers that they must earn back through completing a sentence or otherwise "righting" their wrongs.

In contrast to the Federalist Foundation, the Cato Institute has published articles advocating for the restoration of rights for felons who have completed prison terms. Likewise, the Freedom Partners, funded by Charles and David Koch, who have spent years using their considerable wealth to fund conservative causes via an organization called "Americans for Prosperity," supported recent efforts at re-enfranchising some felons in Florida. The Cato Institute also filed an amicus brief in support of re-enfranchisement efforts in Florida during a court battle over subsequent restrictive legislation. These think tank leanings, all prominent in Republican ideology and legislation, are further evidence of a philosophical split in the party between those who desire a tough on crime approach (against enfranchisement) and those who incorporate libertarian and fiscal conservatism more prominently into their views (for enfranchisement).

Lastly, it is important to examine polling data to understand voter opinion about felon disenfranchisement. After all, in a representative republic, the views of leaders are merely views that are at least tacitly endorsed, if not entirely supported by the electorate. The previously mentioned executive order in Kentucky (enacted by a Democratic governor and suspended by the subsequent Republican governor), enacted a policy supported by two-thirds of voters in the heavily Republican state, according to one poll. Another poll found bipartisan disapproval of the idea that currently incarcerated people should be permitted to vote, but disapproval among Republicans was 85 percent, compared to 60 percent disapproval among Democrats (Kim 2019). Generally, Republican voters support the restoration of voting rights for felons who have completed all aspects of their sentences, but considerably less enthusiasm for more aggressive re-enfranchisement attempts.

DEMOCRATS ON FELON DISENFRANCHISEMENT

Democratic views on felon disenfranchisement fall on a spectrum that ranges from moderately to strongly progressive. Those who are moderately progressive on the issue take the position that once prisoners have served their sentence, they should have the right to vote. But there is disagreement over what it means to serve a sentence. Parole, for example, is a non-incarceration extension of an offender's sentence. If what the voting-rights adherent means is that the right to vote should be reinstated after incarceration and parole, then the individual is minimally progressive. This perspective is already law in twenty-one states. If the adherent is holding that voting rights should be restored after release from incarceration even if the former prisoner is on parole, then the individual is somewhat more progressive; nineteen states allow former prisoners, including those on parole, to vote.

The most progressive position is to allow prisoners to vote while they are incarcerated. As of March 2022, only the District of Columbia and two states, Vermont and Maine, allow incarcerated individuals to vote. This strongly progressive end of the spectrum is represented by the views of Vermont Senator Bernie Sanders, who ran for the Democratic Party presidential nomination in 2020. Sanders believes that individuals incarcerated in prisons and jails should be allowed to vote in every state. His reasoning is that the right to vote is an inalienable and universal right of all citizens, one that cannot be invalidated by being incarcerated. Another candidate vying for the Democratic presidential nomination was Beto O'Rourke, former congressman from Texas. O'Rourke did not go as far as Sanders in saying that all prisoners should be allowed to vote, but he stated that he favored restoring voting rights for prisoners convicted of nonviolent crimes.

No other Democratic contender for the presidential nomination in 2020 went as far as Sanders or O'Rourke in championing prisoner voting rights. All other candidates staked out a more moderately progressive position that favored restoring voting rights once prisoners had completed their sentences. Senator Elizabeth Warren of Massachusetts stated that restoring voting rights for former prisoners who have served their sentence and restoring rights for those who are still in prison are two different issues. She indicated that she was in favor of restoring voting rights for the first group. For the second, however, she would only go as far as saying that it is an issue about which a "conversation" should be held. It was not clear whether Warren was referring to restoring voting rights for those released from prison even if they were on parole or for those who had also completed their parole. Another Democrat vying for the party's nomination was Pete Buttigieg, mayor of South Bend, Indiana. He stated that he believed that voting rights should be restored for prisoners released from incarceration. With respect to those still serving sentences, however, Buttigieg stated that he believed disenfranchisement to be part of their punishment for committing crime and that voting rights should not be restored to those individuals.

Given the outcome of the 2020 national elections, the positions of Democrats President Joe Biden and Vice President Kamala Harris are of special interest. Harris has staked out a position like that of Warren by saying that she favors restoring voting rights to those who have completed their sentences and that restoring voting rights to individuals who are still incarcerated is a conversation that should be held. However, as a former prosecutor, she has suggested that even if this were done for many prisoners, individuals who have been convicted of some violent crimes should not have their voting rights restored while they are incarcerated. President Biden has said that he favors restoring voting rights for felons after they have served their sentence, but like some other Democrats, it is not yet clear whether he believes that voting rights should be reinstated for those who are on parole.

One reason other high-profile Democrats have not joined Sanders and O'Rourke in favoring restoring voting rights for convicted felons while they are incarcerated is likely because most American voters appear to object to such policy. A national survey of registered voters in 2019 showed that 69 percent of poll participants objected. Among poll participants who were registered Democrats, 61 percent objected. Another 2019 poll found that 65 percent of respondents favored restoring voting rights for former prisoners after they had completed their sentences. These results suggest that the politically safest position for a Democratic Party politician is to favor voting rights restoration for those who have been released from prison but not for those still incarcerated.

The matter of restoring voting rights for felons is often viewed by Democrats as being closely related to the issue of racial justice. This is because of the disproportionate percentage of African Americans and Hispanics who have become involved in the criminal justice system. Democrats hold that Republican politicians have made efforts to construct various obstacles that make it more difficult for minorities to vote. One such obstacle is to prevent felons from voting, including those who have been released from incarceration and even those who are on parole. The Democrats' argument is that insofar as these efforts have succeeded, they have further disenfranchised Black and Hispanic voters.

Republicans often claim that one reason Democrats favor restoring voting rights for individuals who have served their sentence completely, are on parole, or even are still in prison is that those individuals are more likely to vote Democrat than Republican. Uggen and Manza (2002) found that in at least one case, a Republican presidential win would have not occurred if released felons had been allowed to vote nationwide. However, this study's conclusions have been brought into doubt by research findings indicating that prisoners and former prisoners actually vote at very reduced rates compared to other citizens. According to this additional research, even if there were more Democrat than Republican felons voting, that fact would be unlikely to alter the results of national elections due to low turnout.

Democrats' efforts to restore voting for former prisoners who are on parole have yielded considerable progress. State houses in Colorado and Nevada have passed laws allowing these individuals to vote. In California, Proposition 17, allowing parolees to vote, was passed in 2019. In Massachusetts, Democratic Party legislators have strenuously lobbied to alter the state constitution to allow incarcerated individuals to vote, which was the case in Massachusetts before the year 2000. If these efforts are successful, Massachusetts will join Vermont and Maine in allowing incarcerated individuals to vote.

In 2021, Senate Democrats proposed S. 481, the Democracy Restoration Act of 2021, which applies to parolees voting in federal elections. The Act states, in part, "The right to vote is the most basic constitutive act of citizenship. Regaining the right to vote reintegrates individuals with criminal convictions into free society, helping to enhance public safety." The Act was not passed by the 117th Congress. If not enacted, it seems likely that Democrats will continue to reintroduce it or a very similar bill in the 118th Congress. The introduction of S. 481 and similar legislation over the years is evidence that the Democratic Party as a whole supports the re-enfranchisement of the formerly incarcerated once they are released from prison, including those who are on parole.

FURTHER READING

Beckworth, Ryan Tegue. 2021. "GOP's Objection to Vote for Felons Imperils Its Own Supporters." *Bloomberg* June 30, 2021. https://www.bloomberg.com/news/articles/2021-06-3--gop-s-objection-to-vote-for-felons-imperils-its-own-supporters.

Brennan Center for Justice. 2022. "Voting Laws Roundup: February 2022." February 9, 2022. https://www.brennancenter.org/our-work/research-reports/voting-laws-roundup-february-2022.

Byrd, Roger, and Harvey McCloud. 2021. *Sisyphus No More: The Case for Prison Education.* Lanham, MD: Rowman and Littlefield.

Civil Death. 2008. *West's Encyclopedia of American Law.* 2nd edition. https://legal-dictionary.thefreedictionary.com/civil+death. Accessed May 30, 2022.

Clark, Lesley. 2019. "The Dems' Voting Bill that McConnell Hates Could Impact his Re- election in Kentucky." *McClatchyDC*, February 1, 2019. https://www.mcclatchydc.com/news/politics-government/election/article225344310.html.

Clegg, Roger, and Hans A. von Spakovsky. 2018. "There Are Good Reasons for Felons to Lose the Right to Vote." *Heritage Foundation*, April 10, 2018. https://www.heritage.org/election-integrity/commentary/there-are-good-reasons-felons-lose-the-right-vote.

Gardner, Amy. 2019. "Text: Florida Agreed to Let Felons Vote. No Republicans Are Trying to Limit Who Is Eligible." *Washington Post*, March 26, 2019. https://www.washingtonpost.com/politics/florida-agreed-to-let-felons-vote-now-republicans-are-trying-to-limit-who-is-eligible/2019/03/25/5b1f9674-4cd9-11e9-93d0-64dbcf38ba41_story.html.

The Guardian. 2020. "Text: How Republicans Gutted the Biggest Voting Rights Victory in Recent History." August 6, 2020. https://www.theguardian.com/us-news/2020/aug/06/republicans-florida-amendment-4-voting-rights?CMP=Share_iOSApp_Other.

Hinton, Elizabeth, LaShae Henderson, and Cindy Reed. 2018. *An Unjust Burden: The Disparate Treatment of Black Americans in the Criminal Justice System.* New York: Vera Institute of Justice.

Kennedy, Ellen J. 2022. "Being Denied Voting Rights Is a Form of 'Civil Death.'" *MinnPost.* September 9, 2022. https://www.minnpost.com/community-voices/2022/09/being-denied-voting-rights-is-a-form-of-civil-death/.

Kim, Catherine. "A Majority of American Don't Want to Give Imprisoned Felons the Right to Vote." *Vox*, May 3, 2019. https://www.vox.com/2019/5/3/18528319/poll-felons-right-to-vote.

Moomaw, Graham. 2022. "Republicans Fall in Line Against Final Push to Expand Felon Voting Rights in Virginia." *Virginia Mercury*, March 3, 2022. https://www.virginiamercury.

com/2022/03/03/republicans-fall-in-line-against-final-push-to-expand-felon-voting-rights-in-virginia.

NBC News. 2020. "Supreme Court Won't Change Florida Voting Rules for Felons." July 17, 2020. https://www.nbcnews.com/politics/supreme-court/supreme-court-won-t-change-florida-voting-rules-felons-n1234071.

Powell, Lauren Latterell. 2017. "Concealed Motives: Rethinking Fourteenth Amendment and Voting Rights Challenges to Felon Disenfranchisement." *Michigan Journal of Race & Law* 22, no. 2: 383–410. http://search.ebscohost.com/login.aspx?direct=true&AuthType=ip,shib&db=lgs&AN=126786498&site=eds-live&scope=site. Accessed July 8, 2022.

Shannon, Sarah, Christopher Uggen, Jason Schnittker, et al. 2017. "The Growth, Scope, and Spatial Distribution of People with Felony Records in the United States, 1948–2010." *Demography* 54: 1795–818. https://doi.org/10.1007/s13524-017-0611-1.

Uggen, Christopher, and Jeff Manza. 2002. "Democratic Contraction? Political Consequences of Felon Disenfranchisement in the United States." *American Sociological Review* 67, no. 6: 777–803. https://doi.org/10.2307/3088970.

Visser, Nick. 2020. "At Least 67,000 Felons Registered to Vote in Florida, Group Says." *Huffington Post*, October 20, 2020. https://www.huffpost.com/entry/florida-felons-vote_n_5f8e3783c5b66ee9a5f2b639.

CHAPTER 11

Gang Violence

SHERI JENKINS KEENAN, JEFFREY P. RUSH, AND KELLEN MCLAUGHLIN

AT A GLANCE

Republicans and Democrats have historically differed on criminal justice system responses to gangs and violent, gang-related crime. Throughout the history of gang violence legislation in the United States, each party has been steered by its own interests, often reflecting the social sentiments of its constituents. The two main areas of contention are gun control policies and immigration.

Regardless of their personal views on gun rights, most Americans are concerned about gun violence's role in gang violence. There is broad bipartisan support for more thorough background checks, with both parties also showing support for closing the "gun show loophole" that allows individuals to purchase firearms at gun shows without a background check. Although both parties claim to support revision of existing gun laws, debate between Democrats and Republicans continues with the proposal of an assault weapons ban and requiring psychological tests and screening for gun ownership. While Democrats advocate for legislation dubbed as "common sense gun reform," Republicans are generally opposed to a complete ban of assault weapons and mandatory psychological tests and screening for gun ownership.

Both parties also differ in their perceptions of immigration and gang violence. Most Republicans believe gangs like Mara Salvatrucha, a Latino gang commonly known as MS-13, exploit the US immigration system and are responsible for committing a disproportionate amount of the violent gun crime. As a result, Republicans advocate for tougher policies on immigration. In the 2016 and 2020 election cycles, Republicans at the federal level and state level used brutal images of gang violence in their campaign advertisements to gain public support. Republicans effectively link migrants, crime, and gang violence in the minds of many voters. Most Democrats favor policies that allow more pathways for potential immigrants and are less likely to associate migration with increased gang violence.

MANY REPUBLICANS...

- Believe that making gun legislation more restrictive would do little to address gang violence.
- Believe weak immigration laws, lax policies, and lack of a secure southern border (i.e., fence or wall) allow the entry of gang members, especially Latino gang members, into the United States.
- Believe gang involvement is driven by socio-psychological factors and that an open immigration system would contribute to the proliferation of these issues.

MANY DEMOCRATS...

- Believe gang violence, especially gun violence, could be mitigated by stricter gun regulations.
- Believe that strengthening immigration policies and building a physical barrier at the southern border would do little to reduce gang violence.
- Believe gang involvement is driven by socio-psychological factors and that gang prevention and intervention programs could reduce gang involvement and gang violence.

OVERVIEW

Roughly 33,000 violent street gangs, motorcycle gangs, and prison gangs are criminally active in the United States. Many are sophisticated and well organized, and all use violence to control neighborhoods and increase their illegal money-making activities such as robbery, drugs, gun violence, prostitution, fraud, and human trafficking.

Gangs "incite fear and violence within our communities" (Knox, Etter, and Smith 2019, 225) and most people associate gangs with violence, crime, guns, and drugs. In almost every major city, gangs are involved in 50 percent of all reported violent crime, and violence by gangs is significant and consistent. Although the violent crime rate (number of violent crimes per 100,000 people) declined from 383.4 in 2018 to 380.8 in 2019, it increased in 2020 to 398.5, the highest since 2010. Gang violence likely contributed to this growth in violence.

In the United States, the emergence of gang activity happened at different times based on geography. Gang emergence in the Northeast and Midwest was fueled by immigration and poverty, with migrants first arriving from Northern and Western Europe. In the West, gangs were fueled by westward expansion and Mexican migrations. These immigrant communities were met with overwhelmed housing and welfare capacities of American cities, which created slum conditions, increased crime rates, and contributed to the development of gangs (Riis 1969). This correlation between immigration, poverty, and the subsequent emergence of gangs provides a historical context for modern Republicans' connection between lax immigration policies and gang violence.

Criminal street gangs emerged around 1820 with the formation of groups like "The Forty Thieves," considered the first important and decisively dangerous gang (Howell

1991; Sante 1991). As organized gangs began to establish their reputations and control their membership, they drew the attention of the American public through police standoffs and innocent civilians caught in the crossfire of rivaling groups. This evolution of gun violence alongside gang violence contributes to contemporary Democrat calls for increased "common sense" gun reform.

One major difficulty legislators face when addressing gang violence is that the definitions of "gang," "gang member," and "gang violence" can vary widely across jurisdictions. Various types of gangs exist, including youth gangs, institutionalized street gangs, prison gangs, and drug trafficking organizations, and the types of activities these groups engage in are just as varied. Most legislation policy across time has focused on "street gangs" and the violent crimes these groups commit. Both citizens and policymakers are especially concerned about these offenses because their perpetration increases resident fear and significantly impacts the community's ability to effectively implement mechanisms of informal social control.

Many jurisdictions rely on the National Gang Center's definition of a "gang," a description that originated from California in the 1990s as a response to gang wars concerning turf and drug trafficking. The following criteria outlines the federal definition of a gang:

- The group has three or more members, generally aged twelve to twenty-four;
- Members share an identity, typically linked to a name, and often other symbols;
- Members view themselves as a gang, and they are recognized by others as a gang;
- The group has some permanence and a degree of organization;
- The group is involved in an elevated level of criminal activity.

Law enforcement agencies believe a group name, group identity, criminal activity, and the use of symbols and signs to represent the group to others to be the most important characteristics of defining a group as a gang (National Institute of Justice 2011).

The definition of "gang member" is also inconsistent across jurisdictions; policymakers often utilize definitions that are "unique to their locality and its explicit gang-related challenges" (National Institute of Justice 2011). Common points to defining a gang member are an admittance to gang involvement from the individual, being identified as a gang member by a reliable witness (often a parent or a guardian), and having identifiable symbols associated with the gang such as clothing or tattoos. Developing a way to define a "gang member" is critical for communities to identify them, to develop effective strategies to handle them, and to effectively prosecute them.

Defining "gang violence" is critical for measuring it and for developing effective policies to address it. Many state definitions specify that the violence must have been committed with the knowledge that it might further the individual's standing in a gang or that a reliable witness could identify the violence as gang activity. Jurisdictions use the terms "gang-involved," "gang-related," or "gang-motivated," and often erroneously use these terms interchangeably when they should be distinct. The distinction among these terms relates to the gang member's intent or motive and whether the violence is related to their status as a gang member.

Some jurisdictions refer to violence committed by a gang member that is irrelevant to their status as a gang member as "gang-involved" or "gang-related." Violence committed with an intent or motive directly related to the offender's gang membership (or potential gang membership) is often termed "gang-motivated." This is the type of gang violence about which jurisdictions should be most concerned because it is directly linked to gang membership. These types of crimes include violence between rival gangs (e.g., drive-by shootings) or crimes committed on behalf of the gang (e.g., carjackings, assaults, homicides).

When examining the presence of gangs in US history, the late 1980s emerge as a point in which gang violence began to grow exponentially. The following decade was characterized by rising rates of gang violence, and many legislative policies throughout the 1990s consisted of a bipartisan intent to be "tough on crime." Accompanying public and media pressure for legislative action during this time pushed for the creation of youth and gang-specific agencies and units, mandatory sentencing, harsher sentencing structures, and increased incarceration. Republicans responded to these cries through the Crime Control Act of 1990 and the Violent Crime Control and Law Enforcement Act of 1994, attempting to mitigate the increasing youth crime throughout the country. During the early part of the 1990s, most policy was bipartisan, with Democrats and Republicans finding common ground on tough on crime policies through the Bush and Clinton administrations.

Father Gregory Boyle's "Kindness" Approach to Rehabilitation

Long before his organization Homeboy Industries became recognized nationwide as the recipient of the Conrad N. Hilton Humanitarian Prize in 2020, Father Gregory Boyle of California was touching the lives of those left behind by legislation. A Jesuit priest, Father Gregory Boyle emphasizes the "importance of kindness" when rehabilitating gang members, an effort he expanded throughout the streets of Los Angeles.

Speaking to *Boston College Magazine*, Boyle recounts that Homeboy Industries has "help(ed) more than 10,000 people change their lives in concrete ways, including through substance-abuse assistance, mental-health support, and tattoo removal." These practices work to address the cracks that federal and state gang-related policies often fail to fill and focus on preventative measures and the rehabilitation of former gang members that is often left to organizations like Boyle's.

Homeboy Industries is one of the most widespread gang intervention and rehabilitation programs in the United States. Boyle advocates that "kindness is a universal language," one that politicians on both sides of the aisle should learn how to speak (*Boston College Magazine* 2022).

Understanding bipartisanship is crucial to grasping the history of gang violence legislation in the United States. While the parties are driven by their own interests, history often shows them steering toward a mutual consensus. Take 2005, for example: under the Bush administration, this year saw the establishment of the National Gang Intelligence

Center (NGIC) to help curb the growth of gangs and related criminal activity. The NGIC was established to support law enforcement agencies through timely and accurate information sharing and to provide strategic and tactical analysis to federal, state, and local law enforcement. A multiagency center, the NGIC integrates its resources to investigate and study the growth, migration, criminal activity, and association of gangs that pose a significant threat to the United States. Composed of representatives from the FBI, the Drug Enforcement Administration, the Bureau of Alcohol, Tobacco, Firearms, and Explosives, the Bureau of Prisons, the U.S. Marshals Service, the Department of Defense, and Customs and Border Protection, historians can see how the gun control interests of Democrats and the border control interests of Republicans reflected in this bipartisan effort. Although both parties have developed policy responses to address gang violence, each party approaches the problem guided by party-specific beliefs about gangs, reasons for gang membership, gang members, and gang violence.

REPUBLICANS ON GANG VIOLENCE

In general, Republicans believe a person's decision to join a gang is a rational choice, guided by that person's free will. They argue that this choice is based on employment decisions, opportunities to improve illegal productivity, and to increase fun, social standing, prestige, and status with other youth. Similarly, Republicans argue that youth receive personal advantages from joining gangs; youth join gangs because membership provides attractive opportunities such as the chance for excitement by selling drugs and making money.

At the beginning of the 1980s, Republican President Ronald Reagan's Violent Crime Task Force, chaired by Attorney General William Smith, was unconcerned about the root causes of crime and recommended increased control and interdiction efforts, increased prosecution of drug cases, and replacing parole with mandatory sentencing. This reflected the Republican-steered War on Drugs, intertwining the issues of the illegal drug trade and gang violence in the minds of the country's conservatives. This desire to mitigate drug flow to and throughout the United States subsequently dominated Republican policy on gangs during the early 1980s.

The mid- to late-1980s were characterized by rising rates of violence, including gang violence, and many legislative policies during this decade intended to be tough on crime. Republicans responded to increasing youth crime and gang involvement in violent crime, and the accompanying public and media pressure for legislative action during this time by pushing for increased law enforcement involvement, the creation of youth and or gang-specific agencies and units, mandatory sentencing, harsher sentencing structures, and increased incarceration. Tough on crime policies like "three strikes and you're out," and "truth-in-sentencing" were enacted to target gang wars in urban areas as groups fought to secure status and territories in drug trafficking.

Existing at the intersection between Reagan's War on Drugs and gang-related policy in the United States is the Anti-Drug Abuse Act of 1986. This piece of legislation steepened the funding that law enforcement received and introduced strict prison sentences for nonviolent offenses (Eisen 2019). In some cases, possession of crack cocaine resulted in life imprisonment. Though Democrats would go on to pass the extensive 1994 crime bill that echoed many of Reagan's practices, liberal critics pointed out that this War on Drugs criminalized many American communities without providing a financial backing to tackle the more violent nature of gang-related activity.

During the War on Drugs, which intended to cease the flow of narcotics into the United States from the southern border, President Reagan implemented immigration policies that benefitted undocumented immigrants already in the country. The Immigration Reform and Control Act of 1986 (also known as IRCA) was the last federal amnesty program for undocumented immigrants, allowing people who had arrived before 1982 and were actively employed to apply for citizenship without fear of deportation.

In 1988, Reagan signed into law the Omnibus Anti-Drug Abuse Act, which implemented the Youth Gang Drug Prevention Program (YGDPP) through the Administration for Children, Youth, and Families, US Department of Health and Human Services. The purpose of the YGDPP was to serve youth at risk of gang and drug involvement because of problems in school, being in a low-income and/or a single parent household, lacking a support system, and with a history of delinquency. This program funded sixteen consortium projects for three years and added nine more projects in 1992 under the presidency of Republican George H. W. Bush with funding for five years at up to $750,000 per year. This federally initiated, coordinated, and monitored strategy to combat gang crime was historically unprecedented.

Many of the projects under this program developed and implemented social intervention strategies consisting of family education, peer counseling, mentoring, youth empowerment, recreation, community restitution, and crisis intervention. Priority funding was also given to programs that targeted female youth, families with intergenerational gang involvement, and youth gangs characterized by refugee and/or immigrant involvement. While a national evaluation (Cohen, Williams, Bekelman, and Crosse 1995) found local programs to be generally effective to reduce drug involvement and delinquency, they were not as effective to reduce or prevent gang involvement. The gang component of the YGDPP was discontinued in 1995.

Elected in 1988, Republican President George H. W. Bush, former vice president to his predecessor, Reagan, had campaigned on an anti-crime, pro-victim platform. With his victory, the War on Drugs and War on Crime sentencing policies of the Reagan era continued into the 1990s. In 1991, for example, the U.S. Sentencing Commission recommended that Congress revisit mandatory minimums, especially the discrepancy between crack and power cocaine. The Republican-controlled Congress overrode the recommendation. In 1993 the National Rifle Association announced it would launch a national campaign to get tough on crime and the first Three Strikes and You're Out laws were enacted. In 1994, James (Jim) Wootton (R) had helped create the Violent Crime Control and Law Enforcement Act, which created the Violent Offender Incarceration and Truth in Sentencing Program; the first law requiring "truth in sentencing" in the United States was passed by Washington State in 1984. Finally, near the end of the Bush administration Attorney General William Barr (R) ran a campaign for further toughening America's penal policies.

In 1991, a program to reduce gang membership was developed by law enforcement officers in Phoenix, Arizona. Throughout the mid-1990a, the Gang Resistance Education and Training (G.R.E.A.T) program was integrated into the curriculum of schools throughout the greater Phoenix area. This program worked as a "gang- and delinquency-prevention program," with the goal of improving the relationship between school-aged children and police officers (Esbensen et al. 2011). Although the G.R.E.A.T. program did not have an extensive theoretical or empirical backing, the curriculum provided a basic structure that was easy to replicate. As a result, the program expanded into schools nationwide under the Bush administration between 1991 and 1993. Evaluations from the National Institute of Justice were ordered under the subsequent Clinton administration, aimed at assessing the role this program played in preventing American children from falling victim to the "school to prison" pipeline. The National Evaluation of G.R.E.A.T in 1994 found that, although risk-seeking behaviors decreased and negative views on gangs increased among children who went through the program, the program did not significantly impact whether a child joined a gang or not (Esbensen et al. 2011). Regardless, G.R.E.A.T. has become an integral part of curriculum across the country, educating children about gang violence as early as elementary school.

While the Clinton administration dominated federal gang-related legislation throughout the mid- to late-1990s, Republicans on the state level continued to push their policies forward. Governor Jim Edgar of Illinois, for example, initiated a Commission on Gangs in 1995, creating a thirty-five-member group to tackle gang violence from a holistic, community approach (Office of Juvenile Justice n.d.). This commission garnered a wide array of perspectives, interviewing victims of gang violence over the course of sixteen public hearings and ultimately producing a recommendation for Governor Jim Edgar on how best to handle gang violence in the state. Accordingly, the Republican governor passed legislation that expanded Illinois' witness protection program, allocating almost $1 million for a program to protect those who testified against gang members (Office of Juvenile Justice n.d.). Following Republican trends throughout the 1980s and 1990s, this state legislation also focused on continuing the harsh prison sentences for violent gang-related activity as well as drug charges.

George Bush's gang violence policy built its foundation on the idea that the United States should "reclaim (its) neighborhoods and (its) streets" (White House Archives n.d.). Much of the Bush administration's focus centered on reducing gun violence and implementing harsher consequences for federal firearms crimes and sales. Continuing in this effort, Bush advocated for the Advancing Justice Through DNA Technology initiative, which was a $1 billion program that worked to identify gang members through DNA samples and other STEM-related evidence. Especially in the wake of events such as 9/11, proposed programs such as these received political criticism as the privacy of American households was threatened. Others revere President Bush's efforts in funding programs that protected women from domestic abuse and provided families with expanded services against gang violence (White House Archives n.d.).

Contemporary Republican attitudes on gang violence have tied the historical issue of illegal drug trade to immigration. In 2015, Republican President Donald J. Trump ran on an anti-gang platform that linked with his anti-immigration efforts. Trump's calls for a border wall to increase national security linked the inflow of immigrants with the inflow of drugs and gang members. Once elected to office, Trump's attack on former president

Barack Obama's immigration legislation proved to be steered by a desire to eliminate the threat of gangs from the United States. Republican voters today follow the rationale that strong borders will beget decreased gang activity; much of the party's policy on gang violence centers around immigration accordingly.

DEMOCRATS ON GANG VIOLENCE

In general, Democrats believe that youth become involved with gangs to deal with or escape abuse, neglect, family and neighborhood dysfunction, classism, and racism. They argue that social, economic, and cultural forces push youth toward gang involvement. Democrats argue that those feelings of marginality give youth no choice but to join gangs for social relationships, a sense of identity, to solve social adjustment problems, and to cope with the normal trials and tribulations of adolescence.

Historically, Democrats have criticized law enforcement's targeting of youth gang members, citing lack of federal support for disorganized neighborhoods, education systems, employment opportunities, drug use, poverty, and racism as the causes of increasing gang violence cases.

In 1976, President Jimmy Carter ran on a campaign of tackling criminal activity from a socioeconomic standpoint. Carter's administration worked to reduce unemployment through social programs and benefits across the United States, a focus they believed would result in decreased rates of criminal gang activity in the country. Jimmy Carter also set the scene for contemporary Democrats and their views on gun control, campaigning on the promise that he would favor a national registration of handguns as well as prohibit the ownership of guns by those who had been previously convicted of a crime (Ford Library Museum 1976).

By many standards, Jimmy Carter's record on immigration matched his successor, Ronald Reagan, and resonated with both Democrats and Republicans of the time. While instituting programs such as the Federal Refugee Resettlement Program to help with the influx of refugees in the aftermath of the Vietnam War, Carter also pushed Congress to pass stricter legislation on the hiring of undocumented Americans. Though the Carter administration believed unemployment was a primary factor that drove criminal gang violence in the United States, historians point out that the president's calls to further prohibit the employment of undocumented immigrants contradicts with his campaign statements.

In 1994, Democratic President William Jefferson "Bill" Clinton, signed into law the Violent Crime Control and Law Enforcement Act, intending to help prisoners find housing, drug treatment, mental health counseling, job training, and education. Historians point out the dual nature of this bill's complicated legacy: on one hand, the 1994 crime bill provided protections for gang-ridden communities and victims of domestic abuse, but on the other hand, it drove more Americans than ever into the "net of the criminal justice system" (Eisen 2019). As the Clinton administration codified the mass incarceration that had begun under Reagan's leadership, fear continued to build in American homes, especially in impoverished communities already struggling under the thumb of gang violence. Though this bill worked to ban types of semiautomatic assault weapons and created the Violence Against Women Act, both of which Democrats champion as a major win for human rights, critics of the Clinton administration argue that this investment in the construction of prisons in the United States could have been allocated to gang preventive measures instead. The 1994 Violent Crime Control bill remains the largest piece of federal crime legislation (Eisen 2019).

In 1998, the National Alliance of Gang Investigators' Associations (NAGIA) was formed. With more than 20,000 members representing twenty-three states and regional gang investigator associations across the country, the NAGIA is a cooperative organization that integrates the expertise of gang investigators nationwide and combines multiple resources to combat the threat gangs pose to national security. Democrats have historically believed in a consolidated federal approach to mitigating gang violence, often starting with the socioeconomic factors that steer youth to entering gangs in the first place. They argue that gangs are a natural and/or normal response to social ills and that those social ills need to be targeted, not the youth.

Furthermore, most Democrats argue that "get tough-on-crime" tactics have long been proven to do little to reduce gang violence. Though Democrats throughout the 1990s contributed to bipartisan efforts and were virtually indistinguishable from Republicans in their support of "get tough" approaches, modern Democrats point out cracks in this system. During the Bush administration, Democrats asserted that policies that aim to burden taxpayers, keep prison beds occupied, and line the pockets of for-profit prisoners and their contractors do nothing but traumatize the American public, especially low-income children of color. In addition, they argue policies like "get tough-on-crime," "Three Strikes and You're Out," and "truth-in-sentencing" are unconstitutional, ignore science and best practices, ignore equity and justice and the science around youth development.

Much of contemporary action by the Democrats seeks to address the factors of identity behind historical gang violence policy. In 2010, Democratic President Barack Obama signed into law the Fair Sentencing Act, which reduced the disparity in sentences between crack and powder cocaine. Democrats argue that marginalized communities in the United States are much more likely to be profiled as gang members and serve longer prison sentences accordingly. While seeking rehabilitation for these people, Democrats argue that the weapons gang members utilize in their institutionalized violence, including assault rifles, should be the issue of contention.

A fair amount of bipartisan legislation has been spearheaded by Democratic administrations hoping to target gang violence. In 2007, Democrat Adam Schiff introduced The Gang Prevention, Intervention, and Suppression Act bipartisan legislation to halt gang violence. This Act would provide new resources for community-based gang prevention and intervention activities. Democrat Attorney General Eric Holder initiated the Smart on Crime Initiative in 2013, which diverted nonviolent, low-level drug offenders to treatment instead of jail. Another bipartisan effort by Democrats took place during the Trump administration when Democrat Gerry Connolly and Republican John Rutherford introduced the Preventing Gang Violence Act that codified a community-based violence prevention grants program.

Like state-level Republican-led community efforts to address gang violence, President Obama is remembered for his restorative, cooperative approach to crime in the United

States, which garnered both praise and criticism. In 2014, President Obama created an eleven-member "task force on 21st century policy" to improve the relationship between law enforcement officers and the American public, specifically, marginalized groups that had suffered from tactics deemed as "racial profiling." The Obama administration emphasized training and education for law enforcement officers on the front lines of America's gang issues. Democrats during the 2010s steered resources toward local governments, prompting local agencies to use the funds to improve the infrastructure and organization of policing throughout the country (Community Oriented Policing Services 2015).

Obama's approach to immigration prompted some to label him the "Deporter-in-Chief," while others cited his leadership for the rise of gangs such as MS-13. Democratic support for legislation such as the D.R.E.A.M. Act and Obama's DACA policy served as a beacon of hope for many undocumented Americans, but these strides in a more "open-border" approach were met with the reality of the Obama administration deporting more immigrants than any previous presidential administration. These deported individuals, many of whom built families and paid taxes within US borders, were often sent back to countries where they faced gang violence. Many Democrats grew frustrated with Obama's extensive deporting policies, arguing that the administration targeted families and workers rather than the undocumented gang members on the streets.

The contemporary Democratic Party seems to be shifting on the lines of gang-related policy. With the election of Democratic President Joseph R. Biden in 2020, many Democratic voters criticize lifelong Democratic politicians and their support for bills that have worked against American communities, especially people of color. Biden, for example, has faced criticism for the negative consequences of the 1994 crime bill, a piece of legislation that he supported over the course of his career in Congress. In addition, young Democrats perceive that Democratic Vice President Kamala Harris has broken down some barriers, but erected others with her tough record on nonviolent crimes during her time as the District Attorney of California. Regardless, most Democrats resonate with the efforts of politicians like Democratic New Jersey Senator Cory Booker, who has worked to reintroduce the Reverse Mass Incarceration Act to the Congressional scene. This legislation lays out a strategy for disincentivizing efforts to fill prison beds; instead, this money is reallocated to states' public safety programs, hoping to decrease crime from gangs at its source. Many Democrats also support the Second Chance Act from the late 1980s, believing efforts such as these will crack down on gang violence through preventative measures rather than relying on the prison system. Aimed at ending the "school-to-prison pipeline," these community-based efforts epitomize modern Democrats and their views toward gang violence policy.

FURTHER READING

Boston College Magazine. 2022. "As Told To: Fr. Gregory Boyle SM '84." Winter 2022. https://www.bc.edu/content/bc-web/sites/bc-magazine/winter-2022/linden-lane/as-told-to-father-gregory-boyle.html.

Cohen, Marcia I., K. Williams, A. M. Bekelman, and S. Crosse. 1995. "Evaluation of the National Youth Gang Drug Prevention Program." In *The Modern Gang Reader*, edited by Malcolm W. Klein and Cheryl L. Maxson, 266–75. Los Angeles: Roxbury, 1995.

Community Oriented Policing Services. 2015. "The President's Task Force on 21st Century Policing." https://cops.usdoj.gov/RIC/Publications/cops-p341-pub.pdf. Accessed September 17, 2022.

Esbensen, Finn-Aage, Dana Peterson, Terrance J. Taylor, Adrienne Freng, D. Wayne Osgood, Dena C. Carson, and Kristy N. Matsuda. 2011. "Evaluation and Evolution of the Gang Resistance Education and Training (G.R.E.A.T.) Program." *Journal of School Violence* 10: 53–70. https://www.nationalgangcenter.gov/content/documents/great-evaluation-and-evolution.pdf.

Eisen, Lauren-Brooke. 2019. "The 1994 Crime Bill and Beyond: How Federal Funding Shapes the Criminal Justice System." Brennan Center for Justice, September 9, 2019. https://www.brennancenter.org/our-work/analysis-opinion/1994-crime-bill-and-beyond-how-federal-funding-shapes-criminal-justice.

FBI. 2019. "2019 Crime in the United States." https://ucr.fbi.gov/crime-in-the-u.s/2019/preliminary-report/home. Accessed September 15, 2022.

Ford Library Museum. 1976. "First Debate: Carter and Crime." September 21, 1976. https://www.fordlibrarymuseum.gov/library/document/0010/1554405.pdf.

Howell, James C. 1991. *Gangs in America's Communities*. Thousand Oaks, CA: Sage.

Klein, Malcolm W., and Cheryl L. Maxson. 2006. *Street Gang Patterns and Policies*. New York: Oxford Press.

Knox, George, Gregg Etter, and Carter F. Smith. 2019. *Gangs and Organized Crime*. New York: Taylor and Francis.

National Gang Intelligence Center. 2015. *2015 National Gang Report*. Federal Bureau of Investigations (FBI). https://www.fbi.gov/file-repository/stats-services-publications-national-gang-report-2015.pdf/view. Accessed September 11, 2022.

National Institute of Justice. 2011. "What Is a Gang? Definitions." Department of Justice. https://nij.ojp.gov/topics/articles/what-gang-definitions#:~:text=Defining%20%22youth%20gangs%22&text=Members%20share%20an%20identity%2C%20typically,elevated%20level%20of%20criminal%20activity. Accessed September 12, 2022.

Office of Juvenile Justice and Delinquency Prevention. n.d. "Juvenile Justice Reform Initiatives in the States: 1994–1996." https://ojjdp.ojp.gov/sites/g/files/xyckuh176/files/pubs/reform2/ch2_e.html. Accessed September 12, 2022.

Riis, Jacob A. 1969. *The Battle with the Slum*. Montclair, NJ: Paterson Smith.

Sante, Lucy 1991. *Low Life: Lures and Snares of Old New York*. New York: Vintage Books.

The White House Archives. n.d. "President George W. Bush: Fighting Crime." https://georgewbush-whitehouse.archives.gov/infocus/achievement/chap16.html. Accessed September 11, 2022.

CHAPTER 12

Gun Control

ANGELA D. MADDEN AND OLIVIA A. EASON

AT A GLANCE

Gun control refers to policy-based and legislative efforts to manage the manufacture, sale, ownership, and use of firearms. Opponents of gun control believe that the Second Amendment to the US Constitution provides citizens with certain rights related to gun ownership and use. The Second Amendment states that, "A well-regulated Militia, being necessary to the security of a free State, the right of the people to keep and bear Arms, shall not be infringed." Opponents (primarily Republican) argue that minimal restrictions on the manufacture, sale, purchase, ownership, and use of guns allow more people to purchase, own, carry, and use guns, which makes communities safer. Proponents (primarily Democrat) argue that strict laws and strong policies are necessary to regulate gun manufacture, sale, ownership, and use because gun crime is a direct threat to individual and community safety. Aside from arguments about the intent of the Second Amendment, the primary issue in the gun control debate is whether unrestricted individual rights to gun sales, ownership, possession, and use threaten the "unalienable rights" of "life, liberty, and the pursuit of happiness" as described in the Declaration of Independence, and "the general welfare" of the people, as described in the Preamble to the US Constitution.

Until the late 1960s, most adults could purchase most firearms and ammunition from stores and through mail-order catalogs, and little legislation had been enacted regarding firearms (except to the extent that it banned or restricted Black ownership or possession). After a spate of violent demonstrations and high-profile assassinations with firearms, however, gun control became more widely debated with growing public awareness of the lack of firearm sale and possession regulation in America.

Although both Democrats and Republicans supported gun control measures until the early 1970s, conservative interpretations of the Second Amendment and the development of the National Rifle Association (NRA) into a powerful lobbying organization, led to an ideological shift in the Republican Party that placed it directly at odds with ideas about gun control, primarily advocated by the Democratic Party. That ideological chasm has only widened and deepened over the past sixty years as gun violence has grown and mass shootings have become almost commonplace. Unification behind gun control legislation becomes even more difficult during times of a divided Congress.

MANY REPUBLICANS...

- Believe that the Second Amendment guarantees an individual's right to own guns and oppose most efforts to restrict their manufacture, sale, purchase, ownership, carry, and use.
- Oppose efforts to restrict the manufacture and sale of firearms, including assault-style firearms, specialized equipment to make rapid firing easier, and high-capacity magazines.
- Support efforts to make it easier for people to conceal and carry firearms in public.
- View gun violence as a combination of social/spiritual decay and a mental health issue.

MANY DEMOCRATS...

- Support responsible and legal gun ownership with "common sense" gun legislation like universal background checks and "red flag" laws.
- Advocate for legislation to ban assault-style, rapid-fire guns with high-capacity magazines.
- Oppose efforts to make it easier for people to conceal and carry firearms in public.
- View the widespread availability of guns and easy access to guns as a primary contributor to increasing gun violence and gun-related suicides and homicides.

OVERVIEW

The intent of the Second Amendment as an absolute right underpins Republican thought about gun control. Democrats believe the right to keep and bear arms should be constrained in appropriate ways to provide for the general welfare of society. James Madison proposed the Second Amendment to protect militias (able-bodied white males aged eighteen–forty-five), armed ordinary civilians who banded together to protect their communities in cases of emergency. Although the Constitutional Convention in 1787 gave the federal government the power to establish a standing army, anti-federalists believed this would deprive states of the right to defend themselves against government oppression. They feared Congress would abuse its power of "organizing, arming, and disciplining the militia" by failing to keep the militia armed properly and that full-time soldiers would be used to oppress the people. Most people believed full-time armies should be reserved for foreign adversaries and that militia members should use their own weapons that most people owned because they were required for survival (hunting, self-protection).

Most Republicans argue that Madison and those who ratified the Bill of Rights intended for the Second Amendment to give *all people* the right to keep and bear arms since all people could be called upon to serve in a militia. Republicans also base gun rights arguments on the ideals of freedom from government regulation (i.e., liberty), and privacy from government intrusion into an individual decision. Democrats justify government regulation on a public safety basis; it is the primary job of any government to keep its citizens safe and the benefit to public safety from firearm regulation outweighs the cost to individual rights. Most Democrats agree that the Second Amendment confers the right to keep and bear arms but prefer to focus on advocating policies and legislation that favor the public's general welfare rights by imposing reasonable restrictions on the sale, purchase, ownership, and use of firearms. Gun control proponents believe that any Second Amendment right to gun ownership can, and should, be constrained like restrictions on other constitutional rights (e.g., limitations on First Amendment rights, "freedom of speech" and "freedom of the press").

For more than forty years after the Second Amendment was ratified, no legislation regulated private ownership of firearms among the white population. In 1837, however, Georgia passed a law banning many small weapons, including pistols. After a subsequent Second Amendment challenge to the constitutionality of this law in *Nunn v. State* (1 Ga. 243, 1846), the Georgia Supreme Court held that the state could not prohibit open carry. This first attempt at gun control became the first to be overturned on Second Amendment grounds.

"Black Codes" enacted by some southern states after the Civil War in 1865 and 1866, prohibited Black persons from bearing arms unless they had a license that was granted under discretionary authority of the white government. White citizens were under no such licensing requirement. Although the Civil Rights Act of 1866, the Freedmen's Bureau Act of 1866, the Fourteenth Amendment in 1868, and the Civil Rights Act of 1871 attempted to rectify this problem, restriction on Black ownership of firearms continued for more than ninety years.

Another major event to impact the gun control debate was the founding of the National Rifle Association (NRA) in 1871. Organized to improve American marksmanship in preparation for war, the NRA promotes itself as a champion of "training, education, and marksmanship." For a century after its founding, the NRA was largely apolitical. In fact, the NRA of the 1930s enthusiastically supported the federal government's first gun control laws such as the National Firearms Act of 1934 (NFA) and the Federal Firearms Act of 1938 (FFA), both signed into law by Democratic President Franklin D. Roosevelt. The group also backed the Gun Control Act of 1968, passed after the assassination of Democratic President John F. Kennedy, which regulated gun shipments and sales, banned some guns, and imposed prohibitions on purchases.

During the 1970s, the NRA's support for gun control efforts significantly shifted after a member, suspected of stockpiling illegal weapons, was paralyzed in a shooting by the Bureau of Alcohol, Tobacco, and Firearms (ATF). The NRA condemned the federal government and began promoting the stance that the Second Amendment protected individual rights to gun ownership (Coleman 2016). In 1975, it formed its Institute for Legislative Action (ILA) to lobby the government for gun rights legislation and installed Harlon Carter as its leader. Two years later at the annual NRA convention in Cincinnati, Ohio, a group of reformers led by Carter engaged in a coup known as the Revolt in Cincinnati (Seuss 2018). Frustrated by the current leadership's wavering stance on gun control and a desire to back away from politics, Carter and his reformers convinced 1,000 lifetime members to oust the existing leadership. Carter was elected executive vice president and immediately adopted a "no compromise," "no gun legislation" defense of the Second Amendment's right to bear arms. Since 1977, the NRA's legislative agenda has focused almost exclusively on opposing any form of gun control and has become increasingly associated with the Republican Party.

No major gun control legislation was passed from 1981 to 1992 during the administrations of Republican Presidents Ronald Reagan and George H. W. Bush. Instead, the Firearm Owners' Protection Act of 1986, rolled back many restrictions enacted in prior decades, made it easier to sell firearms without a license, allowed the sale of firearms at gun shows, and banned any attempts to develop a comprehensive firearm registration system.

In contrast, the first two years of the first administration of Democratic President William Jefferson "Bill" Clinton was very active with the passage of the Brady Handgun Violence Prevention Act in 1993 and the Violent Crime Control and Law Enforcement Act in 1994. Gun control efforts were stymied, however, when the "Republican Revolution" during the midterm elections of 1994 led to the Republican Party gaining unified control of Congress for the first time since 1952 (Feuerherd 2018). The last couple of years of Clinton's second term, however, saw several civil suits against gun manufacturers and sellers and the decade ended with passage of legislation to require trigger locks, waiting periods, and background checks for gun show sales by federally licensed dealers. Sales by unlicensed dealers and online sales were not affected and this lack of regulation became known as the "gun show loophole."

From 2001 through 2008, during two administrations of Republican President George W. Bush, an assault weapons ban expired, gun-rights friendly laws were passed to shield firearm manufacturers from civil liability for crimes committed with their products, laws to restrict dissemination of information about gun sales and purchasers were passed, and the US Supreme Court bolstered Second Amendment arguments when it overturned a thirty-year ban on handguns in the District of Columbia in the 2008 landmark case, *District of Columbia v. Heller* (554 U.S. 570).

This gun rights trend continued under two administrations of Democratic President Barack Obama (2009–17) and one of Republican President Donald J. Trump (2017–21). Despite several high-profile mass shootings, rising rates of violent gun crime, and tragic examples that expose significant loopholes in existing legislation, a bipartisan bill proposed under the Obama administration to expand background checks failed to pass the Senate, a ban on a gun accessory that increases the rate of fire on semi-automatic weapons initiated under the Trump administration was overturned, and a New York law restricting concealed carry was struck down in 2022 by a conservative Supreme Court.

The most significant bipartisan gun control legislation in more than thirty years, the Bipartisan Safer Communities Act, was signed into law by Democratic President Joseph R. Biden in June 2022. Although a bill to ban assault weapons passed the House, Senate Republicans blocked the measure in December 2023, shortly after the United States broke the record for the most mass shootings in a single year. However, gun control advocates scored a major victory with a new U.S. Department of Justice rule to close the gun show "loophole" (Jackson 2024). Under this rule, gun dealers must obtain a federal license and conduct background checks regardless of where they sell their guns. Despite a more bipartisan show of support for restrictions, more recent data indicate that GOP support for strengthening gun laws is slipping (Long and Sanders 2023).

REPUBLICANS ON GUN CONTROL

Republican views on gun control are closely tied to the party's relationship with the NRA, although this was not always the case. Following a spate of gang violence in the late 1920s and early 1930s, the NRA supported gun permits and legislation proposed in 1934 and 1938 by the administration of Democratic President Franklin D. Roosevelt. It did, however, oppose limitations on pistols and revolvers and it was around this time that the organization began to take formal positions against a variety of gun control proposals such as a national gun registry.

After NRA support for the Gun Control Act of 1968 signed by Democratic President Lyndon B. Johnson divided its membership, the 1970's saw the NRA begin earnestly vocalizing the idea that guns *prevent* deaths and encouraged members to actively lobby elected officials against the "slippery slope" of gun rights restrictions. The slippery slope posits that *any* gun control law inevitably leads to mass confiscation of weapons. This tactic is frequently cited by conservative politicians to increase support for gun rights (Reese 2020). During this same decade, the NRA created its lobbying branch (the ILA) and the funding arm of its political action committee, the Political Victory Fund (NRA-PVF). In 1977, the Revolt at Cincinnati replaced many establishment leaders in the organization with activists whose goals included abolishing the newly formed ATF.

Shortly afterward, the organization began issuing "grades" for politicians based on their support for gun rights and urged members to vote accordingly (Achenbach, Higham, and Horwitz 2013). While politicians of both parties courted the organization and vied for NRA dollars, Republicans typically received more funding and support. The reinvigorated NRA quickly allied itself with the "New Right," conservatives within the Republican Party who prioritized social issues (Lacombe 2019). In 1992, 37 percent of NRA funds went to Democratic candidates, but by 2022, Democrats received $0 with 100 percent going to Republican candidates (Open Secrets n.d.).

Even after an assassination attempt on Republican President Ronald Reagan in 1981 wounded the president, two police officers, and Reagan's press secretary, James Brady, Reagan signed the Firearm Owner's Protection Act of 1986, rolling back many of the provisions of the Gun Control Act of 1968. It prohibited a national registry of dealer records, limited ATF inspections of dealers, redefined the meaning of "engaging in the business" of selling firearms, allowed licensed dealers to sell firearms at gun shows in their state, and loosened regulations on the sale/transfer of ammunition. It also expanded the definition of "silencer" and restricted transfer/possession of machine guns. Unsurprisingly, the legislation was supported by the NRA, but opposed by nearly every major law enforcement agency.

Although the relationship between the Republican Party and the NRA has been historically harmonious, some notable exceptions exist. Republicans who supported two bipartisan laws passed during the Clinton administration faced intense backlash, and after Wayne LaPierre, the NRA's outspoken executive vice president, attempted to raise money after the 1995 Oklahoma city bombing, former Republican president George H. W. Bush resigned his NRA membership. Hard feelings were resolved when the NRA supported Bush's son, George W. Bush, in his 2000 presidential bid. That same year at the NRA's annual convention, actor Charlton Heston uttered "from my cold dead hands," which became the rallying cry for both NRA and Republican gun rights arguments (Achenbach, Higham, and Horwitz 2013).

During the first two decades of the twenty-first century, the NRA and NRA-aligned Republican politicians discovered that financial support for gun rights organizations and elected officials skyrocketed as mass shootings became more common. Fundraising emails in the wake of shootings became commonplace. The threat of weapons bans by Democratic candidates was financially lucrative for both the NRA and the Republican Party. In 2008, however, gun rights proponents achieved a significant victory. In *District of Columbia v. Heller*, 554 U.S. 570, 2008, the US Supreme Court overturned a thirty-year-old handgun ban in the District of Columbia and held that the Second Amendment protects the right of an individual to bear arms. *Heller* was the result of a decades-long campaign by the NRA, other gun rights groups, and Republican luminaries such as former Republican president Reagan to codify the idea that the Second Amendment had been misinterpreted for centuries. Following this ruling, gun control laws across the country were overturned (Khan 2012).

The Republican Party platform in 2016/2020 affirmed the party's support of individual gun ownership for self-defense and defense of others. It denounced the potential appointment of "anti-gun" Supreme Court justices, encouraged reciprocity agreements among all states, and lent support to "constitutional carry" laws (i.e., without permit). Additionally, it opposed limits on magazine capacity, lawsuits against gun manufacturers, federal registration of firearms or ammunition, and limitations on assault weapons. The 2024 Republican National Convention in July 2024 altered nothing about these positions despite an assassination attempt on the Republican nominee just days before the meeting.

The 2016 National Convention hosted NRA chief lobbyist Chris Fox as the keynote speaker (Reese 2020). In turn, President Trump, recipient of $31 million in NRA campaign funds, gave the keynote address at the NRA-ILA's Leadership Forum that same year and spoke at the annual meeting each year of his presidency (Lacombe 2019). Although a Manhattan jury in February 2024 found the NRA, former CEO Wayne LaPierre, and two other high-ranking executives civilly liable for mismanagement and misuse of funds, the NRA remains a valuable ally to Republican candidates who advocate for gun rights (Mann and Bowman 2024).

The modern Republican is unabashedly pro-gun, although some have demonstrated appetite for moderate reforms following increasingly large-scale mass shootings in the past couple of decades. In 2008, for example, President Bush signed the National Instant Criminal Background Check Improvement Act, which required firearms dealers to conduct background checks to screen for individuals with certain mental health conditions. Even President Trump helped implement a gun control action. During the first year of his presidency, the deadliest mass shooting in modern American history occurred at a Las Vegas music festival when a man armed with twenty-four legally purchased firearms and more than 1,000 rounds of ammunition, killed 60 people, and injured 867 others. Most of the firearms were assault-type rifles, and some were fitted with "bump stocks" that allow a semi-automatic rifle to fire like a machine gun.

In response to this shooting and a subsequent mass shooting at Marjory Stoneman Douglas High School in Parkland, Florida, that claimed the lives of seventeen people, Trump expressed support for raising the minimum age to purchase certain types of rifles from eighteen to twenty-one, for "red flag" laws, and for expanded background checks although he took no legislative action on these matters. He did issue an executive order for the ATF to define bump stocks as "machine guns," which are heavily restricted. This de facto ban, which took effect in March 2019, required owners of existing bump stocks to surrender or destroy them. Despite surviving several challenges, the 5th Circuit Court of Appeals in New Orleans overturned the ban in January 2023, on the basis that the ATF did not have the authority from Congress to define a bump stock as a machine gun. In April 2023, the Biden administration appealed this decision to the US Supreme Court, which heard oral arguments in February 2024. On June 14, 2024, the Court upheld the 5th Circuit decision that the ATF exceeded its statutory authority and struck down the federal ban on bump stocks.

Following the killing of nineteen elementary age children and two teachers in Uvalde, Texas, Texas Republican Senator John Cornyn joined with fourteen other Senate Republicans and all Senate Democrats to pass the Bipartisan Safer Communities Act, signed into law on June 25, 2022. Fourteen House Republicans also voted for the measure, which increases federal funding for mental health services, school security, expands criminal background checks for gun buyers under twenty-one, expands the prohibitions on owning gun for individuals convicted of certain domestic violence offenses, and funds "red flag" programs (Longley 2023).

These bipartisan moves have not been without backlash. The Texas Republican Party formally rebuked Senator Cornyn for his part in the Bipartisan Safer Communities Act (Schonfeld 2022). Meanwhile, other high-profile Republicans responded to calls for gun control with a variety of alternatives for decreasing gun violence. After Uvalde, for example, both Texas Senator Ted Cruz and Texas Lt. Governor Dan Patrick stressed the importance of locking doors and having only one door in and out of schools. Conservative media companies suggested methods of "hardening" schools and other potential targets with things like ballistic blankets for classrooms, man traps at entrances, more widespread usage of bulletproof glass and metal detectors, and more armed police/civilian guards (Lim 2022).

One of Republicans' most prominently cited methods of addressing gun violence is based on former NRA executive vice president Wayne LaPierre's assertion that "the only thing that stops a bad guy with a gun, is a good guy with a gun," made in the aftermath of the 2012 shooting at Sandy Hook Elementary School, which killed twenty-six people. The idea that more armed citizens creates a safer society has been parroted by Republicans in the wake of shootings and calls for gun reform for the past decade (Lee 2019).

Georgia Schools Arm Teachers

Visitors to some schools in Laurens County, Georgia, are greeted by the following word on bright yellow signs: "Warning. Staff members are ARMED and TRAINED. Any attempt to harm children will be met by Deadly Force." In 2018, schools in the Laurens County School District in rural Georgia became the first in the state to take advantage of a 2014 Georgia law permitting the arming of teachers. Spurred by the Parkland school shooting just months prior, Superintendent Dan Brigman developed a program to train and arm volunteers with handguns in the hopes that they would be able to eliminate a school shooter. Potential participants must undergo a psychological evaluation, background check, and physical and mental training, and about 20 percent of applicants are rejected if they are on certain medication or have histories of mental health challenges. To date, no teachers have had to draw weapons, but one gun was stolen from the vehicle of a participating teacher at East Laurens High School just three days after the program was implemented. Although some are concerned, the program seems to have the support of most teachers, parents, and students (Broady 2019).

Republican voters seem to be developing more moderate views than their elected counterparts with a major increase in Republican support for some form of stricter gun laws. About half of polled Republican voters believe more restrictions should be in place (Page and Tran 2022). These voters are more divided when it comes to specific policies. According to the Pew Research Center, about 85 percent support tougher restrictions on gun ownership for individuals facing mental health challenges while only 37 percent support a ban on assault-style weapons. Nearly two-thirds (64 percent) oppose laws that allow concealed carry without a permit, which is at odds with the party platform's push for constitutional carry laws (Molla 2022).

Leading up to the 2022 midterms, gun control groups outraised gun rights groups \$35 million to \$29 million, respectively, and despite spending roughly \$13.7 million on federal races (\$2 million more than the three major gun control groups spent combined), many NRA-backed candidates performed poorly. The 2022 midterm elections, predicted to be a "red wave," reflected Republican voter support for moderate gun control and an NRA in shambles. Republicans failed to flip the Senate and only narrowly gained control of the House.

DEMOCRATS ON GUN CONTROL

In response to vicious gang violence resulting in thousands of gun deaths in the 1920s and early 1930s, Democratic President Franklin D. Roosevelt signed into law the federal government's first gun control laws, the National Firearms Act of 1934 (NFA) and the

Federal Firearms Act of 1938 (FFA). The NFA heavily taxed and regulated machine guns, sawed-off shotguns, and silencers, required gun owners to register with the federal government, and banned felons from owning weapons while the FFA limited gun sales across state lines, prohibited the sale of guns to fugitives and persons with violent felony convictions, and required gun sellers to be federally licensed and to maintain records on purchasers. The NFA was upheld in *U.S. v. Miller*, 307 US 174 (1939), when the Supreme Court ruled that short-barreled/sawed-off shotguns were not protected under the Second Amendment. This was the only federal case to specifically mention the Second Amendment until 2008.

For nearly thirty years, no significant gun control legislation was passed. During the 1960s, however, a spate of violent gun-involved demonstrations and high-profile assassinations such as that of Democratic President John F. Kennedy in 1963 led to the Gun Control Act of 1968, signed into law by Democratic President Lyndon B. Johnson. With widespread bipartisan support, this was the most comprehensive gun control law to date. It restricted the ability to ship guns across state lines, required an ID to purchase certain bullets, banned guns with "no sporting purpose," imposed age restrictions, prohibited felons, the mentally ill, and others from purchasing, required serial numbers, and imposed stricter licensing requirements. Although the original bill mandated a national registry of all guns and that all gun carriers be licensed, the NRA successfully lobbied against these parts of the legislation.

Proposed in 1988 during the Reagan administration and debated and voted on throughout the administration of President George H. W. Bush, the Brady Handgun Violence Prevention Act was signed into law by Democratic President Bill Clinton in 1993, twelve years after Brady was shot in an assassination attempt on Reagan in 1981. The Brady Act required background checks for purchases from licensed dealers, manufacturers, and importers, and established the National Instant Criminal Background Check System (NICS), run by the Federal Bureau of Investigation (FBI). It took five more years, until 1998, for NICS to be activated.

The Clinton administration also passed the Violent Crime Control and Law Enforcement Act of 1994, which contained the Public Safety and Recreational Firearms Use Protection Act banning certain assault weapons and "high capacity" magazines. A "sunset provision" led to this ban's expiration in September 2004, and it has not yet been revived despite repeated attempts. Restrictions on assault-style weapons, despite being supported by voters across the political spectrum, are stringently opposed by Republicans (and the NRA).

From 1997 to 1999, a flurry of legal activity focused on gun manufacture and sales. Several civil suits filed against gun manufacturers and sellers were dismissed. In Florida, however, the Supreme Court allowed an $11.5 million verdict against Kmart to stand after the store sold a rifle and ammunition to an intoxicated man who then shot and paralyzed his ex-girlfriend (*Kitchen v. Kmart Corporation*, 697 So. 2d 1997). Calling a firearm a "dangerous instrumentality," the Court bluntly concluded that "there is simply no excuse for a gun dealer not to be held accountable for what is alleged to have occurred."

On April 20, 1999, the worst school shooting in US history to date claimed fifteen lives (including the two shooters) and injured twenty-four others at Columbine High School in Littleton, Colorado. The shooters, who were too young to purchase firearms, purchased three firearms from a gun-show through a "straw purchase" by a friend from an unlicensed dealer. A straw purchase is when a person legally able to buy firearms buys them for someone who is not legally able to buy them. The shooters also bought an Intratec TEC-DC9 assault pistol for $500 from a person who knew they were too young to buy weapons.

In response, just hours after another school shooting in Conyers, Georgia, wounded six people, Democratic Vice President Al Gore cast the tie-breaking vote in the Republican-led Congress and passed legislation to require trigger locks on newly manufactured handguns and to require federally licensed dealers at gun shows to impose waiting periods and conduct background checks. This law did not, however, require waiting periods or background checks in transactions between private individuals at gun shows or in online sales (the "gun show loophole").

Two mass shootings in 2012 brought renewed calls for a ban on assault weapons and focused intense pressure on legislators to "do something." On July 20, a shooter killed twelve people and caused seventy others to be injured in a crowded movie theater in Aurora, Colorado, and on December 14, a twenty-year-old gunman killed his mother and then took twenty-seven other lives (including his own) with a semi-automatic AR-15 and two semi-automatic pistols at Sandy Hook Elementary School in Newtown, Connecticut. Gun control advocates focused on the AR-15 and the thirty-round magazines the Sandy Hook shooter had used. These mass shootings brought renewed discussion of an assault weapons ban that spurred lobbying efforts in 2013. While spending by gun rights lobbyists in 2013 jumped 150 percent over 2012 levels (from $6 million to $15 million), spending by gun control lobbyists increased more than 780 percent (from $250,000 to $2.2 million).

In response to the Connecticut and Colorado shootings, Democratic President Barack Obama, presiding over a divided Congress, issued more than two dozen executive orders related to gun control. Supported by the Democratic Senate majority, West Virginia Democratic Senator Joe Manchin and Pennsylvania Republican Senator Pat Toomey cosponsored a bipartisan background check bill, but it was defeated by a filibustering Republican Senate minority.

Another problem with federal gun laws was highlighted in a 2015 mass shooting when a 21-year-old man, federally prohibited from owning a gun, was allowed to purchase a Glock 41 .45-caliber handgun without a federal background check being completed (the "default proceed loophole" or "Charleston loophole"). According to federal law, a seller may sell a gun to a potential buyer if background checks are not completed within three days ("default proceed"). With hopes of starting a race war, this shooter killed nine and injured one Black worshipper at the Emanuel African Methodist Episcopal Church in Charleston, South Carolina. James Comey, the FBI Director, blamed "lapses in the FBI's background-check system" (Nakashima 2015), which led to the federal government reaching an $88 million settlement with victims' families.

In 2016, President Obama once again urged Congress to reconsider a ban on assault weapons after a man used a Sig Sauer MCX semi-automatic rifle and a Glock 17 semi-automatic pistol to kill forty-nine people and wound fifty-three more (five more people were injured in the aftermath) at a nightclub in Orlando, Florida. With Obama in the last year of his last term, however, Congress took no action.

During the three years between 2021 and 2023, America experienced nearly 2,000 mass shootings with 104 incidents in which 4 or more victims were killed. The most deadly occurred on May 24, 2022, at Robb Elementary School in Uvalde, Texas, when a former student used an AR-15 style semi-automatic rifle to shoot his grandmother, then kill nineteen students and two teachers before being shot and killed by law enforcement. Shortly after this deadly act, President Biden signed into law "the first major gun safety legislation passed by Congress in nearly 30 years" (Clyde and Miranda 2022). The Bipartisan Safer Communities Act (S. 1938) was introduced in the Senate by Florida Republican Senator Marco Rubio and modified by an amendment by Connecticut Democratic Senator Chris Murphy. Among other things, this law extends background checks for gun purchasers under the age of twenty-one, further criminalizes arms trafficking and straw purchases, and expands the definition of "domestic violence" to include relationships others than just spouses and cohabitants (e.g., ex-spouses, ex-cohabitants, dating relationships/ex-relationships) to partially address the "boyfriend loophole" in restrictions of gun ownership for domestic violence offenders.

Gun Control Groups Celebrate Public Law 117-159: Bipartisan Safer Communities Act

On June 25, 2022, President Joe Biden signed into law an "historic gun safety, mental health, and school safety bill," the first major federal gun safety law to pass Congress since 1994.

Proposed by Republican Senator Marco Rubio as part of an unrelated bill that was later amended by Connecticut Democratic Senator Chris Murphy, the bill was also cowritten by Texas Republican Senator John Cornyn, Democratic/Independent Arizona Senator Kyrsten Sinema, and North Carolina Republican Senator Thom Tillis. The Bipartisan Safer Communities Act enhances background checks for buyers under twenty-one, provides federal funding to implement state "red flag" laws, including funding to support crisis intervention services, disarms domestic abusers who have abused dating partners, clarifies what it means to be "engaged in the business" of selling firearms so unlicensed people selling guns to strangers know when they are required to obtain a Federal Firearms License and run background checks on all sales, prohibits interstate gun trafficking and straw purchasing, provides funding for community violence intervention programs and school violence prevention programs, and provides resources to expand mental health services and access (Everytown for Gun Safety 2022).

The Biden administration is also currently overseeing several other pieces of important gun control legislation. Proposed by South Carolina Democratic Representative James Clyburn, H.R. 2403, the Enhanced Background Checks Act of 2023 would address the "Charleston loophole" and increase the amount of time that a seller would wait for the FBI to complete a background check from three to ten days, after which the potential buyer could petition for a final firearms eligibility determination. If another ten days pass with no final determination, the seller may proceed with the sale ("default proceed"). The bill was referred to the House Committee on the Judiciary in March 2023.

In March 2021, a bill to reinstate an assault weapons ban was introduced in the House by Rhode Island Democratic Representative David Cicilline. The Assault Weapons Ban of 2021 (H.R. 1808), was passed in July 2022 as the Assault Weapons Ban of 2022 by a vote of 217-213. Five Democrats voted against the bill while two Republicans (Pennsylvania Rep. Brian Fitzpatrick and New York Rep. Chris Jacobs) voted for it. It was sent to the Senate in August 2022, read twice, referred to the Committee on the Judiciary, where it died. However, in January 2023, California Democratic Senator Diane Feinstein introduced S.25, Assault Weapons Ban of 2023. It was read twice and referred to the Committee on the Judiciary. Recent research indicates that the 1994 ban prevented an estimated eleven mass shootings and would have prevented another thirty mass shootings that killed 339 people and wounded 1,139 people had it not expired (Post et al. 2021).

It is estimated that more than 20 percent of firearms are acquired without a background check. To address this "gun show loophole," California Democratic Representative Mike Thompson proposed H.R. 715, Bipartisan Background Checks Act of 2023, which would require background checks on all firearm sales, including those by private unlicensed sellers. This bill also has been referred to the House Committee on the Judiciary. However, the U.S. Department of Justice clarified language about being "engaged in the business" of selling guns and will soon begin enforcing a new rule that anyone who sells guns, whether from a storefront, online, or at a gun show, must be federally licensed and must conduct background checks.

FURTHER READING

Achenbach, Joel, Scott Higham, and Sari Horwitz. 2013. "How NRA's True Believers Converted a Marksmanship Group into a Mighty Gun Lobby." *Washington Post*, January 12, 2013. https://www.washingtonpost.com/politics/how-nras-true-believers-converted-a-marksmanship-group-into-a-mighty-gun-lobby/2013/01/12/51c62288-59b9-11e2-88d0-c4cf65c3ad15_story.html.

Broady, Arlinda Smith. 2019. "Locked and Loaded: Inside a Georgia School District with Armed Teachers." *The Atlanta Journal-Constitution*, March 28, 2019. https://www.ajc.com/news/locked-loaded-inside-georgia-school-district-with-armed-teachers/Gz9OTHYo3cNDfuSgrDJqiM/.

Clyde, Don, and Shauneen Miranda. 2022. "Biden Signs Gun Safety Bill into Law." NPR. June 25, 2022. https://www.npr.org/2022/06/25/1107626030/biden-signs-gun-safety-law.

Coleman, Arica L. 2016. "When the NRA Supported Gun Control." *Time*, July 29, 2016. https://time.com/4431356/nra-gun-control-history/.

Democratic Party Platform. 2020. https://democrats.org/where-we-stand/party-platform/. Accessed September 12, 2022.

Everytown for Gun Safety. 2022. "Monumental Victory for Gun Safety: Everytown, Moms Demand Action, Students Demand Action Celebrate Gun Sense Champion President Joe Biden Signing Bipartisan Safer Communities Act into Law." Press Release, June 25, 2022. https://

www.everytown.org/press/monumental-victory-for-gun-safety-everytown-moms-demand-action-students-demand-action-celebrate-gun-sense-champion-president-joe-biden-signing-bipartisan-safer-communities-act-into-law/.

Feuerherd, Peter. 2018. "The Midterms That Changed America." *JSTOR Daily Newsletter*, September 17, 2018. https://daily.jstor.org/the-midterms-that-changed-america/.

Jackson, Katharine. 2024. "US to Close 'Gun Show Loophole' and Require More Background Checks." Yahoo News. April 11, 2024. https://www.yahoo.com/news/us-close-gun-show-loophole-090512989.html.

Khan, Azmat. 2012. "How Conservatives 'Reinvented' the Second Amendment." *PBS Frontline*, December 18, 2012. https://www.pbs.org/wgbh/frontline/article/how-conservatives-reinvented-the-second-amendment/.

Lacombe, Matthew J. 2019. "The Political Weaponization of Gun Owners: The National Rifle Association's Cultivation, Dissemination, and Use of a Group Social Identity." *The Journal of Politics* 81, no. 4: 1342–6.

Lee, Susanna. 2019. "How the 'Good Guy with a Gun' Became a Deadly American Fantasy." *PBS News Hour*, June 8, 2019. https://www.pbs.org/newshour/nation/how-the-good-guy-with-a-gun-became-a-deadly-american-fantasy.

Lim, Clarissa-Jan. 2022. "23 Creative Solutions Republicans Have Offered to Stop Mass Shootings That Have Nothing to Do with Guns." *Buzz Feed News*, May 26, 2022. https://www.buzzfeednews.com/article/clarissajanlim/republicans-solutions-shootings-doors-guns.

Long, Colleen, and Linley Sanders. 2023. "GOP Support for Gun Restrictions Slips a Year After Congress Passed Firearms Law." *Associated Press-Politics*. August 24, 2023. https://apnews.com/article/guns-mass-shooting-schools-uvalde-biden-83c7ece4a3ffb6ff033a07737303d772.

Longley, Robert. 2023. "Timeline of Gun Control in the United States." *ThoughtCo*. January 8, 2023. https://www.thoughtco.com/us-gun-control-timeline-3963620.

Mann, Brian, and Emma Bowman. 2024. "Jury Finds NRA, Wayne LaPierre Liable in Civil Corruption Case." *NPR*, February 23, 2024. https://www.npr.org/2024/02/23/1232229060/nra-wayne-lapierre-corruption-trial-verdict-new-york.

Molla, Rani. 2022. "Polling Is Clear: Americans Want Gun Control." *Vox*, June 1, 2022. https://www.vox.com/policy-and-politics/23141651/gun-control-american-approval-polling.

Nakashima, Ellen. 2015. "FBI: Breakdown in the Background Check System Allowed Dylann Roof to Buy Gun." *Washington Post*, July 10, 2015. https://www.washingtonpost.com/world/national-security/fbi-accused-charleston-shooter-should-not-have-been-able-to-buy-gun/2015/07/10/0d09fda0-271f-11e5-b72c-2b7d516e1e0e_story.html.

Open Secrets. n.d. "National Rifle Assn. Contributions by Party of Recipient." https://www.opensecrets.org/orgs/national-rifle-assn/totals?id=d000000082. Accessed August 16, 2023.

Page, Susan, and Ken Tran. 2022. "Half of Republicans Support Stricter Gun Laws, a Double-Digit Jump in a Year, USA TODAY/Ipsos Poll Says." *USA Today*, June 7, 2022. https://www.usatoday.com/story/news/politics/2022/06/07/gun-laws-poll-republicans-uvalde/7524705001/.

Post, Lori, Maryann Mason, Lauren Nadya Singh, Nicholas P. Wicklinski, Charles B. Moss, et al. 2021. "Impact of Firearm Surveillance on Gun Control Policy: Regression Discontinuity Analysis." *JMIR Public Health and Surveillance* 7, no. 4 (April). https://doi.org/10.2196/26042.

Reese, Hope. 2020. "How the NRA Went from a Marksmanship Group to a Controversial Political Powerhouse." *Vox*, April 2, 2020. https://www.vox.com/the-highlight/2020/3/24/21191524/nra-national-rifle-association-history-frank-smyth-wayne-la-pierre.

Republican Party Platform: 2016/2020. https://prod-cdn-static.gop.com/static/home/data/platform.pdf. Accessed September 14, 2022.

Schonfeld, Zach. 2022. "Texas GOP Rebukes Cornyn, Rejects Gun Control Legislation Framework." *The Hill*, June 20, 2022. https://thehill.com/homenews/state-watch/3529731-texas-gop-rebukes-cornyn-rejects-gun-legislation-framework/.

Seuss, Jeff. 2018. "NRA: 'Revolt at Cincinnati' Molded National Rifle Association." *Cincinnati Enquirer*, March 8, 2018. https://www.cincinnati.com/story/news/politics/2018/03/08/revolt-cincinnati-molded-nra-did-you-know-jeff-suess-schism-within-national-rifle-association-led/404628002/

CHAPTER 13

Hate Crimes

BRENDAN LANTZ AND ZACHARY T. MALCOM

AT A GLANCE

Hate crimes are criminal incidents in which victims are targeted because of their real or perceived group affiliation, which may include race, color, religion, national origin, sexual orientation, gender, gender identity, age, and physical or mental disability. Laws dealing with hate crimes differ substantially by state, and some state laws are more comprehensive than others. In addition to the above group affiliations, some state hate crime statutes include homelessness, political affiliation, US armed forces service history, and law enforcement and other emergency personnel as protected group affiliations.

While hate crime legislation constitutes a recent development from a historical standpoint, such legislation has been the subject of considerable policy debate from both sides of the political spectrum. Hate crime laws are generally justified by supporters on the grounds that "hate" crimes, in comparison to other crimes, have the potential to "hurt more," or lead to greater harm (Iganski 2001). They do so in three primary ways. First, in comparison to other crimes, hate crimes are associated with greater psychological trauma for the victim. Second, hate crimes hurt more physically than other crimes, in that they are often more characterized by extreme brutality. Finally, hate crimes have a greater community impact, in that they target an individual primarily, and often exclusively, for their innate or immutable characteristics. As such, they often serve to send a chilling message to the broader community to which the victim belongs (i.e., those with similar characteristics) that all members of that community are in danger.

As a political issue, however, the role of government in addressing hate crimes has been contentious. As Democrats have shifted progressively more toward the political left and the promotion of social welfare issues, including the protection of minorities, they have increasingly embraced such laws. Simultaneously, as the Republican Party has increasingly shifted right, toward social conservatism and limited government, members have generally resisted hate crime legislation.

MANY REPUBLICANS...

- Believe that hate crime laws overstep constitutional bounds, most notably the First Amendment, because they punish the thought behind the crime (i.e., bias motivation) and thus lead to the prosecution of "thought crimes."
- Believe that separate legislation addressing hate crimes is redundant with criminal legislation more generally, because such laws punish crimes that are already punishable under other statutes.
- Believe that federal hate crime legislation is representative of government overreach, and that such laws are better handled at the state and local level.
- Believe that hate crime laws, when enacted, should be relatively narrowly defined, extending only to a limited set of immutable characteristics, and often to the exclusion of sexual orientation and gender identity.

MANY DEMOCRATS...

- Believe that hate crimes are fundamentally distinct from other crimes, necessitating separate legislation dealing with hate crimes directly.
- Believe that hate crime legislation serves an important purpose in protecting minority communities from the increased harm associated with victimization for their group membership.
- Believe that hate crime laws should be expansive, extending to a variety of diverse group characteristics, including sexual orientation, gender, and gender identity.
- Believe that, while hate crime laws should be expansive, they should not extend to law enforcement personnel.

OVERVIEW

Although prejudice and bigotry have a long history, hate crimes are a relatively recent legal construct. Indeed, the first state legislation regarding hate crimes was not passed until 1981, when lawmakers in both Washington and Oregon passed anti-hate crime measures. Since then, the federal government, forty-seven states, and the District of Columbia have adopted some form of hate crime legislation. Georgia became the most recent state to pass state hate crime legislation on June 26, 2020, after the shooting death of Ahmaud Arbery energized efforts to pass such a law. The legislation was signed into law by Republican Governor Brian Kemp and received broad bipartisan support (Slotkin 2020).

Notably, while the state of Indiana also recently passed a law regarding hate crimes, the legislation has been the subject of considerable debate and is not currently recognized as a hate crime law by the Anti-Defamation League (ADL 2019a). The three other states with no state-level hate crime legislation as of October 2020 (Arkansas, South Carolina, Wyoming) are all predominantly "red" states with a large proportion of Republican voters.

The first major hate crime legislation to be passed at the federal level was the Hate Crime Statistics Act of 1990 (HCSA), which required the U.S. Department of Justice

(DOJ) to collect and publish hate crime data from local law enforcement agencies. Because the legislation dealt specifically with data collection, and not criminalization, it was largely supported by members of both parties. The only resistance to the law came from four Republican senators who opposed the inclusion of sexual orientation in the legislation. Gender identity, which is conceptually distinct but treated similar to sexual orientation by many lawmakers, was also not included as a protected category.

Three additional federal hate crime laws were passed between 1994 and 1997. The first of these laws, the Hate Crimes Sentencing Enhancement Act, mandated that the United States Sentencing Commission (USSC) revise sentencing requirements for incidents in which a defendant selected a victim because of their group affiliation. The law essentially functioned as a penalty enhancement statute in that it increased the penalty for such crimes by at least three levels. The second law, the Violence Against Women Act (VAWA), provided mechanisms for victims of gender-based crimes to sue their offenders and receive damages. As a result, many viewed certain aspects of the legislation as functionally extending federal hate crime laws to include gender as a protected category. This act, which was cosponsored by Democratic Senator Joe Biden (DE) and Republican Senator Orrin Hatch (UT), passed with bipartisan support. While the considerably contentious history of the VAWA is beyond the scope of this chapter, it should be noted that a more recent iteration of the law was not reauthorized in 2019, largely as a result of Republican opposition to new provisions pertaining to the purchase of firearms. Finally, Congress unanimously passed the Republican-sponsored Church Arson Prevention Act of 1997. This legislation was primarily a reaction to a spike in church burnings at the time and provided for increased penalties for damaging places of worship. Many of the church burnings targeted churches that were home to primarily African American congregations.

While most early pieces of legislation, other than the Church Arson Prevention Act, faced some opposition, resistance was relatively limited in scale. The bipartisan character of support was attributed in part to the fact that hate crime legislation represents “a curious blend of progressive and conservative sentiment” (Perry 2002, 489). Such legislation takes both a compassionate approach to victims of hate crime (appealing to many Democrats) and a punitive “get tough” approach to hate crime offenders (appealing to many Republicans).

The first comprehensive federal hate crime law, however, faced considerably more partisan debate. This legislation, originally titled the Hate Crimes Prevention Act, was first proposed in 1998 but tabled as Congress focused on the impeachment hearings of Democratic President Bill Clinton. Two competing bills were subsequently introduced in 1999, one of which was sponsored by Democratic Senator Ted Kennedy (MA) and the other was sponsored by Republican Senator Orrin Hatch (UT). The primary difference between the two bills pertained to an issue that still largely separates the two parties today—whether to include hate crimes motivated by bias toward sexual orientation. Both bills died in committee. While several more attempts were made in following years, it was not until October 28, 2009, when the Matthew Shepard and James Byrd, Jr. Hate Crimes Prevention Act was signed into law by Democratic President Barack Obama that a comprehensive federal hate crimes law became a reality. The law, in its current form, includes federal protections for crimes committed due to actual or perceived race, color, religion, national origin, gender, sexual orientation, gender identity, disability, and membership in the US armed services.

At the state level, over the last two decades of the twentieth century, many states passed legislation similar to the laws Washington and Oregon had passed in 1981. But even after passage, many of these laws remain subjects of ongoing debate and disagreement. These disagreements primarily orbit around: (1) whether hate crime laws are necessary to begin with and (2) which group affiliations should be protected by hate crime laws. Regarding the former, Republicans have voiced concerns regarding the policing of hate crimes as "thought policing." Put simply, such arguments posit that, because hate crime legislation considers the motivation of the offender and punishes crimes more severely when they involve bias motivation, hate crime laws effectively punish thought. Supporters of hate crime laws counter by pointing out an important qualification to that argument: hate crime laws do not punish thoughts that are unaccompanied by criminal conduct. In other words, individuals are free to think whatever thoughts they like, however bigoted or unpleasant, if they do not act on those thoughts in committing a violation of the law. It is only in such cases of criminal violation that hate crime legislation applies.

Critics of hate crime legislation have also argued that such laws violate the Equal Protection Clause of the Fourteenth Amendment because they give more protection to hate crime victims relative to other victims. While constitutional challenges to this end have generally been unsuccessful, the assertion remains a common talking point among opponents.

Republicans and Democrats also frequently disagree on which groups should be protected by hate crime legislation. These debates typically surface annually or semi-annually as legislators debate whether to add or extend hate crime legislation to new protected groups at the state level. With the notable exception of Indiana, which does not define protected groups, all states with hate crime laws include race, religion, and ethnicity, or national origin as protected categories. Indeed, some states include only these categories. Other states, like New York, include an extensive list of additional protected categories. There is substantial variation at the state level regarding the inclusion of sexual orientation and gender identity as protected categories.

As of 2024, thirty-three states have hate crime laws that include sexual orientation. Most states that do not have such provisions are politically conservative and are led by Republican governors and/or legislatures. Republican support has been even less enthusiastic for the inclusion of transgender status, or gender identity, as protected categories in most hate crime laws. As of 2024, only twenty-two states explicitly include gender identity or transgender status as a protected category, even though hate crimes motivated by sexual orientation and gender identity are among the most frequent hate crimes in America. But although LGBTQ individuals regularly face disproportionate violence and bullying, the exclusion of these categories in many states revolves around higher levels of homophobia and societal disapproval of LGBTQ communities.

REPUBLICANS ON HATE CRIMES

Republicans have largely been resistant to federal hate crime legislation, especially in recent years. Republican lawmakers have argued that the federal hate crime law violates the Fourteenth Amendment because it does not protect all individuals equally and violates the

First Amendment by punishing "thought crimes." Such assertions continue to be leveled against hate crime laws today, despite the fact that hate crime laws have been upheld in the face of several such constitutional challenges. The Republican Party of Texas Platform (2018) even goes so far as to state that Republicans should "urge the complete repeal of hate crime laws, since ample laws are currently in effect to punish criminal behavior toward other persons."

Republicans have been especially adamant in opposing the inclusion of sexual orientation and gender identity in both state and federal hate crime legislation. This has been a consistent stance of Republicans dating back to the first federal legislation dealing with hate crimes, the Hate Crime Statistics Act. Much of this resistance centers around the symbolic function of hate crime legislation. In other words, because hate crime laws express society's disapproval and outrage toward a behavior, there is some concern among Republicans opposed to homosexuality on moral grounds that including sexual orientation as a protected category sends the message that the government approves of homosexuality more generally.

Indeed, when the HCSA was originally being considered, a small, but vocal group of Republican senators led by Jesse Helms of North Carolina vigorously opposed the inclusion of sexual orientation in the law. Helms claimed that the legislation was "the flagship of the homosexual, lesbian, legislative agenda" and that including sexual orientation would undermine traditional family values (Rankin 2013, 590). It is important to note that this law only mandated the collection of data on hate crimes; it did not actually establish sexual orientation-based hate crimes as a federal crime. In other words, Republican opponents at the time did not even wish to allow such crimes to be tracked. In order to effect compromise while still including sexual orientation as a protected category, an additional sentence was added to the end of the legislation, which stated that nothing in the act was to be construed or used to "promote or encourage homosexuality."

This resistance to the inclusion of sexual orientation as a protected category also played a significant role in the delay of the passage of the Matthew Shepard and James Byrd, Jr., Hate Crimes Prevention Act, an act named in part after Matthew Shepard, a gay college student in Wyoming who in 1998 was beaten and tortured so severely for his sexual orientation that he eventually died of his injuries. While the Act was not signed into law until 2009, efforts began at least ten years earlier, when Democratic Senator Edward Kennedy (MA) and Republican Senator Orrin Hatch (UT) both introduced competing bills that would implement hate crime laws at the federal level. The difference between the two laws was the inclusion of sexual orientation as a protected category. And, while the final version of the legislation did include sexual orientation, there was resistance at that time as well. Indeed, Republican senators, led by Jeff Sessions of Alabama, specifically added death penalty provisions to the bill, generally viewed unfavorably by Democrats, in an attempt to stall or prevent the enactment of a hate crime law that included sexual orientation (colloquially referred to as a "poison pill"). The legislation was, however, eventually passed without the inclusion of the death penalty provision.

While sexual orientation and gender identity are conceptually distinct issues, the issue of gender identity has often been subsumed within the debate surrounding sexual orientation, especially during the 1980s. In other words, much of the Congressional conversation surrounding hate crime legislation has been marked by confusion over the difference between gender identity and sexual orientation. In this way, Republicans have also been staunchly opposed to the inclusion of gender identity, or transgender status, in hate crime legislation. Republican Representative Louis Gohmert (TX), for example, attacked the inclusion of gender identity on grounds that it symbolically elevated the transgender community, claiming "it says to the world that a transvestite with gender identity issues will now be more important to protect than a heterosexual" (Rankin 2013, 602). Despite credible scientific evidence to the contrary, several Republicans have also resorted to claims that gender identity is a "choice" and thereby different from immutable characteristics like race or ethnicity (Krouse 2009). This perspective is further evidenced by Republican proposals for so-called bathroom bills, which criminalize the use of public bathrooms that do not conform to an individual's gender as listed on their birth certificates. These laws have also been vehemently opposed by Democrats.

Does Indiana's Hate Crime Legislation Count as a Hate Crime Law?

In April 2019, Republican Governor Eric Holcomb (IN) signed legislation intended to add Indiana to the list of states with hate crime laws, stating that the state had "made progress and taken a strong stand against targeted violence" (McKinney 2019). Critics of the law were quick to question the strength of that stand, however, because the language of the law does not include *any* explicitly protected categories. Because of this omission, and in contrast to most hate crime legislation, the law was supported by many Republicans. Several Democrats, on the other hand, were explicitly against the law. Moreover, the Anti-Defamation League (ADL), which tracks state hate crime laws and generally supports such legislation, stated that the law "does not meet our standard for a real and effective hate crimes bill in 2019" (ADL 2019b). As such, the ADL has not recognized the law as a hate crime law. While the reaction among supporters of hate crime laws has been less than enthusiastic, a small group of scholars has argued that approaching hate crime legislation through a lens that emphasizes group identity only serves to create and exacerbate community divisions (Chakraborti and Garland 2012). While such scholars might be supportive of legislation like that passed by Indiana, it remains to be seen whether such legislation will be effective when used, or whether it largely serves a symbolic purpose.

The Republican Party broke tradition in 2020, electing not to adopt a formal platform. However, the most recent 2016 Republican platform states that Republicans "denounce bigotry, racism, anti-Semitism, ethnic prejudice, and religious intolerance ... [and] oppose discrimination based on race, sex, religion, creed, disability, or national origin and support statutes to end such discrimination" (2016, 9). Sexual orientation and gender identity are notably missing from these enumerated categories. The platform further states that including such categories would "impose a social and cultural revolution upon the American people by wrongly redefining sex discrimination to include sexual orientation or other categories" (2016, 35). In 2020 the Republican Party decided against updating their platform, instead choosing to recycle the 2016 platform again in combination with a resolution of party support for Trump and his chosen policy priorities.

DEMOCRATS ON HATE CRIMES

Compared to Republicans, Democratic lawmakers tend to support hate crime legislation on a much broader scale, and "have been more committed than Republicans to embracing diversity and making provisions for the rights of ethnic, racial, religious, and sexual minorities" (Jenness and Grattet 1996, 140). In general, research on hate crime legislation has indicated that states with Democratic majorities in the legislature are more likely to pass hate crime laws and to protect more group affiliations. The federal Hate Crimes Protection Act was also passed by a Democratic-controlled Congress and signed by a Democratic president (Obama). West Coast and Northeastern states with more liberal populations also are significantly more likely than states in other regions to include categories like sexual orientation in their hate crime laws.

Indeed, Democratic lawmakers have played an integral role in the passing of most hate crime legislation to this point. While hate crime legislation has been challenged constitutionally on several occasions, the most prominent challenge was *Wisconsin v. Mitchell* (508 U.S. 476, 1993). In this case, which centered around Wisconsin's hate crime law, several Democratic members of Congress, including Senator Charles Schumer (NY), submitted a brief to the court arguing that hate crime laws are necessary and justifiable due to the increased harm associated with such crimes, in comparison to other crimes. The outcome of the case established hate crime legislation as constitutional. In contrast to Republicans, many Democrats have also been broadly supportive of the inclusion of sexual orientation and gender identity in hate crime legislation. In an impassioned statement supporting the inclusion of these categories in the Hate Crime Prevention Act, Democratic Representative Jan Schakowsky (IL) argued that: "This is not about thought. This is not about speech. This is about violence. And you or your pastor may not agree with homosexuals or transgenders, but surely you don't think that it is a reason for them to be assaulted" (Rankin 2013, 604).

Democrats have also taken the lead in introducing more recent hate crime legislation, although not all of it has been passed. For example, Democrat Don Beyer (VA) cosponsored with Republican Peter Olson (TX) the National Opposition to Hate, Assault, and Threats to Equality Act of 2020 (NO HATE). This bill proposed to improve agency tracking and victim reporting of hate crimes by establishing hotlines for victims of hate crimes to seek assistance. The legislation also intended to improve data on hate crimes by improving the collection of hate crime data in the National Incident Based-Reporting System (NIBRS). Democrats led by David Cicilline (RI) also introduced recent legislation referred to as the Disarm Hate Act, which would prohibit individuals who have been convicted of misdemeanor hate crimes from buying or possessing firearms. The legislation has been met with heavy resistance from Republican representatives, who have argued that the law would violate the Second Amendment by expanding disarmament to misdemeanor convictions. While the Disarm Hate Act received vocal support from several

2020 Democratic presidential candidates, attempts to pass the legislation in 2020 were hampered due to opposition from the Republican-controlled Senate.

The Democratic-controlled House of Representatives approved the Emmett Till Antilynching Act of 2020, which made lynching a federal hate crime. At the time, the passage of this legislation was viewed as a historic victory, given that efforts to pass such a law have been made by both Democrats and Republicans for nearly 120 years. Democratic Representative Bobby L. Rush (IL), who sponsored the legislation, remarked that the bill would "send a strong message that violence, and race-based violence in particular, has no place in American society" (Sonmez 2020). While the bill was broadly supported by both Democrats and Republicans, of the four representatives who voted against the law, three were Republican and one was an independent. The justification for these nay votes largely reflected decades of Republican resistance to the legislation of hate crimes: Republican Thomas Massie, when asked about his vote against the law, stated that "a crime is a crime, and all victims deserve equal justice. Adding penalties for 'hate' tends to endanger other liberties, such as freedom of speech" (Bailey 2020). These sentiments expressed by Massie echo a long history of resistance to hate crime laws among members of the Republican Party, often centered around issues of equal protection and freedom of speech.

Yet, while the bill passed the House with broad bipartisan support, Senator Rand Paul (R-KY) used procedural moves to block passage of the bill in the Senate. Paul has argued that the act was too broadly worded and could lead to further injustice in the form of "excessive sentencing for minor infractions" (Fandos 2020). Despite this resistance, the Emmett Till Antilynching Act was signed into law in March 2022 by Democratic President Joe Biden.

"Blue Lives Matter" and the Inclusion of Law Enforcement in Hate Crime Legislation

Many Republicans have couched stances against the inclusion of certain protected categories, most notably sexual orientation, in arguments that only immutable characteristics (i.e., race) should be protected. Interestingly, however, there is considerably more support from Republicans, compared to Democrats, for the inclusion of law enforcement personnel as a protected category. In 2016, Louisiana became the first state to pass hate crime legislation including law enforcement personnel, popularly referred to as "Blue Lives Matter" legislation. Kentucky, Mississippi, and Texas have since followed suit, with Alabama significantly pushing to do so as well. Such laws, primarily supported by Republicans, emerged in response to the Black Lives Matter movement generally and, more immediately, to a 2016 Dallas sniper attack in which the offender targeted and killed five police officers. Proponents of the legislation argue, quite simply, that police officers and other emergency personnel risk their lives frequently and thus deserve extra protections. Opponents of the legislation, largely Democrats, argue that most states already provide for the enhanced punishment of those who assault or kill law enforcement officers. More broadly, such opponents also fear that the inclusion of law enforcement as a protected category is contrary to the primary intention of hate crime legislation. Put simply, while hate crime laws are ostensibly written in such a way as to protect everyone from being targeted for their group affiliation, they are intended primarily to protect minorities. Thus, given larger concerns about police–minority community relations, there is significant concern that the inclusion of law enforcement as a protected category may translate, in practice, to legislation that is primarily enforced against minorities, rather than for them (Gerstenfeld 2017; Mason 2020).

The 2024 Democratic Party platform explicitly stated that the party is "committed to ending discrimination on the basis of race, ethnicity, national origin, religion, language, gender, age, sexual orientation, gender identity, or disability status" and to enforcing and strengthening the Matthew Shepard and James Byrd, Jr. Hate Crimes Prevention Act. The platform further evokes a specific focus on gender identity, pledging to fight to end violence against transgender Americans and to "prioritize the investigation of hate crimes against transgender and non-binary people." It also asserted an agenda to close what is colloquially referred to as the "Charleston loophole," by introducing legislation that will prevent individuals convicted of hate crimes from being able to possess firearms. Notably, the platform also specifically attributes growth in hate crimes against Asian Americans and Pacific Islanders to the "xenophobic rhetoric" of former Republican president Donald Trump. As such, Democratic support for hate crime laws is comparatively unequivocal (Democratic Party Platform 2024).

FURTHER READING

Anti-Defamation League. 2019a. "Anti-Defamation League State Hate Crime Statutory Provisions." July 2019. https://www.adl.org/media/13726/download.

Anti-Defamation League. 2019b. "Indiana Will Remain on the ADL List of States without a Hate Crimes Law." April 12, 2019. https://chicago.adl.org/news/7850/.

Bailey, Phillip M. 2020. "Kentucky Rep. Thomas Massie Opposes Anti-lynching Bill Named for Emmett Till." *Courier Journal*, March 27, 2020. https://www.courierjournal.com/story/news/politics/2020/02/26/kentucky-rep-thomas-massie-opposes-emmett-till-anti-lynching-act/4883740002/.

Bell, Jeannine. 2002. *Policing Hatred: Law Enforcement, Civil Rights, and Hate Crime*. Vol. 15. New York: NYU Press.

Chakraborti, Neil, and Jon Garland. 2012. "Reconceptualizing Hate Crime Victimization through the Lens of Vulnerability and 'Difference.'" *Theoretical Criminology* 16, no. 4: 499–514.

Cogan, Jeanine C. 2002. "Hate Crime as a Crime Category Worthy of Policy Attention." *American Behavioral Scientist* 46, no. 1: 173–85.

Democratic Party Platform. Democratic National Committee. August 18, 2020. https://www.democrats.org/wp-content/uploads/2020/08/2020-Democratic-Party-Platform.pdf.

Fandos, Nicholas. 2020. "Frustration and Fury as Rand Paul Holds Up Anti-Lynching Bill in Senate." *New York Times*, June 5, 2020. www.nytimes.com/2020/06/05/us/politics/rand-paul-anti-lynching-bill-senate.html.

Franklin, Karen. 2002. "Good Intentions: The Enforcement of Hate Crime Penalty-enhancement Statutes." *American Behavioral Scientist* 46, no. 1: 154–72.

Gerstenfeld, Phyllis B. 2017. *Hate Crimes: Causes, Controls, and Controversies*. Thousand Oaks, CA: Sage Publications.

Gerstenfeld, Phyllis B. 1992. "Smile When You Call Me That!: The Problems with Punishing Hate Motivated Behavior." *Behavioral Sciences & the Law* 10, no. 2: 259–85.

Grattet, Ryken, Valerie Jenness, and Theodore R. Curry. 1998. "The Homogenization and Differentiation of Hate Crime Law in the United States, 1978 to 1995: Innovation and Diffusion in the Criminalization of Bigotry." *American Sociological Review* 63, no. 2 (April): 286–307.

Hanser, Russell P. 2000. "Book Review: 'Punishing Hate', Punishing Harm." *Journal of Criminal Law and Criminology* 90, no. 3: 1047–82.

Iganski, Paul. 2001. "Hate Crimes Hurt More." *American Behavioral Scientist* 45, no. 4: 626–38.

Jacobs, James B., and Kimberly Potter. 1998. *Hate Crimes: Criminal Law & Identity Politics*. Oxford: Oxford University Press.

Jenness, Valerie, and Kendal Broad. 1997. *Hate Crimes: New Social Movements and the Politics of Violence*. New York: Transaction Publishers.

Jenness, Valerie, and Ryken Grattet. 1996. "The Criminalization of Hate: A Comparison of Structural and Polity Influences on the Passage of 'Bias-crime' Legislation in the United States." *Sociological Perspectives* 39, no. 1: 129–54.

Jenness, Valerie, and Ryken Grattet. 2001. *Making Hate a Crime: From Social Movement to Law Enforcement*. New York: Russell Sage Foundation.

Krouse, William J., and M. Angeles Villarreal. 2009. "Hate Crime Legislation." Congressional Research Service, Library of Congress.

Levin, Brian. 2002. "From Slavery to Hate Crime Laws: The Emergence of Race and Status-based Protection in American Criminal Law." *Journal of Social Issues* 58, no. 2: 227–45.

Levin, Brian. 1999. "Hate Crimes: Worse by Definition." *Journal of Contemporary Criminal Justice* 15, no. 1: 6–21.

Mason, Gail. 2014. "The Symbolic Purpose of Hate Crime Law: Ideal Victims and Emotion." *Theoretical Criminology* 18, no. 1: 75–92.

Mason, Gail. 2020. "Blue Lives Matter and Hate Crime Law." *Race and Justice* 12, no. 2: 1–20.

McKinney, Matt. 2019. "Gov. Holcomb Signs Hate Crimes Bill into Law." RTV6 Indianapolis, April 3, 2019. https://www.theindychannel.com/news/politics/gov-holcomb-signs-hate-crimes-bill-into-law.

Myers, Wesley, and Brendan Lantz. 2020. "Reporting Racist Hate Crime Victimization to the Police in the United States and the United Kingdom: A Cross-National Comparison." *The British Journal of Criminology* 60, no. 4: 1034–55.

Peek, George S. 2001. "Recent Legislation: Where Are We Going with Federal Hate Crimes Legislation-Congress and the Politics of Sexual Orientation." *Marquette Law Review* 85: 537.

Perry, Barbara. 2002. "Hate Crime and Identity Politics." *Theoretical Criminology* 6, no. 4: 485–91.

Pezzella, Frank S. 2016. *Hate Crime Statutes: A Public Policy and Law Enforcement Dilemma*. New York: Springer.

Rankin, Sara K. 2013. "Invidious Deliberation: The Problem of Congressional Bias in Federal Hate Crime Legislation." *Rutgers Law Review* 66: 563.

Republican Party of Texas Platform. 2018. https://www.texasgop.org/platform/.

Republican Party Platform 2016. 2016. The American Presidency Project. July 18, 2016. https://www.presidency.ucsb.edu/documents/2016-republican-part-platform..

Slotkin, J. 2020. "After Ahmaud Arbery's Killing, Georgia Governor Signs Hate Crime Legislation." *Newsweek*, June 26, 2020. https://www.npr.org/sections/live-updates-protests-for-racial-justice/2020/06/26/884003927/after-ahmaud-arberys-killing-georgia-gov-signs-hate-cri mes-legislation.

Smith, David. 2020. "Rand Paul Stalls Bill That Would Make Lynching a Federal Hate Crime." *The Guardian*, June 11, 2020. https://www.theguardian.com/us-news/2020/jun/11/rand-paul-lynch ing-hate-crime-bill-limbo.

Sonmez, Felicia. 2020. "House Passes Historic Anti-lynching Bill after Congress's Century of Failure." *Washington Post*, February 26, 2020. https://www.washingtonpost.com/politics/house-poised-to-pass-historic-anti-lynching-bill-after-more-than-a-century-of-failure/2020/02/26/33df9 1ae-58ae-11ea-9000-f3cffee23036_story.html.

Soule, Sarah A., and Jennifer Earl. 2001. "The Enactment of State-Level Hate Crime Law in the United States: Intrastate and Interstate Factors." *Sociological Perspectives* 44, no. 3: 281–305.

Touchberry, R. 2020. "Four Lawmakers Vote against House Bill to make Lynching Federal Hate Crime, Cite 'Government Overreach.'" *Newsweek*, February 26, 2020. https://www.newsw eek.com/four-federal-lawmakers-vote-against-bill-outlaw-lynching-cite-government-overreach-1489313.

White, Rob. 2002. "Hate Crime Politics." *Theoretical Criminology* 6, no. 4: 499–502.

CHAPTER 14

Immigration and Customs Enforcement

SEAN MADDAN AND MIGUEL V. RANGEL

AT A GLANCE

In the aftermath of the September 11, 2001, terrorist attacks, federal law enforcement agencies went through one of the most transformative realignments in US history. One of the most important changes was the creation of the Department of Homeland Security (DHS). Within the DHS, the consolidation of the newly minted Immigration and Customs Enforcement (ICE) was supported by a wide swath of lawmakers in both the Democratic and Republican parties, as well as by the public. Both the DHS and ICE fall under the purview of the executive branch (president), while Congress has oversight on budgetary and operational matters. ICE, in and of itself, is not controversial and enjoys relatively widespread support for promoting legal immigration practices and for protecting US citizens from attacks by terrorists entering the country illegally with malignant intent; the politics of the present have placed this agency in a controversial position since it is at the forefront of immigration control in the United States.

While both Democrats and Republicans supported the creation of ICE and its mission to combat terrorism and enforce laws in relation to legal immigration, differences exist between the parties in views of how ICE should operate and how general policies of either Democratic or Republican presidential administrations impact the priorities of ICE law enforcement. In general, most believe that legal immigration should be held sacrosanct; for those individuals who violate these laws, there should be penalties. Likewise, legal enforcement of immigration laws that help to keep citizens safe is also supported. However, there are differences between Democratic and Republican immigration strategies in how both these ends are achieved. The party that controls the executive branch determines the priorities of all cabinet agencies/departments. So, while there is agreement on the law enforcement function of ICE, party priorities necessarily impact how ICE goes about its efforts, whether by organizational mandates or by external policies that have an impact on how ICE operates.

Democratic goals for ICE tend to be more moderate. In addition to increased enforcement, Democrats tend to support policies like hiring/utilizing more judges in an effort to more quickly process immigration cases, using catch-and-release policies on immigrants, and allowing local jurisdictions to choose whether or not to assist ICE in its law enforcement efforts. These more moderate policies have profound impacts on ICE operations.

Republican goals for ICE, by contrast, emphasize interdictions and punishments to cut down on undocumented immigration. In addition to increased enforcement, Republicans tend to support policies like mass deportations of immigrants who entered the country illegally, the indefinite detention of entire families, utilizing soldiers on the border, installation of a border wall, keeping immigrants/asylum seekers in Mexico until their court processing is complete, and blocking immigrants who would require public assistance. These more conservative polices also have a profound impact on ICE operations.

MANY REPUBLICANS...

- Advocate for the detention of families at the border, support the physical separation of children from parents, and allow children to be detained in less than optimal conditions.
- Advocate for mass deportations of unauthorized immigrants and asylum seekers, or for transporting them to "sanctuary" states/cities with Democratic governments.
- Support strengthening borders, most notably through construction of a physical border wall between the United States and Mexico.
- Believe that legal immigration should be merit-based and support blocking the entry of immigrants who might require public assistance.
- Indicate that Democratic immigration policies are too lenient, do not secure the borders, and are a waste of taxpayer dollars.

MANY DEMOCRATS...

- Support "catch and release" policies for immigrants entering the United States illegally.
- Advocate for employing more judges to handle the number of immigration cases.
- Support Deferred Action for Childhood Arrivals (DACA) and DACA "Dreamers."
- Support "sanctuary cities" where unauthorized immigrants may be protected from deportation.
- Argue that Republican immigration policies are cruel, not commonsense, and are a waste of taxpayer dollars.

OVERVIEW

In the wake of the terrorist attacks on September 11, 2001, great scrutiny was placed on federal intelligence-gathering and law enforcement agencies. Subsequent congressional investigations into the attacks determined that law enforcement agencies and intelligence organizations should do a better job of sharing information across the entire federal government. Also, new laws were needed to increase the power of federal law enforcement to better collect and share information. To address this shortcoming, a critical change was made to federal intelligence-gathering and law enforcement efforts through two key pieces of legislation: the Uniting and Strengthening America by Providing Appropriate Tools Required to Intercept and Obstruct Terrorism Act of 2001 (USA Patriot Act) and the Homeland Security Act of 2002. The USA Patriot Act of 2001 outlined national security changes deemed necessary to combat terrorist acts and organizations. Primarily, these changes included a substantial expansion of federal law enforcement powers in relation to search and surveillance. Additionally, the USA Patriot Act made it easier for federal law enforcement agencies to share information collected with other law enforcement agencies.

To further help federal law enforcement efforts to collect and share information, a reorganization of several existing federal agencies was implemented. The Homeland Security Act of 2002 (HSA) created the Department of Homeland Security (DHS). The DHS was a new configuration of preexisting law enforcement agencies into a more cohesive unit that could better (1) prevent terrorism and enhance security, (2) secure and manage borders, (3) enforce and administer immigration laws, (4) safeguard and secure cyberspace, and (5) ensure resilience to natural disasters (ICE 2019). As illustrated here, the newly created DHS was a catch-all organization intended to combat terrorism, manage the border and immigration laws, protect cybersecurity threats, and deal with natural disasters—all potential threats to the security of the homeland.

Perhaps the most significant agency to emerge from the creation of the DHS was the Immigration and Customs Enforcement (ICE) agency on March 1, 2003. Through the HSA, parts of the now defunct US Customs Service and the Immigration and Naturalization Service merged to create ICE, which was ultimately placed within the purview of the DHS. ICE's overall mission is to "protect America from the cross-border crime and illegal immigration that threaten national security and public safety" (ICE 2019). ICE's four directorates—Homeland Security Investigations (HSI), Enforcement and Removal Operations (ERO), Office of the Principal Legal Advisor, and Management and Administration—work interactively to uphold its mission. The HSI and ERO are the primary arms of ICE that enforce immigration laws.

The HSI's history dates to the formation of the Customs Service and the Office of the Superintendent of Immigration under the Treasury Department in 1891. Legislation such as The Immigration Act of 1891, Basic Naturalization Act of 1906, 1976 Arms Export Control Act, Immigration Reform and Control Act of 1986, the Illegal Immigration Reform and Immigrant Responsibility Act of 1996, and the establishment of the U.S. Immigration and Naturalization Service in 1933 helped lay out the duties and responsibilities for what has become the HSI.

By 2010, less than a decade after its creation, the DHS was already going through a realignment. This shuffling led to the creation of the HSI as it is known today (Congressional Research Service 2015). The HSI focuses on investigating criminal activity pertaining, but not limited, to financial crimes, commercial fraud and intellectual property theft, cybercrimes, human rights violations, and narcotics and weapons smuggling/trafficking. It has twenty-six field offices throughout the United States (Domestic Operations) and has a transnational presence since it is primarily focused on combating transnational criminal activity (International Operations). This means that it is important for ICE to have strong relationships with law enforcement agencies and officials throughout the United States and abroad. The responsibilities of these divisions vary but they ultimately contribute to enforcing the nation's immigration laws. Domestic Operations is divided into three geographical branches (East, Central, and West), and International Operations is the largest investigative international presence within the DHS.

ERO is the directorate of ICE that identifies, arrests, and removes aliens who are alleged to present a danger to national security or a risk to public safety. Those who enter the United States illegally or otherwise undermine the integrity of immigration laws and border control efforts also are subject to this section of ICE. ERO primarily enforces immigration laws in the interior of the United States.

ERO carries out interior enforcement by coordinating and collaborating with law enforcement partners in agencies at both the federal and state levels. For instance, the 287(g) program aims to enhance community security and safety by forming partnerships with state and local law enforcement agencies. Officers who agree to take part in the program receive the necessary training to carry out limited immigration law enforcement. Through the program, those living in the United States who are foreign-born criminals are identified, arrested, and detained. Criminals who are capable of being removed from the United States are then put into ICE custody once they have served their sentences. State and local agencies benefit because post-released criminals are put into ICE custody rather than sent back into the community. ICE benefits from these partnerships since they reduce the time offenders spend in ICE custody. Partnerships stemming from the 287(g) program led to the convictions of roughly 1,700 aliens in fiscal year 2023 (ICE 2023).

Another key organizational component of ICE is the Office of Congressional Relations. The secretary of the DHS and the director of ICE are political appointees made by the president of the United States, but the legislative branch has direct oversight over ICE. If one party is in charge of the executive branch and another is in charge of the legislative branch, there can be tension in the oversight function. Headquartered in Washington, DC, ICE's Office of Congressional Relations (OCR) represents ICE when interfacing with Congress and responding to all inquiries and requests.

Today, the top ten laws that ICE enforces include: child exploitation, human trafficking, money laundering, counter proliferation (theft of US technology and illicit procurement networks), war crimes, extrajudicial killings and torture, genocide, anti-dumping laws, use and recruitment of child soldiers, and the Lacey Act, which protects illegally obtained animals/plants from being sold in the United States (ICE 2019). Currently, ICE has over

20,000 personnel located in over 400 offices in the United States and across the world. It is ICE that performs many of the practical functions of the entire DHS in relation to immigration offenses.

Due to its role in enforcing immigration laws and political disagreement over the methods it uses to that end, ICE has increasingly found itself at the center of political storms over US immigration policies, whether these policies are generated by the executive, legislative, or judicial branches. In general, political controversies erupt over executive branch priorities. For instance, during Democratic President Barack Obama's two terms, Republicans repeatedly attacked his administration for being "weak" on enforcement of immigration laws, despite the fact that during the Obama years deportations of undocumented immigrants actually increased dramatically. During Republican President Donald Trump's time in office, one of his key policy promises was the building of a wall on the US southern border with Mexico. Democrats have tried to block "the wall" suggesting that the monies used to construct it could be better used on hiring more judges, DHS/ICE personnel, or a smart wall. Under Democratic President Joseph R. Biden, Republicans have renewed their attacks on his administration's border policies. Over the last twenty-four years, regardless of the party in control of the executive or legislative branches, however, ICE is required to follow the policies, mandates, and priorities of the federal authorities controlling the government.

Despite common misconceptions, the unauthorized immigrant population decreased by 14 percent (1.75 million people) from 2007 to 2021 (Passel and Krogstad 2023). In 2021, an estimated 10.5 million unauthorized immigrants were living in the United States. Although the number in 2021 represented a slight increase from the 10.2 million in 2019, it is nearly identical to the number in 2017. Illegal border contacts and arrests, however, exceeded 2 million during both federal fiscal years 2022 and 2023. In December 2023, for example, the U.S. Border Patrol apprehended (taken into custody pending determination of immigration status) or expelled (not placed into custody but denied entry) nearly 250,000 migrants attempting to cross the southern border between Mexico and the United States (Gramlich 2024). The increased number of border contacts in recent years coupled with executive priorities has strained the DHS resources, in general, and ICE resources, specifically. In addition to impacting federal resources, the issue of immigration has divided Congress and become a point of contention in the 2024 presidential campaign. Americans clearly are unhappy, with 80 percent of recent poll respondents believing that the government is doing a "bad job" and 45 percent believing there is a border "crisis." Republicans are much more likely than Democrats to view the situation as a "crisis" (70 percent and 22 percent, respectively), but respondents from both parties are similarly dissatisfied with the government on its handling of the problem (Pew Research Center 2024).

Depending on the party in control of the legislative or executive branches, there is often a push to pass immigration reform, whether comprehensive or piecemeal. While there is general agreement with the desired ends, there is less agreement about the means to obtain a secure border, to eject immigrants illegally in the United States, to deal with special cases (i.e., DACA "Dreamers"), or to process immigration cases more efficiently.

REPUBLICANS ON IMMIGRATION AND CUSTOMS ENFORCEMENT

Historically, Republicans have embraced very conservative policies on both legal and illegal immigration. Republican President George W. Bush pushed for the creation of the DHS and the consolidation of ICE after September 11, 2001, and this conservative trend is clearly denoted in Republican platforms over the past thirty years. During the 1990s, Republicans were very pro-legal immigration; legal immigration was thought to provide a worker base for big businesses that has traditionally supported the Republican party. The conservative message in the 2016 Republican Party platform was much more averse to all forms of immigration, both legal and illegal (see sidebar). Meanwhile, Republican policies and attitudes toward illegal immigration have long emphasized interdiction and deportation, but they became even more severe and punitive during the administration of Republican President Donald Trump. As President Trump (2018) posted on Twitter when writing about ICE, "The people of our Country want and demand Safety and Security, while the Democrats are more interested in ripping apart and demeaning (and not properly funding) our great Law Enforcement!"

The 2016 Republican Platform

On June 16, 2015, Donald J. Trump rode down the escalator in Trump Tower in New York City to announce his candidacy for the president of the United States of America. During his announcement speech, Trump made many hyperbolic statements about immigration, including claims that Mexico was "sending people that have lots of problems and they're bringing their problems. They're bringing drugs, they're bringing crime, they're rapists." When Trump went on to secure the Republican nomination for president in 2016, the party's official platform was crafted to reflect many of his stances in relation to immigration and enforcement:

America's immigration policy must serve the national interest of the United States, and the interests of American workers must be protected over the claims of foreign nationals seeking the same jobs. Illegal immigration endangers everyone, exploits the taxpayers, and insults all who aspire to enter America legally. We oppose any form of amnesty for those who, by breaking the law, have disadvantaged those who have obeyed it. The executive amnesties of 2012 and 2014 are a direct violation of federal law and usurp the powers of Congress as outlined in Article I of the Constitution. These unlawful amnesties must be immediately rescinded by a Republican president. In a time of terrorism, drug cartels, human trafficking, and criminal gangs, the presence of millions of unidentified individuals in this country poses grave risks to the safety and sovereignty of the United States. Our highest priority, therefore, must be to secure our borders and all ports of entry and to enforce our immigration laws. That is why we support building a wall along our southern border and protecting all ports of entry. The border wall must cover the entirety of the southern border and must be sufficient to stop both vehicular and pedestrian traffic. (Republican National Committee 2016)

Republicans have generally expressed support for giving ICE extensive support—and leeway—in prosecutions to stop illegal immigration and deport those who slip across the border and are later found. As with the Obama administration, the Trump administration has continued policies that increase arrests and processing of immigrant cases. Contrary to what might be expected, however, ICE efforts during President Obama's terms resulted in more arrests and deportations than during President Trump's term, as of 2019. Under the Trump administration, raids of businesses have increased to identify immigrants who do not have documentation to work in the United States. These raids, many of which resulted in the taking of hundreds of undocumented employees into government custody, have occurred in both liberal and conservative states throughout the entire country. Additionally, more ICE officers were hired during Trump's tenure, despite reservations from the Office of Inspector General for DHS (2017), primarily in relation to the allocation of new personnel. Republicans have been content with these types of ICE enforcement efforts.

In addition to increased ICE enforcement, Republicans also have pushed for policies to expand detention for all immigrants (including those seeking asylum), not just immigrants with criminal records, to keep immigrants outside of the United States until their cases are heard, and to block the entry of immigrants who might require public assistance. The Trump administration has greatly extended the use of detention for immigrants illegally residing in the United States. Included in this extension is the indefinite detention of immigrants caught crossing the border illegally.

The detention of entire families at the US-Mexico border was the most controversial aspect of the Trump administration's general detention policy. Children were removed from their parents/guardians and placed in a different detention area. There were many reports that this had a detrimental effect on these children. Due to a strained system, poor record keeping, and lack of personal documents, officials running these detention centers were unable to return the children to their parents/guardians in many cases. The tensions and misery at the border were further exacerbated by human trafficking and by immigrants who "rented" children so they could pretend to be a family—a precaution taken to improve their odds of receiving better treatment in case of capture.

Republican policies also emphasize rejecting immigrants seeking asylum from war-torn or politically unstable countries, or immigrants who might require public assistance. Republican policies seek to limit the total number of immigrants through what they describe as a merit-based approach. This approach automatically rejects asylum seekers and those who cannot afford to live in the United States without relying on the state to support them. Trump made this a priority of his immigration policy. Lawsuits were filed in relation to both groups, and on July 1, 2020, this practice was blocked by a Trump-appointed judge in the US District Court in Washington, DC. Later, the US Supreme Court held that the executive branch had the discretion to use these policies and regulations in relation to both immigrants and asylum seekers; the Biden administration abandoned this policy (*Huisha-Huisha v. Mayorkas*, 560 Supp.3d 146, 2022) early during its tenure. Regardless of whether the immigrant is impoverished or an asylum seeker, the Trump administration created the notion of a policy that kept these individuals in either Mexico or Canada until their cases were heard. This kept the United States from having to pay to detain those individuals while they awaited court processing. This type of policy is appealing to fiscal conservatives.

The final two policies embraced by Republicans that impact the work of ICE include the use of soldiers on the border and the construction of a border wall. Since the formation of ICE, it has been a regular practice to send soldiers to the border to provide support to the agencies defending the border. It is important to note that these soldiers cannot participate in law enforcement investigations, arrests, or any other practices that would result in citizen or noncitizen interaction. This is due to Posse Comitatus (1878), a federal policy that prohibits the federal use of the military on US soil. Because of this prohibition, soldiers sent to the border are only allowed to function in an administrative capacity. National Guard members, however, whether sent by Presidents Bush, Obama, or Trump, can assist the various agencies of the DHS. On a practical level, sending military or guard reinforcements to the border is symbolic and primarily political to push the legislative branch into drafting and passing comprehensive immigration reform. While both Democrats and Republicans have historically been supportive in general of sending troops to the border, Democrats have been adamantly opposed to President Trump's use of troops on the border. This opposition stems from the Posse Comitatus Act of 1878, which limits the use of federal military forces to deal with domestic policies in the United States.

As early as the summer of 2015, one of the main pledges Trump made on the presidential campaign trail was to construct a wall along the US-Mexico border that would firmly shut the door on illegal immigration into the United States from the south. In Trump's conception, the proposed border wall would run from California to Texas along the entire land border with Mexico; Mexico would be responsible for the funding of that wall. In the first two years of the Trump presidency, Republicans had control of both chambers of the legislative branch. Despite this fact, no funding for the border wall was allocated by Congress, although funds were provided to replace existing sections of wall. After Democrats won control of the House of Representatives in the 2018 midterm elections, Trump's window for seeking funding for his border wall closed. In early 2019, however, Trump exercised his presidential emergency powers to pull $2.5 billion from military counter-drug enforcement to pay for the wall. This reallocation of funds, however, was condemned by Democrats and other critics as a violation of Congressional authority over federal spending—the legislative branch's so-called power of the purse, and the case ended up before the US Supreme Court, which allowed the funds to be spent while referring the issue back to the lower courts. Despite widespread criticism and litigation, in early 2020, Trump used the same emergency declaration to divert another $3.5 billion from the same military program and $3.2 billion from DOD construction projects. In June 2020, the 9th Circuit Court of Appeals ruled that Trump illegally circumvented Congress for the $2.5 billion and disallowed the $3.6 billion expenditure in an October 2020 decision. After Trump lost the 2020 presidential election to Democrat Joseph R. Biden, however, the US Supreme Court ruled "moot" all legal arguments about using diverted funds without

Congressional authority. Although Trump was able to repair or replace existing wall sections in need of attention, no actual new wall construction was accomplished.

While not a widespread practice, a newer Republican strategy to deal with immigration has been to transport undocumented immigrants to Democratic-controlled states. Republican Governors Greg Abbott (TX) and Ron DeSantis (FL) used this high-profile tactic to load undocumented immigrants onto airplanes or buses destined for states like Massachusetts, Illinois, and New York. DeSantis sent forty-nine migrants from Texas to Martha's Vineyard, Massachusetts (Zuckoff 2023). Although this "publicity stunt" impacted the receiving locations, straining resources and public sentiment, it may actually have facilitated the immigration process for these migrants. In a strange twist, they may be eligible for a "U Visa," a special visa for victims of certain crimes who assist law enforcement in their investigations. If the forty-nine migrants were criminally abducted, each migrant will be eligible for the U Visa which could help make them permanent residents. At the end of 2023, the Bexar County (TX) district attorney was set to present the results of a criminal investigation into DeSantis's actions to a grand jury (Bernstein 2023).

DEMOCRATS ON IMMIGRATION AND CUSTOMS ENFORCEMENT

ICE as an agency is relatively new. It was created in the aftermath of the terrorist attacks on the United States on September 11, 2001. In general, Democratic lawmakers were supportive of the new agency since the reorganized ICE was primarily oriented toward protecting the United States from future terrorist attacks. As the 2000s progressed, the country was largely concerned, not with immigration, but with the war on terrorism, much of which was occurring in Afghanistan and Iraq. It was not until 2008 that the country once again began to critically focus on undocumented immigration. The Obama administration's de-escalation of the War on Terror and the economic implosion of 2008, complete with increasing unemployment rates, forced all Americans regardless of party affiliation, to confront the impacts of undocumented immigration. With the de-emphasis on terrorism, politicians, especially Republicans, began to fill the threat void with the moral threat of undocumented immigration, a common political practice that extends to the 1800s. Whether real or imagined, there is a common misconception that immigrants are "stealing" jobs from American citizens. Economic uncertainty increases the moral threat regardless of the facts.

Between 2008 and 2016 during the Obama presidency, both legal and illegal immigration decreased, primarily due to the economic downturn and the resulting lack of available work opportunities. In addition to the natural decline of immigration due to the US economy's downswing, the Obama administration focused heavily on increased enforcement of illegal immigration cases. Indeed, Republicans generally were content with immigration enforcement under Obama. ICE enforcement was so significant that many Democrats began to oppose the high level of enforcement. It was during this time that ICE began to detain immigrants who were thought to be dangerous or who had extensive criminal histories in their home countries.

Historically, when an immigrant is initially detained, the individual is given a court date and is released into the country; it is expected that the immigrant will then show up to the hearing date to receive their punishment. This practice is known as "catch-and-release." While this has been the general operating practice of immigration agencies, it has become controversial in recent years. Despite the controversy, Democrats are generally supportive of this practice as opposed to detaining individuals until their hearing date. In addition to its cruel and inhumane nature, Democrats believe it is impractical to keep immigrants waiting in adjacent countries while they await their court dates and do not want to use resources on immigrant detention (e.g., clothing, food, shelter).

Abolish ICE?

As a result of the hyper-politics surrounding ICE, the agency's law enforcement efforts have been highlighted through most media outlets. Some of the unintended consequences of increased enforcement have led to negative media portrayals of children being forcibly separated from their parent, and immigrants and refugees dying at the closed US-Mexican border. These news stories led some Democrats to call for major reforms—or outright dissolution—of ICE. In July 2019, Democratic senator and former presidential candidate Elizabeth Warren of Massachusetts wrote an op-ed in which she described how she would change the focus of ICE:

> *Separate law enforcement from immigration enforcement to strengthen our communities.* There are good reasons to keep immigration enforcement and law enforcement separate. When law enforcement is forced to also handle immigration violations, people are less willing to report crimes for fear of revealing their immigration status. Combining these functions sows distrust and harms public safety. As President, I'll put in place strict guidelines to protect sensitive locations like schools, medical facilities, and courthouses from enforcement actions.
>
> *Remake Customs and Border Patrol (CBP) and ICE in a way that reflects our values.* Our immigration agencies should protect Americans and uphold the rule of law, not pursue punitive anti-immigrant policies that target communities of color. I'll hold immigration enforcement to the same due process standards as other law enforcement agencies—no more warrantless arrests or stops deep in the interior of our country. I'll reshape CBP and ICE from top to bottom, focusing their efforts on homeland security efforts like screening cargo, identifying counterfeit goods, and preventing smuggling and trafficking. And to change the culture, I'll insist on transparency and strengthen the authorities of independent internal watchdogs to prevent future abuses. (Warren 2019)

A Democratic policy linked to "catch and release" pertains to court processing. Immigrants generally wait many months between their arrest and court processing. Thus, many Democrats, as well as some Republicans, prefer hiring more judges for immigration cases to reduce this delay. Trump initially expressed support for hiring more immigration judges, but this support waned after 2019. The need for judges, however, has increased in the last several years because judges left their positions at an accelerated rate, primarily due to micromanagement by the Trump administration. Since 2016, immigration lawyers have been retiring at an accelerated rate; it can take up to two years to fill those positions. According to IBISWorld, the average industry growth for immigration lawyers and attorneys in the United States is -1.5 percent from 2015 to 2020. During the Biden administration, legislators crafted a bipartisan bill that would have led to hiring 100 more judges and associated staff. The bill was defeated, however, when former president Trump urged Republicans to vote against it so that the issue would be "live" for his upcoming 2024 presidential campaign.

One of the most gut-wrenching aspects of immigration enforcement involves individuals who were illegally brought to the United States when they were children, and who then become young adults or adults in America. For all intents and purposes, they are Americans, raised in the United States and largely indoctrinated into American culture. These individuals are commonly known as "Dreamers."

During the Obama administration, the DACA Executive Order became the primary US policy to deal with "Dreamers." Under this program, "Dreamers" who did not have a criminal record would be given a partial citizenship status that deferred deportation and provided a work permit; there was no expedited pathway to citizenship under this program. While most Democrats enthusiastically support DACA, most Republicans adamantly oppose it. During the Trump administration, the policy was rescinded, spurring multiple court cases. In June 2020, the Supreme Court ruled against Trump, indicating that the administration had attempted to end DACA in a procedurally incorrect manner. Subsequently, in July 2021, a District Court judge ruled DACA to be unlawful, although the program was allowed to continue for existing recipients and renewals. On October 31, 2022, the Biden administration's DHS issued its "DACA Rule" to formalize the program and strengthen its legal foundation. This rule, however, does not change current eligibility for DACA, make the program available to new applicants, or protect the program from legal challenges. On September 13, 2023, the Fifth Circuit held Biden's DACA Rule to be unlawful, but left DACA in place for existing participants and renewals.

Probably the most controversial position held by some Democrats on immigration issues pertains to so-called sanctuary cities. Sanctuary cities are cities or municipalities that do not cooperate with, and sometimes actively resist, working with ICE in enforcing immigration laws. The Trump administration enacted a policy to withhold federal law enforcement grant funds from sanctuary jurisdictions, but legal challenges did not end in his favor and the policy was repealed by the Department of Justice in April 2021 after Biden's 2020 victory. As of 2024, twenty-nine states and the District of Columbia are sanctuary jurisdictions or have sanctuary cities and/or counties (Vaughan and Griffith 2024).

FURTHER READING

Bankton, Carl L., and Danielle Antoinette Hidalgo. 2015. *Issues in U.S. Immigration*. Amenia, NY: Grey House Publishing.

Beaumont, Ned. 2018. *Beat the Border: An Insider's Guide to How the U.S. Border Works and How to Beat It*. Las Vegas, NV: Amazon.com Services.

Bernstein, Jenna. 2023. "Migrant Case Moves Forward to Texas Grand Jury." *MV Times*, September 18, 2023. https://www.mvtimes.com/2023/09/18/migrant-case-moves-forward-texas-grand-jury/.

Bjelopera, Jerome P. 2015. *Homeland Security Investigations, A Directorate within U.S. Immigration and Customs Enforcement: In Brief*. Washington DC: U.S. Department of Homeland Security.

Congressional Research Service. 2015. *Homeland Security Investigations, A Directorate within U.S. Immigration and Customs Enforcement: In Brief*. Washington, DC: Library of Congress.

Das, Alina. 2020. *No Justice in the Shadows: How America Criminalizes Immigrants*. New York: Bold Type Books.

Davis, Julie Hirschfeld, and Michael D. Shear. 2019. *Border Wars: Inside Trump's Assault on Immigration*. New York: Simon and Schuster.

Democratic National Committee. 2020. 2020 Democratic Party Platform. Accessed August 27, 2020. https://www.presidency.ucsb.edu/documents/2020-democratic-party-platform..

Department of Homeland Security v. Regents of the University of California, 591 U.S. 1, 2020.

Foer, Franklin. 2018. "How ICE Went Rogue." *The Atlantic* 322: 56–70.

Gramlich, John. 2024. "Migrant Encounters at the U.S.-Mexico Border Hit A Record High at the End of 2023." Pew Research Center, February 15, 2024. https://www.pewresearch.org/short-reads/2024/02/15/migrant-encounters-at-the-us-mexico-border-hit-a-record-high-at-the-end-of-2023/.

Hillstrom, Laurie. 2020. *Family Separation and the U.S.-Mexico Border Crisis*. Santa Barbara, CA: ABC-Clio.

Immigration and Customs Enforcement (ICE). n.d. "U.S. Immigration and Customs Enforcement." May 9, 2024. https://www.ice.gov/about-ice.

Immigration and Customs Enforcement (ICE). 2019. *U.S. Immigration and Customs Enforcement Fiscal Year 2019 Enforcement and Removal Operations Report*. Washington, DC: Immigration and Customs Enforcement.

Immigration and Customs Enforcement (ICE). 2023. *U.S. Immigration and Customs Enforcement Fiscal Year 2023 Enforcement and Removal Operations Report*. December 29, 2023. Washington, DC: Immigration and Customs Enforcement.

McElreath, David Hughes, Carl J. Jensen, Michael Wigginton, Daniel Adrian Doss, Robert Nations, and Jeffrey Van Slyke. 2013. *Introduction to Homeland Security*. Second Edition. Boca Raton, FL: CRC Press.

Office of Inspector General. 2017. *Special Report: Challenges Facing DHS in Its Attempts to Hire 15,000 Border Patrol Agents and Immigration Officers*. Washington, DC: Department of Homeland Security.

Passel, Jeffrey S., and Jens Manuel Krogstad. 2023. "What We Know About Unauthorized Immigrants Living in the U.S." Pew Research Center, November 16, 2023. https://www.pewresearch.org/short-reads/2023/11/16/what-we-know-about-unauthorized-immigrants-liv ing-in-the-us/#:~:text=As%20of%202021%2C%20the%20nation's,1.75%20million%2C%20or%2014%25.

Payan, Tony. 2006. *The Three U.S.-Mexico Border Wars: Drugs, Immigration, and Homeland Security*. Westport, CT: Praeger Security International.

Pew Research Center. 2024. "How Americans View the Situation at the U.S.-Mexico Border, It's Causes and Consequences." February 15, 2024. https://www.pewresearch.org/politics/2024/02/15/how-americans-view-the-situation-at-the-u-s-mexico-border-its-causes-and-consequences/.

Republican National Committee. 2016. 2016 Republican Party Platform. July 18, 2016. https://www.presidency.ucsb.edu/documents/2016-republican-party-platform. Accessed February 2, 2020.

Sampathkumar, Mythili. 2019. *Inside ICE*. New York: Enslow Publishing.

Simmons, Christine M., ed. 2014. *Immigrant Detention Facilities: Costs, Standards, and Issues of Sexual Abuse*. Hauppauge, NY: Nova Science Publishers.

Taylor, Derrick. 2014. *Tainted I.C.E.: Immigration and Customs Enforcement*. San Francisco, CA: DBM Publishing.

Trump, Donald J. "Tweet Message." Twitter, July 3, 2018. https://twitter.com/realDonaldTrump/status/1014100908127543296?ref_src=twsrc%5Etfw%7Ctwcamp%5Etweetembed%7Ctwterm%5E1014100908127543296%7Ctwgr%5E496f370a4c4dfe0f65598b8f3e43bd8425b6062a%7Ctwcon%5Es1_&ref_url=https%3A%2F%2Fwww.voanews.com%2Fa%2Ftrump-accuses-democrats-of-demeaning-immigration-agents%2F4464865.html.

Uhlmann, Natascha E. 2019. *Abolish ICE*. New York: OR Books.

United States Congress. 2017. *Release of Criminal Detainees by US Immigration and Customs Enforcement: Policy or Politics?* Washington, DC: Createspace.

U.S. Department of Homeland Security. 2019. *U.S. Immigration and Customs Enforcement's Alternatives to Detention*. Washington, DC: Createspace.

Vaughan, Jessica M., and Bryan Griffith. 2024. Map: Sanctuary Cities, Counties, and States. Center for Immigration Studies. April 12, 2024. https://cis.org/Map-Sanctuary-Cities-Counties-and-States.

Wadhia, Shoba S. 2019. *Banned: Immigration Enforcement in the Time of Trump*. New York: NYU Press.

Warren, Elizabeth. 2019. "A Fair and Welcoming Immigration System." *Medium*. https://medium.com/@teamwarren/a-fair-and-welcoming-immigration-system-8fff69cd674e. Accessed July 31, 2024.

Zuckoff, Raquel C. 2023. "A Journey Continues: Migrants Reflect One Year After Being Flown to Martha's Vineyard." WGBH Boston Public Radio, September 14, 2023. https://www.wgbh.org/news/local/2023-09-14/a-journey-continues-migrants-reflect-one-year-after-being-flown-to-marthas-vineyard.

CHAPTER 15

International Terrorism

KELLY A. MCHUGH

AT A GLANCE

The Federal Bureau of Investigation (FBI) defines terrorism as one of two types, international or domestic. International terrorism occurs when individuals and/or groups commit violent, criminal acts on behalf of foreign terrorist organizations or nations. In the United States, domestic terrorism refers to violent, criminal acts committed by Americans in furtherance of ideological goals (religious, political, social, racial, or environmental). According to the FBI, there were 335 known or suspected acts of terrorism in the United States between 1980 and 2000, with 247 attributed to domestic terrorists, and 88 to international terrorists.

Prior to 2001, acts of terrorism were handled through existing legislation that regulated how private communications could be intercepted and how foreign surveillance and collection of foreign intelligence could be conducted. These restrictive rules, which reflected civil liberties and privacy concerns, prohibited the collection of a wide range of private information for law enforcement purposes and made sharing among agencies very difficult. After the September 11, 2001, terrorist attacks killed and injured thousands of people on American soil, however, legislation was passed by Congress and signed into law by Republican President George W. Bush that significantly changed how terrorism investigations are conducted and how terrorism suspects are treated.

MANY REPUBLICANS...

- Believe international terrorism is a top threat to the national security of the United States and that it is appropriate for the government to implement a comprehensive approach to preventing attacks. This effort encompasses a range of policy domains, including foreign affairs, intelligence gathering, law enforcement, and homeland security.

- Support renewal of provisions of the 2001 USA Patriot Act, which grants federal law enforcement personnel sweeping powers to investigate and prevent potential terrorist plots and punish actual acts of terrorism. While this surveillance may compromise the privacy rights of American citizens, most Republicans believe the benefits to national security to outweigh the cost.
- Believe that foreign nationals suspected of plotting terrorist attacks against the United States should be classified as "enemy combatants" and should not enjoy protection under the US Constitution or international law. As such, many believe it acceptable to hold these individuals in military detention facilities and try them in military courts. Some also argue that more extreme interrogation methods are necessary to obtain critical intelligence from terrorist suspects.

MANY DEMOCRATS...

- Believe international terrorism is a top threat to the national security of the United States and that it is appropriate for the United States to implement a comprehensive approach to preventing attacks. This effort encompasses a range of policy domains, including foreign affairs, intelligence gathering, law enforcement, and homeland security.
- Believe that the federal government should expand its intelligence-gathering capabilities to combat terrorism, but that federal powers should be balanced with accountability mechanisms to ensure that law-abiding US citizens are not subject to unnecessary and unconstitutional surveillance.
- Believe that foreign nationals suspected of terrorism-related crimes against the United States should be afforded protections under international law during their imprisonment and trial. This means that whenever possible they should have their cases adjudicated in civilian courts where they enjoy due process rights such as access to counsel. Moreover, the use of extreme interrogation methods against these suspects not only violates international law but also compromises US values.

OVERVIEW

On September 11, 2001, the United States suffered the worst terrorist attack in its history. Nineteen suicide terrorists affiliated with al-Qaeda, a terrorist Muslim organization founded in the late 1980s by Osama bin Laden, hijacked four airplanes, crashing two into the World Trade Center towers in New York City and one into the Pentagon in Washington, DC. The fourth plane crashed in a rural Pennsylvania field after passengers overpowered the hijackers. In total, 2,977 people were killed, over 6,000 were injured, and the United States suffered billions of dollars in economic damage. Though impossible to quantify, the attacks had a profound impact on both public and elite attitudes about the vulnerability of the United States to international terrorism. As such, in the aftermath of the tragedy, elected officials from both parties endorsed a comprehensive approach to preventing future mass-casualty attacks on US soil. In the months and years after the attacks, the administration of Republican President George W. Bush established the framework for the nation's efforts to combat international terrorism; much of this policy architecture remains in place two decades later.

Following the attacks, the Bush administration declared the United States to be engaged in a War on Terror. In October 2001, a mere forty-five days later, Congress responded by passing the Uniting and Strengthening America by Providing Appropriate Tools Required to Intercept and Obstruct Terrorism Act (i.e., USA Patriot Act). The legislation amended the Foreign Intelligence Surveillance Act (FISA) of 1978, removed many existing judicial barriers to surveillance by the federal government, expanded the definition of terrorism, and sought to provide federal law enforcement personnel with sweeping new powers to detect, prevent, investigate, and punish acts of terrorism.

President George W. Bush Announces the Passage of the USA Patriot Act in 2001

On October 25, 2001, President Bush signed the USA Patriot ACT, granting the federal government sweeping new powers to detect, prevent and punish terrorism.

Today, we take an essential step in defeating terrorism, while protecting the constitutional rights of all Americans. With my signature, this law will give intelligence and law enforcement officials important new tools to fight a present danger. ... For example, this legislation gives law enforcement officials better tools to put an end to financial counterfeiting, smuggling, and money-laundering. Secondly, it gives intelligence operations and criminal operations the chance to operate not on separate tracks, but to share vital information so necessary to disrupt a terrorist attack before it occurs. As of today, we're changing the laws governing information-sharing. And as importantly, we're changing the culture of our various agencies that fight terrorism. Countering and investigating terrorist activity is the number one priority for both law enforcement and intelligence agencies. Surveillance of communications is another essential tool to pursue and stop terrorists. The existing law was written in the era of rotary telephones. This new law that I sign today will allow surveillance of all communications used by terrorists, including e-mails, the Internet, and cell phones. ... This bill was carefully drafted and considered. Led by the members of Congress on this stage, and those seated in the audience, it was crafted with skill and care, determination and a spirit of bipartisanship for which the entire nation is grateful. This bill met with an overwhelming—overwhelming agreement in Congress because it upholds and respects the civil liberties guaranteed by our Constitution. (Bush 2001)

During legislative debate, some members of Congress expressed concerns that the Act would give the federal government the authority to monitor the communications of law-abiding US citizens. Despite these concerns, however, it passed with overwhelming bipartisan support; only one Senator and sixty-six Representatives voted against it; the sole nay vote in the Senate came from a Democrat, as did sixty-two of the nay votes in the House. As a precautionary measure, Congress made several provisions of the Act subject to expiration (or sunset) after five years, requiring Congressional reauthorization to renew.

Since the Act was passed, groups such as the American Civil Liberties Union, the Electronic Frontier Foundation, and the Center for Constitutional Rights have criticized it for infringing upon the constitutionally protected privacy rights of American citizens. Three of its provisions have been especially controversial. The first, Section 203, allows greater information sharing between intelligence agencies, effectively shattering the wall between foreign and domestic surveillance. The second, Section 206, permits federal authorities to use a single wiretap authorization to cover multiple communications devices used by a suspect (a "roving wiretap"). Finally, Section 215, the "business records provision," allows the FBI to obtain confidential data, including a person's financial or medical information, without a judge's approval (Abramson and Godoy 2005). Although its contents have evolved over time—a bipartisan coalition of lawmakers worked to narrow the scope of some provisions, and the US Supreme Court struck down some provisions as unconstitutional—its key elements remain in place, with majorities in both chambers of the Congress electing to reauthorize all of its expiring provisions on five separate occasions since its passage.

Members of both parties have supported the consolidation of executive branch agencies responsible for counterterrorism. Eleven days after the 9/11 attacks, Bush announced that Pennsylvania Governor Tom Ridge, a Republican, would serve as the inaugural director of the Office of Homeland Security. In this capacity, Ridge would oversee and coordinate the work of twenty-two agencies participating in anti-terrorism efforts. This included Immigration and Naturalization Services, the Transportation Security Administration, the Secret Service, and the Federal Emergency Management Agency. In 2002, Congress passed legislation formally establishing the Department of Homeland Security (DHS), making it the fifteenth cabinet-level department. The DHS currently employs more than 200,000 personnel and ranks as the third-largest cabinet department within the executive branch.

After DHS was established, attempts to pass reforms to the country's diffuse intelligence community soon followed. In 2002, the Bush administration established the Commission on Terrorist Attacks Upon the United States, which was tasked with compiling an official history of all attacks and making policy recommendations to prevent future ones. The resulting report, issued in 2004, identified numerous intelligence failures that occurred before the attacks, stemming from a lack of cooperation and coordination among agencies. To reconcile this, Congress passed the Intelligence Reform and Terrorism Prevention Act of 2004. This established the Director of National Intelligence (DNI), a new cabinet-level official authorized to oversee all seventeen US intelligence agencies. The DNI was also envisioned as the principal intelligence advisor to the president.

Following the 9/11 attacks, through a series of executive orders and secret memorandum, the Bush administration created a parallel legal system to detain and try foreign nationals accused of planning or executing acts of terrorism against the United States. Before 9/11, noncitizens accused of terrorism-related crimes were tried in civilian courts, and if convicted, were incarcerated in federal prisons. The Bush Justice Department, however, argued that suspected terrorists should be classified as "enemy combatants," and thus should not enjoy the protections afforded to prisoners of war under international law. In accordance with this view, the president issued an executive order in 2001 that established military commissions to try terrorist suspects. Trials in these commissions were not governed by the Fifth Amendment's guarantee of due process, so defendants were not entitled to legal counsel and could not review the evidence against them. Moreover, by early 2002, the administration began sending terrorist suspects awaiting trial to a US military facility located in Guantanamo Bay, Cuba. Since the base was not in US territory, the administration argued that the prisoners held there could be detained indefinitely without being charged with a crime.

Finally, although it was not revealed until years later, President Bush signed a classified directive in 2001 allowing the Central Intelligence Agency (CIA) to use so-called enhanced interrogation methods to obtain information from suspected terrorists. Included was the ability to subject detainees to humiliation tactics, forcing them to remain in stress positions for long periods of time, and simulating drowning (a practice known as waterboarding). Such practices are prohibited by the *Army Field Manual*, which governs the treatment of international prisoners held in US custody. Enhanced interrogation techniques, however, have been used on detainees at Guantanamo Bay, as well as on prisoners held at top-secret US prisons established overseas, referred to as "black sites" (Peralta 2014).

During the initial years of the War on Terror, despite the unprecedented concentration of power in the executive branch, the exponential growth of the counterterrorism budget, and vigorous debates over the constitutionality of US surveillance and detention policies, the Bush administration had strong support from elected officials in both parties. Owing to Bush's stewardship of post-9/11 anti-terrorism efforts, the Republican Party enjoyed a clear political advantage on this issue. Beginning in 2002, Gallup has periodically asked the public which of the major parties would do a better job of protecting the United States from terrorism. Until 2006, polls demonstrated that the public consistently favored Republicans over Democrats. In 2006, however, the public judged Democrats to be superior on this issue for the first time (Saad 2012).

Several developments help to explain the drop in public support for Republican policies. First, in 2004, news outlets published graphic photos showing the abuse of detainees at the US-run Abu Ghraib prison in Iraq. Bush condemned the actions of the US personnel involved and argued that these were isolated incidents of misbehavior. That same year, however, several details were published of the enhanced interrogation techniques that US personnel regularly used on detainees at Guantanamo Bay. Critics, including human rights groups, members of Congress, and former government officials, argued that these practices were tantamount to torture. In response, the following year, Congress included the Detainee Treatment Act of 2005 in a supplemental defense spending bill. This prohibited Department of Defense personnel from employing any interrogation tactics not sanctioned by the *Army Field Manuel*. Although Bush agreed to the legislation, he included a signing statement in which he reserved the right to set aside this prohibition if he deemed it to be in the national interest.

Other developments called into question the necessity of the expansive measures the administration undertook as part of the War on Terror. In 2005, the *New York Times* revealed the existence of the "President's Surveillance Program" that allowed the National

Security Administration (NSA) to monitor phone calls, emails, and text messages of Americans without a warrant. Finally, the Iraq War, launched in 2003, had become a costly and protracted US military endeavor. Although the Bush administration had initially argued that the removal of Iraqi leader Saddam Hussein would aid in America's global fight against terrorism, by 2006, Iraq was in the midst of a bloody civil war and had become a haven for al-Qaeda.

After Democrat Barack Obama took the Oath of Office to become the nation's 44th president in January 2009, he pledged robust support for continued US efforts to defeat al Qaeda. He also promised, however, to roll back what he and many in his party considered to be the excesses of the Bush administration's counterterrorism policies. His administration did succeed in making some policy changes. Obama banned the use of enhanced interrogation methods against suspected terrorists, reduced the number of detainees housed at Guantanamo Bay, and permitted some suspected terrorists to be tried in federal courts. By and large, however, his administration maintained—and in some cases expanded—the surveillance policies put in place by his predecessor. When faced with criticism from civil libertarians in both parties, Obama consistently supported the renewal of expiring provisions of the Patriot Act and defended the program as essential to preventing future terrorist attacks. He maintained this stance even when former CIA contractor Edward Snowden leaked documents in 2013 that showed the NSA used its Patriot Act powers to engage in the bulk collection of phone records of US citizens.

During its eight years, the Obama administration was forced to contend with the evolving nature of terrorism. The United States' post-9/11 counterterrorism policies were focused on combating international terrorism, but during Obama's presidency, homegrown terrorism emerged as a major threat. American citizens perpetrated both the Fort Hood shooting in 2009 and the Boston Marathon bombing in 2013. The existing counterterrorism framework, which focused on targeting terrorist groups, proved ill-suited to detecting and preventing these types of "lone-wolf" attacks. Moreover, by the middle of Obama's second term, the Islamic State of Iraq and Syria (ISIS) had supplanted al-Qaeda as the top international terrorist threat to the United States. Individuals directed by ISIS or inspired by the group's propaganda orchestrated deadly attacks in the United States, including those in San Bernardino, California, in 2015 and Orlando, Florida, in 2017.

Republican President Donald J. Trump, the third executive to manage the US War on Terror, took a hardline tone during the 2016 election, blaming Obama's rollback of Bush-era policies for the rise of ISIS. As a candidate, Trump promised he would reinstate the use of enhanced interrogation methods against suspected terrorists and increase the number of detainees sent to Guantanamo. Once in office though, he largely continued the policies of the Obama administration. The Trump administration, however, did depart from its predecessors in expressly linking immigration policy and counterterrorism policy. In 2017, Trump issued an executive order categorically banning immigration from eight Muslim majority countries. He and many Republicans argued that stricter border controls were a crucial element in preventing attacks inside the United States.

Since the Bush administration first pledged to defeat international terrorism using "every tool in [its] arsenal—military power, better homeland defenses, law enforcement, intelligence, and vigorous efforts to cut off terrorist financing" (Bush 2002, vi), US anti-terrorism efforts have been characterized by consistency, rather than by change. A review of major policy debates demonstrates that there are significant differences between the two parties on issues such as the proper scope of government surveillance, the degree to which detainees enjoy protections under international law, and the link between immigration and terrorism. Throughout the duration of the War on Terror, however, members of both parties have been united in the belief that the United States must devote significant resources to comprehensive efforts to prevent attacks. In 2018, a report from the nonpartisan Stimson Center estimated that those resources had cost the United States a total of $2.8 billion since 2001 (Stimson Center 2018, 5).

REPUBLICANS ON INTERNATIONAL TERRORISM

In the years following the 9/11 attacks, Congressional Republicans were steadfast in their support for the Bush administration's ambitious counterterrorism policies. Every member of the party voted in favor of the 2001 Patriot Act; when expiring provisions were up for reauthorization in 2005, only eighteen House Republicans opposed their renewal. In addition, a substantial majority of Congressional Republicans supported the legislation creating the DHS in 2002, as well as the 2004 Intelligence Reform Act, which created the DNI.

The ostensible success of the Bush administration's counterterrorism policies proved to be an electoral boon for the party, with Republicans arguing that the sweeping changes put in place had prevented additional attacks. The 2002 midterm elections occurred fourteen months after the terrorist attacks, and the president, along with New York Mayor Rudy Giuliani, traveled around the country to campaign on behalf of Congressional Republicans in competitive races. Ultimately, the party gained additional seats in both chambers. Subsequently, during the 2004 presidential election, the Republican platform gave top billing to the party's commitment to fighting terrorism, and Bush made his leadership of the effort a centerpiece of his campaign. He was ultimately reelected in November, defeating Democratic candidate Massachusetts Senator John Kerry.

During his second term, despite the growing controversy over the administration's detainee policies, Bush generally maintained strong support from members of his party. In 2006, the Supreme Court declared in *Hamdan v. Rumsfeld* (548 U.S. 557) that the military tribunals established by the administration violated international law. In response, the Republican-controlled Congress overwhelmingly passed the Military Commissions Act of 2006, reinstating the tribunals, but adding some legal protections for detainees. In addition, in 2008, Republicans vigorously opposed efforts by Democrats in Congress to insert a measure in the annual Intelligence Authorization Act prohibiting US personnel from using enhanced interrogation techniques. Although the measure passed the Democratic-controlled Congress, it did so with scant support among Republicans. Bush ultimately vetoed the bill, arguing that the continuation of enhanced interrogation techniques was crucial to US national security.

Republican support for enhanced integration measures was by no means uniform, however. Arizona Senator John McCain, a former US Navy pilot who had been subjected to torture during his five and half years as a prisoner of war in Vietnam, emerged as the most outspoken Republican opponent of the administration's interrogation policies. In 2006, he successfully proposed an amendment to the National Defense Authorization Act that restricted the types of interrogation techniques the United States could use on detainees. Up until his death in 2018, McCain remained an ardent opponent of the use of torture by US civilian and military personnel.

Senator John McCain Speaks Out against Torture, 2014

During a debate over whether or not the Senate should declassify a top-secret report on the use of torture by the CIA, Senator McCain discussed his opposition to the practice.

I know from personal experience that the abuse of prisoners will produce more bad than good intelligence. I know victims of torture will offer intentionally misleading information if they think their captors will believe it. I know they will say whatever they think their torturers want them to say if they believe it will stop their suffering. Most of all, I know the use of torture compromises that which most distinguishes us from our enemies—our belief that all people, even captured enemies, possess basic human rights which are protected by international conventions the United States not only joined but for the most part authored. ... What might come as a surprise not just to our enemies but to many Americans is how little these practices did aid our efforts to bring 9/11 culprits to justice and to find and prevent terrorist attacks today and tomorrow. ... But in the end torture's failure to serve its intended purpose isn't the main reason to oppose its use. I have often said and I will always maintain that this question isn't about our enemies; it is about us. It is about who we were, who we are, and who we aspire to be. It is about how we represent ourselves to the world. (McCain 2014)

The policy preferences of Republicans in the realm of foreign terrorism threats remained largely consistent during the presidency of Barack Obama. Congressional Republicans actively opposed efforts by the Democratic president to rollback Bush-era detention policies. In 2011, for example, Congress passed the bipartisan Ike Skelton National Defense Authorization Act by overwhelming margins. The legislation stymied Obama's plans to close Guantanamo Bay, as it contained a provision prohibiting the administration from using funds to transfer or release detainees held there into the United States. In addition, members of the Republican Party remained supportive of the post-9/11 surveillance powers granted to the federal government. Since Congressional Democrats had become increasingly skeptical of the vast authority vested in the executive branch, Republican legislators were crucial in providing the Obama administration with the votes to reauthorize controversial provisions of the Patriot Act. When the Act was due for reauthorization in 2011, Republicans delivered 75 percent of the "yea" votes in the House, and 58 percent of the "yea" votes in the Senate.

Despite the majority, a small faction within the Republican Party emerged as outspoken opponents of the mass surveillance policies that formed the cornerstone of post-9/11 intelligence-gathering efforts. Senators Rand Paul of Kentucky and Mike Lee of Utah consistently expressed reservations about the degree to which measures like the Patriot Act compromised the civil liberties of US citizens. In 2011, they joined three other Senate Republicans in refusing to support the Act's reauthorization. In 2015, when provisions of the Act were again due to expire, Paul conducted an eleven-hour filibuster and succeeded in temporarily delaying the renewal of the Act.

The 2016 election of Republican Donald J. Trump generally resulted in policy continuity, despite his campaign rhetoric. Trump had indicated that he believed waterboarding was an effective interrogation tool and promised that if elected, he would reauthorize its use by the CIA. In accordance with this, during his first month in office, his administration drafted an executive order that would permit the use of the enhanced integration methods abolished by the Obama administration, and reopen the overseas prisons where these practices could be employed. This move was opposed by national security officials in his administration as well as by some Republicans in Congress, including Senators Paul and McCain. Ultimately, Trump elected not to issue the executive order. He did, however, issue another executive order in 2018, pledging to keep the Guantanamo Bay detention camp open indefinitely. Like his predecessors, Trump supported the renewal of expiring provisions of the Patriot Act. In 2019, Congress passed a stopgap measure extending the provisions until March 2020. By May of 2020, both chambers of Congress had passed separate bills reauthorizing the expiring provisions through 2023.The Congress, however, has never sent a final version to the president, and the surveillance powers contained in the Act are expired as of 2020.

DEMOCRATS ON INTERNATIONAL TERRORISM

In the early years of the War on Terror, there was little distinction between the positions of the two parties regarding the appropriate scope of US counterterrorism efforts. In overwhelming numbers, Democrats supported the passage of the Patriot Act in 2001. Most Congressional Democrats also voted in favor of the creation of the DHS in 2002, as well as the 2004 Intelligence Reform Act. During the 2004 presidential election, Democratic nominee John Kerry largely endorsed the policies of the Bush administration and the party's platform echoed Republicans in endorsing comprehensive efforts to defeat global terrorism.

During Bush's second term, however, a key cleavage emerged between the parties, with most Democrats opposing the administration's detainee policies. In 2006, in large numbers, Democrats opposed the passage of the Military Commissions Act, which would permit the president to continue to try detainees in military tribunals rather than in civilian courts. Moreover, after Democrats won control of the House in the 2006 midterm elections, party leaders took steps to limit the Bush administration's use of enhanced interrogation methods on detainees. In 2008, California Senator Dianne Feinstein inserted a provision in the annual Department of Defense Appropriations Act that would prohibit the CIA from using several types of interrogation methods, including waterboarding, electrical shocks, and mock executions. When it came to a vote, it was supported by all Congressional Democrats, except one senator and six representatives.

During the 2008 presidential campaign, the party made clear its opposition to Bush's policies toward detainees. The Democratic nominee, Illinois Senator Barack Obama, promised that if elected, he would close the Guantanamo Bay facility, transfer the prisoners held there to federal custody, and ban the use of enhanced interrogation measures. Once in office, he had mixed success in fulfilling these promises. During his first month in office, Obama signed two executive orders related to reforming the country's antiterrorism policies; one banned enhanced interrogation methods, while the second established the goal of closing Guantanamo Bay within one year, and temporarily halted the use of military commissions to try detainees. Pursuant to this goal, the administration created a task force to review the status of all current prisoners held at the Guantanamo Bay facility. After examining each case, the task force would determine if the prisoner should be released, tried in federal court, or tried by a military commission.

Ultimately, however, the Obama administration was unable to close the detention facility. In a bipartisan vote in 2011, Congress passed the Ike Skelton National Defense Authorization Act, which contained a provision prohibiting military funds from being used to transfer detainees to the United States for trial. Subsequently, in 2011, Obama issued an executive order reinstating the use of military commissions to try suspects. Although Obama was unable to close the Guantanamo Bay facility during his time in office, he did succeed in resettling many of the detainees who were not charged with crimes. When he took office, 242 prisoners were held in the facility; this number dropped to 42 by the time he completed his second term (Human Rights First 2018).

Remarks by President Obama on His Administration's Approach to Counterterrorism, 2016

Near the end of his second term, President Obama spoke to US military personnel at MacDill Airforce Base.

Iit has been my conviction that even as we focus relentlessly on dismantling terrorist networks like al Qaeda and ISIL, we should ask allies to do their share in the fight, and we should strengthen local partners who can provide lasting security. ... And this focus on al Qaeda—the most dangerous threat to the United States at the time—paid dividends. Today, by any measure, core al Qaeda—the organization that hit us on 9/11—is a shadow of its former self. Plots directed from within Afghanistan and Pakistan have been consistently disrupted. Its leadership has been decimated. Dozens of terrorist leaders have been killed. Osama bin Laden is dead. And, importantly, we have built a counterterrorism capability that can sustain this pressure against any terrorist network in South Asia that might threaten the United States of America. ... Now, to say that we've made progress is not to say that the job is done. We know that a deadly threat persists. We know that in some form this violent extremism will be with us for years to come. In too many parts of the world, especially in the Middle East, there has been a breakdown of order that's been building for decades, and it's unleashed forces that are going to take a generation to resolve. (Obama 2016)

In the realm of surveillance, the Obama administration sought to maintain Bush-era policies, despite growing skepticism within the Democratic Party. In 2011, when provisions in Patriot Act were due for renewal, House Democrats opposed the reauthorization by an almost 2-1 margin. By 2015, when portions of the Act were again due to expire, the administration acceded to bipartisan calls to limit the scope of the government's surveillance powers. The reauthorization bill, titled the USA Freedom Act renewed three expiring provisions of the Patriot Act, but also limited the ability of federal intelligence agencies to collect and store data on the telecommunications of Americans. Upon taking office in 2021, the Biden administration did not seek additional powers to surveil individuals suspected of links to international terrorism. Instead, the administration focused on violent homegrown extremism, and published the *National Strategy for Countering Domestic Terrorism* (National Security Council, 2021).

During the Trump presidency, Congressional Democrats emerged as strong opponents of his January 2017 executive order halting immigration from eight Muslim-majority countries. Democrats in both chambers proposed legislation that condemned and sought to reverse the action. Opponents of the measure deemed it a "Muslim ban," arguing that it constituted discrimination against members of the Islamic faith, while doing little to protect the US homeland. In 2017, Senator Dianne Feinstein of California introduced a bill rescinding the travel ban, and Vermont Senator Patrick Leahy, along with thirty Democratic cosponsors, introduced a nonbinding resolution condemning the executive order as contrary to US values of inclusivity. In the House, Democratic Representative Judy Chu of California introduced the NO BAN Act, designed to limit the president's ability to categorically ban immigration flows from specific countries. As of 2020, it had 216 Democratic cosponsors. However, none of these measures received a vote and expired at the end of the 116th Congress.

FURTHER READING

Abramson, Larry, and Maria Godoy. 2005. "The Patriot Act: Key Controversies." NPR, December 16, 2005. https://legacy.npr.org/news/specials/patriotact/patriotactdeal.html?ref=the-republic-sentinel.ghost.io.

Bush, George W. 2001. "President Signs Anti-terrorism Bill." George W. Bush White House Archives. https://georgewbush-whitehouse.archives.gov/news/releases/2001/10/20011026-5.html. Accessed August 3, 2022.

Bush, George W. 2002. *The National Security Strategy of the United States of America*. September 2002.https://www.globalsecurity.org/military/library/policy/national/nss-020920.pdf.

Cohen, Zachary, and Jennifer Hansler. 2019. "State Department Rejects More Than 37,000 Visas Under Trump's Travel Ban." CNN, February 26, 2019. https://www.google.com/amp/s/amp.cnn.com/cnn/2019/02/26/politics/state-department-travel-ban visas.

Human Rights First. 2018. "Guantanamo by the Numbers." October 10, 2018. https://www.humanrightsfirst.org/library/guantanamo-by-the-numbers/.

McCain, John. 2014. "Sen. McCain's Full Statement on the CIA Torture Report." *USA Today*. December 9, 2014. https://www.usatoday.com/story/news/politics/2014/12/09/john-mccain-statement-cia-terror-report/20144015/.

Obama, Barack. 2016. "Remarks by the President on the Administration's Approach to Counterterrorism." Barack Obama White House Archives, December 6, 2016. https://obamawhitehouse.archives.gov/the-press-office/2016/12/06/remarks-president-administrations-approach-counterterrorism.

Peralta, Eyder. 2014. "'Torture Report': A Closer Look at When and What President Bush Knew." NPR, December 16, 2014. https://www.npr.org/sections/thetwo-way/2014/12/16/369876047/torture-report-a-closer-look-at-when-and-what-president-bush-knew.

Saad, Lydia. 2012. "Democrats Pull Even With Republicans as Better on Terrorism." *Gallup News*, September 13, 2012. https://news.gallup.com/poll/157445/democrats-pull-even-republicans-better-terrorism.aspx.

The Stimson Center. 2018. "Counterterrorism Spending: Protecting America While Promoting Efficiencies and Accountability." May 2018. https://www.stimson.org/wp-content/files/file-attachments/CT_Spending_Report_0.pdf. Accessed August 3, 2022.

The Washington Post. 2001. "Text: Bush Signs Anti-Terrorism Legislation." October 25, 2001. https://www.washingtonpost.com/wpsrv/nation/specials/attacked/transcripts/bushtext_102601.html.

The White House. n.d. "The Executive Branch." Accessed July 3, 2020. https://www.whitehouse.gov/about-the-white-house/the-executive-branch/.

CHAPTER 16

Law Enforcement Discretion

LUIS F. NUÑO

AT A GLANCE

Law enforcement discretion refers to the inevitable reality that police officers make choices about which laws to enforce, and how to interact with local residents when enforcing those laws. Enforcing the law is one of the many tasks assigned to police officers, which include order maintenance, peace keeping, crime prevention, and criminal investigation. The focus here will be primarily on political debates about police officers' decisions when making stops and issuing arrests, including the nature of police-citizen interaction during those encounters.

Stop-and-frisk is a police tactic that is heavily reliant on police discretion. The idea behind stop-and-frisk is that low-level citations and arrests are an effective crime-control strategy. Stop-and-frisk is premised on the notion that patrol officers are socialized into an occupational subculture where they learn how to recognize suspicious activity. Stop-and-frisk policing is a subset of broken windows policing. Broken windows policing rests on the notion that police occupational subculture grants them special knowledge to identify social forces that create disorder and contribute to crime. This insider knowledge allows police to detect the signs of a potential drug dealer or an individual carrying a gun. Stop-and-frisk is a police practice that allows officers to stop and search people that give off signs that they might be in possession of drugs or a firearm. Critics contend that this police practice allows officers to discriminate against racial and ethnic minority groups using the decision to preserve public safety as a cover for their biased decision-making. The Democratic and Republican Parties both defended broken windows theory and stop-and-frisk policing until Black Lives Matter protests called into question systemic bias in exercise of law enforcement discretion.

Community activists argue that discretionary powers should be made more transparent, and officers who make rash decisions should be held accountable. A Minneapolis police officer's decision to kneel on the neck of a Black man for nearly nine minutes as he struggled to breathe put the issue of police discretion in the spotlight.

MANY REPUBLICANS...

- Argue that policing is a highly specialized skill and that police should enforce the law the best way that they know how, even if in some instances officer discretionary decisions may come across looking like racial profiling .
- Believe that the rule of law and, by extension, the exercise of discretion in law enforcement exist in the abstract independent of the systemic biases built into American democracy .

MANY DEMOCRATS...

- Believe that police-community relations are at risk of disruption when police repeatedly make the wrong decisions, exercising discretion that appears from the community's perspective to reinforce institutional and systemic bias.
- Believe that independent review can assess the quality of police training, whether there may be some officers more prone to making bad split-second decisions than others, and the impact that certain situations (such as being under duress) can have on officers' ability to make rational decisions.

OVERVIEW

On May 25, 2020, Minneapolis police officers arrested a Black man by the name of George Floyd, pinning him to the ground while one of the officers kneeled on the back of his neck for nearly nine minutes. Witness videos captured the confrontation. Floyd died as a result of the police decisions during this interaction, and his death sparked massive public protests in June, despite a worldwide pandemic. For many who viewed the video, a police officer's decision to choke a handcuffed man to death is a vivid example of systemic bias in law enforcement discretionary behavior. During the video, Floyd pleads for his life, yells "I cannot breathe" at least sixteen times in less than five minutes and calls out for his mother. Not once during this encounter does the officer kneeling on Floyd's neck give way to Mr. Floyd's cries. The other officers actively prevent witnesses from intervening, thus assisting in the killing of a handcuffed Black man.

The rule of law is central to American democracy and is supported at local, state, and federal levels by law enforcement agencies and agents. However, in American democracy there appear to exist two rules of law, one for whites and another for non-whites. For white people, law and order means public civility and justice in the courts for those who violate collective morals codified as criminal law. As former chairman of the Republican National Committee Michael Steele said, "For black folks, especially older black folks, when they hear a white man talking about 'law and order,' that means get your ass in the house before dark" (Alberta 2020). Law enforcement discretionary power reflects the social reality that there exist two rules of law, one that applies to Black people in unofficial street justice and another idealized by white people in the legal discourse.

Public figures recently began to call attention to how police discretionary power is exercised in American society. Professional sports is an arena where social protests about police brutality have gained popular attention. Athletes in National Football League during the fall 2016 season decided to kneel during the playing of the national anthem to call attention to police brutality against people of color in the United States. There emerged a sharp divide in how Americans understood these protests and the issue of police brutality. Older Americans, Republicans, and whites were more likely to believe the protests to be wrong. Younger Americans, Democrats, and Blacks were more likely to support the protests (SSRS survey cited in Intravia, Piquero, and Piquero 2018, 1059).

Democracy requires transparency and accountability. The concepts of law enforcement, transparency, and accountability, however, often are at odds. Defenders of greater police discretion point to the thin blue line that protects free society from dangerous elements of social order. Those who seek to place limits on police discretion point to system biases in how patrol officers interact with the public.

The history of modern policing is linked to the establishment of a racial hierarchy in American society. The first slave patrols appeared in the southern state of South Carolina in the early 1700s, a full century prior to New York City's urban police force in 1829 (Turner, Giacopassi, and Vandiver 2006). The modern urban police department appeared in New York City, Boston, and Philadelphia during the 1820s and 1830s. Throughout much of the nineteenth century, police in the cities of the Northern States served as political appointees for the urban political machines of early democracy. After the Civil War, the South replaced laws regulating slavery with Black Codes to control the movement of free Black people. When Black Codes proved insufficient, extrajudicial, terrorist violence by the Ku Klux Klan and other groups defending whites' interests worked in partnership with local police to maintain the Jim Crow system. "Anything that challenged the racial hierarchy could be seen as a crime, punished either by law or by the lynchings that stretched from Mississippi to Minnesota" (Stevenson 2019). The assumption that police in America operate as a purely administrative bureaucracy to enforce a colorblind rule of law minimalizes the historical ties of policing with efforts to maintain the racial hierarchy in the United States.

Residents' claims of police brutality sparked riots throughout the 1960s in the cities of Detroit, Newark, and Los Angeles. During this period, Richard Nixon and the Republican Party crafted the Long Southern Strategy to politicize policing (Maxwell 2019). Presenting themselves as defenders of "law and order" for the silent majority of voters who had grown weary of confrontations between police and civil rights protesters, Nixon's Republican Party promised to restore law and order to a nation "with the greatest tradition of the rule of law ... plagued by unprecedented lawlessness" (Nixon 1968).

In a buildup of the system of mass incarceration, a "tough on crime" consensus emerged within both the Democrat and Republican Parties. Law enforcement were at the forefront of the mass incarceration system. The political culture and municipal law enforcement practices emerging from the Reagan-Bush-Clinton eras of the 1980s and 1990s expanded police discretionary power. The popularity of broken windows ideology granted police greater authority to criminalize deviance, thus expanding the criminal justice net. During the last two decades of the twentieth century, the American political system strengthened the role of local city police to make arrests in the War on Drugs and War on Crime, leading to increases in incarceration. The War on Drugs and the War on Crime were instrumental in the reallocation of resources to local city police. Military equipment began to be repurposed for local city police uses. Police officers started to look more like military officers engaged in combat against an enemy, rather than public servants responding to residents' requests (Giroux 2015). The Democratic and Republican Parties each pursued law and order campaigning strategies to win local and national elections that strengthened the state's power to punish. Reagan embarked on a "Just Say No" campaign to combat drug use. Bush rode to electoral victory by portraying his opponent, Michael Dukakis, as soft on crime. Clinton attended the execution of a mentally impaired man who saved the dessert accompanying his last meal for after his execution. The Democrat and Republican law and order consensus nurtured the broken windows metaphor and stop-and-frisk policing. By 1999, broken windows and police discretion interlocked with the American consensus on law and order.

Policing in New York City during the Republican administrations of Mayors Giuliani and Bloomberg becomes the epicenter of stop-and-frisk police practices. Stop-and-frisk policing allows officers to exercise discretion to stop suspects in order to pat them down and search for drugs or weapons. The law-and-order doctrine of this new policing in defense of New Yorkers' quality of life is explicitly laid out by Mayor Giuliani and Police Commissioner Bratton in the 1994 document, *Police Strategy No. 5: Reclaiming the Public Spaces of New York*. In the new phase of broken windows policing, which is the precept for stop-and-frisk tactics, New York City police officers were instructed to "define deviance up." Law enforcement were instructed to exercise discretionary powers "to uphold a uniform standard of civility and mutual respect in all the neighborhoods of the city" (Bratton, Giuliani, and NYPD 1994, 7). Previously unenforced deviance would become crimes admissible for prosecution. Loud cars, alcohol sales to underage buyers, patronizing prostitutes, and graffiti all fell under the rubric of low-level disorderly offenses for which patrol officers were instructed to issue citations and make arrests. Over the course of the next twenty years, increased officer discretion to make misdemeanor arrests established an unmistakable pattern of institutional bias in law enforcement. "In 2015, 45 percent of misdemeanor arrests were of black individuals, 35 percent of Hispanic individuals, 13 percent of white individuals, and 5 percent of other racial or ethnic individuals" (Kohler-Hausmann 2018, 51). These patterns reflect the cosmopolitan values of New York City in the era of stop-and-frisk policing.

As we transition to the post-George Floyd era of policing, social protests across the United States and democracies throughout the world are calling for a serious discussion about systemic bias in police discretion. Some police departments have publicly supported the protests. Democrat and Republican Party policies must confront powerful police unions in the post-George Floyd era.

REPUBLICANS ON LAW ENFORCEMENT DISCRETION

With the election of Richard Nixon in 1968, the Republican Party set the tone for tough on crime, law-and-order cultural sensibilities that politicized law enforcement for the remainder of the century. Studies note a strong allegiance among police officers to the conservativeness of the Republican Party (Reiner 2000, 191–4). The Nixon, Reagan, and Bush administrations pursuit of the War on Drugs and Crime, united the Republican Party and local city police in defense of the thin blue line that defines city police as defenders of law and order amid chaos in civil society. The election of New York City Mayor Rudolph Giuliani established a deeper connection between the Republican Party and the defense of granting street-level officers greater discretionary powers as a tool in the battle to lower crime. Mayor Giuliani and Police Commissioner William Bratton advocated for the idea of broken windows policing where patrol officers were granted the freedom to exercise discretion to arrest individuals for violating low-level offenses (Vitale 2008; Kohler-Hausmann 2018).

During the 2016 Republican Party convention, attendees broke out in a "Blue Lives Matter" chant when Sheriff David Clarke delivered his address. Republicans used the ambush-style attacks on law enforcement officers in New York City in December 2014 and similar attacks on six police officers in Dallas in June 2016 as evidence to support their rationale for siding with law enforcement when citizens criticize police misbehavior. The message conveyed by proponents of blue lives matter is that criticism of law enforcement makes an already difficult job even more dangerous. From this standpoint, it is a citizen's duty to allow officers to perform their occupational roles with impunity. Minneapolis police union president, Lt. Bob Kroll, is quoted as referring to protesters as a "terrorist movement" and President Trump as an ally who "put the handcuffs on the criminals instead of us" (Scheiber, Stockman, and Goodman, 2020).

Milwaukee Sheriff David A. Clarke, Jr. Speech at the 2016 Republican National Convention and 2016/2020 Republican Party Platform on Police

In his speech at the 2016 Republican National Convention, Milwaukee Sheriff David A. Clarke Jr. stated:

> Ladies and Gentlemen, I would like to make something very clear, Blue Lives Matter in America. ... Dr. Martin Luther King wrote passionately about the interrelatedness of all communities and states and about our inescapable network of mutuality tying us in a single garment of destiny. He spoke of the basic reality of the rule of law provided that it is applied equally to both the wealthy and the impoverished, both men and women, and yes the majority and the minority. What we witnessed in Ferguson and Baltimore and Baton Rouge was a collapse of the social order. So many of the actions of the Occupy Movement and Black Lives Matter transcends peaceful protest and violates the code of conduct we rely on. I call it anarchy. (Clarke 2016)

The Republican Party platform for 2016 and 2020 supported those in law enforcement:

> The men and women of law enforcement—whether patrolling our neighborhoods or our borders, fighting organized crime or guarding against domestic terror—deserve

our gratitude and support. Their jobs are never easy, especially in crisis situations, and should not be made more difficult by polarized second-guessing from federal officials. The [Obama] Administration's lack of respect for them, from White House intervention in local arrests to the Attorney General's present campaign of harassment against police forces around the country, has been unprecedented. (Republican Party Platform 2016 and 2020)

The Republican Party's defense of law-and-order through limited restraints on police discretionary power allied the party with local and federal police unions. In 2016, the National ICE Council, a union representing Immigration and Customs Enforcement employees, and the Fraternal Order of Police, an association representing local law enforcement, both publicly endorsed Republican presidential candidate Donald Trump. Upon taking office, President Trump and the Republican Party pursued a strategy to remove consent decrees put in place during the administration of Democratic President Barack Obama. Consent decrees are a legal tool that allows federal oversight of police departments with a pattern of police misconduct. Months into the Trump administration, Republican Attorney General Jeff Sessions published an opinion piece in *USA Today* titled "Avoid Harmful Federal Intrusion," which detailed the administration's support for abandoning federal oversight of local police departments with histories of bias in discretionary behavior. Although property and violent crime rates had steadily fallen throughout the prior three decades, Sessions called for strengthening the role of federal, state, and local law enforcement to combat violence. In February 2017, President Trump signed three executive orders to make it clear to federal, state, and local police that his administration would move away from federal oversight of officer misbehavior.

Only 10.3 percent of salary workers across the country were members of unions in 2019. Union membership has declined throughout all occupations in the United States since 1983 when union membership rate was 20.1 percent. Union membership in protective service occupations is 33.8 percent, the highest among all occupational groups (Bureau of Labor Statistics 2021). Larry Cosme, national president of the Federal Law Enforcement Officers Association, and National Sheriff's Association incoming president, Sheriff David Mahoney, lobbied President Trump and South Carolina Senator Tim Scott to protect qualified immunity for law enforcement and prevent the creation of a national database of civilian complaints against police officers. Qualified immunity protects officers accused of misconduct from civil litigation. Cosme is quoted as saying, "Attorney General Barr assured us it wouldn't go far" (Broadwater and Edmondson 2020). The bill introduced by Senator Scott stalled when it was criticized by Democrats as not going far enough to address systemic bias in policing. Police unions prefer enhanced training and equipment for police rather than large-scale overhaul to police discretionary power.

From the point of view of the police unions and allies in the Republican Party, police misconduct results from individual officers who make bad choices not from systemic biases in racial and class inequities built into the functions of the city police. The issue of police misconduct understood from this individualistic perspective sidesteps structural changes for addressing police discretionary behavior. From the police unions' and Republican

Party's perspective, the best strategy to preserve public safety is by granting police officers greater discretionary powers to go after criminals. "Their core belief that police are heroes and protesters are criminals and the only tragic failure in America is a failure to respect authority" (Alberta 2020).

DEMOCRATS ON LAW ENFORCEMENT DISCRETION

With the election of Barack Obama in 2008, the Democratic Party slightly moved away from the law-and-order politics that defined the party in the 1990s. In *Dreams of My Father*, President Obama states, "I learned how not to care. I blew a few smoke rings, remembering those years. Pot had helped; maybe a little blow when you could afford it" (2004, 93). Obama's election represented a shift in cultural experiences and sensibilities of the voting population. A sitting president no longer felt the need to prop up the moralism and hypocrisy that defined the previous decades of zero tolerance for minor infractions, such as recreational drug use. The new social landscape, much like President Obama's racial identity, couldn't be watered down to a simplistic black and white binary. Now the world was filled with many shades of grey. While the order maintenance enforcement continued, the trend toward a more critical approach to the law enforcement discretionary powers of broken windows police strategies was set in motion.

In the summer of 2009, Harvard professor Henry Louis Gates, Jr., was arrested in his own home by a Cambridge police officer. In his comments about Gates's arrest, President Obama confirmed the hardships faced by African Americans hyper-policed in geographic spaces within the American landscape:

> I don't know, not having been there and not seeing all the facts, what role race played in [Gates's arrest]. But I think it's fair to say, number one, any of us would be pretty angry; number two, that the Cambridge police acted stupidly in arresting somebody when there was already proof that they were in their own home, and, number three, what I think we know separate and apart from this incident is that there's a long history in this country of African Americans and Latinos being stopped by law enforcement disproportionately. (Washington Post Staff Reports, 2016)

President Obama's comments recognized discretionary behavior by police that disproportionately targets ethnic and racial communities. "That a *black* president would cast suspicion on America's core institutions was seen as inflammatory if not subversive" (emphasis in original) (Alberta 2020). President Obama went from being the media's construct of a post-racial president to America's first Black president by his recognition as fact the systemic challenges faced by Black and Latinx communities in their interactions with law enforcement during the era of mass incarceration. President Obama is a biracial man raised by a white mother and white grandparents. Yet, with his public declaration that if he had a son, he would look like Trayvon Martin, media commentators reverted to the centuries' old Black and white racial divide. Presidential administrations preceding the Obama administration never acknowledged the reality of systemic racism in America.

The Democratic Party represents diverse groups in society. Minority groups are overrepresented as victims of unfair and unequal treatment by the police and establish their political space in the Democratic Party. Democratic House Representative Ilhan Omar represents Minnesota's 5th Congressional District where police officers killed George Floyd by holding him down as an officer knelt on the back of Floyd's neck while he was handcuffed on the ground for over eight minutes. In an op-ed published in the *Washington Post* on July 15, 2020, Representative Omar notes that her demands to end systemic oppressions were edited and modified by the Republican National Committee to fabricate a claim that she was calling for "getting rid of the entire U.S. economy and government." People who identify as Black, Hispanic, and Asian are more likely to identify as Democrat (Pew Research Center 2018).

Democratic members of Congress are more diverse than their Republican counterparts. According to the Congressional Research Service, in 2024, the racial and ethnic diversity of the 118th Congress is more visible within the Democratic Party than within the Republican Party. Fifty-seven of the sixty-one African Americans in the House of Representatives are Democrats. Three of the four African Americans in the Senate are Democrats. Thirty-eight of the fifty-five Hispanic Americans in the House of Representatives are Democrats. Fifteen of the nineteen Asian Americans in the House of Representatives are Democrats. Two Asian Americans in the Senate are Democrats. When ethnic and racial minorities make claims to government about police discretionary behavior, they tend to find more influence in the Democratic Party than the Republican Party.

Democratic Party Platforms on Black Lives Matter: 2016 and 2020

The following statements on racial justice appeared as part of the Democratic Party platform in 2016 and 2020:

> Democrats will fight to end institutional and systemic racism in our society. We will challenge and dismantle the structures that define lasting racial, economic, political, and social inequality. Democrats will promote racial justice through fair, just, and equitable governing of all public serving institutions and in the formation of public policy. Democrats support removing the Confederate battle flag from public properties, recognizing that it is a symbol of our nation's racist past that has no place in our present or our future. We will push for a societal transformation to make it clear that black lives matter and that there is no place for racism in our country. (Democratic Party Platform 2016)
>
> Democrats will root out structural and systemic racism in our economy and our society, and reform our criminal justice system from top to bottom, because we believe Black lives matter.
>
> We believe Black lives matter, and will establish a national commission to examine the lasting economic effects of slavery, Jim Crow segregation, and racially discriminatory federal policies on income, wealth, education, health, and

> employment outcomes; to pursue truth and promote racial healing; and to study reparations. (Democratic Party Platform 2020)

A series of headline-grabbing events tied to the issue of law enforcement discretionary powers unfolded during the years of the Obama administration. The shooting death of seventeen-year-old Trayvon Martin in Sanford, Florida, by George Zimmerman, a neighborhood watchman in a gated community captured national attention in 2012. The shooting death of an unarmed Black teenager by a twenty-eight-year-old vigilante male claiming self-defense highlighted how, in America, Black bodies are perceived as dangerous. In the summer of 2014, not long after the acquittal of Trayvon Martin's killer, the death of Eric Garner at the hands of police was captured on cell phone video. Garner was heard repeatedly uttering the phrase, "I can't breathe" as officers choked the life out of him. Later that summer, the shooting death of Michael Brown, an unarmed Black teenager in the suburb of Ferguson outside of St. Louis, Missouri, sparked social protests. In the spring of 2015, Freddie Gray, a 25-year-old Black man, died while in custody of the Baltimore Police Department. Eyewitness accounts reported officers use of excessive force while arresting Gray. An investigation into his death revealed that Gray died of a spinal cord injury suffered in the police vehicle as he was taken to the station. Riots broke out in Baltimore following Gray's funeral. These events grew in social import over the past few years. They show discriminatory bias in the application of the rule of law in America. The fact that these stories made headlines during the Obama administration represents the possibility that activists recognized a political opportunity structure that would be responsive to their claims. A cultural shift in politics and sensibilities aligned to reveal troubling patterns in police discretionary behavior.

In March 2015, Obama's Department of Justice (DOJ) released the findings from two investigations related to police misbehavior in the Ferguson Police Department (FPD). The DOJ found patterns of racial profiling and hostility toward the African American community by the FPD and recommended that it involve community stakeholders in the process of reform. Democratic Attorney General Eric Holder's investigation into civilian complaints against police found institutional bias in law enforcement, and recommended federal oversight of local police departments to combat institutional bias in local policing.

Democrats in Congress generally support wide-ranging police reform. House Democrats passed a bill ending qualified immunity for officers, establishing a database to track officers accused of misconduct, and narrowing the occupational roles of law enforcement. Activists' pleas for greater transparency and accountability of police discretionary behavior is caught in between several social forces moving in different directions.

FURTHER READING

Alberta, Tim. 2020. "Is This the Last Stand of the 'Law and Order' Republicans?" *Politico Magazine*, June 8, 2020. https://www.politico.com/news/magazine/2020/06/08/last-stand-law-and-order-republicans-306333.

Bratton, William J., Rudolph W. Giuliani, and New York Police Department. 1994. *Police Strategy No. 5: Reclaiming the Public Spaces of New York*. New York: Police Dept., City of New York.

Broadwater, Luke, and Catie Edmondson. 2020. "Police Groups Wield Strong Influence in Congress, Resisting the Strictest Reforms." *New York Times*, June 25, 2020. https://www.nytimes.com/2020/06/25/us/politics/police-reforms-congress.html.

Clarke, David A., Jr. 2016. Speech at the Republican National Convention. July 18, 2016. https://www.c-span.org/video/?c4612553/user-clip-sheriff-david-clarke-speech-rnc-2016.

Congressional Research Service. 2024. "Membership of the 118th Congress: A Profile." https://crsreports.congress.gov/product/pdf/R/R47470. Accessed July 31, 2024.

Democratic Party Platform. 2016. July 9, 2016. https://www.presidency.ucsb.edu/documents/2016-democratic-party-platform.

Democratic Party Platform. 2020. August 17, 2020. https://www.presidency.ucsb.edu/documents/2020-democratic-party-platform.

Giroux, Henry A. 2015. *Dangerous Thinking in the Age of the New Authoritarianism.* New York: Routledge.

Intravia, Jonathan, Alex R. Piquero, and Nicole Leeper Piquero. 2018. "The Racial Divide Surrounding United States of America National Anthem Protests in the National Football League." *Deviant Behavior* 39, no. 9: 1058–68.

Kohler-Hausmann, Issa. 2018. *Misdemeanorland: Criminal Courts and Social Control in the Age of Broken Windows Policing*. Princeton, NJ: Princeton University Press.

Maxwell, Angie. 2019. "What We Get Wrong about the Southern Strategy: It Took Much Longer—and Went Much Further—Than We Think." *Washington Post*, July 26, 2019. https://www.washingtonpost.com/outlook/2019/07/26/what-we-get-wrong-about-southern-strategy/.

Nixon, Richard M. 1968. "Address Accepting the Presidential Nomination at the Republican National Convention in Miami Beach, Florida." The American Presidency Project. August 8, 1968. https://www.presidency.ucsb.edu/documents/address-accepting-the-presidential-nomination-the-republican-national-convention-miami.

Obama, Barack. 2004. *Dreams of My Father: A Story of Race and Inheritance*. New York: Three Rivers Press.

Omar, Ilhan. 2020. "When I Spoke Out about System Oppression, the Republican Response Was Vicious." *Washington Post*, July 15, 2020. https://www.washingtonpost.com/opinions/ilhan-omar-when-i-spoke-out-about-systematic-oppression-the-republican-response-was-vicious/2020/07/15/5bc79f7a-c6ce-11ea-8ffe-372be8d82298_story.html.

Pew Research Center. 2018. "Wide Gender Gap, Growing Educational Divide in Voters' Party Identification: College Graduates Increasingly Align with Democratic Party." March 20, 2018. https://www.people-press.org/2018/03/20/1-trends-in-party-affiliation-among-demographic-groups/.

Reiner, R. 2000. *The Politics of the Police*, 3rd edition. Oxford: Oxford University Press.

Republican National Committee Party Platform. 2024. https://prod-static.gop.com/media/Resolution_Platform.pdf. Accessed July 31, 2024.

Scheiber, Noam, Farah Stockman, and J. David Goodman. 2020. "How Police Unions Became Such a Power Opponent to Reform Efforts." *New York Times*, June 6, 2020. https://www.nytimes.com/2020/06/06/us/police-unions-minneapolis-kroll.html.

Stevenson, Bryan. 2019. "Slavery Gave America a Fear of Black People and a Taste for Violent Punishment. Both Still Define Our Criminal Justice System." *New York Times*, August 2019. https://www.nytimes.com/interactive/2019/08/14/magazine/prison-industrial-complex-slavery-racism.html. Accessed June 16, 2022.

Turner, K. B., David Giacopassi, and Margaret Vandiver. 2006. "Ignoring the Past: Coverage of Slavery and Slave Patrol in Criminal Justice Texts." *Journal of Criminal Justice Education* 17, no. 1: 181–99.

United States Department of Justice, Civil Rights Division. 2015. *The Ferguson Report: Department of Justice Investigation of the Ferguson Police Department.* Washington, DC.

United States Department of Labor, Bureau of Labor Statistics. 2021. "News Release: Union Members-2020." https://www.bls.gov/news.release/archives/union2_01222021.pdf. Accessed July 31, 2024.

Vitale, Alex S. 2008. *City of Disorder: How the Quality of Life Campaign Transformed New York Politics*. New York: New York University Press.

Washington Post Staff Reports. 2016. "How One Scholar's Arrest Tainted the President's Image as a Racial Healer." April 22, 2016. https://www.washingtonpost.com/graphics/national/obama-legacy/henry-louis-gates-jr-arrest-controversy.html.

CHAPTER 17

Mandatory Minimum Sentences

R. BRUCE ANDERSON, EDWARD KERR, AND MCKENNA MARSH

AT A GLANCE

Mandatory minimum sentences are federal and state laws requiring certain crimes to be punishable by a specific length of time. Courts are required to sentence criminals to at least the designated minimum number of years of imprisonment regardless of any extenuating circumstances. Enacted by Congress or state legislatures, rigid mandatory minimums are the alternative to flexible sentencing guidelines. Existing in both the federal system and in all fifty states and the District of Columbia, drug trafficking, firearms offenses, child pornography, sexual abuse, and fraud are the most common offenses subject to mandatory minimums (United States Sentencing Commission 2019).

Unlike sentencing guidelines, judges have little sentencing discretion when it comes to mandatory minimums. Mandatory minimums trump any sentencing guideline. For example, the federal Armed Career Criminal Act requires a fifteen-year mandatory minimum sentence instead of a sentence of ten to twenty years for anyone with three prior convictions for drug trafficking or violent felonies found in possession of a gun or ammunition.

Mandatory minimum sentencing affects prison populations, the sentencing procedure, racial disparities, prosecutors, judges, the accused, the economy, and politics. While mandatory minimum sentencing has been around for decades, it becomes more relevant as both Democrats and Republicans campaign on criminal justice reform. Interestingly, the two parties have similar views and support bipartisan legislature related to mandatory minimums although there are some intraparty disagreements. Each party's reasoning for its positions on mandatory minimums, however, differs.

MANY REPUBLICANS...

- Are divided in their support for mandatory minimums.
- Have sponsored and cosponsored reform acts primarily to reduce the financial burden associated with mandatory sentencing policies. Reform efforts aim to reduce the number of nonviolent crimes for which mandatory minimums are imposed.
- Believe that supporting mandatory minimums helps them to maintain a "tough on crime" persona, a stance that is important to their electorate.

MANY DEMOCRATS...

- Support abolishing mandatory minimum sentences.
- Argue that mandatory minimums are racially unjust and negatively impact social justice.
- Consider sentencing reform a high priority.
- Have sponsored and cosponsored reform acts to eliminate mandatory minimums for nonviolent drug offenses primarily to reduce racial disparities and increase social justice.

OVERVIEW

Until the 1970s, judges had expansive discretion when it came to sentencing. Offenders could receive anything from probation to the maximum possible sentence for their crimes, depending on the judge's outlook and local sentencing guidelines. In the late 1960s, with increasing numbers of individuals addicted to drugs, lawmakers began to focus on drug-related crimes. In 1971, Republican President Richard M. Nixon declared the War on Drugs, and consequently increased funding for drug control agencies and for implementing mandatory sentencing policies (Drug Policy Alliance n.d.). In the mid-1970s, Martinson (1974) concluded that "nothing works" to rehabilitate individuals, and the "just deserts era" evolved. Throughout the late 1970s and early 1980s, lawmakers and courts emphasized punishment proportionate to the crime and began to consider the offender's history and seriousness of the crime. Legislators and other policymakers decided that potential punishments should induce more fear to convince potential offenders to avoid law-breaking behaviors. Judicial discretion also was too variable.

The 1980s was defined by the Sentencing Reform Act of 1984, which eliminated the idea of rehabilitation, created the United States Sentencing Commission (USSC), made all federal sentences determinate, and authorized appellants to review their sentences. The USSC continues to establish the guidelines for federal sentencing, including determinate and indeterminate sentences. A determinate sentence has a set number of years and leaves little room for judicial discretion (e.g., mandatory minimums), while an indeterminate sentence provides a range of time for which a person might be sentenced (e.g., three–five years).

Mandatory minimum sentences were implemented in the United States under the notion that the sentencing process would become more uniform. Judges would no longer be burdened with making sentencing decisions, convicted persons would no longer be subject to sentencing disparities, and citizens would be protected for longer periods of time. However, both judges and the convicted feel restricted by mandatory minimums. Instead of being able to evaluate aspects of the crime and the offender, judges must impose a mandatory minimum sentence. This becomes an issue when a person found guilty of a less violent crime is sentenced to the same amount of time as someone found guilty of a more serious version of the same crime. Successful appeals of mandatory minimums are also more difficult.

The 1980s also experienced exponential growth in prison populations. Although many believed that mandatory minimum sentences would deter crime, prison populations began to dramatically increase. In 1980, federal prisons held 24,640 prisoners compared to 155,826 in 2021; in 2013, the population peaked at 219,298 (Federal Bureau of Prisons 2022). Part of this increase is attributed to mandatory minimum sentences for drug crimes.

A need for exceptions to mandatory minimums spurred passage of the 1994 "Safety Valve Provision," which allowed offenders who met certain criteria to revise their mandatory minimum sentence. Criteria included certain types of crimes or offenders, but more specifically applied to first-time nonviolent drug offenses not involving a gun. Many who support the safety valve would like to see it broadened to more, if not all, mandatory minimum sentences and to cover more low-level offenders. While the exception saves money and reduces the prison population, it also perpetuates racial disparities as white offenders are more likely to receive a safety valve than Black or Latinx offenders.

A second exception is substantial assistance. Allowed by Rule 35(b) of the Federal Rules of Convicted offender Procedure, 18 U.S.C. § 3553(e), and Section 5K1.1 of the US Sentencing Guidelines, an offender can receive a lesser sentence if they help the government to investigate and prosecute crimes committed by others. It differs from the safety valve because neither Section 3553(e) nor Rule 35(b) are limited to mandatory minimums established for controlled substance offenses. The 5K1.1 Section enables a judge to consider the defendant's substantial assistance when imposing a sentence below the Sentencing Guideline change. Unlike the 5K1.1 Motion, Rule 25 Motion occurs after a defendant has been sentenced and it gives the federal judge the ultimate power to give a sentence below the mandatory minimum.

These exceptions have not reduced racial disparities in sentencing. Black defendants are almost twice as likely to be sentenced to the mandatory minimum than white defendants; from 2005 to 2012 between 26 percent and 30 percent of Black defendants were given mandatory minimums compared to between 14 percent and 16 percent of white defendants (Gillette 2020). One study from Massachusetts also found Latinx defendants disproportionately impacted by mandatory minimums; they were twice as likely to face mandatory minimum sentences compared to white defendants in Massachusetts Superior Court (Bishop et al. 2020). Massachusetts is reliably Democratic, proving that harsh mandatory minimum trends are not tethered to only Republican states.

In 2010, the Fair Sentencing Act was signed into law by Democratic President Barack Obama as Public Law 111-220. Cosponsored by sixteen Democrats, six Republicans, and one Independent, the Act amended the Controlled Substances Act and the Controlled Substances Import and Export Act, eliminated five-year mandatory minimum prison terms for drug trafficking, and directed the US Sentencing Commission to review and amend its sentencing guidelines. One of its main goals was that people convicted of low-level crack cocaine offenses would be fined rather than imprisoned.

The First Step Act of 2018 was another bipartisan reform effort. Introduced in March 2017 by Republican Arkansas Senator Dan Sullivan and cosponsored by twelve Democrats, eight Republicans, and one Independent, the bill was signed into law by Republican President Donald J. Trump in December 2018. Among other initiatives, the Act reduced and restricted the application of mandatory minimums for certain repeat drug offenses involving high-level drug quantities. Instead of a high-level offender with one prior conviction receiving twenty years, they would receive fifteen. A high-level offender with two prior convictions would receive twenty-five years instead of life. Additionally, the law broadened the safety valve exceptions.

In 2021, the EQUAL (Eliminating a Quantifiably Unjust Application of the Law) Act was sponsored by Democratic New Jersey Senator Cory A. Booker and cosponsored by ten Democrats and eleven Republicans. In the House, it was sponsored by New York Democratic Representative Hakeem Jeffries, and cosponsored by thirty Democrats and twenty-six Republicans. Introduced in January 2021, the EQUAL Act aimed to eliminate the federal sentencing disparity between drug offenses involving crack and powder cocaine. Historically, the same substance in different forms incurred disparate mandatory minimums. Specifically, possession of 28 grams of crack cocaine and 500 grams of powder cocaine both incurred mandatory minimum sentences of five years.

Removing Mandatory Minimum Sentences in Virginia

In the 2021 Special Session of the Virginia Senate, SB 1443 was introduced by Democrats John S. Edwards, co-patron Joseph Morrissey, and House Patron Kaye Kory. The three Democrats proposed the elimination of mandatory minimum sentences and modification of sentences to a mandatory minimum term of confinement for felony offenses. Additionally, they advocated for the establishment of a work group to evaluate the feasibility of the sentencing modifications for those already convicted. Supporters of the bill argued that mandatory minimums do not deter crime and restrict judges. As a compromise to eliminating mandatory minimums, the bill's proponents urged Virginia judges to simply follow the existing sentencing guidelines. Republican Senator Mark Obenshain opposed the bill due to concerns over how it would affect violent criminals such as those convicted of sexual crimes relating to children. The conflict between advocates and opponents centered around levels of violence and maintaining uniformity. This bill demonstrated the desire for mandatory minimums for violent crimes and sex offenses, while considering removal of them for drug offenses. The bill died on February 7, 2022 (Associated Press 2022; Evans 2021).

The Smarter Sentencing Act of 2021, sponsored by Illinois Democratic Senator Richard J. Durbin and cosponsored by nine other Democrats, two Independents, and two Republicans, proposed to reduced mandatory minimum penalties for certain drug offenses, would require reporting on the impact of cost savings from the reductions, and would establish a public database of federal criminal offenses. Utah's Republican Senator Mike Lee stated that the Act was "a commonsense solution that will greatly reduce the financial, and more importantly the human, cost imposed on society by the broken status quo. [It] will give judges the flexibility and discretion they need to impose stiff sentences on the most serious drug lords and cartel bosses, while enabling nonviolent offenders to return more quickly to their families and communities" (United States Committee on the Judiciary 2021). Illinois Democratic Senator Durbin concurred when he argued that "mandatory minimum penalties have played a large role in the explosion of the U.S. prison population, often leading to sentences that are unfair, fiscally irresponsible, and a threat to public safety" (United States Committee on the Judiciary 2021). While Lee and Durbin represent different political parties, both agree that reducing reliance on mandatory minimum sentences is beneficial. Although many of the provisions proposed in this and in the original 2013 version of this bill were incorporated into the First Step Act of 2018, a 2023 version attempts to address the only remaining proposed reform, reducing mandatory minimum sentences for certain nonviolent drug offenses (Frolo 2023).

Republicans and Democrats have started to work together on reforming mandatory minimum sentencing laws. While their reasoning to do so differs, their bipartisan efforts demonstrate unity. If mandatory minimums were abolished, those yearning for social justice would see a cut in racial disparities, fiscal conservatives would experience economic relief as it pertains to incarceration, libertarians would enjoy less federal oversight regarding criminalization, and Christians could witness a stage of redemption (Dewan 2020). Criminal justice reform in the United States has been initiated, with both Republicans and Democrats developing approaches to appease their respective constituents.

REPUBLICANS ON MANDATORY MINIMUM SENTENCES

Republicans consider their party as tough on crime. In the Republican Party platform of 1984, Republicans took pride in their passage in the Senate of the federal anti-crime package that established uniform sentencing practices. Similarly, the 1996 platform mentioned support for mandatory minimum sentences regarding drug trafficking, distribution, and other drug-related crime. By 2008, the party added support for mandatory minimums including sentences pertaining to gang conspiracy crimes, violent sexual offenses against children, rape, and assaults resulting in serious bodily injury. A mandatory minimum of life imprisonment was supported for more severe crimes like gang rape, child rape, and rape committed during another felony. Due to the cancellation of the 2020 Republican National Convention, the most recent party platform was released in 2016. This platform is quite detailed, urging a limitation on the government's creation of "new crimes" because of over-criminalization and over-federalization. According to this report, mandatory minimum sentences are essential for keeping violent offenders off the streets and any changes to these laws need to target specific categories like drugs, alcohol, mental health, and nonviolent offenders. When judges can use their discretion, serious mistakes can occur. To combat this risk, any deviation must be disclosed. The platform demonstrates general consistency in support when it comes to mandatory minimum sentencing laws, but also shows a shift in the idea that violent offenders are much more deserving of mandatory minimums than nonviolent offenders. Given that former Republican President Donald J. Trump is the party's presumptive nominee in 2024, it is unlikely that the 2016/2020 platform will significantly change.

Across time, Republican legislation has been divided on sentencing reform efforts. In 1984, legislators expressed broad bipartisan support for the Sentencing Reform Act as a component of the Comprehensive Crime Control Act of 1984. Sponsored in the House by New York Republican Representative Hamilton Fish, Jr., and in the Senate by South Carolina Republican Senator Strom Thurmond, the Sentencing Reform Act of 1984 was signed into law by Republican President Ronald Reagan. This Act established mandatory sentencing guidelines that supporters believed would reduce sentencing disparities. Any deviations from the guidelines are required to have written justification.

The First Step Act of 2018, for example, drew a lot of disagreement and reluctance from some members of the party. Four Republican Senators, Iowa's Charles "Chuck" Grassley, South Carolina's Lindsey Graham and Tim Scott, and Kentucky's Rand Paul, supported it whereas their colleagues, Louisiana's John Kennedy, Arkansas' Tom Cotton, and the Senate Majority Leader from Kentucky, Mitch McConnell, opposed it. The ideological split was due to differing Republican stances on criminal justice reform. Some Republicans believed the party should toe the tough on crime line, while others believed it was time for change. Support for reform also involves reducing the costs of prisons, which appeals to fiscal conservatives (Zhou 2018).

Despite divergent opinions within the party, Republican President Donald J. Trump signed the Act into law. He stated that the legislation "reformed sentencing laws that have wrongly and disproportionately harmed the African American community ... the First Step Act gives nonviolent offenders the chance to reenter society as productive, law-abiding citizens. Now, states across the country are following our lead. America is a nation that believes in redemption" (Lopez 2018). With respect to mandatory minimums, the Act expanded the "safety valve," increased the probability that an individual with three or more convictions will get twenty-five years instead of life, and reduced gun stacking charges so that drug offenders are not serving more time than necessary (Lopez 2018). Arkansas Republican Senator Tom Cotton opposed the Act and claimed it was "misguided and dangerous" and that "conservatives should resist this revolution" as it allows "thousands of federal offenders ... [to] be released earlier than they would be under current law" (Cotton 2018). While Senator Cotton does not represent all conservative grievances, he represents an opinion that prefers offenders be imprisoned for their total sentences, arguing that doing so keeps the public safer longer.

In March 2021, Iowa Republican Representative Steve King and Texas Republican Senator Ted Cruz introduced "Kate's Law," also known as House of Representatives Bill 361 (HR 361) and Senate Bill 45 (SB 45). Kate's Law proposes a five-year mandatory minimum sentence for anyone who illegally reenters the United States and is convicted under 8 U.S.C. section 1326. This means that anyone convicted of an aggravated felony or is convicted at least two times before removal or departure and who subsequently enters or tries to enter the United States is imprisoned for at least five years. As of July 2022, the bill had not been signed into law, but if it is enacted, it would be the first to impose a mandatory minimum sentence for those convicted of reentry after an aggravated felony (FAMM 2018). This bill also represents a conjoining of Republican sentencing reform and immigration laws.

In 2022, Missouri Republican Senator Josh Hawley and four other Republican Senator cosponsors have introduced the PROTECT Act of 2022. After the nomination hearings of then-nominee Supreme Court Justice Ketanji Brown Jackson, Republicans argued that child predators, including those whose offenses involved minor pornography, were punished too leniently. Building off the PROTECT Act of 2003 (Prosecutorial Remedies and Other Tools to end the Exploitation of Children Today), which requires mandatory life imprisonment or death (with some exceptions) for persons convicted of a federal sex offense against a minor if the person has a prior sex conviction involving a minor victim, punishment for possession of child pornography would be raised to the same level as punishment for receipt, incurring at least a five-year sentence. Republican supporters of this bill argue that "it is time for Congress to stand with the victims of those offenses, and to ensure that perpetrators receive the severe punishment these crimes deserve." Opponents argue that the mandatory minimum should be between the terms for the two crimes to "reduce the unwarranted sentencing disparities resulting from inconsistent application of the mandatory minimum penalty" (Rifkin 2022).

Some Republicans oppose mandatory minimums because they wish to reduce prison populations to save money, they wish to appeal to constituents, and they believe that prisoner redemption is in line with conservative religious values. Some Republicans support mandatory minimums because the guidelines represent a tough on crime stance, violent offenders are kept off the streets for longer, and constituents want to see crime being punished. Republicans are more likely to support mandatory minimum sentences for major crimes such as gang crimes, sexual offenses against children, repeat drug offenders and traffickers, and rape. Not every Republican supports the same mandatory sentencing laws, and some push for reform much more than others. Kentucky Republican Senator Rand Paul, a reform supporter, stated, "I'm not afraid of appearing to be not conservative enough" (Peters 2014). Senator Paul eased his stance on mandatory minimums and other convicted offender justice reforms to gain younger and more diverse constituents who felt alienated from the Republican Party. Republican leaders who support mandatory minimums have criticized Democratic President Joseph R. Biden for being "soft on crime" and blame him for an uptick in crime since he took office in 2020 (Hounshell and Askarinam 2022).

It is difficult to predict how future Republicans will view mandatory minimum sentences due to many divergent opinions and inconsistency within the party. Furthermore, support for mandatory minimums is different within the Republican Party depending on the level of government. At the state level, Republicans are more likely to support reform than on the federal level (Hounshell and Askarinam 2022). Generally, the Republican Party wants to maintain its appearance as a party dedicated to "law and order." This can create contradictions as lessening mandatory minimum laws would appear to give offenders another chance, but also would decrease the overall cost that fiscal conservatives worry about. If reform pertaining to mandatory minimums garners support, it is likely that Republicans will develop campaigns around it.

DEMOCRATS ON MANDATORY MINIMUM SENTENCES

Democrats have not always been ardent supporters of abolishing mandatory minimum sentences. The Democratic Party platform of 1984 supported reform of sentencing, but only to the extent that offenders who commit similar crimes would receive similar penalties. At that time, Democrats supported sentencing guidelines for judges to follow and adequate justification when judges deviated from those guidelines. In fact, in 1986 Texas Democrat Representative James Wright introduced the Anti-Drug Abuse Act. Cosponsored by 205 Democrats and 96 Republicans, this Act is one of the most influential pieces of legislation involving mandatory minimum sentences for drug offenders. Notably, it set the same minimum sentence of five years for 5 grams of crack cocaine and 500 grams of powder cocaine. African Americans were more likely to use crack, so this Act affected them disproportionally.

In 1996, the Democratic platform had harsh tough on crime rhetoric but did not mention mandatory minimums. Instead, it focused on "putting more police on the streets and tougher penalties on the books" (Democratic Party Platform 1996). One law passed during this time was the Violent Crime Control and Law Enforcement Act of 1994. Sponsored by Texas Democratic Representative Jack Brooks, and cosponsored by two other Democrats, this Act is credited for causing a massive increase in incarceration in the years that followed its passage. At the time, the United States was experiencing elevated levels of crime and the Act was created in response.

To undo the effects of this act, New Jersey Democratic Senator Cory Booker sponsored the Reverse Mass Incarceration Act of 2019. With his cosponsor, Connecticut Democratic Senator Richard Blumenthal, the Act incentivizes states to lower their prison populations to earn grant money. While the Act has made little progress, similar previous efforts that reduced mandatory minimums proved effective. In 2009, for example, New York eliminated mandatory minimum sentences for some drug offenses among other things and from 2011 to 2014, the state had an 11 percent reduction in crime and a 5 percent reduction in incarceration (Eisen and Chettiar 2015). Similarly, in 2010, South Carolina ended mandatory minimums for drug possession and expanded prison alternatives and parole eligibility with a result of a 14 percent decrease in crime and 6 percent decrease in incarceration through 2011–2014 (Eisen and Chettiar 2015). This demonstrates that eliminating mandatory minimum sentences can result in decreased prison populations.

The 2008 Democratic platform contained slightly less harsh rhetoric, shifting instead to a "smart on crime" approach. In this sense, Democrats believed in being "tough on violent crime, funding strategic, and effective community policing, and holding offenders accountable." It also meant "getting to the root causes of crime by investing in successful crime prevention, including proven initiatives that get youth and nonviolent offenders back on track" (Democratic Party Platform 2008). The 2012 platform expressed support for the Fair Sentencing Act because it aimed to eliminate the racial disparities that came with sentencing drug crimes. Four years later, the 2016 platform contained only a brief mention of mandatory minimums (i.e., "we will reform mandatory minimum sentences").

As time has progressed, however, Democrats have become more vocal about their stance on mandatory minimum sentences.

In September 2017, California Democratic Representative Maxine Waters introduced the Mandatory Minimum Reform Act (MMRA). Receiving total cosponsorship by other Democrats, the Act worked to amend the Controlled Substances Act and the Controlled Substances Import and Export Act. While the MMRA did not become law, the goal was to eliminate most mandatory minimum prison terms imposed on defendants who import, export, manufacture, distribute, or possess with the intent to distribute a controlled substance. In 2019, another effort titled the Next Step Act was proposed by New Jersey Democratic Senator Cory Booker, cosponsor Massachusetts Democratic Senator Edward Markey, and New Jersey Democratic Representative Bonnie Coleman and aimed at sentencing reform, prison reform, reentry policies, and law enforcement conduct. Specifically, the bill eliminated mandatory minimum penalties and the practice of increasing the severity of penalties for drug offenses involving mixtures or substances containing cocaine base. It also decriminalized marijuana and reduced the mandatory minimum prison term for defendants who manufacture, distribute, or possess with intent to distribute a controlled substance, among other things. Mandatory minimums for nonviolent drug offenses with twenty-year mandatory minimums would be reduced to ten years, ten-year mandatory minimums would be reduced to five years, and five-year mandatory minimums would be reduced to two years. Senator Booker stated that this bill is the necessary "next step" to the First Step Act and works to build off the gains made by the previous Act (Booker 2019). In the Senate, not a single Democrat voted against the bill (Grawert and Lau 2020).

The Democratic Party platform in 2020 was the most direct in its intentions regarding mandatory minimums. Specifically, the party expressed concern with the number of people imprisoned, the disproportionate criminalization of those in poverty, and the unequal representation of Black and Latinx communities in prison. As a result, the Democratic Party proposed elimination of mandatory minimum sentences. Any sentence should consider not only the crime, but also it's severity, the defendants' exceptional circumstances, and their prior records. Democrats believe mandatory minimums to perpetuate racial and economic injustices within the criminal justice system.

During campaigns for the Democratic Party nomination leading up to the 2020 presidential election, all candidates except Mike Bloomberg supported eliminating mandatory minimum sentences at the federal level. Bloomberg did not support mandatory minimums but did support the First Step Act and experimenting with shorter sentences (*The Washington Post* 2020). Even though Democratic leaders disagreed on specifics, they all supported the general idea of criminal justice reform.

Despite a past of tough on crime policy during his time in the Senate, President Biden introduced a plan for criminal justice reform. It included a new, $20 billion grant program in which states, counties, and cities could use funding to invest in efforts that help eliminate crime. Inspired by the Brennan Center for Justice, states must eliminate mandatory minimums for nonviolent crimes to get this funding.

Democrats have continued to move toward criminal justice reform. Most Democrats support abolishing mandatory minimum sentences especially for nonviolent drug crimes. They believe that mandatory minimums have resulted in overcrowded prisons, discriminatory sentencing, unfair treatment, and inconsistency. Taking more of a social justice perspective, Democrats want to prevent the unequal treatment of minorities and improve the overall prison system, both calls coming from Democratic constituencies. For Democrats to attract voters, especially in the 2020s and beyond, they must develop policies that support innovative reforms in the criminal justice system. Andrew Yang, former nominee for the Democratic Party presidential nomination, believes that "judges should be free to take the situation as a whole into account when considering charges ... mandatory minimums put pressure on defendants to accept plea bargains they wouldn't otherwise and are unfair between different crimes" (*The Washington Post* 2020). Similarly, Massachusetts Senator Elizabeth Warren stated that

> The federal prison population has grown dramatically in the past decades, driven in large part by rules requiring mandatory minimum sentences and other excessively long sentencing practices. These harsh sentencing practices are not only immoral, there's little evidence that they are effective ...Congress should reduce or eliminate the mandatory minimums provisions of the 1994 crime bill, and give judges more flexibility in sentencing decisions, with the goal of reducing incarceration to mid-1990s levels. (The Washington Post 2020)

Like Yang, Warren believes that eliminating mandatory minimums would aid judges in their sentencing decisions. She also stressed that the practice of mandatory minimums is overall ineffective and unjust to individuals.

FURTHER READING

Associated Press. 2022. "Virginia Senate Kills Bill Ending Most Mandatory Minimums." WVEC, February 7, 2022. https://www.13newsnow.com/article/news/local/virginia/virginia-senate-kills-bill-ending-most-mandatory-minimum-sentences/291-7da2843c-b186-4d7e-bdeb-fde4f4996998.

Bishop, Elizabeth Tsai, Brook Hopkins, Chijindu Obiofuma, and Felix Owusu. 2020. "Racial Disparities in the Massachusetts Criminal System." Criminal Justice Policy Program, Harvard Law School, September 2020. https://hls.harvard.edu/content/uploads/2020/11/Massachusetts-Racial-Disparity-Report-FINAL.pdf. Accessed June 8, 2022.

Booker, Cory. 2019. "Booker, Watson Coleman Introduce Far-Reaching Criminal Justice Legislation: The Next Step Act: U.S. Senator Cory Booker of New Jersey." March 8, 2019. https://www.booker.senate.gov/news/press/booker-watson-coleman-introduce-far-reaching-criminal-justice-legislation-the-next-step-act.

Cotton, Tom. 2018. "Cotton Op-Ed in National Review: 'Fix the First Step Act and Keep Violent Criminals Behind Bars.'" December 17, 2018. https://www.cotton.senate.gov/news/op-eds/cotton-op-ed-in-national-review-and-145fix-the-first-step-act-and-keep-violent-criminals-behind-bars-and-146.

Democratic Party Platform. 1996. The American Presidency Project, August 26, 1996. https://www.presidencyproject.ucsb.edu/documents/1996-democratic-party-platform. Accessed January 12, 2023.

Democratic Party Platform. 2008. The American Presidency Project, August 25, 2008. https://www.presidencyproject.uscb.edu/documents/2008-democratic-party-platform. Accessed January 11, 2023.

Democratic Party Platform. 2016. The American Presidency Project, July 16, 2016. https://www.presidency.ucsb.edu/documents/2016-democratic-party-platform. Accessed January 11, 2023.

Democratic Party Platform. 2020. Democrats.org, August 29, 2020. https://democrats.org/where-we-stand/party-platform/. Accessed January 14, 2023.

Dewan, Shaila. 2020. "Here's One Issue That Could Actually Break the Partisan Gridlock." *New York Times*, November 24, 2020. https://www.nytimes.com/2020/11/24/us/criminal-justice-reform-republicans-democrats.html.

Doyle, Charles. 2019. "Federal Mandatory Minimum Sentences: The Safety Valve and Substantial Assistance Exceptions." Congressional Research Service, February 22, 2019.

Drug Policy Alliance. n.d. "A History of the Drug War." https://drugpolicy.org/issues/brief-history-drug-war. Accessed June 1, 2022.

Eisen, Lauren-Brooke, and Inimai Chettiar. 2015. "The Reverse Mass Incarceration Act." Brennan Center for Justice. https://www.brennancenter.org/sites/default/files/publications/The_Reverse_Mass_Incarceration_Act%20.pdf. Accessed June 12, 2022.

Evans, Whittney. 2021. "Democrats Removing Mandatory Minimum Sentences in Virginia." VPM.org, February 9, 2021. https://vpm.org/news/articles/20268/democrats-removing-mandatory-minimum-sentences-in-virginia.

Fair Fight Initiative. n.d. "Mandatory Minimum Sentence Statistics." https://www.fairfightinitiative.org/mandatory-minimum-sentence-statistics/. Accessed June 4, 2022.

Families Against Mandatory Minimums (FAMM). April 26, 2012. "Mandatory Minimums in a Nutshell." https://famm.org/wp-content/uploads/FS-MMs-in-a-Nutshell.pdf. Accessed June 6, 2022.

Families Against Mandatory Minimums (FAMM). 2018a. "Pending Bills: H.R. 361/S. 45, Kate's Law." April 27, 2018. https://famm.org/tag/mandatory-minimums/.

Families Against Mandatory Minimums (FAMM). 2018b. "Safety Valves." April 27, 2018. https://famm.org/our-work/u-s-congress/safety-valves/.

Federal Bureau of Prisons. 2022. "Federal Bureau of Prisons: Statistics." May 26, 2022. https://www.bop.gov/about/statistics/population_statistics.jsp.

Frolo, Caitlyn. 2023. "Bill Introduced to Lower Mandatory Minimum Sentences for Some Nonviolent Drug Offenses." WSET ABC13 News, April 5, 2023. https://wset.com/news/local/bill-introduced-lower-mandatory-minimum-sentences-some-nonviolent-drug-offenses-smarter-sentencing-act-narcotics-federal-senator-tim-kaine-virginia-democrats-republicans-april-2023.

Gillette, Caroline. 2020. "Do Mandatory Minimums Increase Racial Disparities in Federal Criminal Sentencing?" *Undergraduate Economic Review* 17, no 1: Article 9. https://digitalcommons.iwu.edu/uer/vol17/iss1/9. Accessed June 9, 2022.

Grawert, Ames, and Tim Lau. 2020. "How the FIRST STEP Act Became Law—and What Happens Next." Brennan Center for Justice, June 23, 2020. https://www.brennancenter.org/our-work/analysis-opinion/how-first-step-act-became-law-and-what-happens-next.

Hardy, David C. 2020. "Substantial Assistance, 5K1.1 Motions, and Rule 35 Motions." November 5, 2020. https://www.thehardylawfirm.com/blog/substantial-assistance-and-federal-criminal-sentencing/.

Hounshell, Blake, and Leah Askarinam. 2022. "Republicans and Democrats Begin to Sharply Diverge on Crime." *New York Times*, March 25, 2022. https://www.nytimes.com/2022/03/25/us/politics/republicans-democrats-criminal-justice-reform.html.

Hulse, Carl. 2022. "Drug Sentencing Bill Is in Limbo as Midterm Politics Paralyze Congress." *New York Times*, April 29, 2022. https://www.nytimes.com/2022/04/29/us/politics/congress-drug-sentencing-bill.html.

Lopez, German. 2018. "The First Step Act, Explained." *Vox*, December 19, 2018. https://www.vox.com/future-perfect/2018/12/18/18140973/state-of-the-union-trump-first-step-act-criminal-justice-reform.

Martinson, Robert. 1974. "What Works? Questions and Answers About Prison Reform." *The Public Interest*, 35: 22–54.

Peters, Jeremy W. 2014. "G.O.P. Moving to Ease Its Stance on Sentencing." *New York Times*, March 14, 2014. https://www.nytimes.com/2014/03/14/us/gop-moving-to-ease-stance-on-sentencing.html.

Republican Party Platform. 1856. The American Presidency Project, June 18, 1856. https://www.presidency.ucsb.edu/people/other/republican-party-platforms. Accessed June 6, 2022.

Rifkin, Jesse. 2022. "Taking Judge Jackson's advice, Republicans Introduce the PROTECT Act to Impose Harsher Sentences for Child Pornography." GovTrack Insider, April 12, 2022. https://govtrackinsider.com/republicans-say-ketanji-brown-jackson-was-too-lenient-on-child-pornography.

United States Senate Committee on the Judiciary. 2021. "Durbin, Lee Introduce Smarter Sentencing Act." March 26, 2021. https://www.judiciary.senate.gov/press/dem/releases/durbin-lee-introduce-smarter-sentencing-act.

United States Sentencing Commission. 2019. Mandatory Minimum Penalties for Sex Offenses in the Federal Criminal Justice System. January 2019. Washington, DC: US Government Printing Office.

The Washington Post. 2020. "Mandatory Minimums: Where 2020 Democrats Stand." April 8, 2020. https://www.washingtonpost.com/graphics/politics/policy-2020/criminal-justice/mandatory-minimums/.

Zhou, Li. 2018. "Republicans' Civil War over Criminal Justice Reform, Explained." *Vox*, December 12, 2018. https://www.vox.com/2018/12/12/18131130/mitch-mcconnell-criminal-justice-reform.

CHAPTER 18

Marijuana Legalization

KYLE C. WARD AND BRIAN IANNACCHIONE

AT A GLANCE

The criminalization and slow legalization of marijuana has historically been a hot-button political issue closely tied to racism, xenophobia, and political interests. Up until the early 1900s, the drug was widespread in the United States. By the late 1930s, taxation, enforcement, and an effective propaganda campaign had basically eradicated the drug's growth domestically and greatly reduced its use. During the late 1960s, however, use had significantly increased and views about its criminalization had changed. In 1969, only 12 percent of Americans supported legalizing marijuana, but by 1977 this percentage had risen 25 percent (Carroll 2005).

Since the late 1970s, support among Americans for legalization has increased dramatically, growing from 31 percent in 2000 to 67 percent in 2019 (Daniller 2019). Growing support among the public is reflected in changing political views within both parties; both Republicans and Democrats have increased their support for marijuana legalization over the years.

While a partisan gap still exists between the two parties, with a greater percentage of Democrats than Republicans supporting legalization (78 percent to 55 percent, respectively), the gap is much smaller than those between the parties on issues such as climate change, gun violence, and illegal immigration. Both groups clearly have become more liberal in their beliefs over time, which may be because 43 percent of Republicans and 47 percent of Democrats report having used the drug (Galston and Dionne 2013).

MANY REPUBLICANS...

- Believe that marijuana is a public safety risk and is especially harmful to pregnant women and youth.

- Are showing increasing support for marijuana legalization because of safety concerns and the risk of victimization involved with illegal marijuana markets.
- Advocate for allowing business relationships to prosper in relation to marijuana markets and letting individual states determine their best course of action regarding legalization and regulation rather than the federal government.

MANY DEMOCRATS...

- Support the legalization of marijuana at the federal level.
- Believe that the War on Drugs, including marijuana criminalization and prosecutions, has harmed minority communities.
- Advocate for expunging criminal records for those convicted of marijuana offenses and for using federal resources and tax revenue from marijuana sales to help those communities most impacted.

OVERVIEW

Reports of marijuana in America can be traced back to early seventeenth-century settlers in Jamestown, Virginia. At that time, however, marijuana was primarily cultivated for industrial use, as fiber for ropes and fabrics, and not for consumption. Evidence suggests that some of the founding fathers grew hemp on their estates, including George Washington, Thomas Jefferson, and James Madison. It was not until the nineteenth century that accounts of marijuana use as a psychoactive drug in the United States began to surface. From the late 1800s and early 1910s, medicine cabinets around the country were equipped with cannabis, as well as drugs like morphine, cocaine, and opioids.

Marijuana became a popular drug among Mexican laborers who migrated north into the southern United States in the early twentieth century and by those coming from the Caribbean. The drug was further popularized by the African American community and proliferated through jazz culture. These early trends led to the use of the drug becoming associated closely with two groups, Hispanics and African Americans. During this time, American culture was changing, with mass immigration and the "Great Migration" of African Americans escaping the Jim Crow South starting in the early 1900s. Out of fear that the movement of these groups would spread their drug use, a perceived "marijuana problem" was manifesting among white America, and politicians were tasked with taking action.

States enacted different approaches to regulating marijuana, while the federal government passed the Pure Food and Drug Act of 1906 (PFDA). The PFDA added marijuana to a list of "dangerous" drugs and required appropriate labeling, as seen today with prescription medication that clearly labels the drug and dosage. The PFDA did not provide the mechanisms for enforcement, so further regulations fell to the individual states. Some states added labeling of "poison" to marijuana, while others opted for full prohibition. In 1911, Massachusetts became the first state to make cannabis illegal, and other states slowly followed suit, including New York and Maine in 1914, Wyoming in 1915, and Texas in 1919.

During the early 1920s, as the prohibition of movement of drugs and alcohol gained momentum, the status of cannabis also became widely defined as deviant due to its association with Mexican immigrants and jazz musicians. It was during this time that the drug's psychoactive properties were believed to inspire criminal behavior. Coupled with the drug's racial associations, white Americans bought into and perpetuated a high level of fear related to the drug and called for a national ban.

In June 1930, the federal government established the Federal Bureau of Narcotics, an agency within the Treasury Department. The creation of this agency brought enforcement capability that had been missing from prior pieces of legislation aimed to restrict the distribution and use of narcotics (i.e., the PFDA, the Harrison Act of 1914, and Narcotic Drugs Import and Export Act of 1922). This new Bureau was run by Harry J. Anslinger, who went on to lead a strong propaganda campaign against marijuana. Under Anslinger, the Bureau pushed two images of the marijuana user. First, it promoted the idea that users were like uncontrolled animals, typically depicted as Black or Hispanic, who could not control themselves when using marijuana. Additionally, users were portrayed as sexual deviants prone to rape and taking advantage of unsuspecting, typically white, women. These propaganda efforts were accomplished through media campaigns and through movies like *Reefer Madness*.

The racial and criminal overtones successfully propagandized by Anslinger ultimately led to the Marihuana Tax Act of 1937 (MTA). The MTA did not criminalize the drug but required a stamp for all marijuana grown and distributed in the United States. The high tax and negative stereotypes essentially stopped the production of the drug in the country, resulting in a large drop in use.

During the 1960s, however, marijuana became a symbol of the counterculture movement, especially the "hippies." During his presidency, Republican Richard Nixon took a hard-line approach to drug use, calling drugs America's number one public enemy. The Nixon administration's proactive approach to curtailing illegal drug use led to the passage of the Controlled Substances Act of 1970 (CSA). Under this Act, marijuana became classified as a Schedule 1 drug, a substance with a high potential for abuse or harm and no medical benefits, although there were strong arguments and research indicating the opposite was true. After the passage of the CSA, Nixon called for a War on Drugs that ushered in a period of US history marked by strong drug enforcement and mass incarceration.

Beginning with the Office of Drug Abuse Law Enforcement (ODALE) in 1972, federal agents began aiding local law enforcement with drug related crimes. In 1973, ODALE combined with other narcotics-related federal agencies to form the Drug Enforcement Administration (DEA). The DEA became responsible for the enforcement of the CSA and combating the distribution and trafficking of scheduled drugs throughout the United States. During this time, federal, state, and municipal law enforcement agencies began strict enforcement of drug crimes in America, including the possession of small amounts of marijuana.

The push for the legalization of marijuana for medicinal purposes began almost immediately following the passage of the CSA. In 1976, under a court order, the federal government began distributing marijuana under a "compassionate use" program to numerous patients under physician care. Due to the demonstrated medicinal benefits among self-medicating AIDS and cancer patients, activists began calling for the legalization of medical marijuana. In 1992, San Francisco became the first city to decriminalize marijuana and allow for the opening of the first medicinal dispensary. California followed suit in 1996, becoming the first state to legalize medical marijuana. This occurred during the heat of the "tough on crime" period in American history, leading to federal raids on dispensaries, and high-profile cases where users dying of AIDS and cancer were arrested for the possession and use of this state-legal drug.

From 1996 until the late 2000s, raids on medical marijuana dispensaries continued. These raids essentially ceased in 2009, however, after Deputy Attorney General David Ogden issued the *Ogden Memorandum*, a set of guidelines that specified that the federal government would not interfere with state law regarding medical marijuana if certain stipulations were followed. As of July 2020, medical marijuana was legal in thirty-three states. Once a federal agreement was made relating to the sale and use of marijuana for medicinal purposes in certain states, the push for the legalization of marijuana for recreational use began among some western states.

The legalization of recreational marijuana began in Colorado and Washington in 2012. Both states held an election in which voters decided to legalize the drug. This decision by voters, much like with the legalization of medical marijuana, put the country in a situation where state laws conflicted with federal law. Existing precedent at the time was a 2005 US Supreme Court ruling in *Gonzales v. Raich* (545 U.S. 1), which confirmed the power of the federal government to shut down marijuana operations and argued that state law does not nullify federal law. As his predecessor had done with the *Ogden Memorandum* for medical marijuana, Deputy Attorney General James M. Cole issued the *Cole Memorandum* in August 2013, shortly before legalization could take effect in either Colorado or Washington. *Cole* provided guidelines to federal attorneys regarding states with legalized recreational marijuana. Even with these government protections, the federal legal status of cannabis (Schedule 1 under the Controlled Substances Act) has led to a number of issues regarding banking, taxes, and fear of strict federal enforcement among those who work in the legal marijuana industry. Most recently, in January 2018, Attorney General Jeff Sessions, former Republican Senator from Alabama and outspoken critic of legalized marijuana, directed federal prosecutors to disregard both *Ogden* and *Cole*, allowing them to enforce the laws enacted by Congress regarding recreational marijuana. As of July 2020, Sessions's disregard of his predecessors' memos has not resulted in any major changes to federal enforcement, and eleven states have legalized recreational marijuana.

REPUBLICANS ON MARIJUANA LEGALIZATION

While Republicans traditionally have been less likely to support marijuana legalization than Democrats, their support has increased over the years. In 2005, only 21 percent of Republicans supported legalization, but most (55 percent) said they supported it by 2019 (Daniller 2019).

It could be argued that the creation of the Federal Bureau of Narcotics in 1930 under Republican president Herbert Hoover was the first political move against marijuana. Slaughter (1988) argued that racism encouraged marijuana prohibition, citing the influx of Mexican immigrants caused by the Mexican Revolution of 1910 as the impetus. Some of these individuals smoked marijuana, which distinguished them, and led to police harassment and scorn from the citizenry. The list of those who smoked it, and were harassed for it, expanded to African Americans in the early twentieth century. It was so condemned because of reports that it led to criminal insanity. The Bureau of Narcotics, then, urged states to pass what was known as the Uniform State Narcotics Act, including marijuana on the list of proscribed drugs. By 1937, the Bureau pressured Congress to pass the Marijuana Tax Act, banning the drug to all but authorized medical and industrial users. Harry Anslinger, the Republican head of the Bureau, called for harsher penalties for marijuana after the Second World War, arguing that the use of marijuana led to increased heroin addiction.

These laws, however, led to drastically increased arrests and longer jail and prison sentences, leading Congress to revisit them. In addition, in 1907, Republican President Richard Nixon created the National Commission on Marihuana and Drug Abuse, chaired by the former governor of Pennsylvania, and Republican, Raymond Shafer. Essentially, this commission called for the decriminalization of marijuana. President Nixon disagreed, and most states and Congress followed his lead.

The 1970s brought with them a push to decriminalize marijuana, but that push ended in the late 1970s and early 1980s. Critics now cited the increasing use of the drug among adolescents, along with its increased potency, as reasons to reform marijuana laws. Republican President Ronald Reagan helped usher this conservative push against marijuana legalization. As previously noted, a consistent finding of support or opposition to marijuana legalization can be predicted by political affiliation; in other words, individuals tend to toe the party line. This tendency to follow messaging from the political elite can be traced back to President Reagan and the 1980s. Reagan took a hardline stance against drugs and argued quite vehemently that marijuana was dangerous for children. Evidence that Republicans are less likely to support marijuana legalization is found in anti-marijuana messaging during that era. Although both parties engaged in anti-drug campaigns, Republicans started them with First Lady Nancy Reagan's "Just Say No" campaign. Further, President Reagan drastically accelerated the War on Drugs that Nixon first proposed in 1969 (Slaughter 1988). Billions of dollars were funneled to law enforcement agencies to help rid the country of drugs, cannabis among them. This was coupled with stricter drug laws in an attempt to deter future drug users and harshly punish current ones. This led to a dramatic increase in incarceration; in 1980, 50,000 individuals were incarcerated for nonviolent drug offenses and by 1997 there were 400,000 ("A Brief History" n.d.). Policies such as zero tolerance were implemented, and programs such as D.A.R.E. (Drug Abuse Resistance and Education) were created. The push blocked such programs as syringe access, which was being rolled out to try to reduce the spread of HIV/AIDS. All this led to a politically created drug hysteria. In 1985, only about 5 percent of the population thought drugs were the number one problem in the United States; by 1989, 64 percent did.

Driving under the Influence (DUI) of Marijuana Enforcement

After the legalization of marijuana in some states, enforcement of laws related to driving under the influence have become complicated. Unlike alcohol, the detectability and inhibiting effects of marijuana have yet to be firmly established with anything like the .08 "per se" standard used for blood alcohol content. Using the per se standard, DUI is inferred based simply on the measure of substance in a person's system that exceeds the legal limit, regardless of whether driving is impaired. In Colorado and Washington, the "per se" limit of 5 nanograms of delta-9-tetrahydrocannabinol (THC), the psychoactive ingredient in cannabis, per 1 milliliter of blood (5ng/1mg) permits law enforcement to make the determination that this individual is under the influence of one or more drugs. The debate over this THC cutoff and its indication of impairment has led to the acquittal of defendants in multiple DUI cases in Colorado. In California, no per se measure has been established. Instead, law enforcement officers rely on drug recognition experts who are trained to look for cognitive or other physical signs of impairment during a traffic stop, a tactic also used in Colorado and Washington. Studies looking into the impact of cannabis consumption on driving abilities have not found clear results. For example, a recent study found that THC alone was not a risk factor in fatal traffic accidents in Washington, except when used in the combination with alcohol (Woo et al. 2019).

Reagan's successor, Republican President George H. W. Bush, continued this rhetoric and argued that the use of marijuana was a moral issue on par with the use of harder drugs. By the late 1980s, elementary and middle-school programs such as D.A.R.E. and television commercials featuring a cracked egg on a sizzling hot frying pan representing "your brain on drugs" were common. While these anti-drug stances have become much less overt, they likely have had a lasting impact on Republican ideals, leading to reduced Republican support of drug-friendly policies and legislation.

During his 2016 presidential campaign, Donald Trump noted that he would respect states' rights, and his administration did not enforce federal law against marijuana businesses in states that have legalized it. However, when signing a funding bill in December 2019, President Trump noted that he could ignore Congressionally passed medical marijuana protections if he saw fit (Williams 2020). Further, one of his attorneys generals, Jeff Sessions, rescinded multiple memoranda from prior administrations that promoted a federal "hands-off" approach in states with legalized marijuana. Sessions believed that federal prosecutors should be able to pursue marijuana cases in these states if those prosecutors deemed it important. Sessions's successor, Attorney General William Barr, favored a more lenient approach and believed marijuana should be legalized nationally, rather than on a state-by-state basis.

DEMOCRATS ON MARIJUANA LEGALIZATION

Democrats have always been more in favor of marijuana legalization than have Republicans and that support has steadily increased. In 2011, for example, 37 percent of Democrats supported legalization, but by 2019, 78 percent of them did (Daniller 2019).

As noted previously, Anslinger and the Bureau of Narcotics implemented the Marijuana Tax Act. These Draconian laws led to soaring arrests and overcrowded jails and prisons, forcing state legislatures to scale back punishment. During the 1960s, the first decade of survey studies on this topic, few people supported legalization. However, at the end of the decade and into 1970 people started to push back. This counterculture that formed over the next decade also helped usher in increased support for legalization, doubling support. During this time, the Democratically controlled Congress also passed the Comprehensive Drug Abuse and Control Act in 1970, which lowered the maximum penalty for possession of an ounce of marijuana, continuing the trend away from "stigmatic prison sentences for possession of small amounts of marijuana" (Slaughter 1988, 422). By 1977, Democratic President Jimmy Carter was calling for the decriminalization of marijuana

By the end of the 1970s, however, there was a conservative push-back against the "hippie" rebellion against tradition. Support fell steadily, and by 1988, support for legalization among Democrats had dropped to levels first measured during the 1960s. During this time, Democrats took a hard-line stance on drugs, influenced by the Reagan administration and the "Just Say No" campaign, which was continued by President George H. W. Bush. This was a popular position at the time, and it could be that Democrats wanted to receive the perceived benefits of the messaging.

Low levels of support for legalization remained relatively constant until 1993, during the administration of Democratic President Bill Clinton, when legalization began to be viewed more positively. While Clinton was against marijuana legalization, noting the negative impact it can have on youth, his administration advanced policies that could have shifted public views. Specifically, during Clinton's first year in office, he rarely discussed drug use, had a surgeon general who called for consideration of drug legalization, and appointed an attorney general who wanted to reduce mandatory minimum sentences for drug crimes. This messaging, then, could have increased public support for legalization. It must be noted, however, that he did not act on many of these views. Specifically, he rejected the United States Sentencing Commission's recommendation to end the sentencing disparity between crack and powder cocaine, and he rejected the call from Health Secretary Donna Shalala to end the federal ban on syringe access funding.

The Impacts of Marijuana Legalization on Police Officers

Law enforcement officers' typical duties have been impacted by the change in the legal status of marijuana. Since possession of marijuana is no longer criminal for those of legal age, the smell of marijuana no longer constitutes probable cause to search a vehicle in many legal states, and the ambiguity of DUI standards has complicated enforcement. In addition, law enforcement in states bordering those that have legalized marijuana also face an impact. A recent survey of officers in nonlegalized marijuana states bordering Colorado found that they perceive Colorado's legalization of recreational marijuana to have a negative impact on their enforcement duties. These officers complained of the increase in THC potency, a higher perceived juvenile use, and an increased strain on their resources to enforce their marijuana laws. These perceptions were not consistent throughout departments in all the states, as departments further away from the Colorado borders reported less of an impact than closer counties. From a state comparison, Wyoming police officers perceived a larger impact on enforcement when compared to Nebraska and Kansas, and these differences were impacted by officers' personal perceptions of marijuana. If an officer did not view marijuana as a harmful drug, they did not find Colorado's legalization to have a large impact on their enforcement duties (Ward, Lucas, and Murphy 2019).

During the administration of his successor, Republican George W. Bush, support rose for legalization, which continued and strengthened through the term of Bush's successor, Democratic President Barack Obama. During Obama's administration, 62 percent of Democrats supported legalization (McGinty et al. 2017). Since this time, only Democrats born to the "Silent Generation" (those who came to maturity in the 1950s) are clearly opposed to marijuana legalization (Galston and Dionne 2013).

Although Democrats may be more likely than Republicans to support legalization for several reasons, political affiliation is the most important one. Party affiliation explains support for legalization better than education, religion, and region of the country. Moreover, the debate over legalization is as polarizing as homosexuality and abortion, with legalization becoming a majority opinion and a "non-Republican" perspective. Democrats and Republicans have come to diverge so significantly on legalization because people toe party lines. In California, for example, Proposition 19 would have legalized marijuana use in 2010 but it failed to pass because it lacked bipartisan support; Democrats favored it and Republicans opposed it.

President Joe Biden has not called for full legalization. According to his aides, he fears for public health and is waiting for hard proof that legalizing marijuana will not lead to mental or physical health problems in both teens and adults (Dovere 2020). What he does advocate for, however, is decriminalization of drug offenses and rescheduling of marijuana. He also believes in expunging criminal records and leaving it up to the states to decide legalization. Some criticize this approach and argue that Biden is trying to appeal to both young and old voters, which may lead to a narrow path that is hard to follow (Hughes 2019). This stance was strengthened when Biden and Sanders released their Unity Task Force in July of 2020. In addition, it called for the Justice Department to halt the launching of federal prosecutions in states that have legalized marijuana, and it requested that states invest earnings from tax revenue to repair damage within Black and brown communities that experienced hardship from marijuana incarceration. Nationwide legalization, however, was rejected. The hope, it seems, is to unite the more moderate and progressive wings of the party.

FUTURE READING

Angell, Tom. 2019. "Trump Says He Can Ignore Medical Marijuana Protections Passed by Congress." *Forbes*, December 21, 2019. https://www.forbes.com/sites/tomangell/2019/12/21/trump-says-he-can-ignore-medical-marijuana-protections-passed-by-congress/#2ebbd4514256.

Belenko, Steven R. 2000. *Drugs and Drug Policy in America: A Documentary History*. Westport, CT: Greenwood Press.

Booth, Martin. *Cannabis: A History*. New York: Picador, 2003.

"A Brief History of the Drug War." n.d. Drug Policy Alliance. https://www.drugpolicy.org/issues/brief-history-drug-war. Accessed October 9, 2023.

Caulkins, Jonathan P., Beau Kilmer, and Mark A. R. Kleiman. 2016. *Marijuana Legalization: What Everyone Needs to Know*. 2nd edition. New York: Oxford University Press.

Carroll, Joseph. 2005. "Who Supports Marijuana Legalization? Support Rising; Varies Most by Age and Gender." Gallup, November 1, 2005. https://news.gallup.com/poll/19561/who-supports-marijuana-legalization.aspx.

Cole, James. M. 2013. "Guidance Regarding Marijuana Enforcement." Washington, DC: United States Department of Justice, August 29, 2013. https://www.justice.gov/iso/opa/resources/3052013829132756857467.pdf.

Daniller, Andrew. 2019. "Two-thirds of Americans Support Marijuana Legalization." Pew Research Center, November 14, 2019. https://www.pewresearch.org/fact-tank/2019/11/14/americans-support-marijuana-legalization/.

Dovere, Edward-Isaac. 2020. "The Marijuana Superweapon Biden Refuses to Use." *The Atlantic*, July 6, 2020, https://www.theatlantic.com/politics/archive/2020/07/biden-marijuana-pot-legalize/613777/.

Galston, William A., and E. J. Dionne Jr. 2013. "The New Politics of Marijuana Legalization. Why Opinion Is Changing." Governance Studies at Brookings. https://www.brookings.edu/wp-content/uploads/2016/06/Dionne-Galston_NewPoliticsofMJLeg_Final.pdf. Accessed October 11, 2023.

Hill, Joshua B., and Zoe K. Livengood. 2019. "POT-US: Presidential Rhetoric and Marijuana Legalization." In *More on Legalizing Marijuana: Ongoing Shifts in American Policies*, edited by Nancy. E. Marion and Joshua. B. Hill, 107–24. Durham, NC: Carolina Academic Press.

Hughes, Trevor. 2019. "Where the 2020 Democratic Candidates for President Stand on Marijuana Legalization." *USA Today*, September 7, 2019. https://www.usatoday.com/in-depth/news/nation/2019/09/07/2020-and-legal-weed-where-every-democratic-candidate-stands/2150503001/.

McGinty, Emma E., Jeff Niederdepp, Kathryn Heley, and Colleen L. Barry. 2017."Public Perceptions of Arguments Supporting and Opposing Recreational Marijuana Legalization." *Preventive Medicine* 99: 80–6.

Schwadel, Philip, and Christopher G. Ellison. 2017. "Period and Cohort Changes in Americans' Support for Marijuana Legalization: Convergence and Divergence Across Social Groups." *The Sociological Quarterly* 58, no. 3: 405–28.

Schwartz, David S. 2014. "Presidential Politics as a Safeguard of Federalism: The Case of Marijuana Legalization." *Buffalo Law Review* 62: 599–657.

Slaughter, James B. 1988. "Marijuana Prohibition in the United States: History and Analysis of a Failed Policy." *Columbia Journal of Law and Social Problems* 21, no. 4: 417–74.

Somerset, Sara. B. 2019. "Attorney General Barr Favors a More Lenient Approach to Cannabis Prohibition." *Forbes*, April 15, 2019. https://www.forbes.com/sites/sarabrittanysomerset/2019/04/15/attorney-general-barr-favors-a-more-lenient-approach-to-cannabis-legalization/#581ea42c4c80.

Stohr, Mary K., and Cheyenne Foster. 2016. "No Tokes Over the Line: Marijuana Decriminalization, Medicalization and Legalization as It Affects Decarceration." In *Legalizing Marijuana: A Shift in Policies Across America*, edited by Nancy E. Marion and Joshua B. Hill, 57–69. Durham, NC: Carolina Academic Press.

Turner, John R. 2016. "Recreational Marijuana Implementation in Colorado and Washington; Referendum v. Initiative." In *Legalizing Marijuana: A Shift in Policies Across America*, edited by Nancy E. Marion and Joshua B. Hill, 71–88. Durham, NC: Carolina Academic Press.

Ward, Kyle C., Paul A. Lucas, and Alexandra Murphy. 2019. "The Impact of Marijuana Legalization on Law Enforcement in States Surrounding Colorado." *Police Quarterly* 22, no. 2: 217–42.

Ward, Kyle C., Andrew J. Thompson, Brian M. Iannacchione, and Mary K. Evans. 2019. "Crime, Laws, and Legalization: Perceptions of Colorado Marijuana Dispensary Owners and Managers." *Criminal Justice Policy Review* 30, no. 1: 28–51.

Warmbodt, Zachary. 2019. "How Republicans Learned to Love a Pot Bill." *Politico*, September 25, 2019. https://www.politico.com/story/2019/09/25/house-oks-giving-cannabis-industry-access-to-banks-1512850.

Williams, Sean. 2020. "Donald Trump and Marijuana." *The Motley Fool*, February 16, 2020. https://www.fool.com/investing/2020/02/16/donald-trump-and-marijuana-everything-you-need-to.aspx.

Woo, Youngki, Dale W. Willits, Mary K. Stohr, Craig Hemmens, and Stac Hoff. 2019. "Wreck on the Highway: Intersectionality of Driver Culpability, Tetrahydrocannabinols, Other Intoxicants and Fatalities in Washington State." *Transportation Research Record* 2673, no. 11: 127–40.

CHAPTER 19

Mental Health Care in the Criminal Justice System

ELIZABETH Q. WRIGHT AND DEONNA GIBBS

AT A GLANCE

More than half (56 percent) of state prisoners and 64 percent of jail inmates report a mental health issue, prompting the development of 2,954 crisis intervention teams (CITs) across forty-six states. CITs are partnerships between law enforcement and mental health providers in response to justice-involved or at-risk persons with mental health issues (Williams 2015). Approximately 2 million people with serious mental illness enter local jails annually, and in forty-four states the number of mentally ill admitted into jails exceeds the number of mentally ill persons held at state psychiatric hospitals. In the 1950s and 1960s, a policy of deinstitutionalization (closing state-run mental health facilities) led to a dramatic increase in the number of persons in need of mental health treatment in criminal justice facilities. Community-based facilities meant to replace state-run in-patient mental health facilities did not materialize as planned. As a result, the criminal justice system became the de facto caretaker of people suffering mental health crises who presented in seemingly disruptive or dangerous manners (Widgery 2018).

The first point of contact is often law enforcement, who are increasingly required to differentiate if a person's undesirable behavior stems from mental illness, substance use, situational response, or free will. Furthermore, an officer's situational assessment determines the future path for the accused; "arrest, hospitalization or informal disposition, depending on their view of the severity of the disturbance, the behavior of the offender, and the resource options available to them" (The Sentencing Project 2002, 14).

The availability of mental health resources often depends on the community and its access to statewide, legislative support (financial and system-level). Elected leaders influence the evaluation of existing resources and support for new evidence-based approaches to effectively manage mental illness, in and out of the criminal justice system. Therefore, it is paramount to understand the perspectives of Republican and Democratic leaders on how to best handle mental illness within the criminal justice system. Interestingly, while Republicans and Democrats have sharp distinctions in their approaches on many criminal justice issues (e.g., capital punishment, police reform), their current perspectives both seem to favor more therapeutic responses to mental illness for justice-involved individuals. While Democrats have a history of supporting services and funding for mental health services, Republicans have more recently shifted support toward more therapeutic services, particularly considering high profile mass shootings across the country.

MANY REPUBLICANS...

- Favor modifications to mandatory minimum sentencing guidelines for offenders with mental health issues, but also require disclosure by the court when they depart from state sentencing requirements.
- Tend to attribute mental health disorders to factors within a person's control and are generally less supportive of health care coverage for such disorders.

MANY DEMOCRATS...

- Favor investments in mental health services for people in crisis, so law enforcement does not have to be the primary call for response.
- Support expanded access to mental health services in jails and prisons and recognize that justice-involved persons suffer from serious mental health issues at a disproportionately higher rate than the general population.

OVERVIEW

Mentally ill persons are in every jail, prison, or probation office in the United States. The presence of individuals with mental illnesses in these facilities directly impacts both the criminal justice system as well as the individual. The avenues by which mentally ill persons enter the criminal justice system are through arrest, conviction, and incarceration. These interactions with law enforcement, as well as the stigmas, sanctions, and negative experiences associated with these contacts, can contribute to the development of additional stressors that can worsen existing mental health issues. The prevalence of these additional stressors and their occurrence is exacerbated for minorities and members of lower socioeconomic status.

The criminalization of people with mental illnesses is not a new concept. In fact, early views of mental illness did not distinguish between the conscious or unconscious control of abnormal behavior (Gerig 2017). Individuals who were mentally ill were subject to severe forms of corporal punishment and were often placed in mental asylums and state-run institutions where they were referred to and treated as inmates. The harsh treatment they received in these facilities is reflected in the belief that punishment must be rooted in violence. However, through the advocacy of mental health reformers, eventually many of these sanctions and institutions were outlawed. Instead of being locked away in psychiatric wards, mental health patients began receiving forms of outpatient treatment in mental health centers and community-based facilities. Nevertheless, by the 1950s, it was apparent that efforts to deinstitutionalize the mentally ill did not go far enough. These treatment facilities did not plan adequately for capacity and thus, local jails became stand-ins for psychiatric facilities (Widgery 2018).

Criminalization of the mentally ill continues to affect thousands of individuals and their families, along with individuals who work in the criminal justice system and those who provide mental health and substance abuse services. Despite the significant progress that has been made in the way society views mental illness, in many ways these concepts have come full circle. Law enforcement must still distinguish between the conscious and unconscious control of abnormal behavior, while individuals with mental illness are still viewed and treated as inmates. The way mental health is perceived in society, particularly by government agencies, influences the treatment of the mentally ill and consequently, the support for mental health through federal and state regulation (Munsch, Barnes, and Kline 2020).

Historically, Republicans have held positions that were largely conservative, punitive, and rooted in retribution. When examining the relationship between crime and mental illness, the views of this party tend to operate from a perspective that places responsibility with the individual. For example, Republicans believe that mental health issues play a bigger role in mass shootings than issues surrounding gun control (Munsch, Barnes, and Kline 2020). Hence, they are less likely to support gun control and mental health coverage and benefits.

Throughout history, Republicans have operated from a "rhetoric of retribution" when it comes to crime. In the 1960s, riots and rising fear of crime resulted in the development of a "tough on crime" narrative (Dagan and Teles 2014). Throughout the 1980s and 1990s, fear-inducing stories about crime and the repeated claim that violence and crime were on the rise continued to remain prevalent. Depictions in the media portrayed the idea that the criminal justice system failed to punish criminals adequately due to legal technicalities and permissive laws that reinforced the notion that, to decrease crime, society must increase punishment (Beckett, Reosti, and Knaphus 2016). The mass incarceration that resulted from this tough on crime rhetoric is an era that America is still trying to escape.

Recently, however, there has been a shift in conservative views. Following the recessions of the early 2000s, legislation reexamined the costs and fiscal allocations associated with incarceration. As a result, a new "right on crime" stance for conservatives emerged (Beckett, Reosti, and Knaphus 2016). Republicans adopted the idea to reduce prison populations and take part in a nationwide effort to reject mass incarceration. While this new focus is progressive, the comprehensive reform of the criminal justice system has not been emphasized by this party as much as the fiscal costs associated with mass incarceration. Republicans have placed cost and efficacy at the center of their hopes for criminal justice reform, and some view their support as merely a way for "ambitious conservatives to brandish their cost-cutting credentials" (Weaver, Hacker, and Wildeman 2013, 273). Regardless of their motives, however, Republican support for reducing incarceration could mean a decrease in the use of jails and correctional facilities as placement for the mentally ill.

Generally speaking, Democrats hold a perspective that attempts to understand and address the root causes of crime, be they social or economic problems, mental health-related, or issues within the criminal justice system itself. Thereby, the Democratic Party tends to place less blame on individuals with mental illnesses and is more supportive of gun control and reducing the costs of treatment (Munsch, Barnes, and Kline 2020).

The dominance of conservative voices throughout history has made it difficult for liberals to gain a hearing on criminal justice issues. With the strong support of the carceral state in the 1990s, Democrats took a more punitive position like that of Republicans, branding themselves as "tough in effort." In fact, the conservative influence over the Democratic Party was so significant that liberals essentially "lost their distinctiveness, and thus their political advantage on the issue" (Dagan and Teles 2014, 270). The political influence of the Republican Party and tough on crime rhetoric over decades had greatly diminished the political advantage liberals had on criminal justice reform. Thus, Democrats tend to be viewed as "soft on crime," while Republicans tend to have the authoritative voice in conversations surrounding crime and punishment.

While Democrats have largely remained critics of mass incarceration, the recent enactment of criminal justice reform has put its moral compass in perspective when compared to that of its partisan counterpart. Unlike Republicans, Democrats generally weigh the collateral consequences for families and communities and the "human costs" associated with mass incarceration as opposed to fiscal costs. Similarly, Democrats tend to place less focus on the costs associated with mental health treatment and instead emphasize methods of prevention and early intervention as a more long-term solution (Munsch, Barnes, and Kline 2020).

While there are clear differences among Republican and Democratic Parties, the similarities between them are prominent. Both parties currently prioritize mental health reform, especially as it relates to mentally ill persons in their encounters with the criminal justice system and are generally supportive of mental health care coverage. Members of both parties also want to see a reduction in the overpopulation of prisons. In recent years, efforts to improve this issue through the implementation of sentence reform and minimization of mandatory sentence lengths have shown conservative southern states taking a stance that is traditionally more aligned with that of liberals.

Misaligning and contradictory partisan beliefs indicate a potential level of partisan bias among parties or the tendency to instinctively agree with the ideas of one's own political party (The Sentencing Project 2002). In other words, the framing of acts such as mass shootings as a direct result of either gun accessibility or mental illness is like the dichotomy of tough on crime and soft on crime ideologies. The framing of these partisan beliefs can be so entrenched in party discourse that it becomes difficult to see where they intersect. While both parties may have separate motives, each favors reducing prison populations and expanding mental health treatment options. It is imperative for policy enforcers to acknowledge these positions as analogous, because even "some of the most effective crime-reduction programs overlap with areas of policy where partisan gridlock tends to prevail" (Dagan and Teles 2014, 272). By finding common ground on these issues, both parties can expand their current efforts to improve the treatment of the mentally ill within the criminal justice system.

REPUBLICANS ON MENTAL HEALTH CARE IN THE CRIMINAL JUSTICE SYSTEM

Historically, the Republican perspective on mental illness has been that it is a condition of the individual, and thus it is the individual's responsibility to handle their condition. Additionally, research suggests that those on the politically conservative end of the spectrum are more apt to suggest that persons with mental illness are dangerous to others and indicate they are less inclined to live near those with mental illnesses (Love et al. 2019). As crime rates rose in the 1960s and peaked in the 1990s, Republicans adopted a tough on crime approach to deal with offenders that persisted through the 2000s until relatively recently. The financial cost of maintaining the tough on crime approach, considering declining crime rates, has contributed to Republicans shifting perspectives. More recently, Republican legislators have adopted a right on crime perspective in which alternatives to incarceration are considered. This view reverses the financial abyss that has come about from mass incarceration, but also with perhaps a secondary goal of utilizing evidence-based responses to both supervising and rehabilitating offenders. "To seriously shrink the prison population, however, conservatives will have to accept the construction of alternative government structures; liberals will have to accept that these will remain more paternalistic than they might like" (Dagan and Teles 2014, 266). While shrinking the prison population does not seem to imply that figuring out how to handle mentally ill offenders is a primary concern, it is certainly one of the avenues that has been explored recently for the well-being of the offender and to reduce the cost of incarceration. Although Republicans (conservatives) and Democrats (liberals) may have different motives for change, both ends of the ideological spectrum understand that change is needed.

The tough on crime approach of the 1960s that persisted through the era of Republican President Ronald Reagan clearly perceived criminals to be engaging in crime out of choice. Mental health and criminal conduct were viewed and treated as separate social issues. Among American citizens, adults who identified as Republican attributed more responsibilities to individuals with mental health issues than Democrat-identifying individuals. When examining schizophrenia, Democrats were significantly less likely to attribute any responsibility for the illness to the patient, whereas Republicans were more likely to suggest the patient was somewhat responsible for their illness. Perhaps not surprisingly, Republicans were more open than Democrats to supporting gun purchases by persons with schizophrenia.

The perspective on mental health in the Reagan/New Right era of the 1980s was that "the imagery of the poor and disadvantaged" was "one of a lazy and semi-criminal group who are personally responsible for their own unfortunate circumstances" (Samson 1990, 41). It was believed that if a person was poor, it was their own fault because they lacked incentive to seek out economic opportunities. At the same time, mental health and substance abuse were also seen as individual choices and the responsibilities and funding to support services to help people struggling with either/both mental illness and/or substance abuse was cut drastically. Funding for alcohol abuse, substance abuse, and mental health dropped 25 percent from 1979 to 1984 in every state (Burt and Pittman 1985). Medi-Cal (California's Medicaid program) changed its eligibility criteria that resulted in almost 300,000 people being removed from coverage. Those who remained in the program were under higher restrictions when seeking out mental health services. Type and duration of mental health care was very limited for people under Medicaid type programs.

Mental health parity laws, requiring coverage for mental health services equal to that provided for physical health services, have been proposed by both Democrats and Republicans so that the limitations instituted and retained since the 1980s have been reduced or eliminated. Some distinctions between the parties exist with respect to reforming coverage for mental health services where Republican legislators have more often advocated for limiting the types of mental illness diagnoses eligible for coverage to reduce the financial impact on insurance companies and businesses. In 2002, Republican President George W. Bush publicly endorsed the formation of the New Freedom Commission on Mental Health, which recommended mental health parity in its 2003 final report. This recommendation established parity as a bipartisan issue rather than just a Democrat-led issue. Republican Senator Pete Domenici was perhaps the most consistent and persistent advocate for comparative insurance coverage for mental health; he spearheaded every iteration of mental health parity legislation that existed and was instrumental in getting the National Institute of Mental Health (NIMH) to conduct research on mental health benefits. His passion for the legislation was spurred by his own familiarity with the effects of mental illness. His daughter was diagnosed with schizophrenia, and he acquired firsthand knowledge of the costs associated with treatment and the failure of insurance to assist.

In the 1990s, crime rates, particularly violent crime rates, soared. Democrats aligned themselves with their more retributive-minded Republican counterparts so much so that party affiliation was seemingly absent when it came to being tough on crime during the 1990s. In the 2000s, the rise of the conservative "Tea Party" undermined the Republicans' stance to uphold the status quo in criminal justice and to critically examine criminal justice efficiency and cost effectiveness. The specter of individual responsibility for mental illness was still evident within the Republican Party even as recently as 2010. The Prevention and Public Health Fund, enacted in 2010 during the administration of Democratic President Barack Obama, was enacted to support community-based treatment for mental health. Republican legislators, however, proposed to zero out the fund, perceiving it as wasteful because it focused on bike paths and farmers markets (Sugie and Turney 2017).

Republicans have shifted from the tough on crime perspective of the 1990s to a "smart on crime" perspective in which criminal justice reform is evaluated from both effectiveness and fiscally responsible perspectives. Like a desire to win elections contributed to a tough on crime agenda, the desire for balanced budgets contributed to reform (Rizer and Trautman 2018). The right on crime movement of the early 2010s posited that conservatives needed to take the lead in reforming the criminal justice system, because it was seen as costly and damaging to human potential. Right-leaning state and federal politicians and activists, the American Legislative Exchange Council, and conservative think-tanks simultaneously emphasized the failure of the current correctional system and called for change, including alternatives to incarceration. However, more than one researcher noted that the shift by conservatives to recognize that the corrections system is not functional was done without acknowledgment that conservatives were previously behind expanding prisons for the safety of the public (Beckett, Reosti, and Knaphus 2016). Republicans outnumber Democrats in advocating for prison reform for nonviolent offenders. However, they have the freedom to do so without appearing soft on crime, whereas any shift in the efforts of Democrats, long accused of being soft on crime, does not bear the same weight.

As Trump Calls for More "Institutions," GOP Lawmakers Nationwide Shift Their Focus to Mental Health

Tim Craig of the *Washington Post* wrote about a movement by state-level GOP legislators to increase funding for mental health treatment and to invest in the reopening of institutions for the mentally ill. In 2019, the number of Republican bills sponsoring support for mental health initiatives (about 5,300) were twice as many as five years earlier. While Republicans still proposed fewer bills than Democrat in 2019, who proposed about 10,000, their number of bills has grown consistently since 2016. Wisconsin State Representative Paul Tittl stated that Republicans have always cared about mental health, but "we used to just brush it under the rug." Democrat leaders have doubts about the expansion of mental health services and point to years of limited funding and opposition to Medicaid expansion, which covers mental health treatment. Republican leadership suggested they were following in the footsteps of Republican President Donald Trump in the belief that addressing mental health issues early can prevent violence perpetrated by individuals with mental illness. While President Trump focused on institutions, state-level GOP legislators focused more on community-based care as more humane and fiscally sensitive (Craig 2019).

Policymakers on both the left and right have linked mental health with gun violence, something that Republican President Donald Trump often did, as well. Policymakers increased support and proposed funding for mental health between 2017 and 2022, but these initiatives were often preempted by gun violence. Both parties have adopted different narratives around gun violence, mass shootings, and other intentional violence. Liberals blame gun access as the primary contributing factor and conservatives blame mental illness. Only 4 percent of violent crimes in the United States, however, are committed by people with diagnosed mental illness (Munsch, Barnes, and Kline 2020).

Perhaps the most recent example of Republican-led legislation addressing mental health and criminal justice is the First Step Act. The First Step Act, signed into law by President Trump in 2018, directly impacted defendants and offenders with mental health issues. The Act requires the Federal Bureau of Prisons to train staff on how to respond to incidents involving inmates with mental illness or other cognitive deficits. Additionally, the Act requires that the mental health needs of the offender be considered before determining confinement in a correctional facility.

In sum, Republicans appear to have significantly revised their perspective on mental illness and criminal justice. They have moved from a hands-off, individual responsibility perspective to a recognition that they need to be on the forefront of supporting new and innovative programs that both reduce costs and provide necessary services to justice-involved persons struggling with mental illness. Not only are there benefits to the government, but Republicans now see the benefit in providing support to the criminal justice system as the de facto primary provider of service to mentally ill individuals. For the protection of criminal justice practitioners, as well as for the safety of the mentally ill from criminal justice practitioners who may not be trained to deal with mental health crises, Republicans now advocate for a full system overhaul that better addresses the intersection of mental health and criminal justice.

DEMOCRATS ON MENTAL HEALTH CARE IN THE CRIMINAL JUSTICE SYSTEM

Democrats have a long history of advocating for treatment of the mentally ill, both in and out of the justice system. Under the presidency of Democrat John F. Kennedy, Democrats explicitly demonstrated their support for the treatment of mental health disorders through insurance parity legislation. In 1961, Kennedy called for equal financial coverage for mental health treatment (aligning with physical health treatment) within the Federal Employee Health Benefits Program. Prior to that, insurance companies limited the coverage for mental health care, in both number of sessions allowed and in coinsurance costs taken on by the insured (Barry, Huskamp, and Goldman 2010).

A little over a decade later that parity was lost, and insurance coverage went back to reduced benefits from the previous administration. Subsequent efforts within state legislatures and at the federal level saw improvements and exclusions across time, until 2008 when Republican President George W. Bush signed into law the Emergency Economic Stabilization Act of 2008, which included the Mental Health Parity and Addiction Act (MHPAE), cosponsored by Democratic Senator from Minnesota, Paul Wellstone and Republican Senator from New Mexico, Pete Domenici. Democrats' perspective about this bill is illustrated by the floor statement of Democratic Representative Patrick Kennedy (RI) who helped write the MHPAE. Kennedy stated that, "access to mental health services is one of the most important and most neglected civil rights issues facing the Nation. For too long, persons living with mental disorders have suffered from discriminatory treatment at all levels of society" (Congressional Record 2007).

Generally, Democrats are consistently more supportive of mental health treatment, government support for mental health treatment, and increased spending to address mental health concerns in their communities (Munsch, Barnes, and Kline 2020). In contrast to their Republican counterparts, Democrats are less concerned about the financial costs of treatment for mental health, as they believe that treatment, especially early intervention, costs government less in the long run, before a person's mental health and behavior deteriorates to the point of crisis, delinquent or criminal behavior, and/or interaction with the justice system.

For lawmakers, a personal connection with the struggles associated with mental illness provides a perspective associated with more likely support of legislation promoting treatment and cost coverage (Barry, Huskamp, and Goldman 2010). Research on self-report of mental illness and affiliation with a particular political perspective suggests that "extreme liberals"/extreme left-wing ideologists had a 150 percent increased rate of mental illness compared to moderates (Kirkegaard 2020). This finding provides context for why Democrats have historically been more vocally supportive of prioritizing mental health in both the general and justice-involved populations. If personal experience results in greater support for mental health treatment, and more liberal individuals report experience with mental health issues, it follows that Democratic legislators may be more sympathetic and/or knowledgeable about the need for treatment. Representative Kennedy personally struggled with addiction that he believed uniquely situated him to sponsor and advocate for the MHPAE. Senator Wellstone was dedicated to supporting the needs of the mentally ill in large part due to the treatment he saw his brother receive. His brother had been diagnosed with a severe mental illness when Wellstone was only twelve and his brother was eighteen. He often visited his brother at the institution where he lived, referring to it as a "snake pit" (Greenwood 2018).

Democrats recognized quickly that mentally ill offenders might benefit from a therapeutic approach in the courts versus a punitive approach. In 2000, Democratic President Bill Clinton signed into law a bill that funded 100 "mental health courts" across the United States. The goal was to treat defendants who engaged in nonviolent offenses in which their mental illness was a significant factor (Miller and Perelman 2009). Democrats were not only interested in handling mentally ill offenders differently at the court stage of the process, but they were also interested in better serving mentally ill offenders during incarceration. An analysis of news stories in the 2000s indicated that there was journalistic interest in the challenges of incarcerated offenders with mental health issues. In the analysis, Democratic policymakers discussed their efforts to investigate substandard prison conditions and to recommend reform for prisoners in general, especially for mentally ill offenders. Specifically, they wanted to eliminate solitary confinement for mentally ill offenders, as that often exacerbated their illnesses.

One of the most significant pieces of legislation dealing with mental health and the criminal justice system was signed into law by Democratic President Barack Obama on December 13, 2016. The 21st Century Cures Act passed the House and Senate with strong bipartisan support and sought to address the country's mental health challenges in the criminal justice system as a primary component of the Act. The Cures Act included two significant Acts, the Comprehensive Justice and Mental Health Act and the reauthorization of the Mentally Ill Offender Treatment and Crime Reduction Act. The scope of the Cures Act was broad and addressed all facets of the criminal justice system. Increased funding was included for police training to better handle mental health crises of individuals and to support services to mentally ill offenders in the justice system. The purpose of the bill was to better serve persons with mental illness to prevent their engagement with the justice system, to provide access to necessary mental health assistance instead of placing them in the justice system, to reduce the use of jails as temporary housing for people with mental illnesses, and to collect data on existing issues related to mental health and criminal justice (CSG Justice Center 2016). Some programs sponsored in the Act included law enforcement grants for crisis intervention teams, assistance for individuals transitioning out of systems, advancing mental health as part of offender reentry, school mental health crisis intervention teams, and programs for mental health and drug treatment alternatives to incarceration.

Mental health, particularly in the justice system, has motivated Democrats to stay on course with their support of initiatives to better serve the mentally ill, and to better prepare those that respond to the needs of the mentally ill. In 2019, Democrats proposed approximately 10,000 bills that included a focus on mental health. Democratic-sponsored bills focused on prevention, early intervention, treatment, and reduced costs for those things. Reflective of the shift in their perspective, Republican policymakers also proposed more than 5,000 bills in 2019. While that number is smaller than the number proposed by Democratic policymakers, it is illustrative of the dedication within both parties to address mental illness. Criminal justice reform bills include provisions for alternatives to incarceration for mentally ill offenders and greater support for community-based mental health services to reduce the stigma associated with mental illness and to lessen the utilization of the justice system as a replacement for mental health facilities.

Democrats' Bill Calls for Sweeping Review of Maine's Mental Health System

In 2019, Democratic lawmakers in Maine proposed legislation to create a task force to address the current state of Maine's "fragmented mental health system" and to develop a plan to create new community services to fill gaps left by deinstitutionalization decades prior. "Breen's bill," as it was titled, was supported by the Maine Sheriff's Association (MSA). Law enforcement had been asking repeatedly for community mental health programs so that they, along with hospitals and schools, are no longer relied upon to be first responders to a population that is better served by psychologists, counselors, and social workers. Sheriff Troy Morton, vice president of the MSA, indicated it was telling that law enforcement were very vocal supporters of the bill. He said that law enforcement on the road and jail staff are trying to deal with people struggling with mental health, but they may not have the services that those people need. To address the complexity of better serving Mainers with mental health needs, a task force would be developed, composed of a wide variety of people, including law enforcement and mental health care providers, and would provide a long-term strategic plan for reforming the state's mental health system (Thistle 2019).

According to Widgery (2018, 1), "the criminal justice system and jail are all too often the first or only available response, but not necessarily the best" for people experiencing mental health crises. Criminal justice administrators, front line criminal justice and social service professionals, mental health practitioners, and policymakers have all commented on the need for training and resources for criminal justice practitioners to serve this ever-growing population of justice-involved persons effectively and safely. The policy and resources required to effect change can be developed by state laws, and legislators can motivate stakeholders at state and local levels to advance new approaches in responses to individuals with mental illness. News and scholarly articles both demonstrate that Republicans and Democrats support programs to improve the treatment of the mentally ill within the criminal justice system and by criminal justice professionals across the entire system.

Black (2020) notes a substantial growth in support and funding for law enforcement and mental health collaborations to better respond to persons experiencing mental health crises and to reduce the incidence of fatal shootings. In Colorado, a bipartisan sponsored bill prohibited the use of jails to hold people experiencing mental health crises and provided funding to train law enforcement in handling mentally ill persons in crisis, to develop law enforcement and mental health teams to respond to calls when appropriate, and to increase the number of mental health facilities available so that law enforcement can assist persons in crisis to receive appropriate mental health treatment (Brown 2017). Across the United States, support from local and state politicians led to the implementation of mental health courts in which defendants with significant mental health issues that contributed to their justice system involvement are handled in a therapeutic rather than punitive manner. This involves significant court follow-up to ensure the provision of treatment is made available while also holding the defendant/offender accountable for participation in the treatment plan. Corrections, especially jails, have moved to develop facilities that increase the ability of jail administrators and staff to better supervise inmates with mental illness. The political climate in the early 2020s seems to be more tolerant of justice system reform and assisting prisoners who suffer from mental health challenges, which indicates that it may be an ideal time for the pursuit of additional reform (Black 2020).

Indicative of reform ideologies, both Republican and Democratic legislators are reexamining capital punishment, the most severe possible penalty for crime in the United States. One poll, for example, found that 62 percent of Democrats, 61 percent of Independents, and 55 percent of Republicans opposed the death penalty for offenders with mental illness (Death Penalty Information Center 2022a). Members of both parties are sponsoring bills that prohibit the death penalty for offenders with mental illness on the state level. On March 25, 2022, for example, the majority-Republican Senate in Kentucky passed H.B. 269 to prohibit the death penalty for individuals diagnosed with any of four specific mental health disorders (Death Penalty Information Center 2022b). If signed by Democratic Kentucky Governor Andy Beshear, Kentucky will join Ohio as the second state to disallow the death penalty for the mentally ill. Reform efforts have clearly become more bipartisan with respect to how individuals come to the attention of the justice system because of mental health crises and how the justice system handles mentally ill offenders.

FURTHER READING

Barry, Colleen L., Haiden A. Huskamp, and Howard H. Goldman. 2010. "A Political History of Federal Mental Health and Addiction Insurance Parity." *The Milbank Quarterly* 88, no. 3 (September): 404–33.

Beckett, Katherine, Anna Reosti, and Emily Knaphus. 2016. "The End of an Era? Understanding The Contradictions of Criminal Justice Reform." *The ANNALS of the American Academy of Political and Social Science* 664, no. 1: 238–59. https://doi.org/10.1177/0002716215598973. Accessed July 9, 2022.

Black, Courtney. 2020. "Mental-Health Courts: Expanding the Model in an Era of Criminal Justice Reform." *Washington University Journal of Law and Policy* 63: 299–323.

Brown, Jennifer. 2017. "Colorado Would Outlaw Using Jails for Mental Health Holds." *Denver Post*, March 6, 2017. https://www.denverpost.com/2017/03/06/colorado-proposal-outlaw-jail-mental-health-hold/.

Burt, Martha R. and Karen J. Pittman (1985). *Testing the Social Safety Net: The Impact of Changes in Support Programs during the Reagan Administration*. Washington, DC: Urban Institute Press.

Congressional Record. "S1864-5. Daily Edition." February 12, 2007. 153.

Craig, Timothy. "As Trump Calls for More 'Institutions,' GOP Lawmakers Nationwide Shift Their Focus to Mental Health." *Washington Post*, October 6, 2019. https://www.washingtonpost.com/national/as-trump-calls-for-more-institutions-gop-lawmakers-nationwide-shift-their-focus-to-mental-health/2019/10/06/df769f52-e622-11e9-a6e8-8759c5c7f608_story.html.

CSG Justice Center. 2016. "President Obama Signs 21st Century Cures Act." https://csgjusticecenter.org/2016/12/13/president-obama-signs-21st-century-cures-act/. Accessed July 8, 2022.

Dagan, David, and Steven M. Teles. 2014. "Locked in? Conservative Reform and the Future of Mass Incarceration." *The ANNALS of the American Academy of Political and Social Science* 651, no. 1: 266–76. https://doi.org/10.1177/0002716213502935. Accessed July 12, 2022.

Death Penalty Information Center. 2022a. "New Poll Finds Bipartisan Opposition to Use of the Death Penalty as It Is Actually Administered." March 1, 2022. https://deathpenaltyinfo.org/news/new-poll-finds-bipartisan-opposition-to-use-of-the-death-penalty-as-it-is-actually-administered. Accessed March 20, 2022.

Death Penalty Information Center. 2022b. "Kentucky Legislature Passes Bill Prohibiting Death Penalty for People with Serious Mental Illness." March 29, 2022. https://deathpenaltyinfo.org/news/kentucky-legislature-passes-bill-prohibiting-execution-of-people-with-serious-mental-illness. Accessed March 30, 2022.

Democratic National Convention. 2020. "2020 Democratic Party Platform – Democratic National Committee." https://democrats.org/wp-content/uploads/sites/2/2020/08/2020-Democratic-Party-Platform.pdf. Accessed March 22, 2022.

Federal Bureau of Prisons. n.d. "An Overview of the First Step Act." https://www.bop.gov/inmates/fsa/overview.jsp. Accessed March 22, 2022.

Gerig, Mark S. 2017. *Foundations for Clinical Mental Health Counseling*. 3rd ed. Boston: Pearson.

Greenwood, Dan. 2018. "David Wellstone Continues His Father's Work on Mental Health." *Mankato Free Press*, September 25, 2018. https://www.mankatofreepress.com/news/local_news/david-wellstone-continues-his-fathers-work-on-mental-health/article_aa260a30-c13a-11e8-9890-53af31a782f5.html.

Helms, Ronald, Ricky S. Guitierrez, and Debra Reeves-Guitierrez. 2016. "Jail Mental Health Resources: A Conceptual and Empirical Study of Social Determinants." *International Journal of Offender Therapy and Comparative Criminology* 60, no. 9: 1036–63.

Karma, Roge. 2020. "Democrats are Running on the Most Progressive Police Reform Agenda in Modern American History." *Vox*, September 8, 2020. https://www.vox.com/21418125/biden-harris-pelosi-defund-the-police-criminal-justice-reform-2020.

Kirkegaard, Emil O. W. 2020. "Mental Illness and the Left." February 2020. https://www.researchgate.net/publication/339541044_Mental_illness_and_the_left. Accessed March 20, 2022.

Loury, Glenn C. 2014. "Detention, Democracy, and Inequality in a Divided Society." *The ANNALS of the American Academy of Political and Social Science* 651, no. 1: 178–82. https://doi.org/10.1177/0002716213502930. Accessed March 20, 2022.

Love, Jesper, Monica Bertilsson, Johan Martinsson, Lena Wangnerud, and Gunnel Hensing. 2019. "Political Ideology and Stigmatizing Attitudes Toward Depression: The Swedish Case." *International Journal of Health Policy Management* 8, no. 6: 365–75.

Miller, Sarah L., and Abigayl M. Perelman. 2009. "Mental Health Courts: An Overview and Redefinition of Tasks and Goals." *Law & Psychology Review* 33: 113–23.

Munsch, Christin L., Liberty Barnes, and Zachary D. Kline. 2020. "Who's to Blame? Partisanship, Responsibility, and Support for Mental Health Treatment." *Socius: Sociological Research for a Dynamic World* 6: 1–12. https://doi.org/10.1177/2378023120921652. Accessed March 17, 2022.

Republican National Convention. "Republican Platform 2016. 2020 (Statement)." https://prod-static-ngop-pbl.s3.amazonaws.com/media/documents/DRAFT_12_FINAL%5BI%5D-ben_1268872234.pdf. Accessed March 15, 2022.

Rizer, Arthur, and Lars Trautman. 2018. "The Conservative Case for Criminal Justice Reform." *The Guardian*, August 5, 2018. https://www.theguardian.com/us-news/2018/aug/05/the-conservative-case-for-criminal-justice-reform.

Samson, Colin. 1990. "Inequality, the New Right and Mental Health Care Delivery in the United States in the Reagan Era." *Critical Social Policy* 10, no. 29: 40–57. https://doi.org/10.1177/026101839001002903. Accessed March 21, 2022.

The Sentencing Project. 2002. "Mentally Ill Offenders in the Criminal Justice System." January 2002. https://www.sentencingproject.org/wp-content/uploads/2016/01/Mentally-Ill-Offenders-in-the-Criminal-Justice-System.pdf. Accessed March 19, 2022.

Sugie, Naomi F., and Kristin Turney. 2017. "Beyond Incarceration: Criminal Justice Contact and Mental Health." *American Sociological Review* 82, no. 4: 719–43. https://doi.org/10.1177/0003122417713188. Accessed March 16, 2022.

Thistle, Scott. "Democrats' Bill Calls for Sweeping Review of Maine's Mental Health System." *Portland Press Herald*, May 15, 2019. https://www.pressherald.com/2019/05/15/bill-proposes-sweeping-review-of-maines-mental-health-system/.

Weaver, Vesla, Hacker, Jacob S., and Christoher Wildeman. 2013. "Introduction: Detaining Democracy? Criminal Justice and American Civic Life." *The ANNALS of the American Academy of Political & Social Science*, 651: 6–23.

Widgery, Amber. 2018. "The Legislative Primer Series for Front End Justice: Mental Health." National Conference of State Legislatures, August 2018. https://www.ncsl.org/civil-and-crimi

nal-justice/the-legislative-primer-series-on-front-end-justice-mental-health. Accessed March 23, 2022.

Williams, Richard. 2015. "Addressing Mental Health in the Justice System." National Conference of State Legislatures, August 2015. https://www.ncsl.org/research/civil-and-criminal-justice/addressing-mental-health-in-the-justice-system.aspx. Accessed March 20, 2022.

CHAPTER 20

Police Militarization

STEPHEN T. YOUNG AND BRIAN A. PITMAN

AT A GLANCE

Police during the American colonial period were predominantly made up of regimented civilian patrols. These patrols were originally developed for the purpose of protecting property (including slaves), quelling labor rebellions, and colonizing Indigenous lands. Over time these patrols formalized, modeling themselves after the training and organizational structure of England's London Metropolitan Police Department. This new organizational structure led to more local, state, and federal police divisions focused on the modern standards of policing practices in the United States. It also established rank and file positioning and training that helped pave the way for militaristic standards utilized today.

Police patrols today are drastically different in both their appearance and overall strategies that covertly reflect a model of militarization. Police militarization is "the process whereby civilian police increasingly draw from, and pattern themselves around, the tenets of militarism and the military model" (Kraska 2007, 3). This includes the adoption of military weaponry, organizational and operational methods, and cultural rhetoric and appearance. Civilian police agencies have become nearly indistinguishable from military agencies, in appearance, deportment, training, technology, weaponry, philosophy, and practice. Police's armament is directly connected to the established 1033 program under the Clinton administration. The 1033 program and police militarization more broadly continues to elicit concerns from communities, activists, and lawmakers surrounding the severity of police militarization.

Police militarization is a polarizing issue among Republicans and Democrats, especially after Michael Brown's murder in Ferguson, Missouri, in August 2014. Following Brown's murder, Ferguson citizens protested against policing practices and police responded with brute military force. The events of Ferguson and grassroots pressure led Democratic President Barack Obama to sign an executive order eliminating the provision that allowed the transfer of some military weaponry, including tanks, aircraft, rifles, and grenade launchers, to local police departments. He argued that allowing the provision of said military equipment made the police appear as an occupying force. Republican President Donald Trump reversed this order in August 2017. However, more recent police murders including George Floyd and Breonna Taylor have sparked further public discussion about the level of militarization and overall role of police in US society. More recent discussions have once again shined a light on the level of continued militarization of police in the United States, with a specific focus on the funding required to provide the current level of armament to local police departments. Republicans, generally, support providing police additional training and military equipment. The only change included in their July 2020 Senate bill that would impact police militarization was increased monitoring of no-knock warrants. Meanwhile, some Democrats have proposed an end to the 1033 program, while also advocating for the ban of no-knock warrants.

MANY REPUBLICANS...

- Generally support the Trump administration's push for militarizing police.
- Support police access to military equipment.
- Generally support expanded militarization, both equipment and training, for police.

MANY DEMOCRATS...

- Historically supported police militarization.
- Began to openly oppose police militarization tactics following the events in Ferguson, Missouri.
- Advocate eliminating the 1033 program and no-knock warrants.

OVERVIEW

Police in pre-Revolutionary War America were generally informal watch groups. In cities such as Boston, New York, and Philadelphia, watch groups were made up of volunteers designed to warn the community of impending dangers. In the south, slave patrols were the early police forces, serving as counterinsurgency by policing and surveilling enslaved people (Chin 2013). Constitutional framers sought to ensure a difference between police and military for its citizens (free white men). The Militia Act of 1792 required Congressional approval for the US government to use the military for domestic law enforcement and limited the amount of time this could be in effect. Still, military tactics were frequently used to quell slave rebellions, as laws allowed for the federal government to intervene in domestic slave uprisings.

Before the Civil War police departments were formalized to quell slave and labor rebellions, as well as to surveil emerging immigrant populations. After the Civil War, police and military became conflated, especially as the federal government divided Confederate states into districts controlled by the military under the Reconstruction Act of 1867. During this time, police were under the control of the army, commanders, and other federal police officials. Democratic President Andrew Johnson helped to reintegrate the south into the union, allowing them to establish Black code laws enforced by police departments that were formerly slave patrols.

After the controversial election of Republican Rutherford B. Hayes in 1876, Congress sought to scale back military presence domestically. With accusations that federal police officials were using various intimidation tactics, Congress passed the Posse Comitatus Act of 1878, which outlawed the use of the army for policing purposes without Congressional approval. The law later included the air force, the navy, and the marines. However, the law has rarely been followed by Republican and Democratic presidential administrations in times of race and labor uprisings.

During the 1960s specifically, politicians openly utilized war rhetoric to describe domestic problems alongside mass labor and race uprisings. For example, in his 1964 State of the Union Address, Democratic President Lyndon B. Johnson declared a War on Poverty, and in 1965 used the phrase War on Crime. This laid the groundwork for Republican President Richard Nixon to escalate police militarization. In 1969, Nixon described his anti-drug program using military rhetoric, calling for the "creation of 'special forces' within the [Bureau of Narcotics and Dangerous Drugs] that 'will have the capacity to reave quickly into any area in which intelligence indicates major criminal enterprises are engaged in the narcotics traffic'" (Balko 2013, 73). Later in his first term, he declared a War on Drugs and described drugs as "public enemy number one." To win the War on Drugs, Nixon created the Drug Enforcement Agency (DEA) and asserted that his administration had "declared all-out, global war on the drug menace."

Republican President Ronald Reagan accelerated Nixon's War on Drugs by associating the war with international threats from Latin American countries to garner public support. In 1981, with a Democratic House and Republican Senate Majority, President Reagan signed the Military Cooperation with Civilian Law Enforcement Agencies Act, which increased the US military involvement in fighting the domestic War on Drugs. Under the act, local police agencies could use Department of Defense (DOD) equipment and facilities to enforce domestic law if they were enforcing laws relevant to national security. By the 1980s there were 3,000 military-style raids per year, compared to a few hundred through 1972. One of the more infamous of these raids was the Philadelphia MOVE bombing in the Democratic-led city, where police bombed an occupied house, killed eleven people and destroyed sixty-one homes. MOVE, a group originally known as the Christian Movement for Life, was a Black communal group that advocated natural laws and natural living, justice for all living creatures, and opposition to science, medicine, and technology.

President Reagan then signed legislation in 1986 designating illicit drugs as a national security threat leading to the involvement of the CIA and the State Department in the domestic drug war. The National Defense Appropriation Act for Fiscal Year 1987 required the National Guard to cooperate with local, state, and federal police on serving drug warrants and other anti-drug operations. In 1987, Congress required the DOD and the Department of Justice (DOJ) to notify police agencies about available surplus military equipment. Reagan signed additional legislation that monetarily incentivized local police departments to design SWAT teams and escalate policing of drug crimes. Military-style drug raids increased from 3,000 in the 1980s to 30,000 by the 1990s.

In 1988, Congressional legislation established the Edward Byrne Memorial Justice Assistance Grant (JAG) used by many police departments to purchase military equipment. The Democratic-controlled Congress passed the National Defense Authorization Act (NDAA) in 1990, allowing the DOD to transfer surplus military equipment to local police departments and other local government agencies at no cost. The DOJ under Democratic President Bill Clinton provided grants to local police departments to purchase military equipment. In 1997, the NDAA included Section 1033, which relaxed the definition of military equipment allowed for transfer to police, including, but not limited to, grenade launchers, mine-resistant ambush protected vehicles (MRAPs), surplus aircraft, and watercraft. By 2001, paramilitary police raids increased to nearly 45,000.

Police militarization accelerated further following the 9/11 terrorist attacks. At that time, the United States initiated a War on Terror and police agencies used this as an opportunity to enhance their weaponry and technology. The bipartisan Homeland Security Act of 2002 created Immigration and Customs Enforcement (ICE). ICE resembles local police in tactics and equipment, further conflating the role of police with more militaristic forces. President Bush did scale back the JAG program from $500 million to $170 million, though Democratic presidential candidate Senator Barack Obama (IL) promised to restore the funding prior to his election. The 2008 election cycle provided citizens with more visuals of police militarization at the 2008 Party Conventions in Minneapolis and Denver. Following his election President Obama fulfilled his promise and increased JAG program funding to $2 billion. By 2010 police conducted over 50,000 raids per year.

Public awareness of police militarization escalated during the Occupy movement. This, alongside the rise of social media and cell phone video capabilities, made it easier for all to publish the militaristic practices of police, which included the tear-gassing and pepper-spraying of protestors. Occupy was eventually suppressed and disbanded, leaving very little change to police militarization. Under President Obama, militarized police were instead utilized more often for immigration raids and raids of medical marijuana dispensaries and pain clinics. In 2011 police departments received $500 million in military equipment.

Following the 2014 police murder of Michael Brown in Ferguson, Missouri, police militarization was once again in the spotlight. Protests erupted in Ferguson, and the police responded with militaristic force, including rooftop snipers, tear-gas, and concussion grenades. This police response led many to draw parallels with the US occupation of Iraq, such as Democratic Congressman Emanuel Cleaver (MO) who commented that "Ferguson resembles Fallujah more than it does Ferguson" (Topaz 2014, para 4). The imagery of Ferguson and additional grassroots pressure led to President Obama scaling back the 1033 program. However, the police's militarized response continued in 2016 against water protectors protesting against the Dakota Access Pipeline at the Standing Rock Reservation. There, federal, state, and local police officials coordinated with private security company TigerSwan to attack protestors with dogs, rubber bullets, sound devices, and bean-bag pellets. Water protectors were also under heavy surveillance as part of this counterinsurgency, including the use of drones and helicopters to photograph protectors, in addition to police infiltrating the movement for intelligence gathering.

In May 2020, police militarization would again come into the public consciousness following the police murder of George Floyd in Minneapolis. Protests against police brutality rose up across the United States, and police responded with overwhelming militaristic force. These protests also amplified the killing of Breonna Taylor in Louisville, Kentucky, an ER technician whom police murdered in her home while conducting a paramilitary raid. In response to the uprisings, Republican President Donald Trump threatened to send the military to cities he felt were not quelling the protests sufficiently. In Washington, DC, the US Park Police, Secret Service, and other police agencies tear-gassed and pepper-sprayed peaceful protestors in Lafayette Park so President Trump could walk to St. John's Church to hold up a bible in a now infamous photo-op. At another protest in DC, helicopters were shown flying closely over protestors in attempts to intimidate them. Across the country, departments used chemical weapons and militaristic force to quell protests. President Trump even deployed the US Marshals Service and the Department of Homeland Security (DHS) to Portland, Oregon, where they detained, arrested, and used chemical weapons on protestors, despite some local officials' opposition to their deployment. Portland police cooperated with these federal entities, again, conflating police and military. On July 22, 2020, President Donald Trump announced *Operation Legend*, in which he announced a "surge" of federal police officials from the Federal Bureau of Investigation, the Bureau of Alcohol, Tobacco, Firearms and Explosives (ATF), the Drug Enforcement Administration, the US Marshalls Service, and the DHS into Chicago and Albuquerque, escalating the militarized operation that previously began in Kansas City.

REPUBLICANS ON POLICE MILITARIZATION

The historical stance of the Republican Party on police militarization is fairly clear. Republicans have strongly supported both the War on Drugs and the Section 1033 program. In addition to these Republican creations, they also strongly supported the Violent Crime Control and Law Enforcement Act of 1994. This law strengthened the use of military tactics and equipment for police. These programs fall in line with Republican agenda items concerning police support.

Traditionally, the Republican Party has marketed itself as "pro-police." Recent data demonstrates this support, with three-quarters of Republicans believing that police are doing an excellent job of treating racial groups equally, of using the "right" amount of force, and of holding officers accountable for misconduct errors. Moreover, 87 percent report believing that policing has gotten more dangerous. This belief lends itself to the wedge issue of police militarization, with most self-identified "conservatives" supporting the idea of more militarization. To illustrate, the CATO Institute found that 65 percent of Republicans support police using military weapons and armored vehicles. These numbers reflect the current Republican legislative agenda.

Some Republican members of Congress, however, have challenged the status quo of support for police militarization. Senator Rand Paul (KY) began discussing some restrictions for police militarization as early as 2014 by showing some support to Democratic Rep. Hank Johnson's Stop Militarizing Law Enforcement Act of 2014. A small group of Republicans, including Senator Paul, argue that the 1033 program is fiscally irresponsible and infringes on personal liberties. Republican Senator Tom Coburn (OK) in support said, "It's hard to see a difference between the militarized and increasingly federalized police force we see in towns across America today and the force Madison had in mind when he said, 'a standing military force with an overgrown executive will not long be a safe companion to liberty'" (Grossman 2014, para 8). The bipartisan support by Republican senators alleviated some of the pressure on President Obama when he signed his 2015 executive order meant to limit the scope of the 1033 program.

Senator Rand Paul Opposes Police Militarization

In August 2017, in response to President Donald Trump's reversal of President Obama's diminishment of the Section 1033 program, Republican Senator Rand Paul (KY) wrote an op-ed for the *New York Post* that opened with "That's a mistake." Doubling down on his strong stance in a *TIME* op-ed after the death of Michael Brown in August 2014, Senator Paul said "To support our local police, we must first realize they aren't soldiers. But today the line between the two is being eroded." Paul also made it clear that over one-third of the surplus equipment passed on to local law enforcement was new. Moreover, Paul says, "When we couple militarizing law enforcement with the erosion of civil liberties and due process that allows the police to become judge and jury—national security letters, broad general warrants, pre-conviction asset forfeiture—we see the magnitude of the problem." In this op-ed, Paul declared that he would be reintroducing the "Stop Militarizing Our Law Enforcement Act, which will address this issue by prohibiting the federal transfer of militarized equipment to state and local law enforcement, including MRAP vehicles, drones and armored vehicles transferred through the ... Byrne Justice Assistance Grant and Department of Homeland Security's grant programs" (Paul 2017).

Republican support of the order, however, was short-lived. Following his election, President Trump reinstituted the 1033 program with support from then attorney general and former Alabama Republican senator Jeff Sessions. Attorney General Sessions referred to issues of police militarization as "superficial concerns" and argued that access to military equipment improves policing. He also stated that "the executive order the president will sign today ensures you can get the lifesaving gear that you need to do your job and send a strong message that we will not allow criminal activity, violence and lawlessness to become the new normal" (Nelson 2017, para 4).

According to a *New York Times* analysis, police departments received less funding for fiscal year 2018 compared to 2017. However, despite this reduction there was not a major shift in the Republican Party's stance for police militarization. President Trump demonstrated his support for police militarization rhetorically in 2018, saying: "This is why, as I promised all along—that we are allowing local police to access the surplus military equipment the need to protect our officers and law enforcement agents and save their lives ... Millions and millions of dollars of surplus equipment is going to our police department" (Qui 2018, para 1). In 2019, President Trump announced he was making $600 million worth of surplus military equipment available to police for gang activity and drug trafficking in cities and rural areas.

This legislative stance received even more support through Republican Senator Pat Toomey's proposed Lifesaving Gear for Police Act. The act would codify into law former president Trump's executive order, allowing police departments to obtain federal military equipment. It is one of many in a long line of Republican-led legislation that demonstrates their continued support for police militarization. This includes the recent Senate bill proposed by Republican Tim Scott after the murders of George Floyd and Breonna Taylor, which only targets increased oversight of no-knock warrants without addressing any other facet of police militarization. Only two Republicans, Rep. Tom McClinkton and Senator Rand Paul, have voiced support for more material rollbacks of police militarization such as the end of the 1033 program.

DEMOCRATS ON POLICE MILITARIZATION

Historically, Democrats supported the "war" metaphor that escalated police militarization. Specifically, many Democrats supported actions taken to advance the armament and training of police through policies such as the War on Drugs. Despite the fact that two Republican presidents sought to increase the use of police militarization to "fight" the drug problem, Democratic President Bill Clinton signed the Violent Crime Control and Law Enforcement Act of 1994, written by Democratic Senator Joe Biden (DE), strengthening police access to military equipment. Clinton's administration and supporters in Congress mandated the DOD work closely with the DOJ to equip officers. The party also supported the creation of the Section 1033 program, described previously. The connection between the voting records for these policies demonstrate that between the late 1980s and early 2000s, the Democratic Party demonstrated support for legislation that advanced the militarization of police.

Current polling and Democratic Party rhetoric show a slight divergence from these policies. Research demonstrates that Democrats or those who self-identify as liberal are, on average, less likely to show support for police militarization. Nearly two-thirds of registered Democrats, for example, oppose police militarization. Additionally, 75 percent of those identifying as liberal stated that police use of military weapons and armored vehicles is not necessary to provide safety to communities. This stance is directly tied to current Democratic policies and party agenda that argue police militarization subverts democratic ideals as well as disproportionately harms communities of color.

Democratic lawmakers have supported legislation that would weaken the connection between the military and the police. Specifically, there has been a noticeable change in the policy stance started under the Obama administration following the uprisings in Ferguson, Missouri, as Democrats attempt to separate the party from the legacy of both the War on Drugs and the 1033 program. In May 2015, President Obama announced new limits on federal programs that supplied military style equipment and weapons to local police departments. His executive order banned police from obtaining military equipment such as grenade launchers, armed aircraft, guns/ammunition of .50 caliber or higher, bayonets, and tracked armored vehicles. Additionally, the order added more restrictions for the supply of wheeled armored vehicles, drones, firearms, riot gear, and helicopters, requiring written justification for the need of the equipment requested. These restrictions were meant to follow other Democratic policies attempting to rebuild trust between police and communities following several police killings of unarmed citizens of color. However, these policies did not eliminate the 1033 program. The administration believed that to do so would eliminate tools that enhance officer safety when responding to dangerous situations.

Members of the Democratic Party, however, are not singularly unified on these issues. Specifically, Representative Hank Johnson (GA) submitted multiple bills trying to end the Section 1033 program and the advancement of police militarization. Ironically, Rep. Johnson introduced a bill that would drastically limit the kind of military equipment local police departments could acquire from the DOD prior to the Ferguson events. In 2014, Rep. Johnson actively sought bipartisan support for his bill, Stop Militarizing Law Enforcement Act of 2014. This bill, like others limiting police militarization, never received a House vote.

ACLU Admonishes Attorney General Jeff Sessions for Limiting the Policing of the Police, 2018

In November 2018, Kanya Bennett and Carl Takei published a piece through the American Civil Liberties Union (ACLU) admonishing then attorney general Jeff Sessions for limiting the Justice Department's ability to provide oversight of state and local police engaging in unconstitutional policing practices. The authors state, "Sessions' 'law and order' agenda eliminated or perverted Obama-era efforts to advance constitutional policing on a range of issues." They continue to say, "Sessions cheered on police militarization when Trump eliminated all oversight and regulation of federal transfers of military weapons to law enforcement. And Sessions deemed the 'centerpiece' of his 'law and order' agenda, a War-on-Drugs-type program known as Project Safe Neighborhoods, which the Congress just reauthorized." Most worrisome to the authors is the fact that "with all of the distractions and blind eyes during the 115th Congress, there has been zero oversight from the Congress on just how far Sessions' reach was" (Bennett and Takei 2018).

In 2017, Rep. Johnson submitted a second House bill in an attempt to limit the 1033 program following earlier bipartisan support. Citing the over $5 billion worth of equipment used to militarize police, Rep. Johnson's bill H.R. 1556 would shut down what he refers to as the "pipeline through which law enforcement agencies are able to acquire military grade weaponry without first obtaining approval from the state and local government authority" (Cohen 2017, para. 4). This bill, with strong support from the ACLU and NAACP, again did not receive a floor vote by the Republican-controlled House. In 2019, Rep. Johnson and the Democratic Party continued attempts to limit the provisions of military equipment to local police with H.R. 1714: Stop Militarizing Law Enforcement Act of 2019. Since the killing of George Floyd, the bill, which had 66 original sponsors, 64 of whom were Democrats, now has 116 Democratic cosponsors. More recently, the Democratic House

Majority passed The George Floyd Justice in Policing Act, which eliminates no-knock warrants and the transfer of military equipment to police agencies. Very few Democrats, however, have voiced support for defunding police. Democratic legislators have also spoken out against the deployment of unidentified federal forces in Portland who have detained protestors throughout the city. House Democrats have called for an investigation into the matter.

Under the Biden administration, the Pentagon had loaned over $120 million in military gear from January 2021 to June 2022 (Semler 2022). Alongside the continued transferring of military equipment, there was at minimum, the appearance of pursuits to curb militarization. While the George Floyd Justice in Policing Act did not pass, Biden did pass an executive order, part of which pertained to police militarization. In May 25, 2022, on the two-year anniversary of George Floyd's murder by Minneapolis police, President Joe Biden signed an executive order that, among other things, restricted transfers of military equipment to the police. Specifically, Section 12 required federal agencies to review their programming that authorized these transfers, including bayonets, grenade launchers, certain weaponized drones and grenades, among other items. However, there is a loophole that pertains to military vehicles in that if an agency claims they need it for disaster-related, counter/anti-terrorism, search and rescue, and hostage scenarios, they may keep the vehicle. It also restricted federal agencies and their use of no-knock entries and that these agencies maintain records of these entries.

FURTHER READING

American Civil Liberties Union. 2014. "War Comes Home: The Excessive Militarization of American Policing." *American Civil Liberties Union*, June 2014. https://www.aclu.org/sites/default/files/field_document/jus14-warcomeshome-text-rel1.pdf. Accessed May 3, 2022.

Balko, Radley. 2013. *Rise of the Warrior Cop: The Militarization of America's Police Forces*. New York: PublicAffairs.

Bennett, Kanya, and Carl Takei. 2018. "Before Resigning, Jeff Sessions Handcuffed the Justice Department's Ability to Police the Police." American Civil Liberties Union, November 9, 2018. https://www.aclu.org/blog/criminal-law-reform/reforming-police-practices/resigning-jeff-sessions-handcuffed-justice.

Brown, Alleen, Will Parrish, and Alice Speri. 2017. "Leaked Documents Reveal Counterterrorism Tactics Used at Standing Rock to 'Defeat Pipeline Insurgencies.'" *The Intercept*, May 27, 2017. https://theintercept.com/2017/05/27/leaked-documents-reveal-security-firms-counterterrorism-tactics-at-standing-rock-to-defeat-pipeline-insurgencies/.

Chin, William Y. 2013. "Domestic Counterinsurgency: How Counterinsurgency Tactics Combined with Laws Were Deployed Against Blacks Throughout U.S. History." *University of Miami Race and Social Justice Law Review* 3, no. 1 (July): 31–62.

Clark, Dartunorro. 2017. "Trump Makes It Easier for Police to Get Military Equipment." *NBC News*, November 13, 2017. https://www.nbcnews.com/politics/white-house/trump-makes-it-easier-police-get-military-equipment-n815766.

Cohen, Kelly. 2017. "GOP, Democratic Lawmakers Propose Dueling Bills on Police Militarization." March 17, 2017. https://www.washingtonexaminer.com/gop-democratic-lawmakers-propose-dueling-bills-on-police-militarization.

Ekins, Emily. 2016. "Policing in America: Understanding Public Attitudes Toward the Police. Results from a National Survey." CATO Institute. https://www.cato.org/survey-reports/policing-america. Accessed April 8, 2022.

Fabian, Jordan. 2015. "Obama Bans Some Transfers of Military Hardware to Police." *The Hill*, May 18, 2015. https://thehill.com/homenews/administration/242346-obama-limiting-military-hardware-to-police-departments.

Grossman, Andrew. 2014. "Senators Criticize Growing Militarization of Local Police Departments." *The Wall Street Journal*, September 9, 2014. https://www.wsj.com/articles/senators-criticize-militarization-of-local-police-departments-1410287125

Guariglia, Matthew. 2023. *Police & the Empire City: Race & the Origins of Modern Policing in New York*. Durham, NC: Duke University Press.

Hall, Abigail R., and Christopher J. Coyne. 2013. "The Militarization of U.S. Domestic Policing." *The Independent Review* 17, no. 4 (Spring): 485–504.

Johnson, Jake. 2019. "Vowing Nationwide Crackdown, Trump Touts Tougher and More Militarized U.S. Police." *Salon*, October 31, 2019. https://www.salon.com/2019/10/31/vowing-nationwide-crackdown-trump-touts-tougher-and-more-militarized-u-s-police/.

Kraska, Peter B. 2007. "Militarization and Policing—Its Relevance to 21st Century Police." *Policing: A Journal of Policy and Practice* 1, no. 4 (December): 1–13.

Kraska, Peter B., and Victor E. Kappeler. 1997. "Militarizing American Police: The Rise and Normalization of Paramilitary Units." *Social Problems* 44, no. 1 (February): 1–18.

Mummolo, Jonathan. 2018. "Militarization Fails to Enhance Police safety or Reduce Crime but May Harm Police Reputation." *Proceedings of the National Academy of Sciences* 115, no. 37 (September): 9181–86.

Nelson, Louis. 2017. "Trump to Roll Back Obama's Crackdown on Military Equipment for Local Police." *Politico*, August 28, 2017. https://www.politico.com/story/2017/08/28/police-military-gear-trump-242092

Paul, Rand. 2017. "No, The Feds Shouldn't Give War Machines to The Police." *New York Post*, August 28, 2017. https://nypost.com/2017/08/28/no-the-feds-shouldnt-give-war-machines-to-the-police/.

Pierce, Charles. 2011. "Occupy Oakland and the Militarization of America's Police." *Esquire*, October 26, 2011. https://www.esquire.com/news-politics/politics/a11435/occupy-oakland-6530274/.

Qui, Linda. 2018. "Trump Falsely Claimed that Transfers of Military Gear to Police Departments Are 'At a Record Clip.'" *New York Times*, May 15, 2018. https://www.nytimes.com/2018/05/15/us/politics/trump-military-gear-police-fact-check.html.

Radil, Steven M., Raymond J. Dezzani, and Lanny D. McAden. 2017. "Geographies of US Police Militarization and the Role of the 1033 Program." *The Professional Geographer* 69, no. 2: 203–13.

Rambo, K. 2020. "Evidence Shows Portland Police Working with Federal Officers at Protests, Contradicting City Officials." *OregonLive: The Oregonian*, July 18, 2020. https://www.oregonl

ive.com/news/2020/07/evidence-shows-portland-police-working-with-federal-officers-at-protests-contradicting-city-officials.html .

Renner, Nausicaa. 2019. "As Immigrants Become More Aware of Their Rights, ICE Steps up Ruses and Surveillance." *The Intercept*, July 25, 2019. https://theintercept.com/2019/07/25/ice-surveillance-ruse-arrests-raids/.

Schrader, Stuart. 2019. *Badges Without Borders: How Global Counterinsurgency Transformed American Policing*. Oakland: University of California Press.

Semler, Stephen. 2022. "Police have Received $120 Million Worth of Weapons through a Pentagon Grant Program since January 2021." *Substack*, July 11, 2022. https://stephensemler.substack.com/p/police-have-received-120-million.

Shepherd, Katie, and Mark Berman. 2020. " 'It Was Like Being Preyed Upon': Portland Protestors say Federal Officers in Unmarked Vans are Detaining Them." *Washington Post*, July 17, 2020. https://www.washingtonpost.com/nation/2020/07/17/portland-protests-federal-arrests/.

Sierra-Arévalo, Michael. 2024. *The Danger Imperative: Violence, Death, and the Soul of Policing*. New York: Columbia University.

Simon, Samantha J. 2024. *Before the Badge: How Academy Training Shapes Police Violence*. New York: New York University Press.

Topaz, Jonathan. 2014. "Cleaver: Ferguson looks like Fallujah." *Politico*, August 19, 2014. https://www.politico.com/story/2014/08/emanuel-cleaver-ferguson-reaction-110139

Vitale, Alex. 2017. *The End of Policing*. New York: Verso Books.

CHAPTER 21

Prosecuting Juveniles as Adults

KIMBERLY DETARDO-BORA AND DHRUBA J. BORA

AT A GLANCE

The criminal justice system in the United States was primarily developed to address crimes committed by adults, eighteen years of age or older. Crimes committed by individuals under the age of eighteen are generally managed by the juvenile court, but politicians and legislators have created mechanisms to prosecute juveniles as adults, using a transfer process to remove a youth's case from juvenile court to adult court, known as waiver. The primary types of waivers are judicial waiver, legislative waiver (i.e., statutory exclusion), and prosecutorial waiver (i.e., direct file). A judicial waiver grants the judge sole legal authority to transfer or bind over the juvenile's case to adult court. Judges take into consideration criteria such as the seriousness of the offense and the juvenile's prior arrest record. In addition, the judge must consider the likelihood that the juvenile can be rehabilitated under the guise of the juvenile justice system. Legislative waiver is written into state code and typically specifies how a juvenile's case is automatically waived to adult court for a specific type of felony offense, the use of a weapon during the commission of the offense, or based on an age limit. A prosecutorial waiver provides prosecutors the sole decision-making power to transfer a juvenile's case to criminal court. As of 2019, forty-seven states including the District of Columbia, had judicial waiver laws and twenty-eight states had some form of statutory exclusion provisions, while only thirteen states and the District of Columbia have direct file statutes (Office of Juvenile Justice and Delinquency Prevention 2022).

Since its inception, the waiver of juvenile cases from juvenile court to adult court has been widely debated. As this debate has progressed, it has become more evident that prosecuting juveniles as adults is a complex issue hinged on historical, political, legal, and sociocultural underpinnings. Many Republicans argue that youth who commit violent crimes should be held accountable for their actions and prosecuted accordingly as adults in criminal court. Conversely, many Democrats argue that juveniles should be managed solely in the juvenile court. In addition to disagreement over which type of court should handle cases involving juveniles, the parties have different views on the legal processes that should be employed to address serious violent juvenile crime.

MANY REPUBLICANS...

- Believe in the "just deserts" philosophy, with expanded juvenile transfer laws that allow a juvenile's case to be moved to adult court for certain felony crimes (e.g., murder, aggravated assault, rape, etc.).
- Believe in direct file provisions ("prosecutorial waiver" laws) that allow the prosecutor to transfer a juvenile's case to adult court with limited criteria and oversight.
- Believe in lowering the age limit at which a juvenile can be tried in adult court, thereby deterring youth from committing future offenses.

MANY DEMOCRATS...

- Believe in the concept of *parens patriae*; that a juvenile's case should be retained within the jurisdiction of the juvenile court by raising the upper age limit, thereby allowing the juvenile to receive treatment and rehabilitation under the purview of the juvenile court.
- Have attempted to abolish or limit direct file provisions so that prosecutors do not possess the sole discretion in waiving a case from juvenile court to adult court.
- Support legislative action to create reverse waiver laws, whereby in some states the criminal court can transfer the case that was placed there because of direct file or legislative exclusion to be disposed of in juvenile court instead.

OVERVIEW

Central to the treatment of juveniles in the criminal justice system is the concept of culpability. Culpability is another word for responsibility. While it is difficult to know exactly when youth culpability was legally established, historians claim that youth were punished and sentenced in similar ways as early as the Middle Ages. However, this was not true for children of all ages. Historians found that this era marked a time where most youth ages seven and under could be excused for their behaviors by claiming a defense of infancy or immaturity, whereas for children ages seven to fourteen, the validity of this defense was not so clear. The closer the child was to age fourteen, the more likely the court could produce evidence that the juvenile was deemed to be criminally capable and responsible for their actions (i.e., culpable). By age fourteen, it was assumed that the youth was fully responsible for their actions just like an adult. The application of an infancy or immaturity defense was not acceptable.

The American colonies borrowed many of the same ideas from Europe and English Common Law. In the mid-1600s, even though no pronounced political movement was taking place, early colonists started to house youth separately from adults. More notable reform efforts, however, took place in the late 1800s and early 1900s as child advocates started to connect a youth's wayward behavior to poverty and poor parenting. Eventually, the idea emerged that it was best to formally place youth under the jurisdiction of a juvenile court and in the hands of reform schools or a house of refuge.

The reform movement was punctuated by the landmark Illinois Juvenile Court Act of 1899. This legislation originally was conceived by a group of progressives referred to as the "child savers," many of whom were white, affluent, Protestant women. Out of growing concern for wayward and indigent youth, the child savers sought not only to create a separate juvenile court but also to provide youth training and education. This movement was hinged on the *parens patriae* doctrine, which placed power in the hands of the state to "protect" children. Some historians, however, argued that the *parens patriae* doctrine did nothing more than allow states to sustain its power and legitimize its reach into the lives of poor youth and immigrant families, who were viewed as threats to society. Nonetheless, by 1912, almost half of the states in the United States had a separate juvenile court, and by 1945 some semblance of a juvenile court existed in every state in the country. While *parens patriae* may seem like a more liberal philosophy, liberals have been highly skeptical of the broad discretionary power of the juvenile court that accompanies it. However, establishing a separate juvenile court and separate residential facilities for youth certainly opened the door for rehabilitation and treatment approaches to flourish for several decades.

Interestingly, the late 1960s and early 1970s were replete with both the marks of Democrats and Republicans, who explained societal turbulence in different ways. Much like the child savers, modern Democrats relied heavily on societal explanations to explain youthful offending as juveniles were viewed as products of their environment with poverty and racial inequality (forces beyond the youth's control) to blame for their behavior. Republicans, on the other hand, believed that juveniles possessed the ability to fully rationalize right from wrong and simply were choosing to commit crime. As a result, the late 1960s and early 1970s were characterized as a "win" for liberals. Even though a separate juvenile court was in place, and attempts were made to destigmatize youth from the formal trappings of the juvenile system by relying on alternatives such as diversion into treatment, juvenile offenders were not being afforded the same due process rights as adults. In fact, juveniles were receiving similar penalties as adults.

Having juveniles suffer the same consequences as adults resulted in concerns about due process and led to debate at the highest levels. The US Supreme Court, which found itself at the center of national debate, was left to ultimately teeter between the need to expand juvenile rights (making it more akin to the adult criminal court) while simultaneously maintaining the jurisdiction and flexibility of the juvenile court to oversee juvenile matters. Many of these procedural considerations were spelled out in *Kent v. United States* (1966). The case of Morris Kent instituted important due process rights that juveniles had not been previously afforded. In the end, the Supreme Court ruled that juveniles are entitled to a full hearing and the right to counsel should the judge decide to treat the juvenile as an adult and send the case to criminal court (i.e., "waive" it). In addition, judges would be required to specify how the decision to waive the juvenile's case was made. The Supreme Court also included in this ruling several procedural safeguards so that judges would not make arbitrary decisions. That is, judges would have to consider whether the juvenile was unamendable to treatment in the juvenile system and whether the juvenile posed a threat to society.

The position of keeping youth separate from adults was solidified with the President's Commission on Law Enforcement and the Administration of Justice in 1967 and the Juvenile Justice Delinquency Prevention Act. The 1960s undoubtedly represented the spirit of Democratic thinking as policy change relied heavily on the principles of diversion, decriminalization, and deinstitutionalization. However, even with these landmark decisions that hailed from the Supreme Court and federal guidelines, many politicians became disillusioned with the effectiveness of the juvenile system and both parties found themselves dissatisfied with the juvenile justice system in the 1970s. Primarily, it appeared that treatment and rehabilitation of youth were not effective. The increase in arrests for violent juvenile crimes from the 1960s to the 1980s also solidified the notion that the juvenile justice system was flawed, and that liberal practices of treating youth were not effective enough in punishing youth for their indiscretions. Because of this failure, many liberals and conservatives came together to reestablish a just deserts model.

Within a separate court for juveniles and the seeds of waiver laws in place from *Kent v. United States* (1966), the proverbial pendulum swung in the early to late 1990s. This was a period that signified a "win" for Republicans, who used the climbing arrest rates of juveniles for violent offenses as a reason to solidify the widespread adoption and use of waiver policies. Here, Republicans touted the philosophy of deterrence and retribution as well as the need to protect the community from violent youth. However, it is difficult to pinpoint the exact time or historical event that led juveniles to being increasingly treated as adults within the criminal justice system. Criminologists, however, speculate that factors such as the availability of guns, gang violence, and the increased number of adolescents (i.e., echo boom) during this time culminated in a cause for growing concern about youth violence and the need for public safety. Moreover, some criminologists, politicians, and the media fueled the airwaves with rhetoric about a growing violent cohort of youth known as "super-predators" (Dilulio 1995). As a result, both Republicans and Democrats pushed for the adoption or modification of laws that would move cases involving these youth from juvenile court to adult court.

REPUBLICANS ON PROSECUTING JUVENILES AS ADULTS

Traditionally, the Republican agenda to prosecute juveniles in adult court is strongly hinged on conservative ideology that punishment is the more appropriate response to dealing with juveniles and that the need to protect society outweigh the rights of the juvenile. This position has not wavered over time. From a historical perspective, many Republicans made these arguments as juvenile crimes began to rise significantly from 1960 to 1975, and again with the rise of the so-called super-predators in the late 1980s and early 1990s. In many states, Republican legislators have argued for greater crime control measures, changing the mechanisms for handling cases involving juveniles, creating direct file provisions so that prosecutors could more easily send juvenile cases to adult court, and lowering the age limits at which youth could be tried in adult court.

In the late 1970s, most states generically described that any felony offense was justification for an automatic waiver to adult court or in some cases, state legislation specified the types of felony crimes for which a youth's case could be transferred. In 1979, for example, Vermont's state code listed only the crime of murder by which a juvenile could be transferred to adult court. By 1995, however, it included manslaughter, aggravated assault, armed robbery, kidnapping, aggravated sexual assault, and aggravated burglary as crimes by which a juvenile's case would warrant transfer to criminal court. While only a handful of states made changes to their statutes up until the mid-1990s, state Republicans continued to modify state code into the 2000s. In 2017, for example, in Georgia, Republican Tyler Harper sponsored Senate Bill 160, also referred to as the "Back the Badge Act of 2017." The bill, signed into law by Governor Nathan Deal, increased the punishment for juveniles who commit aggravated assault with a firearm against public safety officers (which also includes firefighters and emergency personnel).

Many Republicans have also advocated for one of the most controversial types of waiver—prosecutorial discretion. In Arizona, Republican Senator Linda Gray put forth Bill 1009 in 2010 that allowed for the county attorney to criminally prosecute juveniles at ages fifteen, sixteen, or seventeen years of age for first and second-degree murder, forcible sexual assault, armed robbery, and any other violent felony offense. In addition, the prosecutor was granted transfer powers for fourteen year olds who committed a felony offense and/or who were considered chronic felony offenders. In 1993, Colorado was among many states that removed legislative waiver from its state statute and created a prosecutorial waiver statute instead. As early as the late 1970s and early 1980s, prosecutors in Florida were given mostly unlimited discretion when waiving youth to criminal court. Today, Florida "transfers more juveniles out of the juvenile court and into the adult criminal justice system than any other state" (Chirino 2019, 235).

Even though the Clinton administration seemed like a time for a shift in policy and an opportunity for Democrats to reposition the juvenile court as the sole authority in juvenile matters, twenty-seven states continued to extend the reach of judicial waiver laws by lowering the age requirement between 1992 and 1999. Iowa specifies the minimum age as ten, while Colorado, Indiana, Missouri, and Vermont specify the minimum age as twelve (Thomas et al. 2019). States like Montana modified their legal code in 1995, so youth ages twelve and older could be waived to adult court for crimes such as murder and sexual assault. More recently, in 2019, there is evidence that violent crimes committed by youth continued to fuel the Republican agenda, especially in states like New Jersey where Republican assemblymen initiated a bill to transfer youth as young as fourteen to criminal court on aggravated assault charges as a result of playing the game "knockout" (Evans 2019). Knockout has been popularized on social media and encourages youth to seek out unsuspecting victims and knock them unconscious. There is an ongoing debate, however, as to whether this is a long-term crime phenomenon among juveniles.

Indiana Senate Republican Proposes Senate Bill 449

In 2018, a thirteen year old at Noblesville West Middle School opened fire and wounded a teacher and classmate. Since the shooting, both victims have experienced long-term complications from their wounds. The juvenile plead guilty and was tried in juvenile court for attempted murder. The judge sentenced him to the custody of the juvenile department of corrections where he was ordered to complete a set of programs and possibly detained until he turns eighteen years old. After this incident, Indiana Republican Senators proposed Senate Bill 449, which would allow the court to waive a youth as young as twelve years old to adult criminal court. The law at the time of the shooting stated that only youth ages fourteen and older could be waived to adult court for certain felony offenses. Senator Erin Houchin, who authored the bill, explained that the focus was on the victims. According to Houchin, "the young woman who was shot in the 2018 incident shouldn't have to be in fear of her shooter walking free after being released from a juvenile correctional facility at the age of 18." Given that youth of color are disproportionately represented in the juvenile system, a member of the ministry community stated that the bill was "white supremacy at its finest." Despite tremendous opposition to the bill, it was passed in February 2020 (Odendahl 2020; Ratliff 2020).

While the Republican agenda to prosecute youth as adults has been steadfast over the past fifty years, there have been many opponents and criticisms regarding the legislation that has been put into place. First, the Republican view has been challenged as being too punitive, namely when it comes to longer and harsher sentences for youth tried as adults. Little to no research supports a deterrent effect when youth are tried and sentenced in the criminal court. In fact, some research has shown recidivism rates to be higher among youth sentenced as adults. Second, some have criticized the Republican approach for being too adversarial; opponents claim that juveniles are not adults but children. This criticism is based on the notion that prosecuting children as adults symbolically alters the way in which children are treated in the United States. Third, when it comes to direct file, many opponents have claimed that these laws are vague, have little to no set standards for waiver, and expand the power of prosecutors, creating a major imbalance in the courts. Last, many argue that judicial waiver, direct file, and statutory exclusion laws disproportionately impact youth of color.

DEMOCRATS ON PROSECUTING JUVENILES AS ADULTS

Historically, Democrats advocate for rehabilitating youth, regardless of the type of offense that was committed. Many Democrats believe that youth lack the ability to fully reason and think about their consequences. This belief is supported by scientific evidence that the human brain is not fully developed until a person is about twenty-five years old, evidence provided as testimony in decisions made by the US Supreme Court in *Roper v. Simmons*

(543 U.S. 551, 2005) and *Miller v. Alabama* (567 U.S. 460, 2012). Democrats also question whether adult sentences for juveniles are truly effective in reducing repeat offending, with some evidence suggesting that juveniles who are waived to adult court are more likely than those retained in juvenile court to repeat offend. Over time, many Democrats have argued and advocated for raising the age of juvenile court jurisdiction, abolishing prosecutorial waiver, and supporting bills that would allow reverse waiver.

The "raise the age" movement and legislative efforts from many state Democrats run counter to the movement by conservatives to decrease the age of juvenile court jurisdiction and/or waive youth to adult court. However, this legislation, for many states, applies solely to delinquency cases. Cases that involve certain violent felonies can still be waived to adult criminal court as specified in the state code. Nonetheless, the movement signals a return to the ideas and philosophy of the child savers and is backed by research evidence that a child's brain is not fully developed until their early twenties (Blakemore and Choudhury 2006).

In forty-seven states, juvenile court jurisdiction is typically up to age seventeen. Only three states stipulate that the maximum age is sixteen (i.e., Georgia, Texas, and Wisconsin). Massachusetts raised the age from sixteen to seventeen in 2013 and was one among a few of the New England states that attempted to raise the age in 2018. Currently, efforts are being made to raise the age to twenty-one. In 2016, in a bipartisan effort, Louisiana adopted a new law to retain seventeen year olds in juvenile court regardless of the offense. Likewise, both Democrats and Republicans in Michigan put forth actual "Raise the Age" legislation, which was signed into law by Governor Gretchen Whitmer. The law allows seventeen year olds to be processed by the juvenile court, thus providing the age-appropriate resources and treatment services that are needed (Jackson 2019).

Regarding waiver mechanisms, many Democrats have tried to limit or abolish them, namely direct file. They have largely argued that prosecutors should not wield such power in the courtroom and that youth waived directly to the criminal court find no alternative but to plead guilty and find themselves in the hands of the adult correctional system, which is not suitable to treat youth. However, efforts by Democrats to limit or abolish prosecutorial wavier have not always been successful. In 2018, Indiana state Democrat Linda Lawson sought to repeal direct file with House Bill 1389, but the bill was defeated. On the other hand, attempts to modify direct file in a bipartisan fashion have been more successful. In Colorado, for example, which has had direct file since 1995, state Democrat senator Claire Levy attempted to limit direct file authority in 2008, but it was vetoed by Governor Bill Ritter. However, several years later, House Bill 1271 was passed and signed by Governor John Hickenlooper in 2012 (Hoover 2012).

California Democratic Senator Proposes Senate Bill 889

In 2019, as an attempt to alter Republican laws enacted during the administration of California Governor Arnold Schwarzenegger, Democratic Senator Nancy Skinner proposed Senate Bill 889. This bill proposed to expand juvenile court jurisdiction to cover eighteen and nineteen year olds and, for youth in juvenile court custody, to extend juvenile court management of those individuals until they reach the age of twenty-four. According to Skinner, "When teenagers make serious mistakes and commit crimes, state prison is not the answer ... The bill is heavily based on decades of scientific research that shows how the prefrontal cortex of a youth is not fully developed and how juveniles are more developmentally and emotionally immature." The bill also aligns additional age-based legislation, for example, where youth must be twenty-one to consume alcohol. Proponents of the bill seek to afford youth more appropriate age-related treatment and services as they are maturing instead of placing them into the hands of the adult system. Senator Skinner reiterated "Processing teenagers through the juvenile justice system will help ensure they receive the appropriate education, counseling, treatment, and rehabilitation services necessary to achieve real public safety outcomes" (Gartrell 2020).

To curb the power of prosecutors and to return juveniles back to the juvenile court for more suitable treatment, many Democrats have supported reverse waiver laws. This allows a juvenile's case that originated in criminal court to be transferred back to juvenile court. The power to reverse transfer a juvenile's case depends on state code. In some states, the prosecutor can make this decision, while in other states the judge makes the reverse transfer decisions. In other states, the burden of proof falls on the juvenile to make the case. It is important to note that for many states, reverse waiver mechanisms were already folded originally into the statutory exclusion or direct file laws when they were written and codified.

Although the past fifty years of legislation to prosecute juveniles as adults has been dominated by Republicans, Democrats, often with Republican support, have made significant progress in the past decade to return youth to juvenile court and decision-making power back to juvenile court judges. Democrats, however, still face ongoing criticism and philosophical debate. Opponents argue that Democrats are too soft on crime, that the traditional juvenile justice system provides no real deterrent effect, and that rehabilitation does not work. Many Republicans also believe that the system's goal should be youth accountability and punishment commensurate with the juvenile's age and crime seriousness, due in part to the fact that many violent youthful offenders have not been amenable to treatment within the juvenile system. Finally, while Democrats generally believe the juvenile court to be the best judge of community and victim interests with respect to juvenile offenders, many Republicans believe those interests are best represented by prosecutors.

FURTHER READING

Ash, Peter. 2006. "Adolescents in Adult Court: Does the Punishment Fit the Criminal?" *The Journal of the American Academy of Psychiatry and the Law Online* 34, no. 2: 145–9.

Blakemore, Sarah-Jayne, and Suparna Choudhury. 2006. "Development of the Adolescent Brain: Implications for Executive Function and Social Cognition." *Journal of Child Psychology and Psychiatry* 47, no. 3/4: 296–312.

Chirino, Kristen. 2019. "Florida's Direct File Statute: A Prosecutor's Playground." *St. Thomas Law Review* 31, no. 2 (Spring): 224–44.

DiIulio, John. 1995. "The Coming of the Super-Predators." *The Weekly Standard*, November 27, 1995. https://www.weeklystandard.com/john-j-dilulio-jr/the-coming-of-the-super-predators.

Evans, Brian. 2019. "2019 Legislation on Youth Prosecuted as Adults in the States." Campaign for Youth Justice, February 4, 2019. http://campaignforyouthjustice.org/20 19/item/2019-legislation-on-youth-prosecuted-as-adults-in-the-states.

Feld, Barry C. 1999. *Bad Kids: Race and the Transformation of the Juvenile Court*. New York: Oxford University Press.

Feld, Barry C. 2001. "Race, Youth Violence, and the Changing of Jurisprudence of Waiver." *Behavioral Sciences and the Law* 19, no. 3: 3–22.

Feld, Barry C. 2003. "The Politics of Race and Juvenile Justice: The 'Due Process Revolution' and the Conservative Reaction." *Justice Quarterly* 20, no. 4: 765–800.

Fritsch, Eric, and Craig Hemmens. 1995. "Juvenile Waiver in the United States 1979-1995: Comparison and Analysis of State Waiver Statutes." *Juvenile and Family Court Journal* 46, no. 3: 17–36.

Gartrell, Nate. 2020. "New California Bill: Only 20-Year-Olds and Up Could Be Automatically Tried as Adults." *The Mercury News*, January 28, 2020. https:/www.mercurynews.com/2020/01/28/new-california-bill-only-20-year-olds-and-up-could-be-automatically-tried-as-adults/.

Griffin, Patrick, Sean Addie, Benjamin Adams, and Kathy Firestine. 2011. *Trying Juveniles as Adults: An Analysis of State Transfer Laws and Reporting*. Washington, DC: U.S. Department of Justice, Office of Juvenile Justice and Delinquency Prevention. https://www.ncjrs.gov/pdffiles1/ojjdp/232434.pdf. Accessed April 13, 2022.

Hoover, Tim. 2012. "Hickenlooper Signs 'Direct File' into Law That Limits Charging Juveniles as Adults." *The Denver Post*, April 20, 2020. https://www.denverpost.com/2012/04/20/hickenloo per-signs-direct-file-into-law-that-limits-charging-juveniles-as-adults/.

Jackson, Angie. 2019. "Michigan Bills to 'Raise the Age' for Adult Prosecution Head to Governor." *Detroit Free Press*, October 16, 2019. https://www.freep.com/story/news/local/michi gan/2019/10/16/raise-the-age-for-juveniles-in-michigan/3995973002/.

Kent v. United States, 383 U.S. 541 (1966).

Martinson, Robert. 1974. "What Works? Questions and Answers About Prison Reform." *The Public Interest* 35: 22–54.

Miller v. Alabama, 567 U.S. 460 (2012).

Myers, David L. 2005. *Boys among Men: Trying and Sentencing Juveniles as Adults*. Westport, CT: Praeger, 2005.

National Conference of State Legislatures. 2020. *Juvenile Age of Jurisdiction and Transfer to Adult Court Laws*. By Anne Teigen. Washington, DC: National Conference of State Legislatures, 2020. https://www.ncsl.org/research/civil-and-criminal-justice/juvenile-age-of-jurisdiction-and-transfer-to-adult-court-laws.aspx. Accessed April 14, 2022.

Odendahl, Marilyn. 2020. "Late-Night Hearing Approves Adult Penalties for Youths." *The Indiana Lawyer*, February 5, 2020. https://www.theindianalawyer.com/articles/late-night-hearing-approves-adult-penalties-for-youths.

Office of Juvenile Justice and Delinquency Prevention. 2022. "Juveniles Tried as Adults." *Statistical Briefing Book*. https://ojjdp.ojp.gov/statistical-briefing-book/structure_process/faqs/qa04110. Accessed June 12, 2022.

Platt, Anthony M. 2009. *The Child Savers: The Invention of Delinquency*. Piscataway, NJ: Rutgers University Press.

Ratliff, Victoria. 2020. "Bill Would Change Age for Children to Be Tried as Adults in Murder Cases." *News and Tribune*, January 30, 2020. https://www.newsandtribune.com/news/bill-would-change-age-for-children-to-be-tried-as-adults-in-murder-cases/article_8100a1c6-42d8-11ea-8276-b71373e5c70e.html.

Roper v. Simmons, 543 U.S. 551 (2005).

Taylor, Melanie. 2015. "Juvenile Transfers to Adult Court: An Examination of the Long-Term Outcomes of Transferred and Non-Transferred Juveniles." *Juvenile and Family Court Journal* 66, no. 4: 29–48.

Thomas, Jeree. 2017. *Raising the Bar: State Trends in Keeping Youth Out of Adult Courts,* 2015-2017. Washington, DC: Campaign for Youth Justice. http://cfyj.org/images/A-StateTrends_Report-Web.pdf. Accessed May 13, 2022.

Thomas, Jeree, Jasmine Aswad, Katie Rankin, and Hannah Roberts. 2019. *Raising the Floor: Increasing the Minimum Age of Prosecution as an Adult*. Washington, DC: Campaign for Youth Justice. http://www.campaignforyouthjustice.org/cfyj-reports/item/raise-the-floor-increasing-the-minimum-age-of-prosecution-of-youth-as-adults. Accessed June 12, 2022.

CHAPTER 22

Reproductive Rights

ANGELA D. MADDEN

AT A GLANCE

Abortion was not a legal issue until the mid-1800s (Gold 2003) or a political issue until the late 1970s. In 1845, the conservative Whig government of Massachusetts criminalized abortion and in 1847, the formation of the American Medical Association (AMA) gave physicians more control over women's reproduction. Arguing that abortion was both immoral and unsafe, the AMA helped make abortion illegal in every state by 1900.

During the presidency of Democrat John F. Kennedy, the American Law Institute (ALI) published the "Model Penal Code on Abortion" calling for states to legalize certain abortions; by 1972, all but five had abortion reforms passed or pending. In 1973, the US Supreme Court established a constitutional right to abortion and prohibited states from enacting laws to restrict abortion during the first trimester (*Roe v. Wade*, 410 U.S. 113).

In the late 1970s, political arguments about abortion's legality focused again on its morality, and religious perspectives became politically influential. Throughout the administrations of Republican Presidents Ronald Reagan and George H. W. Bush (1981–93), conservative Christian groups became increasingly influential, and a conservative US Supreme Court allowed states to restrict abortion without overturning *Roe*.

Republicans unsuccessfully attempted to institute a national abortion ban for more than fifty years (Cameron 2024). After his 2016 election, however, Republican President Donald J. Trump, changed the composition of the US Supreme Court resulting in the 2022 overturn of *Roe*. Since then, pro-choice states have enacted protective legislation and anti-choice states have reinstated inactive bans or passed new ones. Democratic President Joseph R. Biden has signed executive orders to protect some rights, but those lack practical power. Key issues have arisen involving "fetal personhood" and the determination of when life begins. In 2024, a public that is conflicted but generally supportive of abortion rights may use the polls to determine the extent to which religion and the most conservative US Supreme Court in modern history should decide those issues.

MANY REPUBLICANS...

- Support a religious view that life begins at conception, prioritizing the potential life of the embryo/fetus, and advocating for "fetal personhood."
- Support the US Supreme Court's decision in *Dobbs v. Jackson Women's Health Organization* (597 U.S. 215, 2022) to overturn *Roe* and eliminate constitutional protections for abortion.
- Believe abortion should be illegal in all or most cases; 60 percent of polled Republicans report believing this, with conservative Republicans (72 percent) much more likely than moderate or liberal Republicans (38 percent) to report this belief.

MANY DEMOCRATS...

- Support views that life begins when the fetus is "viable," or when it is born, prioritizing the life of the pregnant woman.
- Oppose the US Supreme Court's decision in *Dobbs* and believe that the constitutional protections for abortion established in *Roe* should be reinstated.
- Believe abortion should be legal in all or most cases; 80 percent of polled Democrats report believing this, with liberal Democrats (90 percent) more likely than moderate and conservative Democrats (72 percent) to report this belief.

OVERVIEW

Until the mid-1800s, abortion before "quickening" was acceptable. Quickening, or feeling fetal movement in the uterus, generally occurs between sixteen and twenty-four weeks. Legal and generally accepted prior to the Civil War, abortion's use as birth control by married, white, wealthier, Protestant women threatened traditional sex roles (Dynak et al. 2003) so it became a target for criminalization by the American Medical Association (AMA), formed in 1847. By 1900, abortion was illegal in nearly every state.

It also became illegal under The Comstock Act of 1873 to disseminate or possess information about birth control because it was considered "obscene." Passed by Congress under Republican President Ulysses S. Grant, Comstock made it illegal to send "obscene, lewd or lascivious," "immoral," or "indecent" publications through the mail. It was also a misdemeanor to give away, sell, or possess such materials. With abortion illegal and the dissemination of information about birth control restricted, most women had to carry unwanted or dangerous pregnancies to term.

On October 16, 1916, the first clinic to help American women have more power in their reproductive choices opened in Brooklyn, New York (Planned Parenthood n.d.). With birth control education illegal in the United States, Margaret Sanger traveled to Europe to study birth control methods and used that knowledge to open the "birth control" clinic. It was open for nine days before police shut it down and arrested Sanger for violating Comstock. Afterward, Sanger traveled the country advocating for reproductive choice. Unfortunately, however, she also advocated eugenics—sterilization to control undesirable traits like "feeblemindedness."

Despite her legacy being besmirched by promotion of racist and ableist eugenics, she started in 1923 what would eventually become Planned Parenthood Federation of America, Inc. (PPF). A 1936 court case, *United States v. One Package of Japanese Pessaries* (86 F.2d 737) aided her mission to promote reproductive options when it allowed the dissemination of birth control devices and information in New York, Vermont, and Connecticut.

With rising birth rates after the Second World War, the PPF funded research for a birth control pill, which was approved for sale on May 9, 1960, by the U.S. Food and Drug Administration (FDA) under Republican President Dwight D. Eisenhower after twelve years of controversial testing and research. Approval, however, did not make the pill legal. Many states banned contraception, and abortion was illegal in nearly every state, so states effectively controlled reproduction.

Change was inevitable with the growing civil and women's rights movements throughout the 1960s and 1970s. In 1962, the American Law Institute (ALI) published the "Model Penal Code on Abortion," which called for legalizing abortion when the pregnant woman's life and/or health was at risk, in cases of rape or incest, and when the fetus had a severe defect. Colorado was the first state to use ALI recommendations to reform its abortion statute and sixteen other states followed with similar reforms or repeals.

In 1965, it became legal for married couples to purchase contraceptives, but unmarried couples had to wait until 1972 to have that same right. In the interim, Title X of the Public Health Services Act (1970) established the National Family Planning Program to allow public funding for sex education and family planning services. A major goal of this policy was to reduce the negative financial and health impacts of women having too many children too quickly.

A more conservative era began with the 1969 election of Republican Richard M. Nixon, first among four Republicans to be President for twenty of the following twenty-four years. This shift in the executive branch preceded a subsequent shift in the US Supreme Court. While the Court under Chief Justice Earl Warren (1953–69) is considered the most liberal in US history, the Court under Chief Justice Warren Burger (1969–86) is considered "transitional," more conservative than its predecessor, but less conservative than its successor. Nixon appointed Burger and three other justices, including Burger's eventual replacement, William Rehnquist.

Going into the 1970s, reproductive issues were not central to either party's platform because both were focused intently on the war in Vietnam and the resulting social and economic turmoil. Neither Nixon nor his successor, Gerald R. Ford, expressed strong opposition to abortion and both believed it necessary in some cases. As a result, the US Supreme Court decision that became one of the most polarizing in history received very little attention at the time except from those for whom the ruling had specific relevance.

Because of Title X, the legalization of contraception, and the efforts of PPF and others to wrest reproductive control from the states, all but five states had passed or had pending abortion reform legislation by 1972. Abortion advocates feared, however, that impending conservative trends might push states back toward criminalization, so abortion rights needed to be constitutionally protected. In 1970, "Jane Roe" sued Henry Wade, the district attorney of Dallas County, Texas, to challenge the constitutionality of a Texas law that prohibited abortion except by doctor's orders to save a woman's life. Roe argued that Texas laws were unconstitutionally vague and violated her privacy rights protected by the First, Fourth, Fifth, Ninth, and Fourteenth Amendments (*Roe v. Wade*, 410 U.S. 113, 1973).

In a 7-2 decision, the court held that a fundamental "right to privacy" protecting a woman's choice to have an abortion is inherent in the Due Process Clause of the Fourteenth Amendment. This right, however, is limited because the government also has an interest in protecting potential human life. Throughout a pregnancy, the importance of the woman's interest (privacy) relative to the government's interest (protecting human life) varies, something for which laws must account. State laws that broadly prohibit abortion without considering the stage of pregnancy, among other things, violate privacy rights and are unconstitutional ("Roe v Wade" 2024).

Roe prohibited state laws that regulated abortion during the first trimester. During the second trimester, prior to "fetal viability," states could impose restrictions reasonably related to the health of the mother. Fetal viability refers to the potential for a fetus to live outside the mother. In the 1970s, this occurred around twenty-eight weeks from conception (Stacey 2022), although medical advances have reduced this to as little as twenty-two to twenty-four weeks. In the last trimester, states could regulate or prohibit abortions if their laws recognized exceptions for the health of the mother.

In a subsequent landmark case, *Planned Parenthood of Southeastern Pennsylvania v. Casey* (505 U.S. 833, 1992), the US Supreme Court addressed whether 1988 and 1989 amendments to Pennsylvania's abortion law violated *Roe* by adding requirements like informed consent, a twenty-four-hour waiting period, parental consent for minors, and spousal notification. In a 5-4 opinion, the court developed an "undue burden" standard by which to judge state abortion regulations. An undue burden is a "substantial obstacle" faced by a pregnant person "before the fetus attains viability" ("Planned Parenthood of Southeastern Pennsylvania v. Casey" 2024). Spousal notification was the only provision to fail this test.

From 1973 until 2022, *Roe* and *Casey* provided protection for women who sought to terminate pregnancies. After the 2016 election of Republican Donald J. Trump and his subsequent appointment of three conservative US Supreme Court justices, the court's composition had sufficiently changed to enable a successful challenge to *Roe*. In 2022, the US Supreme Court overturned its own precedents in *Roe* and *Casey* with its decision in *Dobbs v. Jackson Women's Health Organization* (597 U.S. 215, 2022), finding no constitutional right to an abortion. Instead, the court held that the legality of abortion should be decided at the state level.

As *Dobbs* was being considered, Republican legislatures passed new abortion bans or reinstated pre-*Roe* bans while Democratic legislatures enacted protective statutes. *Roe* had legalized abortions prior to fetal viability. With its overturn, however, the viability standard became moot, prompting more than a dozen states to consider "fetal personhood" bills giving human rights to embryos and fetuses and criminalizing abortions as early as from conception (Mosley 2024). The Florida Supreme Court, for example, allowed a six-week ban to take effect on May 1, 2024. In February 2024, the Alabama Supreme Court went even further, ruling that cryogenically frozen embryos are "extrauterine children" subject to wrongful death laws (Maxouris 2024), which has virtually halted in vitro fertilization (IVF) in the state.

Democrats pushed back at the polls. On November 7, 2023, abortion rights motivated voters in Virginia, where Democrats reclaimed the House majority, in Kentucky, where the Democratic governor won reelection, and in Pennsylvania, where a Democrat was elected to the state's Supreme Court. Moreover, Ohio became the seventh state in which voters enshrined protections for abortion rights (Littlefield 2023). In November 2024, voters in three additional states will decide whether to protect abortion access, while eight other states are trying to get the issue on their ballots (Habeshian 2024).

REPUBLICANS ON REPRODUCTIVE RIGHTS

Until the mid-1970s, Republicans were the more liberal party on abortion rights partly because Catholics, for whom abortion is prohibited, preferred Democrats. In 1976, Republican Ronald Reagan challenged incumbent Republican president Gerald Ford. Reagan needed to win the presidential primary in North Carolina, where Republican Senator Jesse Helms steered the party. Helms helped propel Reagan to the party convention by securing southern support with a campaign focused on cultural and social issues.

Although more focused on foreign policy and domestic economic issues, a grateful Reagan agreed to several right-wing policies that Helms and his colleagues wished to force into the party's platform, including opposition to abortion. Ford's team also agreed, fearful of losing delegates and the party nomination. This resulted in a 1976 Republican Party platform that was anti-abortion although most of its representatives and constituents were not. Reagan lost to Democrat James "Jimmy" Carter, but this anti-abortion stance became a permanent fixture in Republican ideology.

In 1979, Baptist minister Jerry Falwell founded a group that he named the "Moral Majority." Heavily steeped in the most conservative evangelical Christian values, this "New Christian Right" evolved in the south and became a powerful voting bloc to "further cement a national abortion ban as a key element of the Republican Party's agenda" (Bartho 2024). To secure the Republican nomination in 1980, Reagan aligned himself with Falwell and the Christian Right but stopped short of embracing their anti-abortion demands.

Reagan was disinterested in abortion as a political issue after he won the presidency, although Helms repeatedly tried to pass anti-abortion legislation. While anti-abortion advocates had little overt support from Reagan's administration, his appointment of three conservative justices proved critical in shifting the US Supreme Court to the right on social issues. Reagan also appointed younger, more conservative judges to nearly half of all federal judiciary positions during his two terms. Swinging the federal judiciary from the left to the right was Reagan's primary legacy for anti-abortion activists.

Reagan's public support of the Christian Right gave them political credibility, anchored them in the Republican Party, and brought the "social and cultural values of the white South to the forefront of American political debate" (Bartho 2024). Reagan also convinced white Christian conservative southerners that the Republican Party was a viable option after decades of Democratic dominance in the region. Reagan's wooing of southern conservatives strengthened the influence of anti-abortion advocates within the party. After Reagan left office, the conflict between fiscally and socially conservative Republicans intensified, and southern Christian conservatives dominated the party.

Leveraging Congressional majorities from 1995 to 2001, Republicans repeatedly attempted to ban abortion nationwide throughout the administration of Democratic President William "Bill" Clinton. The 104th and 105th Congresses passed federal bans on abortion. The bans were vetoed by Clinton, and although the House overrode both vetoes, the Senate was able to sustain them to prevent either ban from becoming law.

In 2002, the Republican Congress finally passed an abortion ban that Republican President George W. Bush signed into law in 2003. The Partial-Birth Abortion Ban Act (18 U.S.C. § 1531) prohibited a specific late-term abortion procedure known as "dilation and extraction." The US Supreme Court upheld the ban's constitutionality in *Gonzales v. Carhart* (550 U.S. 124, 2007) although there were no exceptions for the health of the mother. A few years earlier, the court ruled a similar Nebraska law unconstitutional in *Stenberg v. Carhart* (530 U.S. 914, 2000) because the law included no exceptions for the health of the mother. The 2007 *Gonzales* decision is considered the point at which the court became more restrictive of abortion rights. All five justices in the majority decision were Roman Catholics appointed by Republican presidents.

The election of Republican President Donald J. Trump in 2016 was facilitated by the religious faithful, evangelicals and others of the religious right intent on overturning *Roe* and imposing a nationwide abortion ban (Martinez and Smith 2016). More than one in four (26 percent) voters in 2016 were white evangelical Christians and 80 percent of this group supported Trump over his Democratic opponent, Hillary Clinton. Another 23 percent of voters were Catholic who also supported Trump over Clinton (52 percent to 45 percent).

Trump claimed to be anti-abortion and pro-choice but was consistent in his position that any bans should include exceptions for rape, incest, and the health of the mother. He was also consistent in promising to appoint conservative judges to overturn *Roe* (Mangan 2016). By the time he left office in January 2021, he had appointed Neil Gorsuch, Brett Kavanaugh, and Amy Coney Barrett to join three other Republican presidential appointees and three Democratic presidential appointees. His appointments shifted the court's ideology so that by 2021, when Texas' Republican Governor Greg Abbott signed a "fetal heartbeat" law banning abortions at approximately six weeks with no exceptions for rape or incest, the court did not rule on the law's constitutionality and refused to block it.

In 2018, Mississippi's Republican Governor Phil Bryant signed into law a fifteen-week abortion ban with exceptions for medical emergencies and severe fetal abnormality, but not for rape or incest. Jackson Women's Health Organization, the state's only abortion provider, challenged the constitutionality of the law because it banned abortions earlier than the fetal viability standard established in *Roe*. The district and appeals courts both held the law to be unconstitutional, so Mississippi appealed to the US Supreme Court.

In *Dobbs v. Jackson Women's Health Organization* (597 U.S. 215, 2022), Mississippi did not argue that fifteen weeks was early enough for viability, but instead argued that *Roe* should be overturned or that states should be allowed to ban abortions prior to viability in certain circumstances. Laws that banned abortions prior to fetal viability were not constitutional under *Roe*, but several states had such bans. Mississippi banned abortions at twenty weeks, but Jackson Women's Health Organization did not conduct abortions after sixteen weeks, so the issue was moot. Sixteen other state laws banned abortion at twenty-two weeks, but none had been previously challenged. On June 24, 2022, the court issued its decision to reverse the lower courts and to overturn its own precedents in *Roe* and *Casey*.

In a 6-3 decision, the majority called abortion a "critical moral question" that states should have the authority to regulate. Calling the court's reasoning in *Roe* "faulty," it held that the Constitution did not confer the right to an abortion and that personal autonomy and "right to privacy" arguments to justify abortion could be used to legalize activities such as prostitution and illegal drug use. In a scathing dissent, Justice Kagan argued that the majority decision resulted in "the curtailment of women's rights, and of their status as free and equal citizens" (Dissent Para. 6) and predicted that states would pass all manner of laws to significantly restrict or even eliminate women's control over their own reproduction.

As of April 2024, fourteen states ban abortion with most allowing no exceptions for rape or incest (Choi and Cole 2024). Thirteen are "trifecta" states with Republican governors and Republican majority legislatures. The fourteenth state, Kentucky, has a Democratic governor, but a Republican veto-proof "supermajority" in the legislature. Eight other states ban abortion after a heartbeat can be heard or gestational age is six to eighteen weeks. Six of those states are Republican trifecta states, while two have Democratic governors and Republican legislatures. On April 9, 2024, the Arizona Supreme Court upheld a near-total abortion ban from 1864 that had been inactive under *Roe*. This law had no exceptions for rape or incest and only allowed abortion when the mother's life was at risk. On April 24, 2024, despite Republican attempts to block a vote, three House Republicans voted with twenty-nine Democrats to repeal the law (John et al. 2024). The Senate supported the repeal and Democratic Governor Katie Hobbs signed it on May 2, 2024 (Office of the Governor 2024).

Alabama Supreme Court Says Frozen Embryos Are "Children"

In 2020, a patient at a hospital in Mobile, Alabama, removed several embryos from a cryogenic nursery and accidentally dropped them, destroying the embryos. Three sets of parents whose embryos were destroyed sued for wrongful death. Although a trial court dismissed their claims holding that a cryopreserved embryo was not a "person" or "child," the Alabama Supreme Court disagreed in a stunning reversal. On February 16, 2024, the court held that frozen embryos or "extrauterine children," who are "located outside of a biological uterus at the time they are killed," are "children" and covered under Alabama's "Wrongful Death of a Minor" law. This ruling swiftly had a chilling effect on in vitro fertilization (IVF) in Alabama. During IVF treatment, physicians harvest multiple eggs from a woman's ovaries, fertilize them with sperms outside of the woman's body, then implant them into the uterus hoping to create a pregnancy. Usually, more embryos are created than are implanted, so extra embryos are stored in liquid nitrogen until they are used by the original donors, donated to other parents, or destroyed. Almost immediately, three Alabama facilities providing assisted reproductive services halted IVF treatments because it is unclear whether IVF patients or physicians providing IVF services could face civil or criminal penalties. Although this ruling pertains only to Alabama, it has national repercussions (Callahan 2024; Maxouris 2024).

Republican legislatures are refusing to reconsider abortion bans despite evidence that allowable exceptions are unclear, endangering pregnant women. To address this confusion in South Dakota, which bans all abortions except to save the life of the mother, the Republican legislature directed its Department of Health to create a "medical education" video for health care professionals and the public; Republican Governor Kristi Noem signed it on March 18, 2024 (Scanlon 2024).

Attorney generals (AG) in both Oklahoma and Kentucky are also clarifying exceptions to their abortion bans. Oklahoma's AG notified police and prosecutors that doctors have "substantial leeway" to provide abortions, and Kentucky's AG clarified that miscarriages and ectopic pregnancies are exempt from the ban. Texas and Tennessee face lawsuits seeking clarity on exemptions (Kruesi 2024). In Texas, where abortion is prohibited unless the mother's life is at risk, twenty women have sued because this exception is unclear and abortion providers are reluctant to perform any abortions, forcing many women to travel out of state for an abortion or face a life-threatening pregnancy.

Bans include medication abortions involving two drugs, mifepristone and misoprostol. In 2000, the FDA approved mifepristone, which is considered safe and effective for abortions within ten weeks of conception. In 2022, however, Alliance Defending Freedom, a Christian conservative group that led the campaign to overturn *Roe*, successfully petitioned a Texas court to suspend the FDA's approval of mifepristone. The 5th US Circuit Court of Appeals overturned this decision but ordered restrictions be reinstated that the FDA had been rolling back since 2016, such as bans on telemedicine prescriptions and sending it by mail. The FDA appealed this decision to the US Supreme Court, which heard oral arguments on March 26, 2024 (Choi and Cole 2024). On June 13, 2024, a unanimous Supreme Court held that abortion opponents lacked the legal right to sue the FDA, preserving access to mifepristone (Sherman 2024).

In 2024, Donald Trump is once again the presumptive Republican nominee for president. Although he appointed the justices instrumental in overturning *Roe* and previously backed a federal abortion ban, he has consistently stated since *Dobbs* that abortion rights should be decided by the states (NPR 2024). If elected again, it is likely he will retain that position despite pressure from his white evangelical Christian base.

DEMOCRATS ON REPRODUCTIVE RIGHTS

In the mid-1800s, abortion became a target for criminalization partly because reproductive healthcare and facilitating childbirth were lucrative and partly because patriarchy was threatened by a fledgling women's rights movement. Demanding equality, including the right to attend colleges and universities and the right to enter professions such as law and medicine, women also demanded the right to vote (Eisenberg and Ruthsdotter

1998). Women did not secure this right until 1920, but the suffrage movement laid the groundwork for Margaret Sanger's "birth control" movement in 1916.

Spurring significant backlash, Sanger worked with the increasingly influential women's rights movement to promote "voluntary motherhood." Information about birth control, however, was highly restricted as being "obscene." Because men viewed birth control as a direct threat to patriarchy, restricting women's reproductive options was key to controlling them and relegating them to traditional roles of wife and mother (Goodwin 2020), reflected in a proverb recommending men keep wives "barefooted and pregnant" (Hertzler 1970) or "pregnant in summer, barefoot in winter" (Jamieson 2022).

Abortion also was criminalized to address declining fertility rates (number of children women had during their lifetimes) among wealthier white Protestant women and increasing rates among immigrant populations, especially among Catholics and people of color. White Protestant men feared being outbred and at risk of losing their societal dominance, fears that were fueled by the eugenics movement. Especially popular among white elites at the time, the US Supreme Court upheld the practice of eugenics in *Buck v. Bell* (274 U.S. 200, 1927), a case in which Carrie Buck fought forcible sterilization in Virginia for coming from "bad stock," being "promiscuous," and being "feebleminded." Justice Oliver Wendall Holmes, Jr., wrote the opinion authorizing Buck's sterilization in which he famously stated that "three generations of imbeciles are enough." More than two dozen states passed eugenics statutes after the *Buck* decision and it has yet to be overturned.

During the twelve years of Democratic President Franklin D. Roosevelt's presidency, the anti-abortion movement was supported by liberal Democrats who also supported the New Deal's federal anti-poverty initiatives; more children required more federal support, especially during the Great Depression. Democrats lost big business interests and high-income voters during this time, primarily due to Roosevelt's support of collective bargaining, but they gained support among poor and minority voters. Roosevelt's administration marks the point at which Black and minority voters became increasingly associated with the Democratic party; since 1936, no Republican presidential candidate has gotten more than 40 percent of the Black vote (Bump 2015).

In 1959, when Democratic Massachusetts Senator John F. Kennedy, a Roman Catholic, was asked his views on birth control and restricting aid to countries that enacted population-control policies, he said that "the U.S. government does not advocate any policy concerning birth control in the United States," and that it would not be wise for the United States to withhold assistance to a country pursuing a policy "in its own best interest" (Papers of John F. Kennedy 1960). In May 1960, as Kennedy was the first Catholic running for president, the FDA approved the birth control pill, and he secured the office with promises not to restrict access to birth control. He said that, while he might be opposed to birth control as a Catholic, he had no wish to impose his views on others (Bohrer 2011).

Throughout the mid-1960s and early 1970s, the administrations of Democratic President Lyndon B. Johnson and his successor Republican Richard Nixon advocated family planning programs and expanded access to government-funded health care by emphasizing family planning's contribution to economic success over women's rights and health (Bailey 2013). Two major policy changes related to birth control occurred during this time—the US Supreme Court held that married couples could use contraceptives without government restriction (*Griswold v. Connecticut,* 381 U.S. 479, 1965) and federal funding for local family planning programs was expanded. Using various social and economic data, Bailey (2013) evaluated the impact of these policies on fertility rates and concluded that "individuals' access to contraceptives increased their children's college completion, labor force participation, wages, and family incomes decades later" (p. 341). Family planning contributes to the long-term economic success of a family, and eventually to the long-term economic success of society.

In 1972, the Democratic platform contained no references to abortion primarily because it was legal in most states. At that time, many abortion opponents were Democrats who, like most Catholic voters at the time, believed in an expanded social welfare state and hoped that championing the poor translated to protecting the unborn. Republican abortion opponents did not support such an expansion. This ideological divide was widened by a large infusion of southern white evangelicals into the Republican Party beginning in the late 1970s. These evangelicals, unlike most Catholics, strongly opposed social welfare and favored restricting abortion access over expanding anti-poverty initiatives (Williams 2022).

After *Roe* in 1973, defense of unborn rights conflicted with the feminist movement's argument that abortion rights were immutable women's rights. As a result, Democratic advocacy of women's rights became de facto advocacy of reproductive rights, including abortion rights. Likewise, Republican advocacy of unborn rights based in religion became de facto opposition to abortion rights. Interest groups with "intense policy preferences on abortion aligned with political parties—feminist groups with the Democratic Party and evangelical religious groups aligning with the Republican Party" and these divergent beliefs "helped to pull each party to a more cohesive and consistent pattern of voting" (Thurston 2022).

Shortly following *Roe,* Democrats straddled a line with abortion advocates and opponents. In 1976, Democrats "recognize[d] the religious and ethical nature of the concerns which many Americans have on the subject of abortion," but that it was "undesirable" to amend the Constitution to overturn *Roe* (Democratic National Committee 1976). By 1992, however, Pennsylvania Senator Bob Casey was prevented from speaking a pro-life message inconsistent with the party's platform, which stated that "Democrats stand behind the right of every woman to choose, consistent with *Roe v. Wade*, regardless of ability to pay, and support a national law to protect that right" (Democratic National Committee 1992). In 1996, the platform characterized abortion as a "difficult issue" about which the party "respect[ed] the individual conscience of each American." It called for making abortion "less necessary" and "more rare" (Democratic National Committee 1996). The party's nominee in both 1992 and 1996, Bill Clinton, said that abortions should be "safe, legal, and rare."

Clinton's administrations were fraught with Republican attempts to pass a national abortion ban. As a result, Democratic platforms from 2000 to 2012 still respected individual conscience, but the language about *Roe* got progressively stronger. By 2008, the platform stated that the party "strongly and unequivocally supports *Roe v. Wade* and a woman's right to choose a safe and legal abortion, regardless of ability to pay, and we oppose any and all efforts to weaken or undermine that right" (Democratic National Committee 2008).

Shortly after his inauguration in 2009, Democratic President Barack Obama overturned the Reagan-era "global gag rule" banning federal assistance to foreign family planning organizations providing information about or offering abortions. The party's failure to codify the constitutional protections in *Roe* during Obama's administrations, however, was heavily criticized (Roche 2022). In his 2012 reelection year, the platform called abortion an "intensely personal decision between a woman, her family, her doctor, and her clergy," and that "there is no place for politicians or government to get in the way" (Democratic National Committee 2012).

The Democratic Party under Obama was not unified in its support of abortion rights. On November 7, 2009, during debate about the Patient Protection and Affordable Care Act of 2010 ("Obamacare"), Michigan Democratic Representative Bart Stupak forced a separate roll call vote regarding the Act's impact on abortion (Elving 2015). Stupak wanted an amendment to clarify that nothing in the Act would support abortions or fund health insurance plans that covered abortions. It was an issue that threatened to derail Obama's push for affordable health care. Although every House Republican voted for Stupak's amendment, it only passed because sixty-four Democrats, nearly one-quarter of the House majority, also voted for it.

Seeking the Democratic nomination for president, former first lady Hillary Rodham Clinton, indicated a willingness in 2015 to compromise with Republicans on a constitutional abortion restriction if it accounted for the health/life of the mother. She later selected anti-abortion Virginia Senator Tim Kaine as her running mate. In the 2016 platform to support Clinton's presidential campaign, much more verbiage in the platform was dedicated to emphasizing the Democratic Party's support of abortion rights and the constitutional protections of *Roe* and *Casey*. Both the 2016 and 2020 platforms included pledges to repeal the Hyde Amendment, which has banned states since 1977 from using federal funds for abortion except in cases of rape or incest or when the woman's life is at risk.

Democrats Battle Zombies

When the US Supreme Court issued its decision in *Dobbs* overturning nearly fifty years of precedent in *Roe*, it reanimated several state laws thought to be long dead and buried. In states wishing to ban or impose strict restrictions on abortion, these "zombie" laws were given new lives. In Arizona, the Supreme Court ruled that an 1864 abortion ban, passed before Arizona was a state, could be enforced. Under the law, anyone facilitating an abortion could be sent to jail for five years unless the abortion was necessary to save the life of the mother. Alabama, Arkansas, Mississippi, Texas, and West Virginia revived similar zombie laws that ban all abortions with very limited exceptions. Except for Texas' law, which was passed in 1925, all these bans were passed in the 1800s when women were considered chattel and before they could vote. Democrats and abortion rights groups in these states are waging a war against the undead laws. Overcoming House Republican attempts to thwart votes, Arizona's Democratic Governor Katie Hobbs successfully convinced three Republican legislators to vote with Democrats to repeal the law. In other states, zombie abortion bans are unlikely to be challenged because they are in states with Republican majority governments. In other states, such as Arkansas, voters may get to decide the issue if abortion advocates can get it on November 2024 ballots (Choi 2024).

Since the *Dobbs* decision in 2022, Democratic President Joseph R. Biden has repeatedly urged Congress to codify abortion rights in federal law. His administration also has taken "executive action to protect access to reproductive health care" through "three Executive Orders and a Presidential Memorandum" (The White House 2024). These actions aim to protect women's access to reproductive care including contraception and surgical and medication abortions.

To safeguard the privacy of both patients and healthcare providers, Biden's administration issued a new rule through HHS on April 22, 2024, to support reproductive healthcare privacy under the Health Insurance Portability and Accountability Act of 1996 (HIPAA). Under this rule, protected health information related to reproductive health care cannot be disclosed without permission, which makes it much more difficult for private decisions about healthcare, including reproductive care and abortion, to be used against women seeking that care (United States Department of Health and Human Services 2024). Abortion rights are expected to play a critical role in the 2024 presidential election as Democratic nominee, Vice-President Kamala Harris faces Trump, but the extent to which this issue energizes voters over economic issues and ongoing foreign conflicts remains to be seen.

FURTHER READING

Bailey, Martha J. 2013. "Fifty Years of Family Planning: New Evidence on the Long-Run Effects of Increasing Access to Contraception." *Brookings Papers on Economic Activity*. Spring: 341–409. doi: 10.1353/eca.2013.0001.

Bartho, Jonathan. 2024. "How Ronald Reagan Helped Abortion Take over the Republican Agenda." *Time: Made by History*, April 12, 2024. https://time.com/6966056/republican-abortion-arizona-reagan/.

Bohrer, John R. 2011. "Kennedy, the Pill and Conservatives for Contraception." *Huffpost—the Blog*. May 25, 2011. https://www.huffpost.com/entry/kennedy-the-pill-and-cons_b_572322.

Bump, Philip. 2015. "When Did Black Americans Start Voting So Heavily Democratic?" *Washington Post*, July 7, 2015. https://www.washingtonpost.com/news/the-fix/wp/2015/07/07/when-did-black-americans-start-voting-so-heavily-democratic/.

Callahan, Molly. 2024. "Alabama Court Ruling That Frozen Embryos Are Children and Its Impact on the Future of IVF Treatment." BU School of Public Health, February 23, 2024. https://www.

bu.edu/sph/news/articles/2024/alabama-court-ruling-that-frozen-embryos-are-children-and-its-impact-on-the-future-of-ivf-treatment/.

Cameron, Chris. 2024. "Trump Attacks His Conservative Critics While Defending His New Stance on Abortion." *New York Times*. April 9, 2024. https://www.nytimes.com/live/2024/04/08/us/trump-abortion-election-biden#trump-abortion-critics.

Carter, Joe. 2020. "What You Should Know about the 2020 Republican Party Platform." TGC Current Affairs, August 22, 2020. https://www.thegospelcoalition.org/article/what-you-should-know-about-the-2020-republican-party-platform/.

Choi, Annette, and Devan Cole. 2024. "See Where Abortions Are Banned and Legal—and Where It's Still in Limbo." CNN. March 5, 2024. https://www.cnn.com/us/abortion-access-restrictions-bans-us-dg/index.html.

Choi, Joseph. 2024. "Return of the Zombie Abortion Bills." *The Hill*, April 23, 2024. https://thehill.com/policy/healthcare/4612932-zombie-abortion-bills-2024-election/.

Democratic National Committee. 1976. Democratic Party Platform. July 12, 1976. https://www.presidency.ucsb.edu/documents/1976-democratic-party-platform.

Democratic National Committee. 1992. Democratic Party Platform. July 13, 1992. https://www.presidency.ucsb.edu/documents/1992-democratic-party-platform.

Democratic National Committee. 1996. Democratic Party Platform. August 26, 1996. https://www.presidency.ucsb.edu/documents/1996-democratic-party-platform.

Democratic National Committee. 2008. Democratic Party Platform. August 25, 2008. https://www.presidency.ucsb.edu/documents/2008-democratic-party-platform.

Democratic National Committee. 2012. Democratic Party Platform. September 3, 2012. https://www.presidency.ucsb.edu/documents/2012-democratic-party-platform.

Democratic National Committee. 2020. Democratic Party Platform. August 17, 2020. https://democrats.org/where-we-stand/party-platform/.

Diamant, Jeff, Besheer Mohamed, and Rebecca Leppert. 2024. "What the Data Says about Abortion in the U.S." Pew Research Center, March 25, 2024. https://www.pewresearch.org/short-reads/2024/03/25/what-the-data-says-about-abortion-in-the-us/#how-many-abortions-are-there-in-the-us-each-year.

Dynak, Hadley, Tracy A. Weitz, Carol E. Joffe, Felicia H. Stewart, and Abigail Arons. 2003. *Celebrating San Francisco's Abortion Pioneers*. San Francisco: UCSF Center for Health Research & Policy.

Eisenberg, Bonnie, and Mary Ruthsdotter. 1998. "History of the Women's Rights Movement." National Women's History Alliance. https://nationalwomenshistoryalliance.org/history-of-the-womens-rights-movement/. Accessed September 21, 2023.

Elving, Ron. 2015. "Abortion Vote Shows How Much Democrats' World Has Changed." *NPR—It's All Politics*. January 26, 2015. https://www.npr.org/sections/itsallpolitics/2015/01/26/381472527/abortion-vote-shows-how-much-democrats-world-has-changed.

Gold, Rachel Benson. 2003. "Lessons from Before *Roe*: Will Past Be Prologue?" *The Guttmacher Report on Public Policy-Special Analysis*. March 2003.

Goodwin, Michele. 2020. *Policing the Womb: Invisible Women and the Criminalization of Motherhood*. Cambridge: Cambridge University Press.

Habeshian, Sareen. 2024. "Where Abortion Is on the Ballot in November." *Axios*, April 19, 2024. https://www.axios.com/2024/04/06/abortion-amendment-november-2024-elections-states-map.

Hertzler, Arthur E. 1970. *The Horse and Buggy Doctor*. Omaha: University of Nebraska Press.

Jamieson, Katherine. 2022. "How 'Barefoot and Pregnant' Became a Dark American Joke." *Slate*, October 22, 2022. https://slate.com/human-interest/2022/10/barefoot-and-pregnant-history-origin-of-saying.html.

John, Arit, Natasha Chen, Jason Kravarik, and Shania Shelton. 2024. "Arizona House Votes to Overturn 1864 Abortion Ban, Paving Way to Leave 15-Week Limit in Place." CNN, April 25, 2024. https://cnn.com/2024/04/24/politics/arizona-house-abortion-law/index.html.

Kruesi, Kimberlee. 2024. "Asked to Clear up Abortion Bans, GOP Leaders Blame Doctors and Misinformation for the Confusion." *AP News*. https://apnews.com/article/abortion-bans-exceptions-doctors-lawmakers-7cefca4a248076268c789ea05b367f1a.

Littlefield, Amy. 2023. "Abortion Wins Elections for Democrats. What Should Advocates Demand in Return?" *The Nation*, November 20, 2023. https://www.thenation.com/article/politics/abortion-democrats-elections/.

Mangan, Dan. 2016. "Trump: I'll Appoint Supreme Court Justices to Overturn *Roe v. Wade* Abortion Case." CNBC, Elections. March 5, 2024. https://www.cnbc.com/2016/10/19/trump-ill-appoint-supreme-court-justices-to-overturn-roe-v-wade-abortion-case.html.

Margolis, Michele. 2018. *From Politics to the Pews: How Partisanship and the Political Environment Shape Religious Identity*. Chicago: University of Chicago Press.

Martinez, Jessica, and Gregory A. Smith. 2016. "How the Faithful Voted: A Preliminary 2016 Analysis." Pew Research Center, November 9, 2016. https://www.pewresearch.org/short-reads/2016/11/09/how-the-faithful-voted-a-preliminary-2016-analysis/.

Maxouris, Christina. 2024. "In Unprecedented Decision, Alabama's Supreme Court Ruled Frozen Embryos Are Children. It Could Have Chilling Effects on IVF, Critics Say." CNN, February 20, 2024. https://www.cnn.com/2024/02/20/us/alabama-embryo-law-ruling-supreme-court/index.html.

Mosley, Tonya. 2024. "Abortion Opponents Push for 'Fetal Personhood' Laws, Giving Rights to Embryos." NPR, *Fresh Air*, April 4, 2024. https://www.npr.org/2024/04/04/1242774406/abortion-opponents-push-for-fetal-personhood-laws-giving-rights-to-embryos#:~:text=MOSLEY%3A%20And%20as%20we%20talk,has%20always%20been%20somewhat%20fringe.

Newport, Frank. 2023. "The Politics of Religion." Gallup, September 1, 2023. https://news.gallup.com/opinion/polling-matters/510464/politics-religion.aspx.

NPR. 2024. "Trump's Anti-Abortion Stance Helped Him Win in 2016. Will It Hurt Him in 2024?" NPR, *Consider This*, April 18, 2024. https://www.npr.org/2024/04/18/1198911276/trump-stance-abortion-2024-election-republican-pro-life-change.

Office of the Governor. 2024. "Governor Katie Hobbs Signs Bill Into Law Officially Repealing 1864 Abortion Ban." May 2, 2024. News release. https://azgovernor.gov/office-arizona-governor/news/2024/05/governor-katie-hobbs-signs-bill-law-officially-repealing-1864#:~:text=News%20Release.

Papers of John F. Kennedy. 1960. Pre-Presidential Papers. Presidential Campaign Files, 1960. Speeches and the Press. Press Secretary's Subject File, 1960. Birth Control. Digital Identifier: JFKCAMP1960-1044-003.

Pew Research Center. 2022. "Public Opinion on Abortion." May 17, 2022. https://www.pewresearch.org/religion/fact-sheet/public-opinion-on-abortion/#views-on-abortion-by-political-party-and-ideology-2022.

Planned Parenthood. n.d. "Our History." https://www.plannedparenthood.org/about-us/who-we-are/our-history. Accessed July 31, 2024.

"Planned Parenthood of Southeastern Pennsylvania v. Casey." *Oyez*. https://www.oyez.org/cases/1991/91-744. Accessed April 9, 2024.

Republican National Committee. 2016/2020. "Republican Party Platform." August 24, 2020. https://prod-static.gop.com/media/Resolution_Platform.pdf?_gl=1*162m2j4*_gcl_au*MjEyODE1ODkxNC4xNzEyMDg4ODEx&_ga=2.246544324.1739551362.1713630413-1883267302.1712088812.

Roche, Darragh. 2022. "Barack Obama Blasted for Not Codifying Roe v. Wade: 'Dem Failure.'" *Newsweek*, June 25, 2022. https://www.newsweek.com/barack-obama-blasted-not-codifying-roe-v-wade-democrat-failure-1719156.

"Roe v Wade." *Oyez*. https://www.oyez.org/cases/1971/70-18. Accessed April 5, 2024.

Scanlon, Kate. 2024. "Noem Signs Bill to Create Video Explainer of South Dakota Abortion Laws," *OSV News*, March 27, 2024. https://www.osvnews.com/2024/03/27/noem-signs-bill-to-create-video-explainer-of-south-dakota-abortion-laws/.

Sherman, Mark. 2024. "Unanimous Supreme Court Preserves Access to Widely Used Abortion Medication." *AP News*, June 13, 2024. https://apnews.com/article/supreme-court-abortion-mifepristone-fda-4073b9a7b1cbb1c3641025290c22be2a.

Stacey, Madison. 2022. "What Is Fetal Viability, and How Does It Impact Abortion Cases?" WTHR Indianapolis. May 13, 2022. https://www.wthr.com/article/news/health/fetal-viability-explained/531-c39665b1-1bcd-46d3-88be-4620894b23a5.

Thurston, Chloe. 2022. "The History of Abortion Politics." Institute for Policy Research, August 16, 2022. https://www.ipr.northwestern.edu/news/2022/the-history-of-abortion-politics.html.

United States Department of Health and Human Services. 2024. "The Biden-Harris Administration Issues New Rule to Support Reproductive Health Care Privacy Under HIPAA." April 22, 2024. https://www.hhs.gov/about/news/2024/04/22/biden-harris-administration-issues-new-rule-support-reproductive-health-care-privacy-under-hipaa.html.

The White House. 2024. "Fact Sheet: Biden-Harris Administration Continues the Fight for Reproductive Freedom." March 7, 2024. https://www.whitehouse.gov/briefing-room/statements-releases/2024/03/07/fact-sheet-biden-harris-administration-continues-the-fight-for-reproductive-freedom/.

Williams, Daniel K. 2022. "Many Anti-Abortion Activists Before Roe Were Liberals Who Were Inspired by 20th Century Catholic Social Teaching." *The Conversation*, July 1, 2022. https://theconversation.com/many-anti-abortion-activists-before-roe-were-liberals-who-were-inspired-by-20th-century-catholic-social-teaching-185936.

CHAPTER 23

Sentencing for Drug Offenses

ZACHARY D. BAUMANN AND ANGELA D. MADDEN

AT A GLANCE

The laws governing the sentencing of drug offenders change over time, and understanding these fluctuations has not always lent itself to traditional Republican or Democratic arguments found in other policy arenas. At the federal level, both Republicans and Democrats acted in concert throughout much of the late twentieth century to establish more comprehensive drug laws, increase funding for their enforcement, and enact harsher sentences for offenders. Today, at the state level, both parties seek criminal justice reform, aiming to shrink the size of their prison populations and develop policies that curb drug addiction and abuse more effectively. The history of drug sentencing policy has often been characterized by bipartisan effort; however, the parties' motives have not always been the same.

Perhaps the most substantial philosophical difference between Republicans and Democrats is the purpose served by imprisoning drug offenders. While there appears to be broad agreement concerning the necessity of punishing violent offenders and those perpetuating drug abuse, Republicans and Democrats have traditionally differed in their approach to nonviolent drug offenders. The Democratic Party, relative to their Republican counterparts, argues more strongly against traditional incarceration policies and for increased funding for rehabilitation efforts. A substantial number of Democrats seek to deregulate specific drugs and eliminate the current sentences associated with their distribution and use. Finally, while there has been agreement between Republicans and Democrats that sentencing reform is necessary to alleviate the problem of mass incarceration, there exists a national narrative that Republicans must maintain their "tough on crime" image while portraying Democrats as coddling criminals.

Most drug offenders are prosecuted in state courts, so federal policies have little impact on their sentencing. While Republicans control most state governments, both Republicans and Democrats are working to reform their state criminal justice systems. While they often may be motivated by different objectives, both Republican and Democratic state lawmakers seem to understand the need to enact effective drug laws and reduce prison populations.

Recent federal legislation, however, would legalize cannabis and provide a framework for consistent national regulation. The proposed Marijuana Opportunity Reinvestment and Expungement (MORE) Act would invest primary enforcement authority with the federal government. This bill passed the US House of Representatives in April 2022 and was sent to the Senate, where it was referred to the Committee on Finance. Other proposed legislation would entrust states with enforcement authority and reclassify cannabis from a Schedule I drug to a Schedule III drug.

MANY REPUBLICANS...

- Are credited with creating modern drug sentencing policies at the federal level.
- Support long prison sentences for drug offenders to deter them from future crimes.
- Advocate for using the death penalty against violent drug cartels and kingpins.
- Work with their Democratic counterparts at the state level to reform existing sentencing policies.

MANY DEMOCRATS...

- Work with Republicans at the state and federal levels to create modern drug sentencing laws.
- Support the relaxation of specific rules governing the distribution and use of some drugs.
- Believe that drug use is a public health problem and is more likely to be solved with rehabilitation versus traditional incarceration.
- Work with their Republican counterparts at the state level to reform existing sentencing policies.

OVERVIEW

Drug use and abuse are not modern developments in America. Historical records note concerns about opium throughout the nineteenth century, the abuse of morphine and laudanum by the turn of the twentieth century, and the marketing of other opioid-laced concoctions that would reduce pain and cure common maladies into the twentieth century. In 1914, Congress used its constitutionally defined revenue powers to crack down on the traffic of drugs in the United States. In the Harrison Narcotics Tax Act of 1914, the federal government attempted to stem what it saw as a growing drug abuse problem by exercising its taxing and revenue authority. The Harrison Act required every person who "produced, imported, manufactured, compounded, dealt in, dispensed, sold, distributed, or gave away opium or coca leaves or any other compound used to produce these drugs" to register and pay an individual occupational tax to the Internal Revenue Service. In 1919, a commodity tax was added to these items, and failure to keep strict records of their sale would result in being found guilty of tax evasion. Violations of the Harrison Act could result in a $2,000 fine and/or a five-year prison sentence.

By the 1930s, the responsibility of controlling narcotics shifted from the Internal Revenue Service to the newly established Bureau of Narcotics. The Bureau then shifted its focus from opium and cocaine to marijuana. In 1937, Congress passed the Marijuana Tax Act at the insistence of the Bureau of Narcotics, which imposed a tax of $1 on every ounce of marijuana sold. As bureaucracy and taxation increased, legal avenues to obtain these drugs quickly closed. Seeing a new market after the passage of the Twenty-First Amendment to the US Constitution, organized crime factions that had previously peddled alcohol illegally created a black market to purchase drugs. While possession of illicit drugs was criminal, federal laws focused primarily on the production and distribution of specific prohibited items during this period.

The late 1960s and early 1970s saw a substantial shift in government policy, shifting more attention to drug users than producers and distributors. During this period, the public's fears about drug trafficking and addiction skyrocketed along with civil unrests following the assassinations of Dr. Martin Luther King, Jr., Malcolm X, President Kennedy, and Robert Kennedy. Republican candidate for president, Richard M. Nixon, capitalized on these fears, running on a platform of "law and order." Nixon sailed to the White House. With his mandate for law and order, President Nixon spoke from the White House saying, "America's public enemy number one in the United States is drug abuse," and called for "an all-out offensive" war on drugs in the nation's streets. He categorized marijuana as a Schedule I drug. In 1972, a commission led by Republican Governor Raymond Shafer unanimously recommended that marijuana be decriminalized, a report that Nixon ignored. His administration continued to sentence people to prison for marijuana-related offenses.

In the 1960s, America saw a surge in the popularity of the "free love" and "hippie" movements. Despite this, the Governor of New York, where the iconic Woodstock festival was held, grew apprehensive about the situation. Governor Rockefeller, a Republican, had previously held the belief that drug abuse was a medical problem and should not be treated as a criminal offense. However, following President Nixon's announcement of a War on Drugs in 1973, Rockefeller began to reexamine his stance. Nixon's messaging made the nation feel that America's cities were coming apart at the seams. Rockefeller looked to his aide and said, "For drug pushing, life sentence, no parole, no probation" (Mann 2013). Rockefeller's aide, Joseph Persico, remarked that Rockefeller decided that his previous progressive stances on the issues were not working after he learned of Japan's war on drugs. Subsequently, Rockefeller held a press conference, announcing that his current tactics were not working and that he was changing course. Drug addicts and those who sold to them would be given a minimum sentence of fifteen years to life in prison for possession of drugs, even small amounts of marijuana, cocaine, and heroin. Soon, other states began adopting mandatory minimums for drug offenders, and this severe exception to the rule became the rule.

President Nixon's domestic policy adviser, John Ehrlichman, later admitted the reasoning for Nixon's administration launching such an aggressive war on drugs and instituting such policies on mandatory minimums and no-knock raids by saying:

> You want to know what this was really all about. The Nixon campaign in 1968, and the Nixon White House after that, had two enemies: the antiwar left and black people. You understand what I'm saying. We knew we couldn't make it illegal to be either against the war or black, but by getting the public to associate the hippies with marijuana and blacks with heroin, and then criminalizing both heavily, we could disrupt those communities. We could arrest their leaders, raid their homes, break up their meetings, and vilify them night after night on the evening news. Did we know we were lying about the drugs? Of course we did. (Baum 2016)

By the time Democrat Jimmy Carter was elected president in 1976, eleven states had bucked the federal government and decriminalized marijuana possession. As Carter stepped into the White House, he did so as a president who campaigned on decriminalizing marijuana possession. While the Senate Judiciary Committee voted to decriminalize marijuana in small amounts, Carter was voted out of office by 1980. Republican President Ronald Reagan, championed by the religious right, ushered in a new era of drug sentencing.

President Reagan and his wife Nancy launched the "Just Say No" campaign to encourage kids to stay away from drugs. His administration waged war against crack cocaine and pushed the Anti-Drug Abuse Act through with near-unanimous consent from both parties in Congress in 1986. This new law enacted a mandatory minimum sentence for crack cocaine at a 100:1 ratio of powder cocaine. This means that 5 grams of crack cocaine and 500 grams of powder cocaine would garner an American the same sentence.

America's passion for the War on Drugs began to fizzle out at the turn of the millennium. Faced with ever-growing prison populations and the lack of evidence suggesting current policies were working, state legislatures began to look at drug abuse as a medical issue instead of a criminal one. They looked to diversionary programs instead of sentencing people to prison, with drug courts becoming increasingly popular. Some states even began to decriminalize marijuana. To decriminalize means that individuals will not face criminal penalties for possessing an illegal substance, although possession is still illegal.

To address Reagan's legacy of sentencing disparities associated with crack versus powder cocaine, Democratic Representative Bobby Scott (VA) sponsored the Fairness in Cocaine Sentencing Act of 2009, which garnered cosponsorships by more than sixty members of Congress, including Republican Ron Paul (TX). This bill would have eliminated all disparities in the sentencing of crack and powder cocaine. A compromise sponsored by Democrat Dick Durbin (IL) and cosponsored by Republican Jeff Sessions (AL), the Fair Sentencing Act, emerged from this effort. It dropped the sentence ratio disparity for crack cocaine versus powder cocaine down from 100:1 to 18:1 and eliminated the mandatory minimum sentence for possession of the substances. The bill was signed into law by Democratic President Barack Obama in 2010.

Further changes in drug sentencing would come from Republican Senator Chuck Grassley's (IA) First Step Act of 2018. This Act aimed to decrease prison populations that had ballooned by nearly 700 percent since 1980. The bill shortened mandatory minimum requirements and gave judges more discretion when sentencing nonviolent drug offenders. Among these mandatory minimum reforms came a "safety valve" for judges to use to avoid mandatory minimums for nonviolent drug offenders with no prior criminal record. The bill also took the effects of the Fair Sentencing Act and applied them retroactively for those already incarcerated for drug offenses before 2010, when the law passed. It also called for expanded use of halfway houses and other nontraditional sentencing for drug offenders.

By 2024, public feelings about marijuana had changed from just a few decades prior. In twenty-four states and the District of Columbia, marijuana has been legalized for recreational use, fourteen states allow medicinal use, and the remaining twelve states allow legal limited access to cannabis products with little or no THC, such as CBD oil. In addition, twenty-seven states have decriminalized the recreational use of marijuana regardless of the state's legalization status. Cities like Oakland, , Washington, DC, and Denver, also have decriminalized the psychedelic drug psilocybin (i.e., "mushrooms"), and two states (Oregon and Colorado) have fully legalized specific psychedelics. As the states took the reins from the federal government on reforming the way drug offenders are sentenced and, more specifically, the criminalization of drugs in general, the parties have had to adapt to this new reality when it comes to drug sentencing. Although still illegal at the federal level, several recently proposed pieces of federal legislation may foreshadow impending changes.

REPUBLICANS ON SENTENCING FOR DRUG OFFENSES

The Republican Party has pursued a tough on crime stance toward drug offenders since the implementation of modern drug sentencing laws passed in the early 1970s. Beginning with President Nixon's policies crafting stronger and more varied laws against drug possession and use, Republican presidential nominees and officeholders have focused primarily on punishing offenders as a means of curtailing illegal drug use. However, this emphasis on stricter punishments is being challenged by influential party elites and some Republican officeholders. The party is now attempting to balance its historical position of being tough on crime with the necessity of addressing the opioid epidemic and the large number of state and federal inmates incarcerated for committing nonviolent drug offenses.

President Richard Nixon is often cited as ushering in current drug policies with his War on Drugs and emphasis on restoring law and order. Before 1970, two general types of drug policies existed, the first governing their import into and export from the United States and the second regulating their manufacturing and distribution processes within national borders. The Comprehensive Drug Abuse Prevention and Control Act of 1970 created myriad additional rules governing not just the production and sale of certain drugs but also their possession and the actions and associations of those possessing illicit drugs.

Included in this legislation was the Controlled Substances Act of 1970, which outlined a classification system for controlled substances. Schedule I includes substances or chemicals, such as heroin and LSD, with no accepted medical use and a high potential for abuse. Marijuana is also included in Schedule I. Schedule II drugs have a high potential for abuse, with use potentially resulting in severe psychological or physical dependence. This category includes drugs such as cocaine, methamphetamine, and oxycodone. Schedule III drugs have a moderate to low potential for physical and psychological dependence, such as ketamine and testosterone. Schedule IV substances, such as Xanax, Darvocet, and Ambien, are at low risk of abuse and dependence. Finally, Schedule V drugs have the lowest potential for abuse and include drugs made with low amounts of narcotics, such as cough syrup with codeine.

These rules came to fruition as part of Nixon's "all-out offensive" on drugs and the desire to police those he believed contributed to national unrest. These laws resulted in more punitive sentences for Black and brown versus white drug offenders. Despite some movement away from an all-out offensive, current Republican legislation in this area is still guided by a Republican philosophy that drug use is a failure of individual morals that should be corrected using severe disincentives. More than half a century later, the Controlled Substances Act still guides drug classification.

Republican lawmakers at both the state and federal levels view more enforcement of drug laws and harsher sentences as solutions to the nation's rising dependency problems. Republican New York Governor Rockefeller, for example, is credited with crafting the first mandatory minimum sentences for drug use at the state level. These rules take sentencing discretion out of the hands of judges, requiring them to impose prescribed punishments based on the crime committed by the defendant. Like his predecessor, Richard Nixon, Republican President Ronald Reagan also pledged to be tough on crime and to make sentencing rules stricter at the federal level. Using the Sentencing Reform Act of 1984, Reagan signed into law guidelines for judges to use when sentencing drug offenders. Additionally, in 1986, President Reagan signed the Anti-Drug Abuse Act that established mandatory minimum and maximum sentences for drug offenders.

Reagan and "Just Say No"

On September 14, 1986, President Ronald Reagan sat down with First Lady Nancy Reagan to give a speech to the nation on the campaign against drugs. The commander in chief spoke to parents and grandparents from the West Hall of the White House as it was "back to school time for America's children." Branding drugs as a menace to society that was killing the nation's children, Reagan updated parents on what his administration was doing to keep drugs out of the hands of their children. President Reagan warned parents that drug use "is not a so-called victimless crime" and told them of a new "explosively destructive" danger, "smokable cocaine, also known as crack." The First Lady's remarks concluded by speaking directly to the kids going back to school: "Say yes to your life. And when it comes to drugs and alcohol, just say no" (Reagan 1986).

This speech symbolizes the philosophy underlying drug control policy throughout the late twentieth century. Many policymakers view drug abuse problems as individual-level failures that more vigorous policing and punitive punishments can curb. During Reagan's presidency, the federal government enacted sentencing guidelines for judges to employ in the sentencing phase of drug trials and mandatory minimum prison terms for certain drug offenses.

The administration of Republican President Donald Trump did not take substantial action to reform drug sentencing policy. During his 2016 campaign, however, Trump ran on a tough on crime platform. After winning office, President Trump appointed Republican Senator Jeff Sessions (AL), who was outspoken in his prior opposition to criminal justice reform efforts, to become his attorney general. President Trump proposed spending more money and directing more resources toward solving the opioid epidemic but did not strongly consider reforms to sentencing federal drug offenders. In a 2018 speech, for example, President Trump promoted the idea of implementing the death penalty for drug traffickers.

Observers note fissures emerging in Republican positions on drug sentencing policy. On one side are traditional arguments concerning law and order and the necessity of disincentivizing people from selling and using illicit drugs. On the other hand, some party elites do not see current policies working and believe they may serve to harm society more broadly. These arguments range from the ideological right seeking to shrink the size of government to those who see mass incarceration as a threat to the economy to those who feel a moral obligation to develop more effective treatment policies.

Republican-aligned special interest groups, including the Charles Koch Institute, are calling for criminal justice reform and a reexamination of state and federal sentencing policies. Advocating to preserve human dignity, they see the existing sentencing and policing system as harming offenders' ability to reintegrate into society and contribute to the economy and their communities. These organizations also point to the lack of evidence that the current incarceration system substantially reduces drug addiction rates and evidence that it may contribute to a cycle of incarceration for those who enter the system. Regardless of the argument, Republican lawmakers at the state level are currently exploring ways to reform their criminal justice systems, specifically concerning sentencing reform and charging nonviolent drug offenders.

At the federal level, Republican Congressman Dave Joyce (OH), along with two Republican and two Democratic colleagues, recently proposed a bill to eliminate the federal criminalization of marijuana. In addition to eliminating federal criminalization of people in compliance with state programs, the Strengthening the Tenth Amendment Through Entrusting States (STATES) 2.0 Act would authorize interstate marijuana commerce and impose a federal tax on cannabis sales to support regulation and enforcement efforts. The bill is currently with the House Subcommittee on Highways and Transit.

DEMOCRATS ON SENTENCING FOR DRUG OFFENSES

Democratic positions on sentencing drug offenders have shifted to become more uniform over the past four decades, transitioning from being tough on crime to openly questioning the efficacy of these initiatives today. The Democratic Party's movement on these issues and the emergence of louder voices calling for criminal justice reform on the left reflect fundamental changes in the party's supporters. As the Democratic New Deal coalition gave way to today's more economically, racially, and ideologically aligned party system, Democrats are now staking out policy positions that are more representative of the party's members. Philosophically and practically, Democrats and Republicans have distinct motivations, and these are reflected in how state legislatures and governors amended the laws of the late twentieth century to reduce prison populations.

The rising rates of drug abuse and social unrest in the 1960s and 1970s troubled both Democratic and Republican lawmakers, with many looking for legislative solutions. One of these proposed solutions was the Comprehensive Drug Abuse Prevention and Control Act, which was signed into law by President Nixon but was written and passed by a Democratically controlled Congress. Indeed, 97 percent of House and 100 percent of Senate Democrats voted for this measure. Throughout the 1970s, 1980s, and 1990s, a sizable block of Democratic legislators did not wish to be cast as "soft" on crime and took positions similar to Republicans on drug sentencing policies.

Democratic presidential nominee Jimmy Carter's 1976 presidential campaign contrasts this narrative. In his presidential campaign, Carter's platform decriminalized marijuana and ended President Nixon's War on Drugs. Carter did not view the prosecution of low-level drug users as a credible solution to drug addiction, pointing to the rise in drug use over the Nixon presidency and increasing prison populations. While Carter voiced growing concerns that incarceration and punitive punishments may not be the answer, he could not make substantive changes to sentencing rules. While some Democratic elites and legislators harbored the desire for reform, much of the caucus had no desire to be portrayed as soft on crime. Laws establishing federal sentencing guidelines and mandatory minimums passed Congress in the 1980s with substantial Democratic support.

As the policy positions of some Democratic elites began changing, Democratic officeholders' actions at the federal level continued to support harsher punishments for drug violations. The administration of Democratic President Bill Clinton was responsible for passing the Violent Crime Control and Law Enforcement Act of 1994, which authorized the use of the death penalty for drug kingpins and introduced a three-strikes law at the federal level. Additionally, this law is credited with promoting the "truth-in-sentencing" movement by providing more money to state and local governments to build prisons. This measure, criticized by Republicans as costing too much and accomplishing too little, passed with the support of 75 percent of House Democrats and 89 percent of Senate Democrats.

The hesitancy of Democrats to make policy changes that would make them appear weak on crime extends into the twenty-first century. While voices within the party consistently advocated for rehabilitation rather than punishment, publicly, at the federal level, the administration of Democratic President Barack Obama most clearly defined a new policy direction for the party. Reframing drug addiction as a public health rather than criminal justice problem, President Obama became the first president since President Carter to propose spending more on drug treatment than on drug enforcement. While these budget proposals were unsuccessful, the administration used the Affordable Care Act (i.e., "ObamaCare") to push insurance companies to include coverage for drug rehabilitation treatments in the public health insurance market.

The Obama administration was able to make changes to drug sentencing policy using both legislative and bureaucratic tactics. Legislatively, President Obama signed into law the Fair Sentencing Act of 2010, which reduced the disparity in sentencing offenders charged with possessing powder versus crack cocaine. Bureaucratically, the administration authored the Smart on Crime Initiative (2013), which directed federal prosecutors to spend less time prosecuting low-level drug offenders. He also pushed federal agencies not to intervene in state efforts to legalize the manufacturing, distribution, and use of marijuana for medicinal or recreational purposes. The administration's position toward drug sentencing can, perhaps, be best summarized by Michael Botticelli, who led the White House Office of National Drug Control Policy, when he said, "we can't arrest and incarcerate addiction out of people" (Lopez 2015)

The administration of Democratic President Joseph R. Biden picked up where President Obama's administration left off. In 2022, Biden released his administration's National Drug Control Strategy to Save Lives, Expand Treatment, and Disrupt Trafficking, in which he proposed a "whole of government" approach to overcome the overdose epidemic. Focusing on two critical drivers of overdoses, untreated addiction and drug trafficking, the strategy directs federal agencies to employ data-driven approaches to save lives and get people to treatment, as well as to go after drug traffickers and their profits. To show his support for federal legalization, or at least decriminalization, Biden commuted the sentences of eleven nonviolent drug offenders and issued more than 6,500 pardons for marijuana possession, attempted possession, and use in October 2022 and urged the state governor to do the same (Miller 2023). Governors in several states responded, some forgiving unpaid fines and fees and expunging convictions.

Democrat Senators Argue for Changes to Marijuana Classification

At the behest of the Biden administration, via the Department of Health and Human Services (HHS), the Drug Enforcement Administration (DEA) began reviewing the classification of marijuana as a Schedule I drug in August 2023. In addition to marijuana, Schedule I drugs include heroin and LSD. Although some supporters of reclassification would like marijuana to be reclassified as a Schedule III drug, which includes drugs like anabolic steroids and ketamine, twelve Democratic Senators sent a letter to the DEA in January 2024, requesting that it go a step further (Tsirkin 2024). Led by Massachusetts Senator Elizabeth Warren and Pennsylvania Senator John Fetterman, and supported by Senate Majority Leader Chuck Schumer (NY), the Senators argued for marijuana to be "descheduled," removed entirely from the list of substances regulated by the Controlled Substances Act of 1970. Calling the case for removing marijuana from the list of Schedule I drugs "overwhelming," the Senators argued that "the right conclusion" was supported by a "clear scientific and public health rationale," and would "relieve the burden of current federal marijuana policy on ordinary people and small businesses." According to a recent Gallup poll, most Americans agree, with 70 percent favoring legalization.

Most importantly, Biden promoted marijuana reform in his 2024 State of the Union Address, emphasizing his position that no one should be incarcerated for possession. He also noted that he directed the HHS to review marijuana's designation as a Schedule I controlled substance. Subsequently, the HHS advised the DEA to reclassify cannabis as a Schedule III drug. While this would not legalize marijuana, it would allow cannabis operators to take federal tax deductions related to their businesses.

FURTHER READING

The American Presidency Project, National Political Party Platforms. https://www.presidency.ucsb.edu. Accessed February 12, 2022.

Baum, Dan. 2016. "Legalize It All: How to Win the War on Drugs." *Harper's Magazine*, March 31, 2016. https://harpers.org/archive/2016/04/legalize-it-all/.

Lopez, German. 2015. "Obama's Drug Czar: 'We Can't Arrest and Incarcerate Addiction Out of People.'" *Vox*, December 14, 2015. https://www.vox.com/policy-and-politics/2015/12/14/10106372/drug-czar-michael-botticelli.

Mann, Brian. "The Drug Laws That Changed How We Punish." WBUR, February 14, 2013. https://www.wbur.org/npr/171822608/the-drug-laws-that-changed-how-we-punish.

Miller, Zeke. 2023. "Thousands Convicted of Marijuana Charges on Federal Lands and in Washington to Receive Pardons." *PBS New Hour*, December 22, 2023. https://www.pbs.org/newshour/nation/thousands-convicted-of-marijuana-charges-on-federal-lands-and-in-washington-to-receive-pardons.

National Council of State Legislatures, State Drug Crime Policy. www.ncsl.org.

Quinn, Thomas M., and Gerald T. McLaughlin. 1973. "The Evolution of Federal Drug Control Legislation." *Catholic University Law Review* 22, no. 3: 586–627.

Reagan, Ronald. 1986. "September 14, 1986: Speech to the Nation on the Campaign Against Drug Abuse." Miller Center. https://millercenter.org/the-presidency/presidential-speeches/september-14-1986-speech-nation-campaign-against-drug-abuse. Accessed February 11, 2022.

Tsirkin, Julie. 2024. "Democrats Urge Biden Administration to Deschedule Marijuana." *NBC News*, January 30, 2024. https://www.nbcnews.com/politics/congress/democrats-urge-biden-administration-deschedule-marijuana-rcna136241.

CHAPTER 24

Technology in Policing

KELLY A. MCHUGH

AT A GLANCE

Modern American police departments have benefited from a host of new technological tools that have enhanced their ability to detect, prevent, and punish crime. According to a 2017 study from the National Institute of Justice, 96 percent of state and local law enforcement agencies reported using at least one form of technology in routine police work. The technologies most frequently employed in policing include car cameras, body-worn cameras, access to national and state databases, cell phone tracking devices, and license plate readers (Strom 2017).

The adoption of these technologies, however, has not been without controversy. The Fourth Amendment to the United States Constitution protects privacy by ensuring that citizens are free from "unreasonable search and seizure." In practice, this means that when a law enforcement agency seeks to search an individual's home, monitor their communications, or seize their property, the agency must first demonstrate probable cause and receive judicial permission in the form of a warrant. Many new police technologies, especially those that rely on electronic surveillance, effectively allow law enforcement to bypass the process of gaining a warrant. Moreover, when police are surveilling a suspect using technology such as drones, cell phone trackers, and facial recognition technology, they may inadvertently compromise the privacy of law-abiding bystanders.

MANY REPUBLICANS...

- Believe law enforcement personnel at the local, state, and federal levels should be provided with state-of-the-art tools to aid them in preventing and detecting crime. This includes access to surveillance drones and facial recognition technology.
- Believe drones play a crucial role in modern policing and should be available to agencies at the local, state, and federal level. However, they believe that drone usage

must be closely monitored to ensure that law enforcement personnel do not violate the Fourth Amendment's guarantee that US citizens be free from unreasonable searches and seizures.

- Believe the use of facial recognition software by police departments carries clear privacy risks; while the technology may have value for identifying individuals suspected of crimes, Congress must ensure that it is not used to create a national photo database designed to track the activities of law-abiding citizens.

MANY DEMOCRATS ...

- Believe that decades of "tough-on-crime" policies have resulted in strained relations between local police departments and the communities they serve; the government must ensure that the adoption of any new policing technologies does not serve to further empower law enforcement and exacerbate existing tensions.
- Acknowledge that while drones are useful tools for foreign surveillance missions, when they are used within US borders, they can endanger the civil rights and privacy of Americans. They believe that the federal government must establish and enforce standards for data collection and retention by agencies using drones for surveillance.
- Believe facial recognition technology is a powerful and potentially dangerous tool when used by law enforcement. They believe it should be banned outright or strictly regulated to ensure that the government does not use it to monitor citizens engaging in constitutionally protected behavior, such as attending a political rally or protest.
- Have been highly skeptical of technology that allows law enforcement to surveil and track citizens but have been supportive of the adoption of technology that monitors the actions of law enforcement personnel, such as body cameras and dashboard cameras.

OVERVIEW

Discussions of technology in policing center on how emerging technologies enhance law enforcement efforts to detect and prevent crime. Historically, technological developments have served to fundamentally reshape the practice of policing. For example, the development of automobiles allowed law enforcement to replace labor-intensive foot patrols with car patrols, while the invention of the two-way radio allowed officers to be in constant communication with police headquarters. In general, successive technological developments have made policing more efficient, and thus the public and elected officials from both parties have supported the integration of technology into departments at the local, state, and federal levels. More recently, law enforcement agencies in the United States have begun to integrate high-tech surveillance methods into routine police work. The growing prevalence of two particular technologies—drones and facial recognition software—has engendered considerable controversy, with critics questioning the degree to which the widespread employment of these tools could endanger the civil rights and privacy of US citizens.

Drones, also referred to as unmanned aerial vehicles (UAVs), are small, remotely operated aircraft that can be equipped with surveillance technologies including infrared sensing devices, high definition cameras, and facial recognition capabilities. Drones also can be weaponized and used to remotely target individuals; the Federal Aviation Administration (FAA), however, has banned this usage inside the United States. In recent years, the use of drones in policing has grown dramatically; a study from Bard College found that between 2009 and early 2017, 347 law enforcement and emergency response agencies obtained drone technology (Gettinger 2017, 1). Typical uses for UAVs include trailing a suspect, search and rescue operations, traffic monitoring, and crime scene investigation.

The widespread use of drones by law enforcement began after the passage of the FAA Modernization and Reform Act of 2012, which called on the FAA to take steps to integrate drones into US airspace by 2015. The act enjoyed bipartisan support; it passed the House by a vote of 248-169, and the Senate by a vote of 75-20, before being signed into law by Democratic President Barack Obama. In the years following the passage of the Act, however, members of both parties have proposed legislative measures designed to ensure that the use of drone technology by law enforcement does not violate the Fourth Amendment's guarantee against unreasonable search and seizure.

Facial recognition software is another technology that is becoming increasingly common in modern policing. This biometric tool uses a mathematical model to map an image of a person's face, by measuring features such as the overall length of the face and the distance between a person's eyes. Once created, the unique facial signature can be matched to an image in an existing photo array, such as an archive of police mug shots, a state database of driver's licenses, or even social media postings. Security experts refer to this type of technology as passive surveillance; since these data can be obtained from closed-circuit television cameras mounted in public places, a large number of individuals can be under constant surveillance, even if they are not the subjects of criminal investigations.

In 2011, the New York Police Department was among the first US law enforcement agencies to employ facial recognition technology to match images from video surveillance to its database of mug shots. Since then, its use has grown exponentially; according to the Center on Privacy & Technology at Georgetown Law, as of 2016, one in four law enforcement agencies has access to the technology, and half of American adults have an image of their faces stored in a database that can be searched by a law enforcement agency (Garvie, Beedoya, and Frankle 2016). The most common use for this technology is to match a camera-obtained image of a suspect to an existing photo identification. Law enforcement, however, can also use it to actively monitor a crowd at a concert or sporting event, or periodically query photo databases to generate new leads in cold cases.

Due to the newness of facial recognition technology, the federal government has not adopted any comprehensive measures to regulate its usage in law enforcement. Members of both parties, however, have expressed alarm about the potential for abuse of facial recognition software technologies. Currently, both sides are engaging in robust debate regarding whether the technologies are potentially so detrimental to constitutionally protected rights that they should be banned outright, or whether they have utility in policing, and should instead be permitted but strictly regulated. Several localities have already banned or issued moratoria on the use of this technology by police, including

California, New Hampshire, and Oregon, as well as the cities of San Francisco (CA), Oakland (CA), and Somerville (MA).

Law enforcement professionals argue that the use of surveillance drones and facial recognition technology simply represents a logical evolution of policing, allowing officers to detect and prevent crime more effectively. Writing in the *New York Times* in June 2019, New York Police Commissioner James O'Neill called biometric technology a "uniquely powerful tool in our most challenging investigations." He argued, "it would be an injustice to the people we serve if we policed our 21st-century city without using 21st-century technology" (O'Neill 2019). Civil libertarians, however, caution that the widespread adoption of these tools endangers the constitutional rights of Americans. Reacting to the acquisition of drone technology by police departments, the American Civil Liberties Union warned, "the mere presence of these police cameras can create a chilling effect on people exercising their rights to free speech, protest, and other lawful activities" (Sisitzky and McCormack 2018).

Moreover, civil rights organizations have warned about the discriminatory application of these tools. Facial recognition technology was initially developed using photos of white males. A 2016 study from the Massachusetts Institute of Technology found that the technology was most accurate when matching photos of light-skinned men. It was less accurate, however, when used on darker skin tones, including Native Americans, African Americans, and individuals of Asian descent. The technology generated the highest number of false positives when it was used to match camera images of dark-skinned women to photos in a database. This means that when police use facial recognition technology to identify a suspect, people of color face a higher risk of being misidentified and falsely accused of committing a crime.

Many police departments also utilize a technology variably known as "cell site simulators" or "IMSI catchers." This tool mimics the signal coming from a cell tower, tricking a cell phone into connecting with it. Once connected, the technology allows police to track the location of the phone, and also access any unencrypted data. While this technology can be useful when police are seeking to track a suspect, in the process, the device also captures cell phone data from all individuals within a given search area.

While there have been calls for the federal government to regulate and limit the use of many forms of policing technology, members of both political parties have endorsed the increased use of body-worn cameras by police departments. Following the death of George Floyd while in the custody of Minneapolis police in May 2020, both Democrats and Republicans in Congress have supported comprehensive efforts at police reform. These efforts include plans to increase the amount of grant money the Department of Justice allocates to local agencies for the purchase of body cameras.

In general, the controversy over the integration of technology into police work resurrects the classic debate between surveillance and security, a debate that does not break down easily along party lines. Within the Republican Party, there is a key cleavage between those who support the party's traditional "law and order approach" and deference to police, and civil libertarians suspicious of excessive power being vested in law enforcement. A similar divide is also evident in the Democratic party. In the 1990s, Democratic party leaders sought to undercut Republican critiques that the party was soft on crime, supporting the hiring of more police officers, creating three-strikes laws, and building more prisons. More recently, however, some members of the party have argued that decades of tough on crime policies have resulted in police forces that are excessively powerful, and whose actions can endanger the civil rights of US citizens, particularly Black and Brown persons.

REPUBLICANS ON TECHNOLOGY IN POLICING

At the national level, the Republican party has been far more accepting of drones as a legitimate tool for policing then they have been of facial recognition technology. Support for the former, however, is by no means uniform. In the years following the passage of the FAA Modernization and Reform Act, libertarian-minded members of the party proposed several bills designed to curtail the ability of law enforcement to use drones for domestic surveillance. Two measures originated in the House of Representatives in 2013. First Austin Scott (SC) introduced the Preserving Freedom from Unwarranted Surveillance Act of 2013, requiring law enforcement to obtain a search warrant before conducting drone surveillance of a suspect; Rand Paul (KY) introduced the Senate version. Second, Ted Poe (TX) introduced the Preserving American Privacy Act of 2013, which proposed to prohibited law enforcement from using drones to surveil people in private areas, such as homes. Neither measure made it past committee level.

Republican Senator Charles Grassley on the Promise and Peril of Drones

US Senator Chuck Grassley from Iowa discussed the need for safeguards for drone usage in policing during a 2013 US Senate Committee on the Judiciary hearing on "The Future of Drones in America: Law Enforcement and Privacy Considerations":

> On the civilian side, many questions about drone technology remain. Drones can go almost anywhere and can maintain surveillance for days. They may carry sophisticated technology that greatly enhances surveillance. The potential benefits of drone technology is limited only by the imagination. And development in new technology often leads to the creation of new jobs. But we must always remember that the power of new technology creates a greater responsibility to respect the privacy rights of our citizens. While drones can expand the reach of a criminal investigation, they can also create an increased risk of invading the privacy of Americans. We need to make sure that we have sufficient legal safeguards in place to promote innovation while balancing public safety and the privacy of law-abiding citizens. We should carefully consider what the government can lawfully do under the Constitution. But, as a matter of policy, we should go further and examine what limitations are appropriate as a society to protect our privacy. Just because the government may comply with the Constitution does not mean that they should be allowed to constantly surveil us like Big Brother. The thought of government drones buzzing overhead and constantly monitoring the activities of law-abiding citizens runs contrary to the notion of what it means to live in a free society. (Grassley 2013)

During subsequent sessions of Congress, a small group of Republicans in both chambers continued to propose legislative measures to regulate the use of drones by police. In the House, Poe, along with Democrat Zoe Lofgren (CA), reintroduced the Preserving American Privacy Act in 2015 and 2018. In both years, the bills died in committee. In between, a bipartisan group of four Senators, including Republicans Tom Cotton (AR) and Mike Lee (UT), introduced the Drone Federalism Act of 2017. This legislation was designed to allow states, rather than the federal government, to implement regulations on drone usage. Although the primary aim of the measure was to allow hobbyists and businesses greater leeway to use drones, the bill also made the federal government responsible for protecting the airspace over private property. Finally, in 2019, Lee introduced the Drone Integration and Zoning Act, which proposed to ban drone flights at an elevation of under 200 feet over private property and would also apply to drones used by law enforcement. Neither measure advanced beyond committee consideration.

Since none of the preceding measures received a floor vote, the debate over the FAA Reauthorization Act of 2018 offered members of Congress another opportunity to address the lax regulatory landscape governing the use of drones. This bill, which proposed five years of funding for the FAA, contained forty provisions relating to domestic drone use. Overall, the bill took a permissive attitude toward drone usage by both private and public entities in requesting that the FAA accelerate the ongoing integration of UAVs into US airspace. It did, however, direct the agency to conduct a study of the privacy issues stemming from the growing prevalence of drones. After debate and amendments, the measure ultimately contained no restrictions on the circumstances under which law enforcement could employ drones in police investigations. The bill received strong bipartisan support, passing by a vote of 393 to 13 in the House and 93 to 6 in the Senate. Republican President Donald Trump signed the bill into law in January 2019.

While the Republican party generally has been deferential to law enforcement in its regulation of drone usage, members of the party have been far more critical of the use of facial recognition by police. In 2010, the FBI launched Next Generation Identification, a biometric database to supplement its national fingerprint database. A 2016 audit by the Government Accountability Office found that there were insufficient accountability and oversight mechanisms governing the collection and use of this data. Moreover, by 2017, eighteen states had established memorandums of understanding with the FBI, allowing the federal government to request searches of driver's license photos ("Facial Recognition Technology" 2019).

In response, the House Committee on Oversight and Reform held hearings to examine whether the FBI had violated the 1974 Privacy Act, which governs the collection and use of personal information on US citizens. The Committee Chair, Republican Jason Chaffetz (UT), chastised the FBI and expressed concern that it was building a national photo database that could be used to monitor law-abiding citizens. The Committee revisited the issue during a hearing in 2019. Ranking Republican Member Jim Jordan (OH) and Democratic Chairman Elijah Cummings (MD) expressed similar concerns about the possible abuse of this technology and argued in favor of halting funding for any new or expanded use of facial recognition technology by federal agencies. The two representatives were in the process of drafting a bill to limit the use of facial recognition technology, but the effort stalled after Cummings's death in October 2019 (Johnson 2019). In the Senate, Lee along with Democrat Chris Coons (DE), cosponsored the Facial Recognition Technology Warrant Act of 2019. This measure would require law enforcement to obtain a warrant if the agency planned to conduct facial-recognition surveillance of a suspect for more than seventy-two hours. Ultimately, the measure did not advance beyond committee.

Although Congressional Republicans have expressed alarm about the privacy implications of facial recognition technology, the administration of Republican President Donald J. Trump took a more permissive attitude toward biometric surveillance, especially when used for border control. In 2017, Trump issued an executive order titled "Protecting the Nation from Foreign Terrorist Entry." In this order, the administration asked the Department of Homeland Security (DHS) to expedite the completion of a biometric entry/exit tracking system. This system would require DHS to photograph all individuals entering and leaving the United States (including American citizens), effectively creating a new photo database. The administration argued that this would allow DHS to easily identify individuals traveling on fraudulent documents and aid in the apprehension of suspected terrorists and criminals. In 2019, however, following bipartisan criticism of the policy, the administration announced that US citizens would be exempt from being photographed. Subsequently, in 2019, the *Washington Post* reported that both the FBI and Immigration and Customs Enforcement (ICE) were regularly accessing state driver's license databases to locate individuals with outstanding warrants. Some states permit undocumented immigrants to obtain driver's licenses, and ICE used these databases as part of an enhanced effort to identify and deport these individuals (Harwell 2019).

Following the death of George Floyd, Senate Republicans have also grown increasingly supportive of the expanded use of body cameras by police. In June of 2020, Senator Tim Scott of South Carolina authored the JUSTICE Act, which among other provisions, provided increased funding for police departments to purchase the technology. The measure was cosponsored by forty-eight of his Republican colleagues but never received consideration by the full chamber. It expired at the end of the 116th Congress.

DEMOCRATS ON TECHNOLOGY IN POLICING

In general, Democrats have been more skeptical than Republicans regarding the integration of drones and facial recognition technology into routine police work. Over the past decade, members of the party have called for police reform, seeking ways to improve strained relations between local police departments and communities comprised primarily of Black and Brown citizens. In particular, many Democrats have criticized the militarization of the police, arguing that the adoption of military-style equipment and tactics by local police departments has exacerbated these tensions. In legislative debates over the use of drones and facial recognition technology by police, many Democrats have expressed concern that these new tools could serve to further empower law enforcement, with Black and Brown communities being disproportionality impacted by aggressive policing.

Under Democratic President Barack Obama, the United States frequently used UAVs in overseas operations, with the government deploying both surveillance drones and weaponized drones in countries including Pakistan, Somalia, and Yemen. While

Democrats generally have supported their use abroad as tools of war, they have expressed considerable concern about the privacy implications of drone usage by domestic law enforcement. As a result, following the passage of the 2012 FAA Modernization Act, the Obama administration created a working group within DHS to study the impact of drones on the privacy, civil rights, and civil liberties of Americans. From this study, the DHS provided the following recommendations in 2015 for local, state, and federal agencies employing UAVs: (1) articulate clear policies concerning the protection of privacy rights, (2) make these rules publicly available, and (3) refrain from surveilling individuals while they are engaged in constitutionally protected activities. That same year, President Obama issued a memorandum titled "Promoting Economic Competitiveness While Safeguarding Privacy, Civil Rights, and Civil Liberties in Domestic Use of Unmanned Aircraft Systems." This memorandum sought to balance the utility of drones with the potential for privacy violations by setting standards for data collection and retention by executive departments and agencies of the federal government using drones.

Democratic members of Congress have also been active in seeking limitations on the use of drones by law enforcement. Members of the party have advanced several measures designed to address concerns about the growing militarization of the police and the role drones could play in accelerating this trend. Democratic Georgia Representative Hank Jordan introduced the Stop Militarization of Law Enforcement Act four times between 2013 and 2019. This measure would prohibit state and local law enforcement agencies from purchasing armed or weaponized drones. Similarly, in 2014, Democratic Florida Representative Allen Grayson introduced the No Drones for DHS Act. This bill would categorically forbid the agency from purchasing, operating, or maintaining UAVs. Neither of these measures ever received a floor vote.

Another set of legislative proposals condoned the use of drones by law enforcement but sought to provide citizens with adequate privacy protections. Senator Ed Markey (MA) introduced the Drone Aircraft Privacy and Transparency Act three times between 2013 and 2017. The legislation would amend the 2012 FAA Modernization Act and require that any law enforcement agency seeking a license to operate drones first provide the Department of Transportation (DOT) with a data minimization statement detailing how they would protect the privacy rights of those surveilled. Moreover, the act would prohibit law enforcement personnel from using drones for surveillance without a warrant; if an agency violated this rule, the DOT would be required to revoke that department's authorization. Democratic Vermont Representative Pete Welsh introduced a companion bill in the House. The measures did not advance beyond committee consideration in either chamber.

As have been their Republican counterparts, Congressional Democrats have been highly skeptical of the growing use of facial recognition technology by law enforcement. Within the party, a division has emerged between those who believe the technology has value but must be strictly regulated and those who believe it is inherently dangerous to civil liberties and should be banned. As a result, members of the party have spearheaded several legislative proposals designed to limit the ability of law enforcement to use this technology. None of these measures, however, have advanced beyond committee consideration. In 2019, Democratic Senator Chris Coons (DE) joined Republican Mike Lee (UT) to sponsor the Facial Recognition Technology Warrant Act, described previously. During that same session, Michigan Congresswoman Rashida Talib authored H.B. 3875, which would prohibit police departments from using federal funding to purchase facial recognition technology, and New York Representative Elliot Engle proposed the FACE Protection Act, which would require law enforcement agencies to obtain a warrant before accessing images stored in a government database.

Democratic Representative Elijah Cummings on the Need to Regulate Biometric Surveillance

Representative Elijah Cummings from Maryland indicated the need for oversight in the use of facial recognition technology in policing to protect civil rights and liberties, at a 2019 hearing before the House Committee on Oversight and Reform:

> Both the conservatives and liberals alike have real questions about when they are being monitored, why they are being monitored, who is monitoring them, and what happens to this information after it is collected. ... Whatever walk of life you may come from, you may very well be a part of this process. You could be at a rally supporting gun rights or protesting gun violence. You could be marching for the right to life or a woman's right to choose. You could be pressing for the repeal of the ACA or the expansion of health care. In all of these cases, the government can monitor you without your knowledge and enter your face into a database that could be used in virtually unrestricted ways. We need to do more to safeguard the rights of free speech and assembly under the First Amendment, the right to privacy under the Fourth Amendment, and the right of equal protection under the law under the Fourteenth Amendment. (Cummings 2019)

The debate over the use of facial recognition technology also featured in the 2020 Democratic presidential primary. Senator Bernie Sanders (VT) and businessman Tom Steyer indicated that they favored outright bans on the technology, arguing the potential for abuse by law enforcement was simply too great. Other candidates, including former South Bend, Indiana, mayor Pete Buttigieg, Senator Elizabeth Warren (MA), and Senator Michael Bennett (CO) argued that the technology has value for police work, but must be strictly regulated to safeguard the constitutional rights of citizens (Molla and Stewart 2019).

While Democrats have been highly skeptical of technology that allows law enforcement to surveil and track citizens, they have been supportive of the adoption of technology that monitors the actions of law enforcement personnel. In response to a series of controversial use-of-force incidents by police involving minority suspects, Congressional Democrats introduced numerous proposals to require law enforcement personnel to wear body cameras to document their interactions with the public. In 2018, Eleanor Holmes Norton, Democratic Representative from Washington, DC, introduced the Federal Police Camera and Accountability Act, which would require federal law enforcement to wear body cameras and to have dashboard cameras installed in their vehicles. In 2019, Democratic Representative Steve Cohen (TN) introduced the Police CAMERA Act of 2019; the measure had twenty-four Democratic cosponsors and would authorize the Department of Justice to make grants to state and local police departments to purchase body cameras. The same year, Representative Adriano Espaillat (NY), along with thirty-two Democratic cosponsors, introduced the Body Camera Accountability Act, which would require all federal immigration and border employees to wear body cameras. None of these measures have received a floor vote. Currently, no binding federal requirements govern the use of body cameras by law enforcement, and to date, only a handful of states have enacted such measures.

In June 2020, Representative Karen Bass (D-CA) sponsored the George Floyd Justice in Policing Act of 2020, which among other provisions, required federal law enforcement personnel to wear body cameras, and mandated that the footage be preserved for six months. The measure passed the House, with all 233 Democrats voting in favor. It was never considered by the full Senate and expired at the end of the 116th Congress. As a 2020 Democratic presidential nominee, Joe Biden also called for more widespread use of body cameras as part of a broader plan to address systemic racism in police departments. In a June 2020 op-ed, he pledged to allocate $300 million to police departments that adopt a set of reforms, including the use of body cameras. In March of 2022, President Biden signed an executive order addressing accountability in policing. Among its provisions was a requirement that all federal law enforcement personnel wear body cameras.

FURTHER READING

Biden, Joe. 2020. "Biden: We Must Urgently Root Out Systemic Racism, from Policing to Housing to Opportunity." *USA TODAY*, June 10, 2020. https://www.usatoday.com/story/opinion/2020/06/10/biden-root-out-systemic-racism-not-just-divisive-trump-talk-column/5327631002/.

Boyd, Aaron. 2019. "After Criticism from Congress and Privacy Advocates, the Border Security Agency Says It Will Pull Back a Proposed Rule Change." *Nextgov*, December 5, 2019. https://www.nextgov.com/emerging-tech/2019/12/customs-reverses-course-mandatory-facial-scans-us-citizens/161702/.

Cummings, Elijah. 2019. "Facial Recognition Technology: Part I. Its Impact on Our Civil Rights and Liberties." Hearing Before the Committee on Oversight and Reform, 116th Congress, May 22, 2019. https://docs.house.gov/meetings/GO/GO00/20190522/109521/HHRG-116-GO00-Transcript-20190522.pdf.

Electronic Frontier Foundation. n.d. "Street-Level Surveillance: Cell-Site Simulators/IMSI Catchers." Accessed June 7, 2020. https://www.eff.org/pages/cell-site-simulatorsimsi-catchers.

"Facial Recognition Technology (Part 1): Its Impact on Our Civil Rights and Liberties, Before the United States House Committee on Oversight and Government Reform, 116th Congress," May 22, 2019. Joy Buolamwini, Founder, Algorithmic Justice League. https://www.congress.gov/116/meeting/house/109521/witnesses/HHRG-116-GO00-Wstate-BuolamwiniJ-20190522.pdf.

Erondu, Nkechi. 2018. "Five Trends in Police Body Camera Legislation." *Urban Wire*, October 26, 2018. https://www.urban.org/urban-wire/five-trends-police-body-camera-legislation.

Garvie, Clare, Alvaro Beedoya, and Jonathan Frankle. 2016. "Unregulated Police Face Recognition in America." *The Perpetual Lineup*, October 16, 2016. https://www.perpetuallineup.org.

Gettinger, Dan. 2017. "Drones at Home: Public Safety Drones." Bard College Center for the Study of the Drone, April 2017. https://dronecenter.bard.edu/files/2017/04/CSD-Public-Safety-Drones-Web.pdf.

Grassley, Charles. 2013. "Prepared Statement of Ranking Member Chuck Grassley of Iowa." US Senate Committee on the Judiciary hearing on "The Future of Drones in America: Law Enforcement and Privacy Considerations." March 20, 2013. https://www.grassley.senate.gov/news/news-releases/future-drones-america-law-enforcement-and-privacy-considerations.

Hardtsey, Larry. 2018. "Study Finds Gender and Skin-type Bias in Commercial Artificial-intelligence Systems." *MIT News*, February 11, 2018. http://news.mit.edu/2018/study-finds-gender-skin-type-bias-artificial-intelligence-systems-0212.

Harwell, Drew. 2019. "FBI, ICE Find State Driver's License Photos Are a Gold Mine for Facial-recognition Searches." *Washington Post*, July 7, 2019. https://www.washingtonpost.com/technology/2019/07/07/fbi-ice-find-state-drivers-license-photos-are-gold-mine-facial-recognition-searches/.

Johnson, Khari. 2019. "Facial Recognition Regulation Is Surprisingly Bipartisan." *VentureBeat*, November 11, 2019. https://venturebeat.com/2019/11/11/facial-recognition-regulation-is-surprisingly-bipartisan/.

Molla, Randi, and Emily Stewart. 2019. "How 2020 Democratic Candidates Would Regulate Facial Recognition." *Vox*, December 5, 2019. https://www.vox.com/policy-and-politics/2019/12/3/20965470/2020-presidential-candidates-facial-recognition.

O'Neill, James. 2019. "How Facial Recognition Makes You Safer." *New York Times*, June 9, 2019. https://www.nytimes.com/2019/06/09/opinion/facial-recognition-police-new-york-city.html.

Sisitzky Michael, and Simon McCormack. 2018. "New NYPD Drone Policy Represents a Serious Threat to Privacy." The American Civil Liberties Union, December 7, 2018. https://www.aclu.org/blog/privacy-technology/surveillance-technologies/new-nypd-drone-policy-represents-serious-threat.

Strom, Kevin. 2017. "Research on the Impact of Technology on Policing Strategy in the 21st Century, Final Report." National Criminal Justice Reference Service. https://www.ncjrs.gov/pdffiles1/nij/grants/251140.pdf. Accessed June 18, 2022.

CHAPTER 25

Three-Strikes Policies

ELIZABETH GLOYD, WANDA LEAL, AND WHITNEY GASS

AT A GLANCE

Violent crime rates steadily increased during the 1980s and 1990s, especially among juveniles. Media outlets capitalized on this trend by sensationalizing violent crime and stoking fear among the public, shaping public opinion to believe that violent crime was out of control. In response to public outcry and violent crime emerging as a top national priority, both Democratic and Republican policymakers undertook "get tough on crime" approaches.

Democrats, who often are criticized by Republicans as "soft on crime," aimed to counter that criticism with the Violent Crime Control and Law Enforcement Act, signed into law by Democratic President Bill Clinton in 1994 with the backing of a Democratic-majority Congress. This Act was the largest crime bill in the history of the United States, which provided $9.7 billion in funding for prisons, $6.1 billion in funding for prevention programs, $2.6 billion in additional funding for the FBI, DEA, INS, US attorneys, and other justice department components, and about 100,000 more police personnel to be hired. One of the most significant provisions on federal legislation within this bill was the implementation of a three-strikes policy, which required mandatory life imprisonment without the possibility of parole for federal offenders with three or more convictions for serious violent felonies or drug trafficking crimes. Essentially, three-strikes policies, both at the federal and state levels, were designed around repeat violent, serious offenders who were not deterred from committing crime under the policies enacted at that time. While states passed similar three-strikes legislation, the only state to aggressively exploit three-strikes policies was California.

This policy has had many serious repercussions for the criminal justice system that resulted in members of both parties advocating for its reform. Many consider that the Violent Crime Control and Law Enforcement Act of 1994 to be one of the most significant driving forces in the movement known as prison warehousing and mass incarceration in the United States. State and local governments were being financially incentivized by federal funding to expand the correctional system by increasing the construction of prisons and jails to handle the increasing number and length of prison sentences, exacerbated by the removal of the possibility of early release of those already incarcerated. This bipartisan effort led to the passage of the First Step Act (FSA) in 2018, despite initial hold-outs from far-right Republican Congressmen, Cotton (AR), Cruz (TX), and Kennedy (LA), who argued that reforming this law would make the criminal justice system too lenient on crime. The FSA eases the federal three-strikes policy by issuing a twenty-five-year sentence rather than a life sentence for those with three or more convictions, as well as provides more discretion to judges to deviate from the mandatory minimums in sentencing nonviolent drug offenders. The FSA is considered to be a significant step in the struggle to reduce mass incarceration. However, experts remind legislators that the FSA should be just that, the first step, not the only step in criminal justice reform.

MANY REPUBLICANS...

- Believe that chronic, violent offenders influence crime rates and should be incapacitated with longer sentences in prison.
- Support the use of punitive punishments to act as a deterrent among criminals, or at least as a means of incapacitation, as a way to prevent and reduce crime.
- Argue that the more severe the punishment for crime, the more likely crime will be reduced through the fear/threat of punishment.

MANY DEMOCRATS...

- Believe that the passage of the Violent Crime Control and Law Enforcement Act in 1994 was too punitive and caused many unintended consequences.
- Support reforming punitive criminal justice policies to focus more on rehabilitation opportunities to reduce the number of individuals incarcerated in the United States, as well as provide ways to prevent criminal behavior.
- Argue that punitive policies and law-and-order punishment has disproportionately targeted minority communities, especially for minor level offenses.

OVERVIEW

From the mid-1980s until the early 1990s, crime increased throughout the United States, especially youth violence and robbery. During this increase in violent crime, sensationalized media coverage depicted the youth as "super-predators" who were impulsive, violent, and showed no remorse. News reports of this time argued that these violent juvenile offenders should be held responsible for their crimes. The increased violent crime rate coupled with two high-profile murders in Washington and California helped promote the need for stricter sentencing and punishment practices for chronic criminals. As such, legislation centered on the idea of increasing punishment to achieve law and order began to become popular in the early 1990s.

Politicians quickly realized they could use the public's media-fueled fear as a political tool during the election cycle. Viewing three-strikes legislation as the answer to the widespread fear among their constituents during the 1990s, they argued strenuously for the urgent need to keep dangerous, chronic offenders off the streets. As a result, politicians convinced the public that crime control was the solution to the problem and therefore, stricter crime control measures should be their number one priority.

One key piece of legislation from this era was, and continues to be, incredibly controversial. Three-strikes laws were passed to limit the early release of violent offenders. These laws proposed life in prison without the possibility of parole (LWOP), the ultimate, non-death penalty sentence, for chronic offenders, specifically those convicted of three violent or serious felonies. Three-strikes legislation plays on the expression of "three strikes and you're out" in baseball where a player who earns three strikes is subsequently recorded as an out. Generally, three-strikes policies consider an offender "out" if they commit three felonies. While the first two strikes commonly consist of serious or violent felonies, any felony often qualifies as the third strike.

In 1993, the state of Washington was the first to place three-strikes legislation on the ballot, which passed by voter initiative. California followed a year later with the passage of Proposition 184, often referred to as the "three-strikes" initiative, which establishes that repeat offenders committing their third felony offense will receive a mandatory sentence of three times the prison term currently in effect, or an indeterminate sentence of a mandatory twenty-five years to life in prison, whichever sentence is greater. Both laws were sparked by cases in which individuals were murdered by released prisoners. The considerable media coverage arising from these two brutal cases, in combination with rising violent crime rates, created a "moral panic" amongst a concerned public that feared the potential early release of violent offenders. A moral panic is a widespread fear that an individual or a group of individuals threaten the values, safety, and interests of conventional society that is often perpetuated by media, fueled by politicians, and often results into the implementation of new laws and policies designed to target the individual or group of individuals that are believed to be the source of the panic.

In Washington, Diane Ballasiotes was raped and murdered by a convicted sex offender who had recently been released from prison. Ballasiotes's murderer, Gene Raymond Kane, was transitioned back into society despite a prison psychologist claiming that his chances for successful reintegration were "quite poor" (Siegel 1990). When asked about Kane's prison release, the Secretary of the State's Department of Corrections said, "the suspect could not have been retained indefinitely in maximum security. Law and court decisions demanded his release imminently" (Siegel 1990).

The California law resulted from the kidnap and murder of twelve-year-old Polly Klass by parolee Richard Allen Davis. Davis was released after serving eight years of his sixteen-year sentence, despite having an extensive history of violent behavior including assault, kidnapping, and other violent crimes. Republican Governor Pete Wilson signed the three-strikes initiative into law in March 1994. Six months later the Los Angeles county jail was overcrowded with increasing jury trials (150 percent to 300 percent in most counties). As a result, the state began building twenty prisons in addition to the twelve already under construction and the twenty-eight existing ones.

In 1994, with bipartisan support, President Clinton signed the Violent Crime Control and Law Enforcement Act into law containing a three-strikes provision mandating life imprisonment for any offender convicted of a third violent felony if they had two or more prior violent or drug trafficking felony convictions, even at the state level. By 1997, twenty-four additional states had enacted versions of the three-strikes legislation. It is important to note that while most three-strikes laws are similar, states vary in terms of specifics. Some states include nonviolent felonies, some necessitate violent felonies, some only require two strikes, and some states allow for redemption through parole. For example, offenders convicted under three-strikes legislation in Colorado are eligible for release after serving at least forty years of their sentence and New Mexicans are eligible after serving at least thirty years (Austin et al. 2000; Blomberg and Lucken 2017).

Almost immediately, potential problems with this type of law became clear. In California, one issue involved offenders who committed their third "strike" offense many years after their first two strikes or whose third strike was a minor offense. In 1995, for example, Jerry Williams was convicted of felony petty theft for stealing a pizza from a group of children. For Williams, who had four prior convictions for robbery, this became his third strike. During the final sentencing, Deputy District Attorney Bill Gravlin stated that the physical theft of the pizza was not the primary issue in this case; the fact that Williams was a habitual offender was (Slater 1995).

Leandro Andrade also was sentenced under the three-strikes law in 1995 for stealing $153.00 worth of DVDs from K-Mart. At the time of the theft, Andrade had several prior convictions, including minor property crimes, shoplifting, and burglary, and was sentenced to two consecutive imprisonment sentences of twenty-five years to life. Andrade's appeal of his sentence made it all the way to the US Supreme Court. With conservative Justice Sandra Day O'Connor writing for the majority, the Court held that while the sentence was severe, it was not disproportionate to the offense and therefore his sentence did not violate his Eighth Amendment protection from cruel and unusual punishment (Alexander 2010). However, in conservative Justice David Souter's dissenting opinion he suggested that if Andrade's sentence was not disproportionate, then the principle of disproportionate sentencing had no legal meaning. These two cases are not unique. Under California's three-strikes law, 344 other individuals are serving sentences of twenty-five years to life for shoplifting (Chemerinsky 2003). In fact, California is the only state in which any felony offense can trigger a three-strikes sentence leaving two-thirds of the state's offenders imprisoned for nonviolent offenses.

Although many states enacted three-strikes legislation during the get tough on crime movement, the laws have had a relatively small impact on current sentencing practices across the country, have been costly, and largely ineffective. In fact, many states who passed three-strikes policies did so only as a symbolic measure and never utilized the policies in full effect. That is, the twenty-eight states that passed three-strikes legislation by 1995 (with Arizona passing legislation in 2005 and Massachusetts in 2012) all had done so to only send a message to chronic offenders about the possibility of life in prison without the likelihood of parole for their third strike. However, California is the only state to have aggressively pursued their three-strikes legislation as a mechanism to reduce crime among chronic, violent offenders in a way that no other state, or even the federal government, had imagined. In California, for example, the three-strikes law costs its correctional system an estimated $6.7 billion a year (Dyer 2000), with no significant impact on the state's crime rate.

With more attention on the unintended consequences of three-strikes legislation, there has been a push to reform the law. In 2012, voters in California enacted the Three-Strikes Reform Act, otherwise known as Proposition 36, to address the consequences of the original law. This reform created a procedure to petition in court a reduced sentence for offenders convicted of nonviolent crimes and eliminated life sentences for any nonserious or nonviolent offenses. President Donald Trump signed the First Step Act (FSA) into law at the end of 2018, changing the federal three-strikes law's mandatory minimum sentence from life imprisonment to a twenty-five-year sentence. However, the new federal law was not retroactively applied to inmates previously convicted, primarily due to the influence on President Trump's 2016 presidential campaign of many law enforcement groups that opposed such retroactive application. While the FSA was considered a significant move in the right direction when it comes to criminal justice reform, many believe that there should be more bills passed to address the unintended consequences to the Violent Crime Control and Law Enforcement Act of 1994. However, at the current moment, legislators at the federal level have not placed onto record any additional criminal justice reform bills, but many Democrats have argued that more is needed in the realm of criminal justice to fix many of the consequences to the harsh, punitive sentencing policies previously implemented.

REPUBLICANS ON THREE-STRIKES POLICIES

While it is generally acknowledged that Republicans tend to favor more punitive ideals of punishment and sentencing than Democrats, this pattern does not hold true with respect to three-strikes laws. In the early 1990s, both conservatives and liberals at both state and federal levels engaged in "one-upmanship," with each proposing more and more punitive legislation and stricter measures of crime control. Although the passage of more punitive policies such as the three-strikes laws gave the appearance of being tough on crime, their actual success was questionable. At the state level, only six of twenty-two states that had passed three-strikes legislations had secured any convictions under the law by 1996. At the federal level, Kansas' Republican Senator Bob Dole suggested that the few federal convictions indicated that Democratic President Bill Clinton was weak in enforcing the law. He also argued that President Clinton was giving away "get out of jail free" cards to violent criminals because he was not strictly enforcing the new policy (Gordon 1996).

President Bill Clinton's 1994 State of the Union Address Receives Acceptance from Both Sides of the Aisle

In his 1994 State of the Union Address, Democratic President William Jefferson "Bill" Clinton tackled several criminal justice related policies. In the address, President Clinton stated, "First we must recognize that most violent crimes are committed by a small percentage of criminals who too often break the laws even when they are on parole. Now those who commit crimes should be punished. And those who commit repeated violent crimes should be told, 'When you a commit a third violent crime, you will be put away, and put away for good; three strikes and you are out.'" His statement was met with a standing ovation from both sides of the aisle. President Clinton addressed the need for more police personnel and community policing strategies as a way to reduce and prevent juvenile crime in high-crime areas. President Clinton also focused on drug-related crime, which he stated was a factor in the increasing crime rates. After laying out several criminal justice reforms needed, President Clinton made a plea for legislators to make a bipartisan effort to pass a punitive crime bill to address the issue of crime, but to also remember the source of crime in the United States.

Since California was at the epicenter of the three-strikes movement, it is especially important to discuss the changes that have occurred there with respect to three-strikes laws. California's Proposition 66, which would have reduced the length of the sentence for a third strike, was placed on the ballot in 2004. While Proposition 66 was heavily supported by two-thirds of California voters prior to the election, it faced staunch opposition, largely led by California's Republican Governor Arnold Schwarzenegger. Before the election, a Republican-driven late surge in fundraising and advertisements suggested that the passage of Proposition 66 would allow "rapists, murders, and child molesters" back into the community (Martin 2004), which eventually led to the bill's failure. Proposition 66, however, was not the last attempt by California to amend its three-strikes legislation. In 2012, under Democratic Governor Jerry Brown, California voters overwhelmingly passed the Three Strikes Reform Act of 2012 (Proposition 36), which reduced sentences for three-strikes convictions if the third strike was nonviolent or nonserious.

As the negative consequences of three-strikes laws have continued to become more apparent, the need for more widespread criminal justice reform has become more obvious. The bipartisan 2015 Sentencing Reform and Corrections Act (SRCA) introduced by Republican Senator Chuck Grassley (IA) and Democratic Senator Dick Durban (IL) was the first major step toward criminal justice reform. This bill would have had federal legislation follow the states' example of reducing sentences under the three-strikes law from life imprisonment without the possibility of parole to twenty-five years. Ultimately, however, the SRCA failed to pass the Republican-held Congress, largely due to opposition by Republican Senators Tom Cotton (AR) and Jeff Sessions (AL). When Jeff Sessions was appointed attorney general by the Trump administration in 2017, Senators Grassley and Durban reintroduced the SRCA to Congress for a second time. The SRCA once again stalled in Congress primarily due to continued opposition from Attorney General Sessions.

In 2018 after Jeff Sessions resigned as attorney general, Republican Representative Doug Collins (GA) introduced the Prison Reform and Redemption Act, later renamed the First Step Act (FSA), which cleared the Republican-held Senate with an 87-12 vote and subsequently was signed into law by President Trump in late 2018. However, it was not without initial opposition from Senators Cotton, Kennedy (LA), and Cruz (TX). The FSA was the federal system's effort to follow the states that had reduced the punitiveness of three-strikes laws by lowering the sentence for a third offense from life imprisonment to twenty-five years.

Although the Republican platform supports the idea of the get tough approach to crime control and prevention, many Republicans feel that the Violent Crime Control and Law Enforcement Act of 1994 was too punitive because of the unintended consequences that had occurred. Republicans want to reform three-strikes legislation to still include longer sentences in prison for chronic, violent offenders, and did so with the FSA of 2018. However, far-right critics argue that reforming policies focused on deterring crime will arguably lead to an increase in violent crime in the United States. Ultimately, the cost of mass incarceration due to these get tough policies, especially in California, was the fundamental turning point for Republicans to support the need for reform in three-strikes legislation.

DEMOCRATS ON THREE-STRIKES POLICIES

During the 1980s and the 1990s, punishment in America became more punitive, and politicians began to capitalize on the politicization of the criminal justice system and public fear of crime. During his presidential campaign, and just before the New Hampshire primary in 1992, then governor Bill Clinton (AR) who oversaw the execution of a mentally impaired Black man remarking afterward, "I can be nicked on a lot, but no one can say I'm soft on crime" (Alexander 2010, 56). Keeping true to his word, when he was elected president of the United States, he endorsed federal three-strikes legislation for which he received a standing ovation from both Republicans and Democrats during his 1994 State of the Union speech.

After Clinton's election, and in response to the party's increasing support for tough on crime measures, Delaware Senator Joe Biden worked with Democratic representatives Jack Brooks (TX) and Charles E. Schumer (NY) to compose the Violent Crime Control and Law Enforcement Act of 1994. At the time, Democrats held the majority in both the House of Representatives and the Senate and voted in support of the bill (235 to 195 in the House and 61 to 38 in the Senate). This bill even had the support of then representative and eventual Vermont Senator, Bernie Sanders. Within this crime bill, the three-strikes provision required mandatory life imprisonment for offenders convicted of a third violent felony if they had two or more prior violent or drug trafficking felony convictions, even at the state level.

In August 1994, President Clinton signed the $30 billion bill into law. Democrats hailed this as a victory because its passage demonstrated that they were not soft on crime as characterized by Republicans. Consequently, the Clinton administration's tough on crime initiatives resulted in the largest increase in the number of prison inmates at both the federal and state levels than any other president in American history. As a result of social and political demands for effective responses to rising violent crime, the ideological line between Democrats and Republicans in this era became blurred. The Clinton administration, while espousing and enacting generally liberal Democratic principles, enacted crime control legislation that was more akin to Republican ideology to alleviate public fear of crime and to win votes.

President Clinton's wife, Hillary Clinton, who was secretary of state under President Obama and the Democratic nominee for president in 2016, also originally supported the crime bill. She stated, "Just as in a previous generation we had an organized effort against the mob. We need to take these people on. They are often connected to big drug cartels, they are not just gangs of kids anymore. They are often the kinds of kids that are called 'super-predators'—no conscience, no empathy. We can talk about why they ended up that way, but first, we have to bring them to heel" (Graves 2016). In April 2015, however, Clinton pushed for an end to the era of mass incarceration and for criminal justice reform (BBC America 2015). Her husband echoed that sentiment in a speech to the convention of the National Association for the Advancement of Colored People (NAACP) when he said "I signed a bill that made the problem [of racial disparity in the criminal justice system] worse and I want to admit it" (BBC America 2015).

Democratic State Senator Corey Booker and Vice President Kamala Harris have been candid about their opposition to the 1994 crime bill that enacted the three-strikes provision. Prior to becoming a state senator, Kamala Harris was elected as California's attorney general on January 3, 2011. It was during her tenure as attorney general that Senator Harris required the San Francisco district attorney's office to only charge an individual under the three-strikes law if their third strike was for a serious or violent crime (Lopez 2019). Senator Harris's actions aligned with Democrats opposition to three-strikes legislation in California after grasping the need to reform these policies. This opposition to three-strike policies in California among the Democratic Party, and the unwillingness of practitioners to fully implement these policies, allows for more sweeping changes in criminal justice policies. California's Proposition 36 passed in November 2012 and modified the 1994 three-strikes law to: (1) only impose a life sentence when the conviction was a serious or violent felony, (2) re-sentence offenders who were convicted under the previous three-strikes law if their third strike was not violent or serious and if the judge in the resentencing determined that the new sentence would not pose a significant threat to public safety, (3) continued to impose a life sentence if the third strike was for certain nonviolent crimes such as sex, drug, or weapon offenses, and (4) maintained life sentences for felons whose third strike was for a nonserious, nonviolent crime if the prior two convictions were for rape, murder, or child molestation (Teji 2012).

Republicans and Democrats Come Together to Reform the Federal Sentencing Guidelines in a Bipartisan Effort

The First Step Act amends the current federal sentencing guidelines that were enacted in the Violent Crime Control and Law Enforcement Act of 1994, which provides the justification of the sentencing enhancement known as "three strikes." The Act was sponsored by Republican Doug Collins (Georgia) and was successfully voted for in a Democrat-held House of Representatives and a Republican-held Senate. After revisions and amendments were made, the First Step Act was signed into law on December 18, 2018, by Republican President Donald Trump. The FSA eases federal three-strikes initiative by issuing a twenty-five-year sentence to offenders convicted of three or more convictions, rather than the current life imprisonment without the possibility of parole. However, one of the biggest limitations to the FSA is not applying the new law retroactively. This means that offenders who were sentenced under the three-strikes initiative will not have their sentences commuted, rather it will only apply to offenders who have not been convicted of their third strike. While the FSA is considered a significant step in the right direction for criminal justice reform, many believe that more is needed to correct the unintended consequences of the Violent Crime Control and Law Enforcement Act of 1994.

After viewing the Violent Crime Control and Law Enforcement Act of 1994 and California's Proposition 184 as a failure of the Democratic Party, many Democrats use the political platform of criminal justice reform. Arguably, Democrats oppose the idea of focusing only on the use of incapacitation and deterrence as the means for reducing and preventing crime, contrary to that of the Republican Party. However, Democrats know that to receive bipartisan support from the Republican party to reform punitive, get tough punishments, the argument for financial conservativism is needed. Focusing on the cost of mass incarceration, especially its impact in California, Democrats were able to garner support from Republicans to pass the FSA of 2018 and California's Proposition 36 to reform the impact of three-strikes policies.

FURTHER READING

Alexander, Michelle. 2010. *The New Jim Crow: Mass Incarceration in the Age of Colorblindness*. New York: New Press.

Ardaiz, James A. 2000. "California's Three Strikes Law: History, Expectations, and Consequences." *McGeorge Law Review* 32, no. 1: 1–36.

Austin, James, John Clark, Patricia Hardyman, D. Alan Henry. 2000. "Three Strikes and You're Out.' *Punishment and Society* 1, no. 2: 131–62.

BBC America. 2015. "Bill Clinton Regrets 'Three Strikes' Bill." BBC, July 16, 2015. https://www.bbc.com/news/world-us-canada-33545971.

Benekos, Peter J., and Alida V. Merlo. 1995. "Three Strikes and You're Out: The Political Sentencing Game." *Federal Probation* 59, no. 1: 3.

Blomberg, Thomas G., and Karol Lucken. 2017. *American Penology: A History of Control*, 2nd edition. New Brunswick: Transaction Publishers.

Chemerinsky, Erwin. 2003. "The Constitution and Punishment." *Stanford Law Review* 56: 1049–80.

Datta, Anusua. 2017. "California's Three Strikes Law Revisited: Assessing the Long-Term Effects of the Law." *Atlantic Economic Journal* 45: 225–49.

Driscoll, Sharon, and Michael Romano. 2014. "Three Strikes: An Update after Propositions Reform Sentencing for Nonviolent Offenders and Milestone of 2000th Prisoner Released Approaches. Stanford Law School, Three Strikes Project." December 15, 2014. https://law.stanford.edu/2014/12/15/three-strikes-an-update-after-propositions-reform-sentencing-for-nonviolent-offenders/.

Dyer, Joel. 2000. *The Perpetual Prisoner Machine: How America Profits from Crime*. Boulder: Westview Press.

Gordon, Marcy. 1996. "Survey Finds Federal, State Governments Rarely Use 'Three Strikes' Law." Associated Press, September 9, 1996. https://apnews.com/705519e5c8696f069be8273037d391e3.

Graves, Allison. 2016. "Did Hillary Clinton Call African American Youth 'Superpredators'?" *Politifact*, August 28, 2016. https://www.politifact.com/factchecks/2016/aug/28/reince-priebus/did-hillary-clinton-call-african-american-youth-su/.

Grawert, Ames, and Tim Lau. 2019. "How the FIRST STEP Act Became Law—and What Happens Next." Brennan Center for Justice. https://www.brennancenter.org/our-work/analysis-opinion/how-first-step-act-became-law-and-what-happens-next. Accessed January 12, 2023.

Greenwood, Peter W., C. Peter Rydell, Allan F. Abrahamse, Jonathan P. Caulkins, James Chiesa, Karyn E. Model, and Stephen P. Klein. 1994. *Three Strikes and You're Out: Estimated Benefits and Costs of California's New Mandatory-Sentencing Law*. Santa Monica: Rand.

Janiskee, Brian P., and Edward J. Erler. 2000. "Crime, Punishment, and Romero: An Analysis of the Case Against California's Three Strikes Law." *Duquesne Law Review* 39: 43.

Lopez, German. 2019. "Kamala Harris's Controversial Record on Criminal Justice, Explained." *Vox*, September 12, 2019. https://www.vox.com/future-perfect/2019/1/23/18184192/kamala-harris-president-campaign-criminal-justice-record.

Martin, Mark. 2004. "Proposition 66/Efforts to Reform 'Three Strikes' Law Likely to Be on Ballot Again." *SF Gate*, November 4, 2004. https://www.sfgate.com/politics/article/PROPOSITION-66-Efforts-to-reform-three-2638541.php

Mondragon, Sandy. 2019. "California's Three Strikes Law-proposition 36: A Policy Analysis." PhD diss., California State University, Long Beach.

Sabol, William J., and Thaddeus L. Johnson. 2020. "The 1994 Crime Bill: Legacy and Lessons–Impacts on Prison Populations." *Federal Sentencing Reporter* 32, no. 3: 153–6.

Schiraldi, Vincent, Jason Colburn, and Eric Lotke. 2004. *Three Strikes and You're Out: An Examination of the Impact of Strikes Laws 10 Years after Their Enactment*. Washington, DC: Justice Policy Institute.

Siegel, Barry. 1990. "COLUMN ONE: Locking Up 'Sexual Predators': A Public Outcry in Washington State Targeted Repeat Violent Sex Criminals. A New Preventative Law would Keep

Them in Jail Indefinitely." *Los Angeles Times*, May 10, 1990. https://www.latimes.com/archives/la-xpm-1990-05-10-mn-1433-story.html.
Slater, Eric. 1995. "Pizza Thief Receives Sentence of 25 Years to Life in Prison." *Los Angeles Times*, March 3, 1995. https://www.latimes.com/archives/la-xpm-1995-03-03-me-38444-story.html#:~:text=Jerry%20Dewayne%20Williams%20was%20sentenced,a%20slice%20of%20pepperoni%20pizza.
Teji, Selena. 2012. "Prop. 36 Is a Modest and Necessary Three-Strikes Reform." Center on Juvenile and Criminal Justice, September 4, 2012. http://www.cjcj.org/news/5515.

BIBLIOGRAPHY

Abt, Thomas. 2019. *Bleeding Out: The Devastating Consequences of Urban Violence and a Bold New Plan for Peace in the Streets*. New York: Basic Books.

Barkow, Rachel. 2019. *Prisoners of Politics: Breaking the Cycle of Mass Incarceration*. Cambridge, MA: Belknap Press.

Blomberg, Thomas G., and Karol Lucken. 2017. *American Penology: A History of* Control, 2nd edition. New Brunswick: Transaction Publishers.

Bollinger, Lee C. and Geoffrey Stone, eds. 2024. *Roe v. Dobbs: The Past, Present, and Future of a Constitutional Right to Abortion*. Oxford, England: Oxford University Press.

Clinard, Marshall, and Peter Yeager. 2017. *Corporate Crime*. New York: Routledge.

Digard, Léon, and Elizabeth Swavola. 2019. *Justice Denied: The Harmful and Lasting Effects of Pretrial Detention*. New York: Vera Institute of Justice.

Fredrickson, Leif, Christopher Sellers, Lindsey Dillon, Jennifer Liss Ohayon, Nicholas Shapiro, Marianne Sullivan, Stephen Bocking, et al. 2018. "History of U.S. Presidential Assaults on Modern Environmental Health Protection." *American Journal of Public Health* 108: S95–S103. https://doi.org/10.2105/AJPH.2018.304396.

Garland, David. 2001. *The Culture of Control: Crime and Social Order in Contemporary Society*. Chicago: University of Chicago Press.

Gerstenfeld, Phyllis B. 2017. *Hate Crimes: Causes, Controls, and Controversies*. Thousand Oaks, CA: Sage Publications.

Hinton, Elizabeth, LaShae Henderson, and Cindy Reed. 2018. *An Unjust Burden: The Disparate Treatment of Black Americans in the Criminal Justice System*. New York: Vera Institute.

Klein, Maxwell W., and Cheryl L. Maxson. 2006. *Street Gang Patterns and Policies*. New York: Oxford Press.

Lacey, Nicola, and David Soskice. 2019. "Crime and Punishment in the US: Political Systems And Technology Regime Change." LSE Legal Studies Working Paper 16 (November). https://dx.doi.org/10.2139/ssrn.3492701.

Lacombe, Matthew J. 2019. "The Political Weaponization of Gun Owners: The National Rifle Association's Cultivation, Dissemination, and Use of a Group Social Identity." *The Journal of Politics* 81, no. 4: 1342–6.

Munsch, Christin L., Liberty Barnes, and Zachary D. Kline. 2020. "Who's to Blame? Partisanship, Responsibility, and Support for Mental Health Treatment." *Socius: Sociological Research for a Dynamic World* 6: 1–12. https://doi.org/10.1177/2378023120921652.

Percival, Garrick L. 2020. *Smart on Crime: The Struggle to Build a Better American Penal System*. London: CRC Press.

Pickett, Justin T. 2019. "Public Opinion and Criminal Justice Policy: Theory and Research." *Annual Review of Criminology* 2 (January): 405–28.

Platt, Anthony M. 2009. *The Child Savers: The Invention of Delinquency*. Piscataway, NJ: Rutgers University Press.

President's Task Force on 21st Century Policing. 2015. *Final Report of the President's Task Force on 21st Century Policing*. Washington, DC: Office of Community Oriented Policing Services.

Reitz, Kevin R., ed. 2019. *American Exceptionalism in Crime and Punishment*. New York: Oxford University Press.

Sabol, William J., and Thaddeus L. Johnson. 2020. "The 1994 Crime Bill: Legacy and Lessons–Impacts on Prison Populations." *Federal Sentencing Reporter* 32, no. 3: 153–6.

Schrader, Stuart. 2019. *Badges Without Borders: How Global Counterinsurgency Transformed American Policing*. Oakland: University of California Press.

Steiker, Carol, and Jordan M. Steiker. 2020. "The Rise, Fall, and Afterlife of the Death Penalty in the United States." *Annual Review of Criminology* 3 (January): 299–315.

Sugie, Naomi F., and Kristin Turney. 2017. "Beyond Incarceration: Criminal Justice Contact and Mental Health." *American Sociological Review* 82, no. 4: 719–43. https://doi.org/10.1177/0003122417713188.

Tonry, M. 2020. *Doing Justice, Preventing Crime*. New York: Oxford University Press.

ABOUT THE EDITOR AND CONTRIBUTORS

EDITOR

Angela D. Madden earned a PhD in Criminology from Indiana University of Pennsylvania, an MA in Criminology and Criminal Justice from East Tennessee State University, and a BS in Psychology from Tusculum College (TN). She is the founder and director of the Themis Center for Justice Policy, Practice & Research, established in 2003, and from 2013 to 2022, she was a professor and researcher at the University of Memphis (TN). Prior to that, she taught at Marshall University (WV), Washburn University (KS), the University of Louisville (KY), and Indiana State University.

In addition to teaching, she has nearly thirty years of experience in the design, implementation, and evaluation of programs and policies related to problems that impact individuals and communities, such as firearm violence, domestic violence, substance use disorders, mental health, homelessness, and reentry, among others. Since 2013, she has primarily written or significantly contributed to nearly fifty grant proposals to obtain more than $25 million in funding for local, state, and federal agencies, nonprofits, and service providers, with more than $8 million awarded. She also has nearly three dozen peer-reviewed publications including journal articles, book chapters, and encyclopedia entries, as well as dozens of technical reports detailing interim and final program evaluation outcomes for agencies. She serves as Research Partner on a long-running gun-violence reduction effort funded by the Tennessee Office of Criminal Justice Programs and jointly implemented by the US Attorney's Office for the Western District of Tennessee, the Office of the Shelby County District Attorney, the Shelby County Sheriff's Office, the Memphis Police Department, and various other local, state, and federal agencies. Semi-retired from academia, she enjoys being an instructor for the University of West Florida.

CONTRIBUTORS

R. Bruce Anderson is the Dr. Sarah D. and L. Kirk McKay, Jr. Endowed Chair in American History, Government, and Civics and Miller Distinguished Professor of Political Science at Florida Southern College (Lakeland, Florida). He holds a PhD in Political Science from Rice University. His most recent publications are *Policy Making and Southern Distinctiveness* (2021), and "Dobbs, American Federalism, and State Abortion Policymaking: Restrictive Policies Alongside Expansion of Reproductive Rights," in *Publius: The Journal of Federalism* (2023).

Sherah L. Basham is an assistant professor in the Department of Social, Cultural, and Justice Studies at the University of Tennessee at Chattanooga (TN). She holds a PhD in Criminal Justice and has over twenty years of experience in the criminal justice field in the areas of investigations, campus security, and higher education. Her research interests include policing, campus law enforcement, emergency preparedness, and community policing.

Zachary D. Baumann is Assistant Professor of Political Science at Nebraska Wesleyan University.

Chastity Blankenship is a former Associate Professor of Social Science at Florida Southern College in Lakeland, Florida. In addition to a PhD in Sociology, she earned an MA in Applied Sociology, and a BA in Sociology from the University of Central Florida. Her dissertation investigated student perceptions of race and gender portrayals within college textbook images, and she enjoys teaching and learning about race, class, and gender within educational media.

Dhruba J. Bora is chair of the Department of Criminal Justice, Criminology, and Forensic Sciences at Marshall University (WV). He worked on several grants funded by the Department of Justice on community policing as well as domestic violence, and published articles on campus safety and security, crime prevention, and counterterrorism. In 2019, he coauthored the second edition of *West Virginia's Criminal Justice System* with two other colleagues.

Roger Byrd is Associate Professor of Social Sciences at Brewton-Parker College (GA), with twenty-two years of prior experience as a Georgia State Representative. At BPC, he instructs in a variety of academic programs, including political science, criminal justice, government, and business. He also works as an adjunct professor for East Georgia State College. He is the director of Prison Programs, overseeing the school's implementation of postsecondary educational opportunities and Second Chance Pell programming within local prison facilities.

Kimberly DeTardo-Bora is Professor of Criminal Justice, Criminology, and Forensic Sciences at Marshall University (WV). Her research interests include cyber-criminology, women and the justice system, juvenile justice, and theoretical criminology. She is coauthor of *Juvenile Delinquency and Justice in the United States* and has published in scholarly venues such as *Action Research, Corrections Compendium, The Journal of Qualitative Criminal Justice and Criminology, Security Journal,* and *Women and Criminal Justice.*

Olivia A. Eason is a second-year Adjunct Instructor of Criminal Justice at Brewton-Parker College. She has also served as a juvenile probation and parole specialist II at the Georgia Department of Juvenile Justice for four years and prior to that worked as an advocacy coordinator with Tri-County CASA. Eason obtained both her BA in Political Science and her MS in Criminal Justice from Georgia College and State University.

Bradley D. Edwards is an associate professor in the Department of Criminal Justice & Criminology at East Tennessee State University (ETSU). His previous publications include four textbooks, as well as book chapters and articles in the areas of policing, corrections, ethics, and corporate misconduct.

Randy R. Gainey is Professor of Sociology and Criminal Justice at Old Dominion University (VA). He holds a PhD in Sociology from the University of Washington, and an MA and BA in Sociology from Western Washington University. Widely published, his most recent work is a state-wide survey of cybercrime victimization and its correlates. He is also working on a project involving quantitative and quantitative data focused on individual and contextual factors affecting criminal justice processing of domestic violence cases. He has expertise in racial/ethnic disparities in sentencing, alternative sanctions (electronic monitoring), life course perspectives on crime and deviance, and neighborhood social disorganization and crime. He has published in *Criminology*, *Crime & Delinquency*, and the *American Journal of Criminal Justice*, among others.

Whitney Gass is Associate Professor of Criminal Justice at Southern Arkansas University where she has taught since 2009. She earned her BA at Southern Arkansas University, her MA at the University of Louisiana Monroe, and her PhD at University of Arkansas at Little Rock. She serves on the Arkansas Board of Corrections as a liaison to the Arkansas Correctional School. She is a qualitative researcher who focuses on stress, burnout, and coping.

Deonna Gibbs holds a bachelor's degree in Psychology from Middle Tennessee State University and is pursuing an Education Specialist degree in Mental Health Counseling. She is a student in the Professional Counseling program with a concentration in Clinical Mental Health Counseling.

Elizabeth Gloyd is Assistant Professor of Criminal Justice at Southern Arkansas University. She earned her BS (2010) from Florida State University, MS (2012) from Florida Atlantic University, and PhD (2019) in Criminology and Criminal Justice from Florida State University. She has published her work focusing on enforcement activities, and military service on criminal justice outcomes in journals such as *Journal of Drug Issues*, *Journal of Developmental and Life-Course Criminology*, and *Crime & Delinquency*.

J. Andy Hansen is Associate Professor of Criminology and Criminal Justice at Western Carolina University (NC). He holds a PhD in Criminology and Criminal Justice from the University of South Carolina. With a focus on policing and police administration and management, he has published articles in the *American Journal of Criminal Justice*, *Police Practice & Research*, and *Justice Quarterly*, among others.

Brian Iannacchione is professor and chair of the Department of Criminology and Criminal Justice at the University of Northern Colorado. He holds an undergraduate degree from Penn State University, an MA from Boise State University (ID), and a PhD from Indiana University of Pennsylvania. He conducts research on the impact of marijuana legalization, police perceptions of marijuana legalization, and sentencing disparities.

Sheri Jenkins Keenan, PhD, is Associate Professor of Criminal Justice in the Department of Social Science at Alabama A&M University. Her research interests focus on policing special populations with an emphasis on juveniles: delinquency, mental illness, school safety, school-to-prison pipeline, gangs/threat groups, Racial/Ethnic Diversity (RE/D), and Adverse Childhood Experience (ACEs).

Edward Kerr is an associate with Campbell, Trohn, Tamayo, and Aranda in Lakeland, Florida. He earned his Juris Doctorate from the Washington and Lee School of Law and a BS degree in Biology from Florida Southern College (FL), where serves on the Alumni Board of Directors.

Albert M. Kopak is Professor of Criminology and Criminal Justice at Western Carolina University (NC). He earned a PhD in Justice Studies from Arizona State University and an MS and BS in Criminology from Florida State University. His research has focused on the connections between substance use disorders, criminal justice-related outcomes, and research to develop evidence-based practices that minimize the long-term impact of criminal justice system involvement on someone's life, while addressing substance use, mental health, and other factors.

Brendan Lantz is Associate Professor of Criminology and Criminal Justice and director of the Hate Crime Research and Policy Institute at Florida State University. He received his PhD from Pennsylvania State University. He has conducted extensive research on hate crimes and violence, including research funded by the National Institutes of Health, National Institute of Minority Health Disparities, and National Science Foundation, among others.

Wanda Leal is an assistant professor in the Department of Criminal Justice and Criminology at Sam Houston State University (TX). She received her PhD in Criminology and Criminal Justice from Florida State University. Her research interests include substance use and abuse, sports and crime, criminological theory, and life-course criminology.

Sean Maddan is Professor of Criminal Justice in the Department of Social Sciences and the associate dean of the College of Arts and Sciences at Texas A&M International University. He has authored numerous articles that have appeared in many outlets including *Justice Quarterly*, *Crime and Justice*, *Journal of Criminal Justice*, and the *American Journal of Criminal Justice*, among others. Author and coauthor of several books, he recently published a second edition of his coauthored text on sex offenders.

Zachary T. Malcom is a graduate of Florida State University. In 2020, he was the recipient of a highly competitive internship with the FSU Center for the Advancement of Human Rights internship to study the history of Confederate memorialization in the United States.

McKenna Marsh is a student at Nebraska Wesleyan University pursuing a bachelor's degree in Political Science. Following graduation, she plans to continue her education in law school.

Kelly A. McHugh is Associate Professor of Political Science and chair of the Department of History and Political Science at Florida Southern College. Her teaching and research focus on international relations and US foreign policy, and her scholarship has been published in outlets including *Political Science Quarterly*, *Global Peace, Change & Security*, and *Democracy & Security*. She received her PhD from the University of Delaware.

Kellen McLaughlin is a student at Nebraska Wesleyan University pursuing a bachelor's degree in English and Political Science. He has served as the public relations coordinator to the Student Affairs Senate, as editorial staff on *The Flintlock*, and is a member of Pi Sigma Alpha, the Political Science Honor Society.

Luis F. Nuño is Assistant Professor of Sociology at California State University, Los Angeles. He received his PhD in Sociology and Historical Studies from the New School for Social Research. His research focuses on mass incarceration, the criminalization of undocumented statuses, stigma management strategies of marginalized groups, and gentrification.

Donna Ossorio is Assistant Professor of Criminology and Sociology at Delta State University (MS). She holds a PhD and MS in Juvenile Justice from Prairie View A&M University, and a BS in Psychology from the University of Houston. Her areas of teaching and research interest include juvenile justice and delinquency, and youth and family violence. She has published in the *Journal of Humanities and Social Science* and the *Journal of Education and Social Science*, among others.

Brian A. Pitman is Assistant Professor of Criminology at Lander University in Greenwood, SC. He received his PhD from Old Dominion University in 2019, his MA from the University of North Carolina-Wilmington, and his BS from the University of North Carolina-Pembroke.

Miguel V. Rangel earned his MA and BS degrees in Criminal Justice from Texas A&M International University (TAMIU). He has been actively involved in various research and development initiatives within TAMIU's College of Arts and Sciences. His efforts have led to the creation of new degree programs, submission of external and internal grant proposals, and the timely graduation of graduate students.

Jeffrey P. Rush holds a doctorate in Public Administration from the University of Alabama, MS (Criminal Justice), and a MA (Educational Leadership) from the University of Alabama, Birmingham. He retired from full-time university teaching after thirty years; however, he continues to teach as an adjunct. Rush has forty plus years of experience in law enforcement and serves as a Deputy Sheriff with the Alabama Peace Officers Standards and Training Commission (APOSTC). He also continues to work private security for special events, concerts, executive protection, and churches.

Madison Santore graduated *cum laude* from Florida Southern College in Lakeland, Florida. She was a member of the National Honor Society, Mu Alpha Theta (Math Honor Society), the Science Honor Society, and the English Honor Society. She presented her Senior Honors Thesis, "The Effect of College Majors on Students' Perceptions of Sexual Offenders," to the 2021 meeting of the Southern Criminal Justice Association.

Mary Smith-Tengroth is a graduate of East Tennessee State University's (ETSU) Criminal Justice & Criminology MA program and is continuing her education at Loyola University Chicago.

Ruth Triplett is a professor in the Department of Sociology and Criminal Justice at Old Dominion University in Norfolk, Virginia. Her research interests include testing and development of Social Disorganization Theory and Social Learning Theory, policing and community satisfaction, and the history of criminology. Her articles have appeared in various journals including *Deviant Behavior*, *Justice Quarterly*, *Journal of Criminal Justice*, and *Policing*.

Kyle C. Ward is an associate professor in the Department of Criminology and Criminal Justice at the University of Northern Colorado. He earned a BA in Forensic Psychology from John Jay College of Criminal Justice (NY) and a PhD in Criminology from Indiana University of Pennsylvania. His research interests generally include jail and prison reentry, policing, rural crime, impact of marijuana legalization, risk assessment, and evidence-based crime prevention programs and policies.

Dale Wilson is Associate Professor of Criminal Justice at Campbellsville University (KY). He earned a BS from Eastern Kentucky University, an MA from Liberty University, and a PhD from Capella University.

Elizabeth Q. Wright received her PhD in Criminal Justice from Sam Houston State University and has been teaching criminal justice students for approximately twenty years.

She has experience as a Juvenile Corrections Liaison and as a volunteer victim advocate and has served on the boards of two nonprofits. Her research and service are in the areas of violence against women, trauma and the justice involved, implementing trauma-informed care, and stress and resiliency building.

Stephen T. Young is Associate Professor of Criminal Justice, Criminology, and Forensic Sciences at Marshall University (WV). He received his PhD from Old Dominion University in 2017. His primary areas of study are rural criminology and carceral studies.

INDEX

Abbott, Greg, 169, 262
abortion, 116, 218, 257–70, 307
bans, 257, 261, 262, 264, 266, 267, 270
opponents, 264, 266
providers, 262, 264
rights, 16, 257, 259, 261–2, 264, 266–8
abuse, domestic, 129–30
accountability, 2, 16, 71, 186, 189, 195
ACLU. *See* American Civil Liberties Union
addiction, 87, 229, 275, 281–2
ADL (Anti-Defamation League), 63, 67, 71, 150, 154, 157
aggravated assault, 99, 248, 251
Alabama, 112, 153, 156, 214, 253, 255, 263–4, 267, 314
Alaska, 1, 6, 27
alcohol, 88, 127, 137, 203, 213, 216, 239, 254, 278
Alcohol, Tobacco, and Firearms. *See* ATF
al-Qaeda, 62, 176, 180, 184
American Civil Liberties Union (ACLU), 20, 90–1, 93, 178, 242–3, 286, 293
amicus curiae, 26, 117
ammunition, 135, 139–41, 143, 199
Anti-Defamation League. *See* ADL
Arizona, 20, 27, 31, 128, 251, 267
Arkansas, 27, 29, 75, 150, 267–8, 311
Ashcroft, John, 89
assassination, 53, 135, 137, 139–40, 143, 275
asset forfeiture, 11–21, 50
asylum seekers, 162, 167
ATF (Alcohol, Tobacco, and Firearms), 137, 139, 141, 239

bail, 1–9, 40, 113
bonds, 2–4
cash/money/monetary, 2, 5–7, 9
reform, 1–9
Bail Reform Act, 3–8
Barr, William, 128, 192, 216
Barrett, Amy Coney, 262
Bass, Karen, 292
Bennett, Michael, 291
Beshear, Andy, 231
Beshear, Steve, 7
Bevin, Matt, 116
Beyer, Don, 155
Biden, Joseph R. "Joe," 7, 40, 53, 77, 79, 81, 82, 97, 98, 101, 106–7, 109, 119, 132, 138, 145, 151, 156, 165, 168, 171, 205, 207, 218, 241, 243, 257, 268, 271, 281, 292, 301
bill of rights, 25–6, 47, 51, 54, 137
bipartisan, 48, 116, 131, 203, 303
Bipartisan Safer Communities Act, 138, 141, 145
Black Codes, 137, 189
Bloomberg, Michael, 120, 190, 207
Blumenthal, Richard, 206
Boehner, John, 40
Booker, Cory A., 132, 202, 206–8, 302
border, 23, 124, 128, 162–3, 165–8, 172, 191, 245, 308
border wall, 129, 162, 166, 168
Boyle, Father Gregory, 126

Brady Handgun Violence Prevention Act, 53, 138, 143
Brandes, Jeff, 91
Bratton, William, 190, 191, 196
Brennan Center, 55, 116, 120, 133, 207, 209–10, 304
Brooks, Jack, 206, 301
Browder, Kalief, 1
Brown, Jerry, 19, 21 30
Brown, Kate, 82
Brown, Michael, 195, 235, 238, 240
Brown Jackson, Ketanji, 115, 205
Bryant, Phil, 262
bullying, 65, 152
bump stocks, 141
Bureau of Alcohol, 127, 137, 239
Bureau of Labor Statistics, 192, 197
Bureau of Narcotics, 215, 217, 275
Busbee, George, 29
Bush, George H. W., 48, 81, 87, 102–3, 105–6, 128, 138, 140, 143, 216–17, 257
Bush, George W., 4, 14, 18, 37, 39, 40, 51, 64, 66, 89, 97, 100, 102–3, 106, 126, 129, 133, 166, 168, 175, 177, 183, 185–6, 226, 228, 238, 262
Buttigieg, Pete, 7, 118
Byrd, James, 53, 151, 153, 157

CAF (civil asset forfeiture), 11–19, 21
California, 6–7, 125–6, 132, 168, 172, 180, 185, 216, 218, 295, 297–304
cameras, 283, 292
  body-worn, 283, 284, 286, 289, 291–2
  closed-circuit television, 285
  dashboard, 284, 292
cannabis, 86, 212–16, 219, 281
capital punishment, 73–82, 222
Capito, Shelley, 91
Carroll, Julian, 4
Carter, James "Jimmy," 41, 87, 104–5, 130, 133, 217, 261, 269, 276, 280
Casey, Bob, 266
Cato Institute, 117, 239, 244
CBP (Customs and Border Patrol), 170
Central Intelligence Agency. *See* CIA
CFPB (Consumer Financial Protection Bureau), 39–41, 43–4
Chaffetz, Jason, 288
Chicago, 3, 7, 26, 55, 239, 270, 307
child pornography, 17, 199, 205, 210
child savers, 249, 253, 256, 308
Christie, Chris, 5, 91
Chu, Judy, 185
Church Arson Prevention Act, 151
CIA (Central Intelligence Agency), 179, 182–3, 237
Cicilline, David, 146
Cincinnati, 56, 138–9, 148
CISA (Cybersecurity and Infrastructure Security Agency), 60
CITs (crisis intervention teams), 221, 230
civil asset forfeiture. *See* CAF
Civil Asset Forfeiture Reform Act, 21
civil death, 112, 120
civil liberties, 19, 60, 69–71, 77, 81, 175, 177, 183, 240, 290–2
civil rights, 5, 45, 56, 76, 80, 102, 157, 284, 287, 290–2
Civil Rights Act, 80, 137
civil unrest, 80, 275
Civil War, 13, 36, 113, 137, 180, 189, 236, 258
Clean Air Act, 100, 102–3
Clean Energy Revolution, 106–7
Clean Water Act, 100, 102, 104–5, 107
Cleaver, Emanuel, 238
Clinton, Hillary, 262, 267, 302, 304
Clinton, William Jefferson "Bill," 14, 37, 41, 48, 53, 75, 88, 92, 95, 105–6, 126, 129–31, 138, 140, 143, 151, 189–90, 217, 229, 235, 238, 241, 251, 262, 266, 280, 295, 298–302
Clyburn, James, 145
CNN, 185, 269–70
Coburn, Tom, 27, 239
cocaine, 75, 131, 202, 206, 212, 217, 275–7
  crack, 126–8, 131–2, 202, 206, 217, 274, 276, 278, 280
Cohen, Steve, 292
Coleman, Bonnie, 207
Collins, Doug, 301, 303
Colorado, 7, 103, 143–4, 214, 216, 218, 231–32, 251, 253, 277, 298
communications
  digital, 59, 61
  electronic, 68
  private, 68, 175
Community Oriented Policing Services, 94, 132–3, 308
Comprehensive Crime Control Act, 5, 7, 13, 14, 128, 163, 204, 217, 277, 280
Comprehensive Justice and Mental Health Act, 229
Comstock Act, 258
concealed carry, 23, 28, 31–3
Concealed-Carry Reciprocity Bill, 31

Connecticut, 4, 6, 144, 259, 266
Connolly, Gerry, 131
consent decree, 192
conservative religious values, 78, 91, 205
conservatives, 4, 79, 108, 116, 139, 204, 223, 225–7, 250, 291, 299
  fiscal, 115, 168, 203–5
constitutional carry, 27
constitutional rights, 21, 24, 46, 61, 137, 177–8, 286, 291, 307
Consumer Financial Protection Bureau. *See* CFPB
Controlled Substances Act, 201, 207, 213–14, 277–8, 281
Conway, George, 117
Coons, Chris, 289–90
corporate misconduct, 36, 42, 311
Cornyn, John, 28, 141, 145
Costa, Jim, 48
Cotton, Tom, 204, 300–1
countering violent extremism. *See* CVE
counterinsurgency, 245, 308
counterterrorism, 178, 180, 181, 184, 186, 310
Covid-19 pandemic, 20, 93
crime prevention, 187, 206, 310
Crime Reduction Act, 229
crime victims, 45–54, 56, 57, 79
  fund, 49–50, 53
  rights, 45–57
criminalization, 151, 158, 211, 222–3, 258–9, 264, 269, 277, 313
criminal justice reform, 1, 5–6, 47, 55–7, 203–4, 207–8, 223–4, 226, 230, 232–3, 273, 279, 296, 299–300, 302–3
criminal law, 55, 158, 188
crisis intervention teams (CITs), 221, 230
Cruz, Ted, 116, 141, 204
Cummings, Elijah, 288, 291
Cures Act (21st Century Cures Act), 90, 229, 232
custody, 165, 195, 252, 286
customs, 13, 127, 161
Customs and Border Patrol (CBP), 170
CVE (countering violent extremism), 63–4, 67–70
cyberbullying, 64–5, 68
Cybersecurity and Infrastructure Security Agency (CISA), 60
cyberviolence, 59–63, 64–5, 67–71

DACA (Deferred Action for Childhood Arrivals), 132, 162, 165, 171
  "Dreamers," 162, 165, 171
Davis, Gray, 92
Dayton, Mark, 18
DEA (Drug Enforcement Administration), 127, 213, 237, 239, 281, 295
Deal, Nathan, 91
death penalty, 73–83, 153, 231–2, 274, 279–80, 308
Death Penalty Information Center, 73, 79–80, 82–3, 231–2
death row, 74, 76, 79, 82
decriminalization, 218, 250
Deferred Action for Childhood Arrivals. *See* DACA
deinstitutionalization, 221, 250
delinquency, 128, 256, 308, 312–13
democracy, 113, 189–90, 233
Democracy Restoration Act, 115, 120
Democratic National Committee, 157, 172, 232, 266–7, 269
Democratic National Convention, 49, 232
Democratic Party Platform, 15, 55, 106–7, 146, 157, 172, 194–6, 206, 209, 232, 269
Department of Defense. *See* DOD
Department of Homeland Security. *See* DHS
Department of Justice (DOJ), 19–20, 79, 82–3, 89, 92, 95, 97, 100–1, 103, 107–9, 150–1, 195, 197, 237–8, 241
deportation, 128, 162, 166–7
deregulation, 35, 39, 43
DeSantis, Ron, 77, 114, 169
detention, 162, 167
  pretrial, 3, 5–6, 8, 307
deterrence, 48, 250, 303
deterrent, 75, 81, 83, 296
DHS (Department of Homeland Security), 60, 66–7, 69, 161, 163–8, 172–3, 178, 181, 183, 239, 289–90
digital literacy, 70–1
discretion, 2, 6, 8, 23–4, 73–4, 167, 188, 200, 203, 248, 276, 296
  in sentencing, 199, 278
discrimination, 3, 154, 157
disenfranchisement, 111–21
District of Columbia v. Heller, 26–7, 30, 138, 140
diversion, 85–95, 249–50
DNA, 76–7
Dobbs v. Jackson Women's Health Organization, 258, 260, 262, 264, 267–8, 307
DOD (Department of Defense), 127, 179, 183, 237–8, 242
Dodd-Frank Act, 39–43
DOJ. *See* Department of Justice
Dole, Bob, 299
Domenici, Pete, 226

domestic violence, 51–3, 145, 309–10
drones, 238, 240–1, 243, 283–93
Drug Abuse Resistance Education, 215
drug
  cartels, 12, 166, 302
  courts, 89–90, 92, 95, 276
  offenders, 85–95, 115, 204–6, 273–8, 281, 296
  offenses, 14, 90, 92, 200, 202–3, 206–7, 209, 215, 218, 273, 275, 277–9, 281
  possession, 18, 92, 187, 206, 275, 277
  sales/trafficking, 12, 17, 125, 127, 199, 202, 240, 275, 281
  traffickers, 75–6, 80, 279, 281
  treatment, 90, 130, 230, 280
  use, 86–91, 94, 130, 212–13, 217, 263, 274, 277, 278, 280
  users, 90, 215, 275
Drug Enforcement Administration. *See* DEA
Drug Policy Alliance, 19, 21, 200, 209, 219
Dukakis, Michael, 4, 47, 81
Durbin, Richard J. "Dick," 82, 202–3, 276, 300–1

ECP (Environmental Crimes Project), 100, 106
ECS (Environmental Crimes Section), 101, 103, 105–6
Edgar, Jim, 129
Edwards, John S., 202
Eighth Amendment, 2, 15, 75, 81
Eisenhower, Dwight D., 259
electronic monitoring, 5, 311
Emergency Economic Stabilization Act, 228
Endangered Species Act, 100, 105
enemy combatants, 176, 178
England, 13, 25, 31, 235
Engle, Elliot, 291
English common law, 13, 248
ENRD (Environmental and Natural Resources Division), 101, 105
Enron, 37, 41, 43
Environmental and Natural Resources Division (ENRD), 101, 105
Environmental Protection Agency. *See* EPA
EPA (Environmental Protection Agency), 36, 97, 100–8
EQUAL Act, 202
equality, 62, 77, 264
Equality Act, 155
Equal Protections Clause, 113, 152
Espaillat, Adriano, 292
evangelicals, 102, 262, 266
Evers, Tony, 52
excessive force, 49, 195
executions, 73–75, 77–83, 190, 301
executive branch, 18, 161, 164–5, 167, 178–79, 182, 186, 259
Export Act, 201, 207, 213
expungement, 6, 274
extremist, 61, 63, 67, 70–1
  groups, 62–3
  ideologies, 59, 61–4, 67, 71
  Islamic, 64
  online, 59–65, 67, 69–71
  violent, 64–5, 67, 70, 184

FAA (Federal Aviation Administration), 285, 288
facial recognition
  software, 284–5
  technology, 283–93
  use of, 288, 291
Facial Recognition Technology Warrant Act, 289, 291
Fairness in Cocaine Sentencing Act, 276
Fair Sentencing Act, 131, 201, 206, 276–7, 280
False Claims Act, 36, 43
Families Against Mandatory Minimums. *See* FAMM
FAMM (Families Against Mandatory Minimums), 205, 209
Federal National Mortgage Association (Fannie Mae), 37–8, 44
FBI (Federal Bureau of Investigation), 99, 101, 108, 127, 133, 143–5, 147, 175, 178, 239, 288, 293, 295
FDA (Food and Drug Administration), 259, 264–5
Federal Aviation Administration (FAA), 285, 288
Federal Bureau of Investigation. *See* FBI
Federal Emergency Management Agency, 178
Federal Firearms Act, 137, 143
federalism, 220, 310
Federal Police Camera and Accountability Act, 291
Federal Sentencing Guidelines, 303
Federal Voting Rights Act, 113
Feinstein, Dianne, 146, 183, 185
felony, 202, 247, 251–2, 298
Ferguson, Missouri, 191, 195, 197, 235–6, 238, 241, 245
  Ferguson Police Department, 195, 197
Fetterman, John, 281
Fifth Amendment, 13, 179
Firearm Owners' Protection Act, 138, 139
firearms, 25, 135, 137
  purchase, 26, 30, 123, 143
  sales, 135, 138, 146
First Amendment, 61, 137, 150, 153, 291
First Step Act. *See* FSA

FISA (Foreign Intelligence Surveillance Act), 177
Fish, Hamilton, 204
Florida, 27, 31, 89, 114, 117, 141, 143–4, 180, 195–6, 251, 310, 312, 314
Floyd, George, 48, 188, 236, 238, 241–3, 286, 289, 292
Food and Drug Administration. *See* FDA
Ford, Gerald R., 39, 102, 105, 259, 261
Foreign Intelligence Surveillance Act (FISA), 177
Foreign Intelligence Surveillance Court, 69
Foreign Terrorist Organization, 62, 175
Fourteenth Amendment, 11, 27, 112, 137, 152, 260, 291
Fourth Amendment, 13, 26, 283–5, 291
fraud, 36–7, 39, 43, 53, 124, 199
Freddie Mac, 37–8, 44
Freedom Act, 60, 66, 68, 185
FSA (First Step Act), 115, 202–4, 207, 208, 210, 227, 232, 276, 296, 299, 301, 303–4
furlough, 4, 47
Furman v. Georgia, 74, 78

gang
  activity, 123–32, 240, 302
  involvement, 124–5, 127–8, 130
  members, 124–9, 131
  prevention, 124, 131
  violence, 123–27, 129–33, 139, 142, 250
Gang Resistance Education and Training (GREAT), 128, 133
Garland, Merrick, 82
GEC (Global Engagement Center), 69, 72
gender, 59, 149–51, 157, 219, 293, 310
  identity, 59, 149–55, 157
Georgia, 1, 6, 73–76, 78, 137, 142, 144, 150, 251, 253, 303
"get tough" approaches, 131, 151
Giuliani, Rudolph "Rudy," 191
Glass-Steagall Act, 39, 41
Global Engagement Center (GEC), 69, 72
Gohmert, Louis, 154
Goldwater, Barry, 49
Gonzales v. Raich, 214
Gonzales v. Carhart, 262
Gorsuch, Anne, 103
Gorsuch, Neil, 262
Gramm-Leach-Bliley Act, 41
Grant, Ulysses S., 102, 258
Grassley, Charles "Chuck," 204, 276, 287, 293, 300–1
Gray, Linda, 251
Great Depression, 38, 78, 80, 265
Gregg v. Georgia, 74–75, 78–79
grenade launchers, 238, 241, 243
Grennhalgh, Karen, 116
group identity, 125, 147, 154, 308
groups
  marginalized, 132, 313
  terrorist, 63, 180
Guantanamo Bay, 179–80, 182, 184
gun
  control, 25, 29–30, 32, 46, 130, 135–47, 224
  crime, 123, 138
  dealers, 138–9, 143–6
  laws, 25, 27, 30, 139, 142
  manufacturers, 138, 140, 143
  owners, 29, 147, 308
  ownership, 24–5, 29, 123, 130, 135, 137, 142, 145
  reform, 123, 125
  rights, 123, 139–40, 291
  safety, 23, 145–6
  violence, 124–5, 136, 211, 227
Gun Control Act, 137, 139, 143

Hadley, David, 19
halfway house, 6, 277
handguns, 26, 31, 53, 130, 138, 142, 144
Hank Johnson's Stop Militarizing Law Enforcement Act, 239
harassment, 68, 71, 192
Harper, Tyler, 251
Harris, Kamala, 5, 7, 119, 132, 268, 302
Harris, Katherine, 48
Harrison Narcotics Tax Act, 213, 274–75
Hassan, Maggie, 18
Hatch, Orrin, 151, 153
hate, 59, 61, 149–59
  crime victims, 53, 152, 155
  crimes, 71, 149–53, 155–9, 307, 312
Hate Crime Research and Policy Institute, 312
Hate Crimes Prevention Act, 53, 151, 153, 155, 157
Hate Crimes Sentencing Enhancement Act, 151
Hate Crime Statistics Act, 150, 153
Hawley, Josh, 205
Health and Human Services. *See* HHS
health care, 267, 291
  reproductive, 268
Health Insurance Portability and Accountability Act, 268, 271
Helms, Jesse, 153, 261
Heritage Foundation, 16, 21, 103, 117, 120
heroin, 87, 275–77, 281

HHS (Health and Human Services), 65, 89, 128, 268, 271, 281
Hobbs, Katie, 263, 268, 270
Hochul, Kathy, 6
Hogan, Larry, 18
Holcomb, Eric, 154, 158
Holder, Eric, 14, 17, 19, 42, 69, 131
Holmes, Oliver Wendall Holmes, 265
Homeboy Industries, 126
Homegrown Violent Extremism (HVE), 67, 69
Homeland Security, 64, 69, 72, 172–73, 176, 178, 185, 240
Homeland Security Act (HSA), 60, 66, 163
Homeland Security Investigations (HSI), 163–4, 172
homelessness, 91, 149, 309
homicide, 53, 79, 98–9, 126, 136
homosexual, 46, 48, 153, 155
homosexuality, 153, 218
Hoover, Herbert, 215
Horton, Willie, 4, 9, 47, 48, 81
Houchin, Erin, 252
House Committee on Oversight and Reform, 288, 291
HSA. *See* Homeland Security Act
HSI. *See* Homeland Security Investigations
Hudson, Richard, 28
human rights, 131, 182, 260
human trafficking, 46, 49, 51, 53, 124, 164, 166–67
HVE (Homegrown Violent Extremism), 67, 69
Hyde, Henry, 14

ICE (Immigration and Customs Enforcement), 55, 161–73, 192, 238, 289
Idaho, 27–8, 54
Ike Skelton National Defense Authorization Act, 184
Illinois, 2–3, 6–7, 14, 24, 29, 91, 129, 169
immigrants, 53, 129, 132, 162, 167, 169–71
  undocumented, 128, 130, 162, 165, 169, 289
immigration, 123–24, 129–30, 132, 161, 163, 165–6, 169, 172–73, 181
  illegal, 163, 166–9, 211
  laws, 165, 171, 205
  legal, 161–2, 166
  policies, 124, 167
  reform, 128, 163
Immigration and Customs Enforcement. *See* ICE
Immigration and Naturalization Service, 163
imprisonment, 89, 176, 199
incarceration, 86, 91, 225, 301, 303
incentives, 15–16, 39, 104, 225
  economic, 13, 98
incest, 259, 262–3, 267
independents, 29, 78, 202, 231
Indiana, 15, 21, 25–26, 79, 118, 150, 152, 154, 157, 251, 291
infractions, minor, 92, 156, 193
inmates, 48, 74, 76, 115, 222–3, 227, 299
Innocence Project, 76–7
integration, 69, 88, 288
Intelligence Reform and Terrorism Prevention Act, 178, 181, 183
Internal Revenue Service, 274–5
interrogation, 176, 179, 181
intervention, early, 224, 228, 230
Iowa, 116, 204, 251, 287, 293
Iraq, 63, 169, 179–80, 238
Islamic State of Iraq and Syria (ISIS), 180
ISP (internet service provider), 66
in vitro fertilization (IVF), 260, 263–4, 268, 270

Jackson Women's Health Organization, 258, 260, 262
JAG (Justice Assistance Grant), 7, 238, 240
Jeffries, Hakeem, 202
Jim Crow, 8, 77, 82, 303
Johnson, Andrew, 237
Johnson, Hank, 239, 242, 290
Johnson, Lyndon B., 3, 6, 52, 139, 143, 237, 265
Jordan, Jim, 288
Joyce, Dave, 279
judiciary, 82–83, 115, 146, 203, 210, 287, 293
juries, 48, 73–4, 147, 240
  grand, 13, 169
JUSTICE Act, 289
Justice Assistance Act, 51
Justice Assistance Grant (JAG), 7, 238, 240
"Just Say No," 190, 215, 217, 276, 278
juveniles, 247–55, 295, 305, 312
  court, 247–55
  crime, 248, 250, 300
  justice, 129, 133, 247, 249–50, 252, 254–56, 311, 313
  offenders, 249, 254
Juvenile Justice Delinquency Prevention Act, 250

Kaine, Tim, 267
Kansas, 27, 218
Kate Puzey Peace Corps Volunteer Protection Act, 53
Kate's Law, 204, 209
Keenan, Bob, 17

Kemp, Brian, 150
Kennedy, Edward "Ted," 151, 153
Kennedy, John, 5. 204, 296, 301
Kennedy, John F., 137, 143, 228, 257, 265, 268, 270, 275
Kennedy, Patrick, 228, 229
Kennedy, Robert, 6, 275
Kennedy v. Louisiana, 77, 81
Kentucky, 1, 4, 5–7, 25, 31, 111, 115–17, 120, 156, 183, 204, 231, 239–40, 261, 263–4, 287, 309, 314
Kerry, John, 181, 183
King, Martin Luther, 62, 191, 275
King, Steve, 204

Lacey Act, 164
Lakeland, 310, 312, 314
LaPierre, Wayne, 141
Las Vegas, 141, 172
Lautenberg, Frank, 68
law and order, 45, 48, 188–90, 192, 205, 275, 242
law enforcement, 14–15, 20, 22, 127, 192, 213, 240
  discretion, 187–97
  officers, 11, 88, 128, 132, 156, 191, 216–17
Law Enforcement Act, 53, 88, 126, 128, 130, 138, 239–41, 295–6, 298–9, 301, 303
Law Enforcement Assistance Administration (LEAA), 52
laws
  federal forfeiture, 12, 16
  international, 72, 176, 179, 181
  red flag, 30–1, 136, 141, 145
  three strikes, 304
  zombie, 267
Lawson, Linda, 253
Leahy, Patrick, 185
Lee, Mike, 203, 290
legislation, bipartisan, 48, 131
legislative branch, 39, 164–5, 168
Levy, Claire, 253
Libby, Nate, 54
libertarians, 117, 203
  civil, 12, 180, 286
Lieu, Ted, 7
life imprisonment, 127, 203, 299–301
life sentence, 47, 115, 275, 296, 302
Lincoln, Abraham, 36
litigation, civil, 36, 192
Lofgren, Zoe, 288
loophole, 19, 138, 139, 243
  boyfriend, 53, 145
  gun show, 123, 138, 144, 146–7
Louisiana, 77, 81, 116, 156, 253
LSD, 86, 277, 281
Lucido, Peter, 18
lynching, 156–7, 159, 189

machine guns, 139, 141, 143
Madison, James, 25, 32, 136, 212
Maine, 27, 54, 112, 118, 212, 230
Manchin, Joe, 144
Mandatory Minimum Reform Act (MMRA), 207
Manhattan Bail Project, 3
Marihuana Tax Act, 213
marijuana
  classification, 281
  decriminalize, 207, 214–15, 217, 220, 276, 280
  dispensaries, medical, 214, 238
  legalization, 19, 211–20, 257, 259, 281–2, 312, 314
  medical, 214
  possession, 19, 217, 281
  recreational, 214, 218
  use, 14, 212, 214–16, 277, 281
Marijuana Tax Act, 215, 217, 275
Markey, Edward, 207
Marsy's Law, 54
Martin, Trayvon, 193, 195
Martinez, Susana, 17
Maryland, 5, 18, 291
Massachusetts, 2, 4, 118–19, 169–70, 201, 212, 253, 257, 299
Massie, Thomas, 156–7
mass incarceration, 5, 7–9, 56, 82, 130, 189, 193, 213, 223–25, 273, 296, 301–3, 307
mass shootings, 136, 138–41, 144–6, 222–24, 227
McCain, John, 181–3, 186
McConnell, Mitch, 66, 115–16
media outlets, 170, 295
medication abortions, 264, 268
Megan Meier Cyberbullying Prevention Act, 68
Megan's Law, 54, 57
mental health, 46, 64, 78, 87, 90, 130, 141, 145, 149, 203, 221–3, 225–30, 231–4, 308–9, 311–12
  courts, 229, 231–3
  services, 141, 145, 222, 226–8
  treatment, 88, 94, 221, 224, 227–9, 231, 233, 308
Mental Health Parity and Addiction Act, 228
Mental Health Services Administration, 89, 94–5

Mental Health Treatment Act, 91
mental illness, 91, 221–31, 312
Mentally Ill Offender Treatment and Crime Reduction Act, 229
Mexico, 162, 165–8
Michigan, 11, 17–20, 100, 253, 267, 291
midterm elections, 102, 138, 142, 168, 181, 183
migrants, 124, 165, 169
militaristic, 238–9
militarization, 235–6, 239, 243–44, 289
military, 53, 63, 74, 87, 168, 184, 236–7, 239, 241, 311
  equipment, 190, 236, 238, 240–4
  tactics, 236, 239
  tribunals, 181, 183
  weapons, 239, 241–2
Military Commissions Act, 181, 183
militia, 24, 26, 136–7
Miller, Zell, 29
Minneapolis, 48, 238
  police, 243, 286
Minnesota, 228
minorities, 12, 37, 113–14, 119, 149, 157, 191, 194, 208, 222
minority communities, 111, 113–14, 296
minors, 7, 52, 260
misdemeanor, 2, 6, 8, 53, 65, 100, 258
misinformation, 62, 64, 70, 270
Missing Children's Assistance Act, 50
Mississippi, 28–9, 156, 189, 262, 267
Missouri, 28, 79, 195, 235–6, 238, 241, 251
Mitchell, Holly, 19
MMRA (Mandatory Minimum Reform Act), 207
Model Diversion to Treatment Act Legislation, 88
Money Bail Act, 7
money laundering, 164
moral panic, 297
murder, 4, 47, 67, 76, 78, 81, 116, 241, 248, 251–2, 297, 300, 302
Murphy, Chris, 145

NAACP (National Association for the Advancement of Colored People), 242, 302
Nadler, Jerry, 70
NAMSDL (National Alliance for Model State Drug Laws), 88–9, 94
Narcotic Drugs Import and Export Act, 213
narcotics, 128, 164, 213, 215, 217, 237, 275, 278
National Alliance for Model State Drug Laws. *See* NAMSDL
National Association for the Advancement of Colored People (NAACP), 242, 302
National Center for Victims of Crime, 51
National Child Sex Offender Registry, 53
National Commission on Marihuana and Drug Abuse, 215
National Conference of State Legislatures, 21, 32, 234, 255, 282
National Counterterrorism Center, 69
National Crime Victimization Survey (NCVS), 99
National Crime Victim Law Institute, 56
National Criminal Justice Reference Service, 293
National Defense Appropriation Act for Fiscal Year, 237
National Defense Authorization Act (NDAA), 182, 238
National Drug Control Policy, 89, 94, 281
National Drug Control Strategy, 281
National Environmental Policy Act, 100
National Family Planning Program, 259
National Firearms Act, 137, 142–3
National Gang Intelligence Center, 127, 133
National Guard, 168, 237
National ICE Council, 192
National Incident Based Reporting System (NIBRS), 99, 155
National Instant Criminal Background Check Improvement Act, 140
National Institute of Mental Health (NIMH), 226
National Institute of Minority Health Disparities, 312
National Institute on Drug Abuse, 93–4
National Missing Children's Day, 50
National Oceanic and Atmospheric Administration, 101
National Rifle Association. *See* NRA
National Security Agency (NSA), 66, 180
National Security Council, 185
National Sheriff's Association, 192
National Victim Center, 51
National Wildlife Refuge System, 27
National Women's History Alliance, 269
National Youth Gang Drug Prevention Program, 132
NCVS (National Crime Victimization Survey), 99
NDAA (National Defense Authorization Act), 182, 238
neighborhoods, 77, 129, 130, 190–1, 311
Nevada, 82
New Deal, 78, 80, 102, 104, 265, 279
New Jersey, 1, 5, 54, 91, 206–8, 251
New Mexico, 17, 228
New Orleans, 141

New York, 8, 70, 181, 191, 196, 202, 204, 285–6, 291
New York Police Department, 196, 285
New Zealand, 70
Next Step Act, 207–8
NIBRS (National Incident Based Reporting System), 99, 155
NIMH (National Institute of Mental Health), 226
Ninth Amendment, 26
Nixon, Richard M., 5, 13–14, 18, 39, 75, 78, 86, 97, 102, 108, 189–90, 196, 200, 213, 215, 237, 259, 275, 277–8, 280
Noem, Kristi, 28, 264
nonviolent offenders, 88, 92, 203–4, 206, 227, 304
Northam, Ralph, 30–2
North Carolina, 28, 57, 219–20, 244, 312
NRA (National Rifle Association), 128, 135, 137–40, 142–3, 147–48, 308
NSA (National Security Agency), 66, 180

Oakland, 244–45, 277, 286, 308
Obama, Barack, 14, 27, 42, 53, 60, 68–9, 97, 100–101, 105–6, 130–2, 144, 151, 155, 165, 167–9, 180, 182, 184, 186, 192–3, 196, 218, 226, 229, 232, 238, 240–1, 267, 276, 280–1, 285, 290, 302
Obenshain, Mark, 202
obscene, 258, 265
Obstruct Terrorism Act, 60, 163, 177
Office for Victims of Crime, 51, 53, 55–6
Office of Juvenile Justice and Delinquency Prevention, 133, 247, 255–6
Ogden Memorandum, 214
Ohio, 1, 25, 30, 79, 83, 138, 231, 261
Oklahoma, 28
Olson, Peter, 155
Omar, Ilhan, 194
O'Mara, Thomas, 48
Omnibus Anti-Drug Abuse Act, 128
O'Neill, James, 286
online
  hate, 59, 71
  violence, 70
open carry, 25, 27, 29, 31, 33
opioid, 85, 89–90, 212, 274, 277, 279
opium, 274–5
organized crime, 13, 15, 18, 61, 99, 133, 191
Orlando, 144, 180
overdose, 93, 281

parens patriae, 248–9
Paul, Rand, 1, 5, 7, 116, 156–7, 159, 183, 204–5, 239–41, 244, 287
Paul, Ron, 276
Pennsylvania, 2, 13, 21, 29, 144, 215, 261, 309, 312, 314
Perkins, Chad, 79
Pew Research Center, 32, 78, 80, 83, 90, 94, 142, 165, 172–3, 194, 196, 269–70
Philadelphia, 7, 189, 236–7
pistol, 137, 139, 144
Planned Parenthood, 258–60, 271
plea, 81, 87, 208, 300
Poe, Ted, 48
police
  brutality, 189, 238
  discretion, 187, 190
  militarization, 235–45
  misconduct, 192
  reform, 222, 286, 289
  training, 188, 229, 241
  unions, 190, 192, 196
Police CAMERA Act, 292
policing
  aggressive, 48, 289
  broken windows, 187, 190–1, 196
  stop-and-frisk, 187, 190
Policing Act, 243, 292
political
  appointees, 164, 189
  climate, 90, 231
polls, 31, 117, 119, 179, 231, 257, 261
pollution, 35, 39, 101, 105, 107
Posse Comitatus Act, 168, 237
poverty, 124, 130, 207, 237, 249
Preserving American Privacy Act, 287–8
President's Commission on Law Enforcement, 44, 250
Pressley, Ayanna, 82
Pretrial Integrity and Safety Act, 5
pretrial release, 3–5, 8–9
Preventing Gang Violence Act, 131
Prevention and Public Health Fund, 226
prison
  federal, 178, 201
  furlough programs, 81
  reform, 9, 81, 207, 210, 227, 255, 301
prisoners, 1, 52, 92, 115, 118–19, 130, 179, 181–2, 184, 229, 231
  of war, 179, 181
Prison Policy Initiative, 9
Prison Rape Elimination Act, 53

privacy rights, 61, 176, 260, 287, 290
probation, 20, 68, 87, 111, 116–17, 200, 275
progressives, 12, 249
prohibition, 13, 25, 53, 137, 141, 168, 179, 212–13
prostitution, 114, 124, 263
protesters, 191, 193, 239, 243
protests, 189–90, 238–9, 244, 284, 286
Public Health Services Act, 259
Purdue, Bev, 93
Pure Food and Drug Act, 212

qualified immunity, 192, 195

race, 5, 59, 74, 76, 149, 152, 154, 156–8, 196, 237, 244, 255, 310
racial
  disparities, 93, 113–14, 199–201, 203, 206, 208, 302
  justice, 16, 119, 194
  profiling, 132, 188, 195
racism, 130, 154, 194, 211, 215
  systemic, 193–94, 292
radicalization, 64, 69, 71–2
rape, 4, 47–8, 53, 76–7, 81, 203, 205, 213, 248, 259, 262–3, 267, 302
Rauner, Bruce, 6, 91
Reagan, Ronald, 4–5, 14, 18, 27, 39, 46, 50, 53, 81, 87, 102–4, 127–8, 130, 138–40, 143, 190, 204, 215, 217, 225, 232, 233, 237, 261, 268, 276, 278, 282
Reagan, Nancy, 215, 278
recidivism, 88, 115
Recovery Act, 89, 100, 102
Recreational Firearms Use Protection Act, 143
reentry, 112, 205, 309
Reform Act, 285, 287
refugees, 128, 130, 170
Regier, Matt, 17
rehabilitation, 52, 76, 78, 80–1, 126, 131, 200, 248–50, 254, 274, 280
religion, 59, 149, 151–2, 154, 157, 218, 257, 266, 270
repeal, 39, 41, 253, 259, 263, 267–8, 291
reproductive rights, 257–71, 310
Republican National Committee, 49, 166, 173, 194, 271
Republican National Convention, 140, 191, 196, 203, 233
Republican Party Platform, 16, 21, 49, 57, 77, 81, 104, 108, 148, 154, 159, 166, 173, 181, 192, 210, 233, 269, 271, 301
restitution, 20, 54, 79, 113–14, 117
restoration of rights, 113, 117
retribution, 223, 250
Reverse Mass Incarceration Act, 132, 206, 209
revolt at Cincinnati, 148
Reynolds, Kim, 116
rhetoric, 157, 206, 216, 235, 250
Ricketts, Pete, 17
rifle, 141, 143–5, 235
right to vote, 112–13, 117–18, 120, 264
riot, 189, 195, 223, 241
risk assessment, 8, 314
Ritter, Bill, 253
Robb Elementary School, 145
Rockefeller, John D., 278
Rodriguez, Diego, 20
Roe v. Wade, 257–60, 262–4, 266–7, 269–71, 307
Roosevelt, Franklin D., 104, 137, 139, 142, 265
Roosevelt, Theodore, 102
Ros-Lehtinen, Ileana, 51
Rubio, Marco, 145
rule of law, 170, 188–9, 191, 195
Rush, Bobby L., 156
Rutherford, John, 131

safety valve, 201, 204, 209, 276
Sanchez, Linda, 65, 68
sanctions, 88, 92, 222–3, 311
sanctuaries, 25, 30–1
sanctuary cities, 162, 171, 173
Sanders, Bernie, 7, 117–19, 139, 218, 291
Sandy Hook Elementary School, 50, 55, 141, 144
Sanfelippo, Joe, 51–52
Sarbanes-Oxley Act, 37, 41, 43
Schakowsky, Jan, 155
Schiff, Adam Schiff, 131
schizophrenia, 225–6
Schmidt, Jean, 80
school-to-prison pipeline, 132, 312
Schumer, Charles "Chuck," 16, 21, 155, 281
Schwarzenegger, Arnold, 300
Scott, Austin, 287
Scott, Bobby, 276
Scott, Rick, 17, 91
Scott, Tim, 192, 204, 241, 289
search
  unreasonable, 13, 26, 284–5
  warrant, 287
Second Amendment, 24–8, 30, 32, 135–8, 140, 143, 147
Second Chance Act, 132
seizure, 12–15, 17, 20, 26, 66, 284–5

self-defense, 26, 28, 140
Sensenbrenner, Jim, 60, 65, 66
sentences, 81–2, 113–19, 153, 164, 199–203, 207, 276, 281, 296–8, 300–1, 303
  indeterminate, 200, 297
  mandatory minimum, 47, 87, 128, 199–210, 217, 275–6, 278, 280, 296, 299, 304
sentencing, 48–9, 115, 200–1, 206, 273, 276–7, 279, 296–97, 299, 311
  disparities, 201, 204, 217, 276, 312
  drug offenses, 273, 275, 277, 279, 281
  guidelines, 199, 201–2
  mandatory, 126–7
  reform, 200, 207, 273, 279, 300
Sentencing Project, 221, 224, 233
Sentencing Reform Act, 200, 204, 278
Sentencing Reform and Corrections Act (SRCA), 300–1
Sessions, Jeff, 16–17, 90, 153, 192, 214, 216, 240, 242, 276, 279, 300–1
sex, 11, 154, 302
  offenders, 54, 313
sexual
  abuse, 52, 173, 199
  assault, 49, 52, 251
  offenses, 47, 114, 205
  orientation, 59, 68, 149–58
Shafer, Raymond, 275
Shalala, Donna, 217
shall-issue, 24, 26, 27, 29
Shepard, Matthew, 53, 151, 153, 157
Sherman Antitrust Act, 36
shooters, 143–4, 252
shootings, 74, 126, 137, 140–2, 252
Sinema, Kyrsten, 145
Sisolak, Steve, 82
Sixth Amendment, 13
Skelton National Defense Authorization Act, 53
Skinner, Nancy, 253–4
slave patrol, 197, 236–7
slavery, 158, 194, 197
slippery slope, 61, 139
Smarter Sentencing Act, 202
Snyder, Rick, 17
social
  conditions, 52, 78
  contract, 80, 111
  inequality, 35, 194
  justice, 71, 80, 200, 203
  media, 39, 59, 61–5, 71, 238, 251
  movement, 45, 158
  order, 55, 189, 191, 307
  protests, 188, 190
  research, 94, 313
soldiers, 162, 168, 240
solitary confinement, 1, 229
South Carolina, 145, 204
South Dakota, 28, 264
spousal notification, 260
SRCA (Sentencing Reform and Corrections Act), 300–1
Steele, Michael, 188
stop-and-frisk, 187
Stop Militarizing Law Enforcement Act, 242
straw purchase, 144–5
Stupak, Bart, 267
substance, 202, 207, 213, 216, 225, 276–77, 281
  abuse, 88–90, 94–5, 225–6
  abuse services, 223
  controlled, 17–19, 88–9, 207, 277, 281
  illegal, 276
  import, 201
  use, 85, 88, 90, 221, 312
  use disorder, 88–89, 91, 309, 312
Substance Use Disorder Treatment Act, 91
suicide, 1, 68, 72
supermajority, 263
super-predators, 250, 296, 302
surveillance, 3, 147, 163, 176–77, 185, 245, 284, 286–7, 290
  domestic, 178, 287
  drones, 283, 286, 289
systemic bias, 187–8, 190, 192

Talib, Rashida, 291
Taylor, Breonna, 236, 239, 241
TANF (Temporary Assistance for Needy Families), 88
teachers, 141–2, 145, 252
Temporary Assistance for Needy Families (TANF), 88
Tennessee, 25, 29–30, 54, 105, 264, 309–10
Tenth Amendment, 28, 279
terrorism, 14, 18, 46, 59–60, 63, 66–70, 72, 161, 163, 166, 169, 175–81, 186
  domestic, 70–2, 175, 185
  international, 14, 60–1, 175–85
Terrorism Prevention Act, 178
terrorist, 70, 161, 177
  attacks, 14, 51, 60, 66, 70, 161, 163, 169, 175, 177–8, 180–2, 238
  domestic, 70, 175
  international, 61, 180

suspected, 178–80, 289
suspects, 176, 179
Texas, 28, 30–1, 48, 74–6, 118, 141, 145, 154–5, 156, 168–69, 204, 206, 253, 259, 262, 264, 267 276, 287, 296, 301, 312
THC, 216, 277
theft, 51, 99, 164, 298
Thomas, Clarence, 14
Thompson, Mike, 146
three-strikes policies, 127, 280, 287, 295, 297–305
Three-Strikes Reform Act, 299
Thurmond, Strom, 5, 204
Tillis, Thom, 145
Timbs v. Indiana, 15
Tittl, Paul, 227
Toomey, Pat, 144, 241
"tough on crime," 49, 53–4, 87, 126, 223–4
Toxic Substances Control Act, 102
training, 52, 90, 129, 133, 137, 164, 231, 235–6
transfer, 12, 18, 182, 184, 235, 238, 243, 247–8, 251, 255
transparency, 60, 170, 189, 195
trial, 2–3, 20, 38, 49, 68, 75–6, 78, 81, 176, 179, 184
trifecta state, 79, 263
Trump, Donald J., 1, 15, 17, 28, 40, 52, 64, 70, 77, 79, 82–3, 90, 97, 100–4, 106–8, 114–16, 131, 138, 140–1, 157, 165–9, 171, 173, 180, 183, 185, 191–2, 202, 204, 216, 227, 232, 236, 239–44, 257, 260, 262, 264, 278–9, 288–9, 299, 301, 303
truth in sentencing, 127, 131
Truth in Sentencing Program, 128
Tyler Clementi Higher Education Anti-Harassment Act, 68

UAVs (unmanned aerial vehicles), 285, 288–90
Uniform Crime Reports (UCR), 99
Uniform Firearms Act, 25–7, 29
Uniform State Narcotics Act, 215
United States Sentencing Commission (USSC), 151, 199–200, 210
unmanned aerial vehicles. *See* UAVs
USA Patriot Act, 14, 60–1, 65–71, 163, 176–7, 180–3, 185
US Customs Service, 163
US Government Printing Office, 210
US Marshals Service, 239
USSC. *See* United States Sentencing Commission
US Secret Service, 178, 239
US Sentencing Commission, 202
US Supreme Court, 3, 12–15, 26, 39–40, 74–7, 81, 113–15, 140–1, 143, 167–8, 171, 181, 249, 257, 259–62, 264–7
Utah, 27, 29, 73, 151, 153, 288, 290
Uvalde, 141, 145

VAWA (Violence Against Women Act), 49, 51, 53, 57, 131, 151
Vera Institute, 3, 8, 120, 307
Vermont, 7, 23, 112, 117–19, 185, 251, 259, 290–1, 301
veterans, 87, 90
Veterans Justice Outreach Program, 90
victimization, 46, 51, 53, 99, 150, 212
victims
cybercrime, 46, 51
federal, 47, 50
financial crime, 46, 53
rights, 55–6
Victims of Crime Act (VOCA), 50–1
Vietnam, 87, 181, 259
Violence Against Women Act. *See* VAWA
Violent Crime Control Act, 53, 88, 126, 128, 130–1, 138, 241, 295–6, 298–9, 301, 303
Virginia, 2, 24–5, 29–31, 73, 82, 116, 202, 209, 212, 261, 265, 314
VOCA (Victims of Crime Act), 50–1
Voter Rights Act, 80
voting rights, 111–20

waiver, 247, 251–2, 255
judicial, 247, 251–2
prosecutorial, 247–8
Walker, Bill, 6
war
on crime, 75, 78, 128, 189, 237
on drugs, 5, 7, 13–14, 18, 78, 80, 86, 127–8, 189, 190, 200, 209, 212–13, 215, 219, 237, 239, 241–2, 275–7, 280
on terror, 68, 169, 177, 179, 181, 183, 238
warrant, 180, 283, 289–91
Warren, Elizabeth, 118–19, 170, 208, 281, 291
Washington, 29, 128, 220
water, 106–9
pollution, 98–9, 106
protectors, 238
waterboarding, 179, 183
waterways, 39, 107
navigable, 99
pollute, 40

Waters, Maxine, 207
weapons
  assault, 123, 138, 140, 142–4, 146
  chemical, 239
  concealed, 23, 25, 27, 29–30, 32
  illegal, 137
Wellstone, Paul, 228
Welsh, Pete, 290
West Virginia, 91, 144, 309–10, 315
white supremacists, 64, 67
Whitmer, Gretchen, 21
Wickersham Commission, 3
Wilson, Pete, 298
Wisconsin, 1, 6, 24, 31, 51, 54, 57, 60, 93, 227, 253
Witness Protection Act, 50
women's rights, 45, 48, 259, 263, 265–6, 269
Work Opportunity Reconciliation Act, 88
Wright, James, 206
Wyden, Ron, 69
Wyoming, 27, 150, 153, 212, 218

Youth Gang Drug Prevention Program (YGDPP), 128

zero tolerance, 193, 215
zombie laws, 267–8